A MULTIPOLAR PEACE?

Great-Power Politics in
the Twenty-first Century

CHARLES W. KEGLEY, JR.
University of South Carolina

GREGORY A. RAYMOND
Boise State University

St. Martin's Press
New York

Senior editor: Don Reisman
Manager, publishing services: Emily Berleth
Publishing services associate: Kalea Chapman
Project management: Till & Till, Inc.
Art director: Sheree Goodman
Cover design: Edward Smith Design, Inc.

For information, write:
St. Martin's Press, Inc.
175 Fifth Avenue
New York, NY 10010

ISBN: 0-312-10270-4 (hardcover)
ISBN: 0-312-09957-6 (paper)

Published and distributed outside North America by
THE MACMILLAN PRESS LTD
Houndmills, Basingstoke, Hampshire RG21 2XS and London Companies and
representatives throughout the world.

ISBN 0-333-61851-3

A catalog record for this book is available from the British Library.

■ TO OUR MOTHERS ■

In loving memory of Elizabeth Meck Murry (1917–1981)
and
For Irene Skalicky Raymond

PREFACE

Since the end of the Cold War, many people have come to believe that we stand on the threshold of a new era. Over the past few years they have seen revolutionary changes burst upon the world stage with a suddenness that both shocks and bewilders. Whether these changes portend a more peaceful future remains unclear. As the Chorus in Sophocles' tragic play *Ajax* reminds us, "Much may mortals learn by seeing, but before he sees it, none may read the future. . . ."

Although we cannot read the future, social scientists can construct plausible forecasts of what alternative futures could occur based on their knowledge of past patterns and unfolding trends. One forecast often voiced today by government officials, members of the media, and researchers in universities and think-tanks pertains to the global distribution of military and economic might. According to their interpretation of the available evidence, military and economic strength in the early twenty-first century is very likely to be increasingly dispersed among an expanding number of relatively equal great powers. In contrast to the simple bipolar structure that characterized the Cold War, there is a strong possibility that a complex multipolar system will emerge. The purpose of this book is to bring into focus for the serious student of world affairs the characteristics and probable consequences of such a system, and to highlight the issues, theoretical controversies, and policy dilemmas that they pose.

The underlying theme of this book is that there are different types of multipolar systems, some of which are more war-prone than others. If national capabilities become diffused in a condition of rough parity during the twilight of this millennium, we all have a stake in the great powers crafting foreign policies that avoid the most unstable variants of multipolarity. Whereas some policies may calm the turbulence and friction of a multipolar world, others are likely to make matters worse. Our vision of what is desirable for the future should inform the foreign policy decisions of the present. The path to a multipolar peace must begin with carefully chosen steps. Moreover, preparations for it must commence today. The future is now.

The chapters that follow provide a framework for evaluating such choices. The book is divided into three parts. In Part I, we discuss the unfolding trends in contemporary world politics and describe how a multipolar future might differ from the more familiar bipolar world of Cold War competition.

In Part II we comparatively review what the history of multipolar systems tells us about the sources of stability in six previous periods that were characterized by a diffusion of power among more than two relatively equal great powers. Particular attention is given to different types of multipolar systems, as defined by variations in their size, the degree to which alliances were polarized into rigid blocs, and the extent to which prevailing international norms supported a permissive or a restrictive code of great-power conduct.

Part III focuses on the strategies that the United States and other great powers might adopt to deal with the challenges of a twenty-first century multipolar world. Several possible paths to a peaceful multipolar future exist, ranging from unilateral action to special bilateral partnerships to various forms of multilateral cooperation. The costs, benefits, and trade-offs associated with each are examined, and the advantages of a concert-based collective security system are discussed.

Acknowledgments

We have incurred many debts of gratitude while preparing this book. Special thanks must go to Linda Schwartz and Christine Raymond for their understanding and willingness to tolerate our nightmarish schedules as each new deadline appeared.

At the University of South Carolina we are grateful for the assistance provided by Michael Gubser, Steven W. Hook, Jeffrey Morton, Mpwate Ndaume, and Christina Payne.

At Boise State University, Patricia Trofast of the Political Science Department assisted with the word processing, and Randy Swope of the Simplot Micron Technology Center created many of our computer graphics. Robert Sims, Dean of the College of Social Sciences and Public Affairs, provided a supportive environment for research and writing. Gregory Raymond's research in The Hague, Geneva, and elsewhere in Europe was generously supported by grants from the Higher Education Research Council of the Idaho State Board of Education.

Thanks also go to our colleagues who reviewed earlier drafts of the manuscript and provided valuable suggestions: Pamela R. Howard, University of South Carolina; Paul Gordon Lauren, University of Montana; Patrick Morgan, University of California at Irvine; James Lee Ray, Florida State University; and John M. Rothgeb, Jr., Miami University. In addition, we are indebted to Peter

Gladkov, Jack Levy, Alpo M. Rusi, Harvey Starr, and John Vasquez for their support for our work.

Finally, we deeply appreciate the contributions of the professional staff at St. Martin's Press to the development of this project. Our editor and friend, Don Reisman, was especially helpful and encouraging. Gabriela Jasin provided invaluable assistance at every stage of our work with St. Martin's. Finally, we are grateful to Russell Till for his professional management of the book's production.

A Multipolar Peace? continues a productive collaboration that began with our first book in 1975. Hopefully, readers will benefit from the insights from this, our latest joint effort, and will find our work helps them to think about the relative advantages and dangers of alternative paths to peace.

Charles W. Kegley, Jr.
Gregory A. Raymond

CONTENTS

PART I
VISIONS OF THE POST–COLD WAR WORLD

1 • New International Realities   3

Dangers in a Disorderly New World Order   4
The Specter of Multipolarity   8
Continuity and Change in the Structure of World Power   17

2 • Rethinking Cold War Lessons   22

What Was the Long Peace?   23
Potentially Mythical Causes of the Long Peace   27
Cold War Myths and Dangerous Extrapolations   40

3 • Must We Fear a Multipolar Future?   46

Realist Theory, Multipolarity, and the Post–Cold War World   46
The Geometry of Multipolar Systems   53
Multipolar Systems in History   57

PART II
UNDERSTANDING THE PAST

4 • Polarity and Uncertainty   67

Does the Number of Great-Power Competitors Matter?   68
Does the Stability of the Great-Power Hierarchy Matter?   72
Polarity, Power Transitions, and Peace   85

5 • Polarization and Escalation   89

Alliances and Alignment in World Politics   89

Why Great Powers Forge Alliances   90
The Ambivalent Realpolitik Image of Alliances   91
The Consequences of Polarized Alliances   101
Great-Power Coalitions and Escalation to War   117

6 • International Norms and Great-Power Cooperation   121
The Normative Context of Great-Power Interactions   122
Normative Constraints on Great-Power Rivalry?   132
The Normative Foundations of Multipolar Peace   140

PART III
CHOICES FOR THE FUTURE

7 • Paths to Peace   149
The Range of Great-Power Choice in a Multipolar System   151
Comparing Strategies for Peace   162

8 • The United States: Recluse, Leader, or Balancer?   166
Constraints on U.S. Policy Options   167
Setting U.S. Priorities   180

9 • A World of Special Relationships?   191
Special Relationships in the Past   192
Special Relationships in the Future   195
Implications for Great-Power Choices   207

10 • A Concert-Based Collective Security System?   212
The Revival of Interest in Collective Security   213
Requirements for Concert-Based Collective Security   218
Alternative Frameworks for Concert-Based Collective Security   220
The Future Is Now   229

REFERENCES   237

NAME INDEX   265

SUBJECT INDEX   272

ABOUT THE AUTHORS   278

PART I
Visions of the Post—Cold War World

· 1 ·

NEW INTERNATIONAL REALITIES

We're in the middle of a transition that will be obvious to historians 100 years from now. Unless we recognize what's taking place and reorganize the West to deal with it, the problems of the next 20 years will eat us alive. . . . What we have to understand is that the bi-polar world of the post-war era, in which the U.S. and the Soviet Union dominated world events and set the agenda for their respective alliances, is over. We are now moving into a . . . world in which power and influence [are] diffused among a multiplicity of states. . . .

—U.S. DEPUTY SECRETARY OF STATE
LAWRENCE EAGLEBURGER, 1989

This book is about a future, one populated by several roughly equal great powers. It is not the only possible future; it is simply one that many scholars, diplomats, and journalists believe will emerge early in the twenty-first century.

We call such a future world "multipolar" in order to contrast it with situations where either one (unipolar) or two (bipolar) countries possess overwhelming power. For years, international relations theorists have debated whether multipolar systems composed of several great powers are more or less stable than unipolar or bipolar systems. Our purpose here is not to continue that debate. Assuming that a multipolar future is highly probable, we intend to focus on the conditions under which it will be peaceful. As you will see in the chapters ahead, there are many different types of multipolar systems, some of which are less war prone than others. Our goal is to isolate the characteristics of multipolar systems that make them stable and to identify the strategies that the great powers in them have pursued in order to make them so.

Of course, only time will reveal whether we will be living in a multipolar world at the beginning of the next century. Nevertheless, we submit that the odds are high enough and the stakes important enough that we should begin thinking about the ramifications of a multipolar future now instead of waiting to be overtaken by events; in other words, it would be wise and prudent to plan how to avoid the least stable types of multipolarity.

But how can we do this when multipolarity is just far enough over our time horizon that its shape is difficult to see clearly? Our proposal is simple: We intend to look to the past for guidance. Since the birth of the modern state system in 1495, there have been six periods of multipolarity. Some periods have experienced more conflict and war than others. Our aims in this book are to locate the sources of their instability and then assess their implications for any future multipolar system. In addition, we will suggest what paths are open to the great powers for avoiding these destabilizing influences as we move toward the millennium.

To succeed in this search for paths to a multipolar peace, we need to know the hazards that will be encountered along the way. Thus we begin our quest by taking stock of the familiar but dangerous terrain of the post–Cold War world. Here, in the introductory chapter, we set the inquiry into perspective by examining the unfolding properties of contemporary world politics that will structure how analysts are likely to interpret great-power relations in the twilight of the twentieth century. This opens the way in Chapter 2 for an examination of the lessons suggested by the bipolar Cold War system from which we have recently emerged. Chapter 3 introduces different types of multipolarity and prepares us for a comparative analysis of past multipolar periods (Part II) and our prescriptions (Part III) for preserving peace in a new, twenty-first century multipolar world.

DANGERS IN A DISORDERLY NEW WORLD ORDER

When John Lewis Gaddis (1986) coined the phrase "the long peace" to dramatize the virtual absence of war among the great powers since 1945—the longest period of history without a war between major powers—it provoked a vigorous debate about the factors that prevented the Cold War from turning hot. Since then, this debate has inspired hope that the postwar peace will endure, fears that it will end, and disagreement about the policies that might ensure the former and prevent the latter.

Rapid, unanticipated changes often create apprehension about the future of world affairs. As policymakers and scholars have attempted to understand the profound transformations occurring since the end of the Cold War, they have found it difficult to free themselves from old habits of mind; yet it is imperative that they do. With the disintegration of the Soviet Union, the reunification of Germany, and the eruption of ethnonationalist conflicts in southeastern Europe and elsewhere, policymakers face a future whose geopolitical shape will be unlike the world of their memories. "If we could first know where we are and wither we are tending," Abraham Lincoln once observed, "we could better judge what to do, and how to do it." Because the Cold War is barely over, we face great uncertainty about where we are and the direction in which world affairs are headed. Judging what to do and how to do it presents a formidable challenge, which explains why policymakers across the globe "have yet to sort out the complexities of a world suddenly wrenched from the rigid discipline of two power centers" (Schmemann, 1993: A4).

"Great things are achieved," Giuseppe Mazzini noted in 1910, "by guessing the direction of one's century." Trend is not destiny, but if present trends continue, the new international system is likely to be influenced by

- the increasing destructiveness, accuracy, and proliferation of modern weaponry and, despite the end of the Cold War, intensified thirst for security through military preparedness;
- the continuing internationalization of national economies;
- the passage of political clout from governments to private transnational actors such as multinational corporations;
- the widening gap between the world's rich and poor, exacerbated by exponential population growth among those impoverished countries lacking an adequate technological infrastructure;
- the unabated deterioration of the global ecosystem; and
- the resurgence of hypernationalism and outbreak of civil wars bred by ethnic conflicts.

In many respects, recent global changes have spawned myriad new problems. Speaking before the Atlantic Council in early 1992, Les Aspin, Chair of the U.S. House Armed Services Committee (and later secretary of defense under President Clinton), predicted that the rigid Cold War world of "good guys and bad guys" would give way to a complex, fluid world of "grey guys" and diverse threats. As he explained, the threats of the new era represent a significant departure from the threats that dominated the Cold War:

> In the old world, there was only one thing that posed a threat. It was the Soviet Union. In the new world, there will be diverse threats.
>
> In the old world, the very survival of our nation was at stake. In the new world, the interests of our nation will be at risk.
>
> In the old world, we knew what threatened us. In the new world, we will have to learn what threatens us.
>
> In the old world, the policy of deterrence reduced the threat of nuclear war. In the new world, deterrence will not always stop an adversary from threatening Americans and American interests.
>
> In the old world, the two superpowers had thousands and thousands of nuclear weapons and were prepared to use them. In the new world, many nations and groups will vie to acquire nuclear weapons. (Aspin, 1992: 2)

Because a wide spectrum of problems has risen on political agendas in the wake of the Cold War, the concerns of today's foreign policymakers are fundamentally different and more diverse from what they were just a short time ago. Though the danger of nuclear weapons and interstate warfare continues, it would be foolish to neglect the dangers posed by such emergent threats as trade-bloc competition, neomercantilism, trade protectionism, the continuing impoverishment of the least developed countries, acid rain, deforestation, global warming, soaring population growth, the AIDS epidemic, international drug trafficking, the depletion of the earth's finite resources, and destruction of its protective ozone layer.[1] These problems command attention, especially since human survival no longer appears as precarious as it did during the most frigid period of the Cold War. Now that fears of nuclear annihilation have receded, the economic and ecological dimensions of national security have assumed greater prominence.

Still, while the impact of these new nonmilitary threats to global welfare promises to be potent, they do not necessarily mean that geoeconomics or ecopolitics will replace geopolitics. The distribution of power and threats to great-power peace demand continuing attention, and therefore military power balances among the most powerful states will remain of paramount importance.[2] For without the successful coordination of great-power relations, no other threats can be managed. Preserving peace is the *sine qua non* to prosperity and progress.

There is no reasonable assurance that the so-called "new world order" will be orderly (see Box 1.1). Despite the revolutionary transformations that have occurred in world politics since the dismantling of the Berlin Wall in 1989, military threats have not disappeared. To a large extent, many properties of international politics have not changed since the Soviet Union began to dissolve in 1991. The most salient feature of world politics—the relentless competitive struggle for power in an anarchical environment—is still in evidence everywhere, not just in the separatist revolts that have fractured formerly united countries, but also in the behavior of the strongest states toward one another. Communism may be in decline, but the competition at the top continues. For example, in 1992 Boris Yeltsin renounced communism, but not the prerogatives that go with great-power status. Similarly, the leaders of the ascending great powers, Germany, Japan, and China, have continued to express appreciation of the need for power and of the quest for the privileges conferred by that power.

1. Sadly, this list is not exhaustive, as there are many threats that portend "twenty-first century blues" (Ryan, 1993). One might add, for example, the potential transnational problem of multidrug-resistant strains of tuberculosis. What is truly frightening is that "the human immunodeficiency virus looks like an example rather than a culminating disaster" (Preston, 1992: 62).

2. As Paul Kennedy (1993b: 129, 130) has written, "the continued relevance of nation-states and military power was amply demonstrated in the 1990–91 Gulf War." Rather than thinking about the newer nonmilitary threats as "replacing" the more traditional threats to security, it makes more sense to think of them as "*coming alongside*" the older ones.

BOX 1.1
THE COLD WAR'S WAKE: MORE PERIL THAN PROMISE?

"[The Western victory in the Cold War was] so complete that it threatens to destabilize many habitual relationships [at the very time] the United States itself manifests too many characteristics of national decline for comfort."
—David Calleo (1992: 174–178)

"The old world order provided a stability of sorts. The Cold War exacerbated a number of Third World conflicts, but economic conflicts among the United States, Europe and Japan were dampened by common concerns about the Soviet military threat. . . . Rather than an end of history, the post–Cold War world is witnessing a return of history in the diversity of the sources of international conflict."
—Joseph S. Nye, Jr. (1992b: 84–85)

"The international system has always been characterized by instability and there is little evidence that the future will be markedly different. Indeed, the ebbing of the Cold War may produce an upsurge of regional political turbulence."
—Ted Galen Carpenter (1991: 32)

"It can be confidently predicted that the combination of human fallibility and nuclear arms will inevitably lead to nuclear destruction."
—Robert S. McNamara (1993: A13)

"We are witnessing today . . . a return to ethnicity, to nationalism, to self-determination, to the struggle for influence and power."
—Ronald Steel (1992: 173)

"Far from ushering in a period of 'kinder, gentler,' and more purely cooperative relations among the industrial democracies, the end of the Cold War is likely to mark the dawning of the era of tougher bargaining and greater self-assertion."
—Aaron L. Friedberg (1992: 102)

"With the Cold War's end have come the erosion of the discipline of alliances, the diminution of restraints on nationalistic excess, [and] a preoccupation with economic competitiveness abroad. . . ."
—Barber B. Conable, Jr., and John C. Whitehead (1993: 5–6)

"The next forty-five years in Europe . . . are likely to be substantially more violent than the past forty-five years. . . ."
—John J. Mearsheimer (1992b: 48)

"The end of the cold war has made the world safe for regional wars and not just in the third world."
—William E. Odom (1993: A15)

In this setting, the great powers' historic penchant for perceiving each other as rivals has not vanished. As Michael J. Sandel (cited in McNamara, 1991: 12) observed, "The end of the Cold War does not mean an end of global competition between the superpowers. Once the ideological dimension fades, what we are left with is not peace and harmony, but old-fashioned global politics based on dominant powers competing for influence and pursuing their national interests." Whereas we can rejoice in the fact that a real change has occurred in previously antagonistic great-power relations now that the Cold War has ended, we must recognize that differences in the interests of the great powers have not disappeared. It is likely that "the more traditional struggles of great powers" will resume (Kennan, 1989: 25). In short, the "high politics" of military security is likely to remain the world's primary concern well into the twenty-first century.

THE SPECTER OF MULTIPOLARITY

To some optimists, the tides of change that swept across the Eurasian landmass following the collapse of communism signaled "the end of mankind's ideological evolution and the universalization of Western liberal democracy as the final form of government" (Fukuyama, 1989: 3). They have taken confidence and comfort in many encouraging developments, including not just the recent wave of democratization (Huntington, 1991b), but also the new superpower disarmament accords (INF, START), the ability of the United Nations after years of Cold War paralysis to flex its peacekeeping muscles (Rochester, 1993), the steps toward European political integration suggested by the Maastricht Accords, and the resurgence of support for strengthening international law (Moynihan, 1990) and reducing barriers to free trade.

To others, these sea changes suggested not history's end, but its resumption. To them, the Cold War image of two superpowers astride the globe has given way to a different configuration of states, a system composed of a handful of great-power rivals. The end of the Cold War does not mean the end of political, economic, ideological, or even military rivalry among these powers. On the contrary, it could mean "increased instability, unpredictability, and violence in international affairs" (Huntington, 1989: 6).

To this school of thought, therefore, the future threatens to resemble its ugly past. It is ripe with potential for renewed great-power conflict alongside the continuing danger of nuclear proliferation (Zuckerman, 1993) and a new arms race (Klare, 1993), mounting protectionism between new trade blocs (Thurow, 1992a), the threat posed by cultural divisions as a growing source for international conflict (Huntington, 1993a and 1993b), and the prospect that in a world in which "fewer than 10 percent of the 186 countries on earth are ethnically homogeneous" (Talbott, 1990: 70) nationalist revolts will spread civil war, invite great-power intervention (Stedman, 1993), and transform the new democratic governments "into something ugly and dangerous" (Kober, 1993: 63).

In this simultaneously integrating and disintegrating world, the changing structure of the international system as defined by the relative power of its strongest states is of critical importance. And that change is unambiguously profound. "We are leaving the atypical period of a bipolar world in which two superpowers reigned supreme," President Bush's deputy secretary of state proclaimed when jarring and unforeseen shifts rocked the strategic landscape from the Baltic to the Adriatic (Eagleburger, 1989: 244). Similarly, Paul Nitze (1992: 27), a special adviser to President Reagan, suggested that the global community was in the midst of "a transition to a world quite different from the one we have known since 1945." What these former U. S. government officials saw on the diplomatic horizon was a multipolar future, created by the rise of new rivals to American leadership concomitant with the decline of the United States relative to these challengers:

> The United States is less strong today, a lot less strong—economically, politically, culturally—than it was in the 1960s. Europe and Japan have meanwhile become relatively stronger. . . . The heady days of hegemony are gone, never to return. The United States needs to accept that it is just one major power among many in a world of great disorder, a disorder that promises to increase considerably into the next century. (Wallerstein, 1993a: 145, 151; see also 1993b)

The question raised by the specter of multipolarity is whether such a future will usher in a period of great-power peace and cooperation, or a perilous one characterized by great-power conflict and confrontation.

Given widespread recognition of the fact that "world order does not spring up organically [and] that it is made up by the major powers" (Odom, 1993: A15), at this defining moment a heated debate has erupted over the long-term prospects for peace under a system composed of three or more great powers of approximately equal strength. As might be expected, people visualize the menu of choices presented by a system of diffused global power in very different ways. Concern about a multipolar future ultimately stems from the fact that when power has been evenly distributed among several great powers in the past, they have tended to act assertively, independently, and competitively. Behind the ceremonial smiles and handshakes, former friends have drifted apart and a climate of suspicion and mistrust has arisen. Conceivably, a new multipolar distribution of power could culminate in a renewed struggle for supremacy that could end the longest period of great-power peace in modern history.

Indeed, if we look to the past to anticipate the future, we have reasons for fear. As we will see in subsequent chapters, the end of every previous great-power war was followed by an initial hopeful burst of cooperation and institution building to forge a stable new order among the victorious powers. But each of these great-power designs—symbolized by the Peace of Westphalia

(1648), the Treaty of Utrecht (1713), the Concert of Europe (1815), the League of Nations (1919), and the United Nations (1945)—all ultimately proved ephemeral. In each case, as a multipolar distribution of power underwent changes in the great powers' relative power, collaboration gave way to competition. Sooner or later, every previous multipolar system has collapsed, as one or more of the major powers have expressed their dissatisfaction with the existing hierarchy and regime and endeavored by force to overturn the status quo. Rivalry has routinely culminated in a hegemonic struggle for supremacy that has ended in a new catastrophic general war.

Yet we have no way of knowing that the future will resemble this gloomy past. Patterns and practices can change, and it is possible that policymakers can learn from past mistakes and avoid repeating them.

For that, they must peer intensely into history. Strictly speaking, the world situation is always unprecedented, but is never *entirely* unlike situations in the past. The similarities can suggest lessons. And even if the past cannot provide us with perfect analogies, "we need to seek episodes and patterns that may provide guidance for how international politics might develop or for the choices various countries—particularly our own—might face" (Jervis, 1992: 262–263). From that kind of inquiring search, it may be possible to break the cycle of global war that has pervaded world history and create a future in which the threat of massive destruction might be reduced, perhaps avoided.

To frame the questions that must be confronted, we need to introduce the dimensions of the problems and trends that define the nature of multipolar systems and the behaviors associated with them.

The Problem of Relative Decline

Power can be distributed in many ways: It may be concentrated in the hands of one preponderant state, as in the ancient Mediterranean world at the zenith of the Roman Empire, or it may be diffused among several rival states, as it was during the Italian Renaissance when Venice, Florence, Milan, Naples, and the papal states possessed approximately equal strength.

According to many scholars, the distribution of power that will emerge early in the next century could resemble the European multipolar balance-of-power system of the nineteenth century. Such a system might encompass the United States, Russia, Japan, China, and Germany, and conceivably a politically integrated European Community if the ambitious European Union treaty that its members signed in February 1992 lays the foundation for a European federation and a common policy posture in world affairs.

Whereas some analysts envision a relatively short transition between the bipolar system that characterized the Cold War and a new multipolar period, others foresee a more lengthy passage, characterized by a period of American unipolarity. "No doubt, multipolarity will come in time," writes Charles Krauthammer (1991: 23–24). "In perhaps another generation or so there will be great powers coequal with the United States, and the world will, in structure, resemble the pre–World War I era." But it will not happen soon because the United States still "is the only country with the military, diplomatic, political and economic assets to be a decisive player in any conflict in whatever part of the world it chooses to involve itself."

At present, counters Geir Lundestad (1992: 205–206), "no country is really able to challenge the United States for the Number One position as such." But "the United States has undoubtedly been suffering a relative decline, and will most likely continue to do so in certain important respects." The "domestic composition of production is shifting toward becoming a low-wage, low-technology manufacturing and raw materials economy." Moreover, this decline will be difficult to reverse because rather than just losing market position, "the supply base of the economy is unraveling: the component and parts technologies, materials and machinery sectors, and related industrial skills necessary to sustain competitive manufacturing and development are eroding, or are already gone" (Borrus and Zysman with Bell, 1992: 143, 146). Once the world's largest creditor nation, the United States has become the largest debtor nation, with net debt projected to be as high as $1 trillion by the mid-1990s (Chace, 1992: 22).

These symptoms of economic weakness and "diminished expectations" (Krugman, 1990) do not bode well for the long-term political and even military supremacy of the United States because the economic foundations of national security are perhaps more important than ever in today's fast-paced global economy (Sandholtz et al., 1992), and the gap between the financial means and the political ends of global leadership continues to widen (Tonelson, 1993b). In an environment in which the distribution of financial power is arguably equal in importance to the distribution of military power for the relative rank of the great powers, differential growth rates can make an extraordinarily rapid impact on their standing in the international hierarchy (Morita, 1993).

More troubling still are the massive social problems facing the United States: violent crime, drug abuse, gaps in health care delivery, and deteriorating educational performance. Whether these and other domestic difficulties will accelerate the relative decline in American power vis-à-vis other countries and usher in an age of multipolarity remains an open question (see Chapter 8, and Gwin and Feinberg, 1989; Miller, 1994; Nau, 1990; Nye, 1990; Kennedy, 1993b; Layne, 1993). Nevertheless, it is imperative to determine the systemic consequences if such changes occur, since available evidence suggests that the U.S. position in the world power hierarchy is shifting because of the gains made by other countries (Hughes, 1991: 21).

Power and Polarity

Before the consequences of an emergent multipolar system can be assessed, the conceptual underpinnings of the terms that describe its character must be

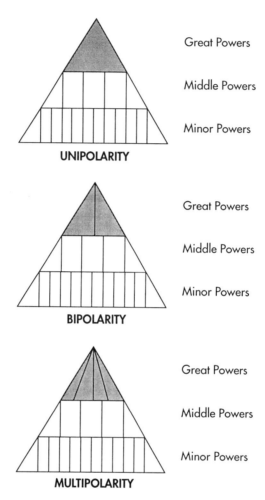

FIGURE 1.1. The Hierarchy of World Power. *Source:* Adapted from Richard Rose-crance, *International Relations: Peace or War?* (New York: Mc-Graw-Hill, 1973), p. 115.

defined. In essence, polarity refers to the distribution of power among the members of the state system. As Figure 1.1 illustrates, unipolar systems have one dominant power center, bipolar systems contain two centers of power, and multipolar systems possess more than two such centers.

To discuss polarity is to talk about power. Simply stated, power refers to the capacity to control the behavior of others. Power is *relational* because it pertains to the ability of the actor attempting to exercise power to make the target continue a course of action, change what it is doing, or refrain from acting. A powerful person, in other words, can significantly reduce the probability of something he or she does not want to happen and increase the probability of a preferred outcome (Deutsch, 1978: 30–31).

Power is frequently described as the currency of politics. Yet, as David Baldwin (1989: 26) points out, "the problem of measuring political power is very much like the problem of measuring purchasing power in an economy without money." Lacking consensus on a standard unit of account for measuring political power, statesmen customarily have turned their attention to itemizing national capabilities. Their focus on the putative or potential power of a nation assumes that actualized power is difficult to gauge except after the fact when influence is achieved (Knorr, 1970). Consider the following analogy:

> A certain gasoline engine is said to *have* fifty horsepower. We are not under any illusion, however, that a quantity of fifty horsepower is possessed or owned by that engine. All that we are willing to accept is that it *rates* at fifty horsepower when it is running under certain specified conditions. We understand that horsepower results from interacting processes involving fuel, air, combustion, and mechanical motions, all of which occur in going through the engine. The horsepower of the engine is a performance trait. (McClelland, 1966: 73)

Similarly, power in international politics is also a performance trait. Analysts who rivet our attention on national capabilities do so because they believe that power is a function of these capabilities. Power results from interacting processes involving a country's human and nonhuman resources. And an analysis of power, Robert A. Dahl (1970: 15) reminds us, "is no merely theoretical enterprise but a matter of greatest practicality. For how one acts in political life depends very heavily on one's beliefs about the nature, distribution, and practices of 'power'."

Capabilities and Context

If the wellsprings of power lie deep within the bedrock of capabilities, from which specific resources will power flow? As illustrated in Table 1.1, scholars who agree that national power derives from a country's resource base sometimes disagree over the composition of that base. Like chefs at a chili cookoff, everyone has his or her own list of ingredients. Normally some combination of geographic, demographic, economic, and other tangible factors are mixed with intangible factors like leadership, morale, and the cultural resources that Joseph Nye (1990: 32) calls "soft power." Though the recipes may differ, the results are usually the same: Power is equated with those capabilities that enhance a country's war-making ability.

The importance customarily accorded military prowess arises from the tendency to regard force as the ultimate arbiter of serious interstate disputes. States are sovereign; that is, no higher authority stands above them with the legitimacy and coercive ability needed to undertake the diverse functions that

TABLE 1.1
Contending Views of the Elements of National Power

Crabb (1965: 7)	Hartmann (1983: 41–67)	Kulski (1968: 98–101)	Lerche and Said (1963: 59)	Morgenthau (1985: 127–183)
Geography	Geographic element	Size, location	Geographic position	Geography
Economic resources	Economic element	Economic resources and raw materials	Resource endowment	National resources
Technological resources		Technological resources	Educational and technical level	
Military forces	Military element	Military potential	Military power	Military preparedness
Population	Demographic element	Population characteristics	Population and manpower	Population
National character	Historical–psychological–sociological element			National character
			National morale	National morale
	Organizational–administrative element	Quality of national leaders and elites	Political economic and social structure	Quality of government
Ideology				
		Industrial capacity	Industrial and agricultural productive capacity	Industrial capability
			International strategic position	
				Quality of diplomacy
		Land, maritime, and air transportation capacity		

TABLE 1.1 (Continued)
Contending Views of the Elements of National Power

Organski (1968: 124)	Palmer and Perkins (1957: 35–91)	Stoessinger (1969: 15–27)	U.S. Army (1960: 2)	Van Dyke (1966: 199–200)
Geography	Geography	Geography	Geographic component	Geographic base
Resources	Natural resources	Natural resources	Economic component	Economic system
Economic development	Technology	Economic and industrial development		Scientific and inventive potentialities
			Military component	Armed establishment
Population	Population	Population		Demographic base
		National character	Sociological component	
National morale	Morale	National morale		
Political development	Leadership	Government: national leadership	Political component	Governmental organization and administration (wisdom of leadership)
	Ideology	Ideology		Ideas
				Productive capacity
				Strategic position
				Transportation and communications
				Intelligence

governments perform in domestic political systems. Without a higher authority to adjudicate interstate disputes, self-help becomes the court of last appeal. A nation's military strength, combined with the perception that it was willing to use it, has traditionally been "a vital backstop to the various diplomatic, political, economic, and other techniques that it might employ in conducting its foreign relations" (Rothgeb, 1992: 7).

While military strength may be effective in controlling the behavior of friends and foes in some contexts, it is ineffective in others. Power is *situationally specific*: The components of a nation's resource base are relatively low in fungibility or usability. The military capabilities that allow an actor to influence one set of countries in a certain issue-area may be useless in influencing other countries on a different matter (Baldwin, 1989: 134–138). The West's military force did not give it the power to reverse the policies of OPEC during the 1970s "oil decade," for example. A state's true power, therefore, is defined in terms of the kinds of targets or actors that it can control and the types of behavior that a power wielder can deploy to exercise influence over the target. A great power is a state that is able to exercise control over a *wide domain of targets* and an *extensive scope of behaviors*, usually by virtue of having a *broad range of rewards and punishments* at its disposal. When more than two great powers exist, and when a rough parity exists in the domain, scope, and range of their might, the structure of the state system may be thought of as multipolar. In this book, our emphasis is on those great powers at the apex of the international hierarchy because it is their behavior that will have the greatest influence on future developments worldwide.

This is unabashedly a "high politics" perspective framed in the logic of realpolitik, which customarily has been relied on to study the evolving relations of the great powers and the consequences of their changing character. As we will illuminate below, the assumptions underlying realist theory, in both its classic and neorealist (Waltz, 1979) versions, have much to recommend it for this purpose. Realism, we aver, best informs analysis of the dynamics surrounding the rise of a potentially preeminent power and the realignments of the other great powers in reaction to its ascending hegemony.

However, before proceeding with a description of these assumptions, it is important to clarify and specify the theoretical orientation that will organize our approach in this book. Because realism directs our attention to the distribution of power within the state system, we will use it as the *starting point* for our analysis of polarity configurations. But as the reader will see in subsequent chapters, we part company with realism on a number of principles. In contrast to many realists, we do not view the nation-state as the sole actor of international importance; nor do we see the state as a unitary actor. Furthermore, we give much greater emphasis than do the realist and neorealist approaches to the possibility of change and cooperation by maintaining that the great powers' core interests are not inherently incompatible and that powerful rivals can collaborate rather than compete in order to enhance their mutual interest in promoting prosperity and in preventing rivalries from collapsing into a destructive war.

In addition, we place considerable stress on the liberal premise that progress is possible because the great powers can maintain order in an anarchical system by agreeing to follow norms or rules to regulate their relations, in part because it is in their enlightened self-interest to do so. This capacity is reflected in rules the great powers have sometimes embraced, we will show, to delegitimize war and to orchestrate their alliance relationships to successfully maintain a pacifying balance-of-power equilibrium.

Our approach also differs from realism by assigning importance to the impact of domestic politics on a powerful state's international behavior, in conformity with the liberal expectation that democracies do not wage war against each other (Doyle, 1995) and that the recent spread of democratic governance can potentially usher in a new era in world affairs (especially if these developments persist). And we attempt to understand the future of great-power relations by stressing not the independence of economic processes from the political–military arena, but rather their increasingly tight interdependence. In fact, our orientation focuses on the growing convergence of the economic and military spheres of contemporary international life; accordingly, it differs from conventional realism by showing how developments and great-power relations in the economic arena vary from and are influencing those in the military arena, in ways that bode both hope for lasting great-power cooperation and the danger of renewed conflict.

Hence, in combination, perhaps the most important differences between our view and that of realism lie in how we conceptualize multipolarity, the prospects for change and great-power cooperation, and the kind of policy prescriptions we consequently recommend to increase stability in an emerging multipolar system. This perspective toward analysis thus bridges the gulf between realism and neorealism on the one hand and the so-called neoliberal theories on the other (see Kegley, 1993 and 1995a; Ray, 1995b).

That approach will take on meaning as we proceed. Let us begin by outlining the foundations provided by the realist framework, which, as noted, is the starting point for our investigation.

CONTINUITY AND CHANGE IN THE STRUCTURE OF WORLD POWER

Although most students of world politics believe that the distribution of power matters, they argue about which *kind* of distribution is most conducive to peace. Statesmen and academicians disagree as to whether peace is a product of a preponderance of power or a diffusion of power. As a result, the historical record must be examined to resolve this controversy. In multipolar systems, when three or more great powers possess a high proportion of the wealth and weapons in the entire system but none has a clear-cut advantage, is a major war likely? Does the number of such poles matter? The goals of this book are to explore these questions and to apply the answers to the multipolar future we face.

The historical and comparative evaluation of multipolar systems can be best informed by a framework that (1) makes power and its distribution the center of its focus and (2) recognizes both continuities and changes in the international system's essential properties. What conditions do we assume are permanent, or constant, and what conditions do we assume tend to change over time?

For explanatory purposes, we will follow realist assumptions, which customarily guide the study of great-power relations. This perspective views power and its distribution as key variables for understanding past patterns and forecasting future outcomes. Realists contend that

> The *structure* of a system refers to the distribution of capabilities among similar units. In international politics the most important units are states, and the relevant capabilities [are] their power resources. . . . The structure of the system (the distribution of power resources among states) profoundly affects the nature of the [system]. . . . (Keohane and Nye, 1989: 20–21)

The only qualification that we add to this orienting premise is that in the overall scheme of things, it is the distribution of power *among the most powerful states* that ultimately matters most, and the degree to which these great powers are clustered into polarized alliances is an equally important structural phenomenon. This focus on the distribution of power and the clustering of the powerful is justified by a simple stubborn fact—the most disruptive and destructive system-transforming wars have undoubtedly been between the great powers:

> There is a strong *a priori* reason to expect that . . . patterns [of war and their consequences] may be quite dissimilar in the behavior of major powers and minor powers. . . . Most international war has been conducted by states classified as great powers. In fact, very few war-prone countries fall outside the great-power category. (Geller, 1988: 367)

To highlight change is not, however, to dismiss continuities. We must be mindful that some features of world politics are relatively permanent while others are subject to variation over time; these variable features, when they change, will most influence the incidence of war and the duration of peace. Table 1.2 summarizes the assumptions about these distinctions that our modified realist framework will employ. This list is largely self-explanatory, but the assumptions behind it require brief comment and elaboration.

First, in the realist view, "power counts decisively in international relations, and . . . the crucial data are to be found in the answer to the question, which states have how much of what kind of power?" (Claude, 1989: 79). The pursuit of power is a primary motive underlying state behavior, and this drive is as-

TABLE 1.2
Constancy and Change in Great-Power Politics: Realist Assumptions

Permanent Properties	Changing Characteristics
Centrality of power	Distribution of power
Great-power pursuit of power	Great-power force ratios
Hierarchy of nations	Rank of the great powers in the system's hierarchy
Threat of hegemonic dominion	Rise and demise of threat of empire building
Salience of military capabilities	Relationship of economic resources to military might
Polarity	Number of great powers
Great-power rivalry	Intensity of great-power competition
Absence of central authority in an anarchical system	Degree of voluntary great-power sacrifice of sovereignty and efforts at cooperation

sumed to be permanent; as Frederick the Great audaciously expressed it, "The politics of sovereigns . . . labors to consolidate the safety of the State and to extend as much as possible . . . the number of its possessions [and] the power . . . of the prince" (cited in Schuman, 1969: 78). Hence, it is an axiom that "Potential war being thus a dominant factor in international politics, military strength becomes a recognized standard of political values" (Carr, 1939: 109).

Yet, realism does not assert that the supposedly universal drive for power results in its even distribution. That condition rarely exists, and when it does, it is only temporary. Relentless competition for predominance invariably produces disparities of strength among the powerful. One reason is that the great powers' capabilities grow at different rates as they attempt to maximize their individual strength relative to the others:

> The truth of the matter is that states are interested only in a balance (imbalance) which is in their favor. Not an equilibrium, but a generous margin is their objective. There is no real security in being just as strong as a potential enemy; there is security only in being a little stronger. (Spykman, 1942: 21–22)

As a result of this drive for a comparative and competitive (Porter, 1990) advantage in power, "the relative strengths of the leading nations in world affairs never remain constant" (Kennedy, 1987: xv). The distribution is constantly shifting, evolving either in the direction of world domination by a sole surviving predator or in the direction of shared power among many equal competitors.

Second, the structure of this distribution is hierarchical; stratification among the actors in the system cannot be avoided. The international system is a class system, with states falling into different categories of power depending on their relative capabilities. As a system of unequals, "a distinction" can always be made "between relatively strong and relatively weak actors," and this distinction is predicated on the assumption "that members of each class are more or less equal with the other members of their class" (Thompson, 1988: 29). But while the existence of such a hierarchy is assumed to be a permanent condition, this does not mean that the rank of states within the hierarchy is resistant to change. Movement of countries between the classes has been commonplace as states ascend and decline in the pecking order. The hierarchy persists, but the rank order of states changes, and these changes are responsible at particular junctures for the outbreak of the most catastrophic wars: "The hegemonic onslaughts of Habsburg Spain between 1585 and 1648, of Louis XIV between 1672 and 1713, of Napoleon from 1792 to 1815, and in the twentieth century's two world wars, resulted from the failure of the central system to cope with the rise and decline of states" (Doran, 1991: 132). As George Modelski (1972: 165) puts it, "the Great Powers and their striving for status have served to bring out the worst features of the nation-state system."

Third, hierarchy breeds competition, and competition in a system of unequals driven by envy and a struggle for status precipitates war. What varies is the frequency with which great-power contestants resort to war, as well as the intensity of the competition among rivals in different epochs. But as the period of détente between the United States and the Soviet Union indicates, sometimes the great powers voluntarily regulate their competition by accepting rules for the contest and by cooperating to avoid war.

Finally, whereas the distribution of power will be permanently skewed in a division between the "haves" and the "have-nots" in any multipolar system, realism assumes that the number of centers of power can and will change, and that the changes are consequential.

To summarize, the high politics of peace and security is largely a process controlled by the powerful. How those great powers relate to one another is conditioned by their perceived interests and relative capabilities. Changes in relative power, in the rank of states in the global hierarchy, and in the number of great powers are observable; and these changes are predicted to cause convulsions in multipolar systems.

> Actors enter social relations and create social structures in order to advance particular sets of political, economic, or other types of interests. Because the interests of some of the actors may conflict with those of other actors, the particular interests that are most favored by those social arrangements tend to reflect the relative powers of the actors involved. . . . Over time, however, the interests of individual actors and the balance of power among the actors do change as a result of economic, technological, and other developments. As a consequence, those actors who benefit most from a change in the social system and who gain the

power to effect such change will seek to alter the system in ways that reflect the new distribution of power and the interests of its new dominant members. Thus, a precondition for political change lies in a disjuncture between the existing social system and the redistribution of power toward those actors who would benefit most from a change in the system. (Gilpin, 1981: 9)

In the chapters ahead we will examine various propositions that are suggested by the preceding line of reasoning. We will evaluate what the history of previous multipolar systems tells us about the sources of stability in periods characterized by a diffusion of power among several relatively equal great powers. This will provide a basis for proposing policies that today's great powers might pursue in order to raise the odds that an emerging multipolar system will be peaceful.

To place our analysis in its proper context, we must first look to the recent past and assess the impact of the Cold War on contemporary great-power relations.

· 2 ·

RETHINKING COLD WAR LESSONS

America's role in this sea change in world politics is straightforward: We must leave behind not only the Cold War but also the conflicts that preceded it.

—U.S. SECRETARY OF STATE JAMES BAKER,
Statement to the House Foreign
Affairs Committee, 1990

On returning to Washington from the first Big Three summit conference in Teheran in 1943, President Franklin D. Roosevelt told a national radio audience: "I got along fine with Marshal Stalin. . . . I believe that we are going to get along very well with him and the Russian people—very well indeed" (*Public Papers and Addresses of Franklin D. Roosevelt*, 1943: 558). At the Yalta conference fourteen months later, Joseph Stalin echoed Roosevelt's optimism. According to James F. Byrnes, director of the Office of War Mobilization, Stalin had been lavish in his praise of the United States; in fact, "Joe was the life of the party" (Yergin, 1977: 67).

Yet the party was almost over. The period between the Teheran (1943) and Yalta (1945) summit conferences was the high point of Soviet–American relations. With their armies sweeping toward the Oder and the Rhine rivers and the common military threat, Germany's hegemonic quest, about to be defeated, mutual suspicions in Moscow and Washington hardened into policy disagreements over the future of the postwar world. The day before his suicide, Adolf Hitler predicted that the "laws of both history and geography" would compel the Soviet Union and the United States to engage in "a trial of strength" (Bullock, 1962: 772–773). He thus echoed the prophecy of his geostrategic counselor, Major General Karl Haushofer, who had predicted in 1938 that "Potentially, the United States is the world's foremost political and economic power, destined to dominate the world once it puts its heart into power politics" (in Schweller, 1993: 92) and that the Soviet Union was destined, as the globe's other great land mass, to devote all its energies to combatting this force.

22

As allied collaboration plummeted in a downward spiral of charges and countercharges, it seemed as if Hitler's ominous prediction would come to pass. On the one hand, Stalin (1946) insisted that the defeat of Germany did not eliminate the danger of foreign aggression, and his heir-apparent, Andrei Zhdanov (1947), identified American expansionism as the major threat to world peace. On the other hand, W. Averell Harriman, U.S. ambassador to the Soviet Union, warned of a "barbarian invasion of Europe" (Truman, 1955: 71), and George F. Kennan, his chief assistant, asserted that the Soviet leadership sought to destroy "our traditional way of life" (*Foreign Relations of the United States*, 1946: 706). Lacking the glue of a common external threat, the Grand Alliance of World War II dissolved amidst distrust, apprehension, confusion, and bitter recriminations. It was as if Alexis de Tocqueville's prediction of 1835 had finally come to pass: The Americans and Russians now held "the destinies of half of mankind" in their hands.

But war did not erupt between the Soviet Union and the United States. Despite nearly five decades of intense rivalry and numerous serious disputes, the superpowers avoided a trial of military strength.

How do we explain this rather surprising pattern of prolonged—though hostile—peace under bipolar conditions? Definitive answers elude us, and any attempt to find them must surmount a number of analytic obstacles. Not only are the sources of the "long peace" during the Cold War tangled in a web of interdependent factors, but it is exceedingly difficult to gauge their relative importance. Nevertheless, knowledge about the factors that contributed to peace when a bipolar distribution prevailed may help to prevent new great-power conflicts from escalating to bloodshed in the years ahead, when a new multipolar era could pit any pair of numerous rivals against one another. For this reason, this chapter will examine the characteristics of the bipolar Cold War phase of history that came to a peaceful end in 1991.

WHAT WAS THE LONG PEACE?

The phrase "long peace" has gained popularity because it underscores the fact that the bipolar period from 1945 to the present comprises the longest span of great-power peace since the birth of the modern world system. The phrase also invites misunderstanding, falsely suggesting that the long peace was (1) peaceful, (2) stable, and (3) institutionalized. It was none of these.

Was the Long Peace Peaceful?

When we speak of the long postwar peace, we misrepresent reality because the period since 1945 appears more accurately to have been a "long war" if we observe the entire international system instead of just the subsystem of great powers. Following World War II, a highly unstable tier of Third World nations emerged alongside a stable great-power one. Among the former, armed conflict cost the lives of 21.8 million people (Sivard, 1989: 23). Figure 2.1 summarizes the changing levels of warfare from 1945 to 1988, during which 269 wars occurred (Tillema, 1991). As J. David Singer (1991: 59) points out, "the level of bloody combat between and within national political entities [did] not diminish appreciably. . . . [It took] a different form and occurred in a different neighborhood." The magnitude and severity of Third World conflict amidst the absence of war among the great powers emphasize the fact that the postwar system was far from peaceful. Accordingly, since the phrase "the long peace" refers only to peace *among the great powers*, hereafter it will be used with this restricted meaning in mind.

Was the Long Peace Stable?

The Cold War that coincided with the long peace was fraught with tension and littered with chronic disputes that could have escalated to war at any moment. Because the superpowers perceived the nature of their conflict as zero-sum, "the leaders of each bloc [tried] to destroy and revolutionize their rivals [and sought] to wear down the other [by] using force to maintain and expand their

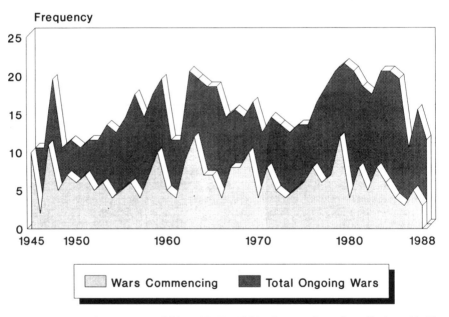

FIGURE 2.1. The Occurrence of War, 1945–1988. *Source:* Based on Herbert K. Tillema, *International Armed Conflict Since 1945* (Boulder, Colo.: Westview, 1991).

blocs" (Pelz, 1991: 74, 75). Indeed, this crusade for hegemonic domination reduced the international system

> to the primitive spectacle of two giants eyeing each other with watchful suspicion. They [bent] every effort to increase their military potential to the utmost, since this is all they [had] to count on. Both [prepared] to strike the first decisive blow, for if one [did] not strike it the other might. Thus, contain or be contained, conquer or be conquered, destroy or be destroyed, [became] the watchwords of Cold War diplomacy. (Morgenthau, 1985: 379)

To use a simple metaphor, the ubiquity of threats to international peace during the Cold War made the stability of the bipolar system more like that of a ball on a ridge than one resting on a plane.

Part of what made the Cold War so tense was that anxieties were heightened by the extraordinary importance the two superpowers attached to recruiting new allies and keeping old ones inside the fold. The Soviet–American conflict spread to virtually every corner of the international system, casting a Cold War patina on regional conflicts around the globe. In all, 251 crises occurred between 1945 and 1985, some of which threatened the very survival of humanity (Brecher and Wilkenfeld, 1991: 86–87), as well as repeated military interventions (see Figure 2.2). Many of these also threatened to escalate into system-wide conflagrations, and all made the conflicts a deadly enterprise everywhere outside the circle of great powers. Although the superpowers may have learned through experience how to diffuse their serious disputes, lesser powers that enhanced their military strength through the military penetration of their neighbors did not develop crisis-management skills commensurate with the new war-making capabilities made possible by the arms they received from their powerful patrons. Overemphasis on the absence of great-power war since 1945 thus may mislead us because it ignores proxy wars between client states, wars in which only one major power fought, military interventions, and repeated crises that at least on one occasion brought Moscow and Washington to the brink of nuclear holocaust.

Will the Long Peace Endure?

Many people erroneously assume long-surviving conditions will endure. The long postwar peace is one of these conditions that might evoke a false sense of continuity and confidence. When the Cold War abruptly ended, there was much celebrating about the "end of history" (Fukuyama, 1992) and the expected obsolescence of great-power war (Mueller, 1992a, 1992b, and 1989). The ideological contest between democratic capitalism and totalitarian communism, which threatened to engulf the world in war, had finally ended. Great-power peace was expected to continue.

History suggests that this kind of persistence forecasting based on trend

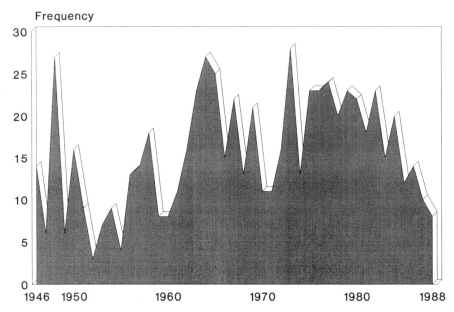

FIGURE 2.2. Military Interventions during the Cold War. *Source:* Based on Frederic S. Pearson, Robert A. Baumann, and Jeffrey Pickering, "International Military Intervention: Global and Regional Redefinitions of Realpolitik." Paper presented at the Annual Meeting of the American Political Science Association, Washington, D.C., August 29–September 1, 1991.

extrapolation is unwarranted. Change is constant. In the past, wars repeatedly have followed periods of peace, even long ones. Recall that

> In 1853, encouraged in part by the long peace after the Napoleonic Wars, the *Manchester Examiner* asserted that "the principles of the Peace Society . . . have unquestionably gained ground among us; statesmen shrink from war now. . . . The period of major-power peace following the Franco–Prussian War . . . spawned several works which forecast the demise and eventual disappearance of international war. The 1911 edition of the *Encyclopaedia Britannica* contained an article [that prophesied] the causes of war would ultimately be eliminated. (Ray, 1991: 330–331)

The great-power peace that persisted during the Cold War could easily break down if the conditions that promoted it erode. Indeed, the achievement of peace rests on inherently fragile foundations; the pillars on which it precariously sits may be too weak institutionally to assure that it will survive, especially if the advent of a multipolar distribution of power weakens their strength.

A safer and saner world depends upon rejecting conventional wisdoms that are more conventional than wise. Until we discover the contribution that various factors made to the long peace during the Cold War, we should "take with a grain of salt any stories . . . about who were the heroes in the Cold War" (Odom, 1992: 29). By questioning the foundations of the long peace during the Cold War, we may illuminate the danger of relying on simple, but possibly fallacious, historical lessons which rationalize counterproductive policies now that the Cold War climate has changed.

POTENTIALLY MYTHICAL CAUSES OF THE LONG PEACE

What prevented the Cold War from turning hot? Many of the "lessons of the past" drawn by contemporary foreign policymakers rest on weak logical and empirical foundations and form a mythology that could undermine accurate understanding of international politics in the twilight of the twentieth century.

Moreover, such myths, if embraced, could lend credence to a number of ill-founded policy prescriptions for extending the long peace in a new multipolar world. Recently advanced interpretations of the causes of the long peace offer little agreement on an accepted set of conclusions. Even less likely is a consensus about the most constructive paths for the great powers to follow in the post–Cold War world, despite their collective interest in preventing another global war.

To separate sense from nonsense, we must critically evaluate a series of prevailing propositions about the reasons for the preservation of superpower peace during the Cold War. Among the most salient of these propositions are (1) alliances deterred great-power warfare; (2) preparations for war preserved peace; and (3) nuclear weapons made war obsolete. Indeed, debate about the nature of the Cold War springs from differences of opinion regarding the bipolar distribution of power and about how these three influences so closely associated with that distribution contributed to the long peace within it (see Box 2.1). Let us examine the logic behind each of these three propositions.

Did Alliances Contain Great-Power Aggression?

Alliances are argued to have been especially instrumental in contributing to the long peace. Following the Second World War, policymakers in Washington and Moscow subscribed to the theory that alliances could deter aggression and augment their nation's defense in the event that deterrence failed, which is why they sought to recruit allies so energetically. When the Cold War ended, this conviction seemed to be confirmed, and the role of alliances in particular was credited with containing Soviet expansionism. "Containment worked," argued President Bush in May 1989, "because our alliances were and are strong."

Yet some analysts hold the opposite opinion. It cannot be conclusively demonstrated, they assert, that alliances were a constructive force in postwar world

BOX 2.1
WHAT WAS BIPOLARITY DURING THE COLD WAR? SOME DEFINING FEATURES AND POSTULATED CONSEQUENCES

During the Cold War the distinction between bipolar and multipolar international systems became commonplace in both popular and academic discussions of international politics. Often this distinction has served merely as a shorthand way of describing the alliance behavior of states during the Cold War period as distinguished from behavior during other periods. Its importance for the academic literature on international politics, however, lies not in its use as a description of states' behavior but as an explanation of it. Used in this way, "bipolarity" refers to that peculiar distribution of power, some scholars claim, that accounts for both the antagonism that developed between the United States and the Soviet Union and the fact that that antagonism, though intense, did not lead to a major war between them. It explains, in other words, why there was a "war" between East and West and also why that war remained "cold."

. . . The word "bipolarity" has at least four distinct meanings in the literature on post–World War II international politics: (1) a condition in which states are polarized into two hostile coalitions; (2) a condition in which there are only two states capable of a strategy of global deterrence; (3) a system of only two states; and (4) a system in which power is distributed in such a way that two states are so powerful that they can each defend themselves against any combination of other states. The first definition is a description of behavior and not an explanation of it and, in any case, is clearly not what recent discussions of the significance of the end of bipolarity have in mind. The second definition is almost universally said to refer to a condition that is independent of bipolarity; moreover, it cannot be what people have in mind who claim that the world is once again characterized by multipolarity. The third definition does not apply to any historical international systems, much less the one that existed during the Cold War. Finally, the fourth definition, far from explaining U.S. and Soviet behavior during the Cold War, makes their behavior inexplicable. Thus bipolarity as an explanatory concept is either undefined, irrelevant to post–World War II international politics, or implies behavior that is inconsistent with the behavior it is supposed to explain. Nevertheless, bipolarity is commonly accepted as one of the most important properties of international politics during the Cold War, and the significance of its disappearance is earnestly debated in many quarters.

—R. Harrison Wagner (1993: 77, 89)

politics. By encircling the Soviet Union in a *cordon sanitaire* of hostile states allied in a common cause, the West may have hardened Soviet resistance, as George F. Kennan (1967), the intellectual father of the containment doctrine, tried to warn. In this sense, the militant containment to which Kennan so vehemently objected could have prolonged the Cold War instead of bringing it to an end (Talbott, 1990: 70).[1]

Georgi Arbatov, director of the Institute for the USA and Canada in Moscow, expressed this view while meeting with the authors in Rome during November 1991:

> The version about President Reagan's "tough" policy and intensified arms race being the most important source of *perestroika*—that it persuaded communists to "give up"—is sheer nonsense. Quite to the contrary, this policy made the life for reformers, for all who yearned for democratic changes in their life, much more difficult. . . . In such tense international situations the conservatives and reactionaries were given predominant influence. That is why . . . Reagan made it practically impossible to start reforms after Brezhnev's death (Andropov had such plans) and made things more difficult for Gorbachev to cut military expenditures.

Despite the fact that alliances were created to contain aggression, it is necessary to ask whether they had an unintended consequence—dividing the antagonists into counterpoised blocs unwilling to strike compromises to end the Cold War. While the answer is unclear, the direct role often ascribed to Cold War alliances in fostering extended deterrence should not be accepted on blind faith. To understand why, it is useful to examine more closely the types of alliances that formed in this bipolar system and the role they performed.

The post–World War II era of alliance politics can be divided into two phases. One phase can usefully be termed a Cold War of *Position*; the other, a Cold War of *Movement* (Morgenthau, 1970: 98). The former entailed efforts by Washington and Moscow to limit external influence over geographic regions that each considered of vital interest in their respective spheres of influence. The latter involved vigorous searches for new partners throughout the globe that could be recruited by either superpower against its rival. One way to approach the question of whether alliances were a supporting pillar of the edifice of the post–World War II great-power peace is to differentiate between the early period dominated by alliances associated with the Cold War of Position and the later period dominated by alliances associated with the Cold War of Move-

---

1. Strictly speaking, American policymakers implemented a form of containment that was at odds with Kennan's original conceptualization of the Soviet Union as an ideological–political (rather than a military) threat to the United States. Instead of encircling the Soviets with allied states, Kennan (1967: 364) recommended that Washington "wait for the internal weakness of Soviet power, combined with frustration in the external field, to moderate Soviet ambitions and behavior."

ment. Although combat did not erupt between the great powers during either period, each successive phase in the post-1945 evolution of alliance building had different consequences for national security and international stability.

Alliances in the Cold War of Position

Despite the promise of universalism that was embodied within the Atlantic Charter (1941) and the Declaration of the United Nations (1942), the early postwar era witnessed a novel version of the principle *cujus regio, ejus religio* (whose the region, his the religion) applied to those territories that were liberated from Axis control. Stalin made clear his position: "Whoever occupies a territory imposes on it his own social system . . . as far as his army can reach" (cited in Djilas, 1961: 114). In accordance with that principle, both Washington and Moscow used alliances to consolidate their power in the territories their respective armies had reached. Far from being flexible coalitions of fairly equal members, these alliances developed into blocs. That is to say, groups of secondary powers clustered around one of the two superpowers.

Driven by an American desire to contain Russian expansionism and an equally strong Soviet desire to build a buffer zone that would preclude another invasion of the USSR, the alliance blocs of the immediate postwar period took on the characteristics of a war of position. For the United States, a line of political entrenchment was constructed by means of the Inter-American Treaty of Reciprocal Assistance (1947), the North Atlantic Treaty Organization (1949), the ANZUS (Australia–New Zealand–United States) Pact (1951), and a number of bilateral alliances designed to both reinforce U.S. geopolitical interests and protect noncommunist centers from communist penetration (for example, Japan [1951], the Philippines [1951], and Spain [1953]). For the Soviet Union, a more secure frontier was established through a series of agreements reached between 1945 and 1948 with various Eastern European countries, agreements that were later institutionalized under the auspices of the Warsaw Treaty Organization (1955). When combined with previous arrangements with the Mongolian People's Republic (1936), a new treaty with Finland (1948), and a formal pact with the People's Republic of China (1950), the alliances with Moscow's western neighbors produced a belt of friendly states around much of its border.

Alliances in the Cold War of Movement

In addition to the alliances that were used to delineate specific spheres of influence, both great powers also engaged in an intense, almost predatory competition for new allies outside of the main geostrategic theater. Beginning with the efforts of Secretary of State John Foster Dulles and First Secretary Nikita Khrushchev, the United States and Soviet Union began to woo states from the periphery of the world system. Globalization of the superpower alliance race during this period of "pactomania" resulted in numerous alliances with Third World states. The Southeast Asia Treaty Organization (1955), the

Central Treaty Organization (1959), and the Soviet alliance with Cuba (1961) exemplified the attempts made by Washington and Moscow to outflank each other. The Cold War was no longer a set-piece encounter between deadlocked giants; it had become a contest of improvisation and maneuver throughout the globe.

Underpinning this search for new allies was a belief that neutral nations would tend to gravitate toward the powerful. Irresolution on the part of either superpower allegedly would allow the adversary to pull nonaligned third parties into its orbit. As President John F. Kennedy put it, "If the United States were to falter, the whole world would inevitably move toward the Communist bloc." Similarly, the Kremlin interpreted the ebb and flow of its influence over other countries as a product of the evolving "correlation of forces." Both sides implicitly assumed that alliance formation was governed by bandwagoning— the propensity for weak states to ally with the strongest state. In President Lyndon Johnson's words, there were "a hundred little nations" watching how the United States and the Soviet Union responded to international challenges, nations that presumably would make decisions to align or dealign based on what they observed.

By the mid-1970s, leaders in the White House and the Kremlin included what might be called "proto-alliances" in their flanking maneuvers. Rather than forging defense treaties of the sort that the United States signed with South Korea in 1953 and the USSR concluded with North Korea in 1961, they began to make less obtrusive agreements pledging more modest commitments. The proto-alliances designed during the Carter and Reagan administrations were highly discrete arrangements based on a mix of ad hoc diplomatic contact, arms transfers, economic aid, facilities construction, and the positioning of U.S. military bases on the allies' soil (see Deibel, 1987: 114). Like the earlier Dulles alliance system, these new security arrangements were diffuse in geographic scope, embracing such countries as Morocco, Saudi Arabia, Oman, Honduras, Pakistan, and Thailand. Similarly, the proto-alliances nourished by General Secretary Leonid Brezhnev and his successors were far-reaching: Buttressed by treaties of friendship and cooperation that promised consultation on issues of common defense, this new form of security arrangement was negotiated with Vietnam, Iraq, Yemen, Angola, Mozambique, and several other Third World countries.

The Contribution of Alliances to the Long Peace

A review of the long postwar peace thus suggests the presence of two overlapping phases of alliance formation: In the first, alliances were used to draw demarcation lines around areas of perceived vital interest along the western and northeastern Eurasian strategic fronts; in the second, a more geographically extensive system of alliances was built in the hope of cultivating allies to the rear of the rival superpower. Threats to peace were frequent throughout both phases, yet none of the many superpower disputes escalated to war. Moreover, great-power peace prevailed even when some of these tight alliances began to unravel and were replaced by new, loose combinations of informal proto-alliances.

At first glance it thus would seem that alliances were unrelated to the preservation of the long great-power peace. War occurred neither during the period of rapid alliance formation nor during the following period of alliance dissolution. Yet a second, more careful examination is needed, for it was not the magnitude of alliance aggregation that mattered so much as did the purposes for which both kinds of alliances were put.

Alliances and Extended Immediate Deterrence. The conventional wisdom of realist thought holds that alliances help preserve peace by enabling a state to deter an attack upon itself or upon some client in two ways. First, allies provide the means to deny the potential aggressor from realizing in battle its immediate territorial objectives by expanding the number of enemies it must confront and conquer. Second, allies enhance a defender's ability to punish an aggressor through military retaliation.

The conclusion suggested by this line of reasoning is that alliances reduce the probability of war; yet the accuracy of this prediction is not to be accepted on intuitive grounds because changes in the level of alliance aggregation may not be directly linked to the onset of war (see Chapter 5). If the long peace during the bipolar Cold War period was a product of deterrence through alliance building, then we should find evidence that alliances prevented a superpower attack in those situations that were ripe for war.

But a perusal of Soviet–American relations since 1945 does not yield such evidence. The alliances that were erected at the beginning of the Cold War were conceived at a time when neither side was willing to risk a major armed conflict. Following the Japanese surrender on August 14, 1945, leaders in Washington felt mounting public pressure to demobilize; those in Moscow faced the enormous task of reconstruction. The Kremlin estimated that 26 million Soviet citizens had perished in the maelstrom of the Second World War; additionally, the country had suffered half of the total material destruction in Europe, amounting to one-quarter of the USSR's reproducible wealth. By 1948, the United States had cut back from a wartime peak of approximately 8 million troops to roughly 1.4 million, while the Soviet Union reduced its military force from 12 million to somewhere between 2.5 and 4 million (Wolfe, 1970: 10–11).

Though reluctant to engage their rival on the battlefield, Moscow and Washington seemed headed in that very direction due to several international events: the Azerbaijan incident, the coup in Czechoslovakia, the Berlin blockade, and, most important, the Korean War, all of which led both sides to revamp their security policies. The United States instituted sweeping organizational changes under the National Security Act of 1947, adopted new global military policies with the Truman Doctrine, crafted an ambitious economic assistance program with the Marshall Plan, and undertook a complete reassessment of its strategic situation in National Security Council Memorandum No. 68. At the same time, the Soviet Union began a full-scale drive to produce an atomic bomb, reorganize its defenses, and launch a major military modernization program. The former World War II allies had become rivals for primacy, conducting foreign policy primarily in terms of their opposition to the other's initiatives.

Though alliances were a key component of such security policy innovations, it is unlikely that they deterred the superpowers from fighting over the future direction of the postwar world. While allies proved useful in symbolizing each superpower's potence and in preempting the opponent's geostrategic momentum, they were probably not essential, as nuclear weapons mitigated the need for allies to deter an attack of either superpower's territory (Burns, 1964). Alliances, however, did perform a balancing function, and in this sense the polarized alliances and rigic blocs formed during the Cold War's bipolar period were not unlike other periods in which formal military alliances were built. But even in these previous periods, military alliances did not contribute directly to successful deterrence (see Huth and Russett, 1984). Therefore we do not have a good reason to attribute the long peace that resulted after World War II to the constraining influence of alliances.

Peace during the early years of the Cold War thus may have owed less to the pacifying effects of alliances than to the twin constraints of demobilization and reconstruction, plus a complex mix of American nuclear superiority, Soviet preponderance in conventional forces, and the network of economic and political ties that developed between the superpowers and their protegés. Whereas the United States could threaten nuclear punishment if its homeland was attacked and could be expected to defend those third parties with whom it had important and direct material interests, the decisive Soviet advantage in conventional arms forces allowed the USSR to hold Western Europe hostage for American restraint. Because extended deterrence was bolstered by ties of trade, investment, and assistance (see Organski and Kugler, 1980: 176–179; Kugler, 1984; Huth and Russett, 1988), there are reasonable grounds for arguing that alliances did not make a direct, independent contribution to preventing the Cold War from becoming hot.[2]

Nonetheless, it would be wrong to infer that alliances made no contribution

---

2. In rebuttal, it has been argued that the Cold War alliances like NATO were so successful that they prevented many situations from ever becoming ripe for war. Critics of this counterargument maintain that if the Soviet Union never seriously contemplated overrunning Western Europe, we have no basis for concluding that NATO was responsible for Soviet restraint (Vasquez, 1991); the Atlantic Alliance cannot be given credit for stopping something that was not sought in the first place. It is true, these critics admit, that there has not been a general war in Europe since April 4, 1949, when the North Atlantic Treaty was signed, and it is also true that NATO was created in part to deter such a conflict. But they assert that it does not necessarily follow that NATO directly prevented such a war and underline their logic by noting that no war occurred in the tense 1945–1949 period before NATO was formed.

to the long postwar peace. Their impact is more accurately described as having been contingent upon the kind of commitment that was made: Those alliances associated with the Cold War of Position tended to advance the cause of peace by fostering tacitly coordinated problem solving, whereas those associated with the Cold War of Movement were counterproductive, fostering overcommitment and a compulsion to test the adversary's willingness to defend allies whose allegiance and ultimate importance were questionable. Let us elaborate on this assertion, for the inferences derived from this bipolar period have broad implications for the multipolar world of the future.

Alliances and the Coordination of Expectations. The rivalry between the Soviet Union and the United States during the Cold War can be best conceptualized as a geographically diverse group of what can metaphorically be termed "mixed-motive games," each containing elements of mutual dependence and conflict, partnership and competition (Schelling, 1960: 89). Many of the rules of these games had different structures and somewhat different implications for conflict management (George, 1986: 251). Two types of game structures lent themselves to the development of normative rules that allowed the two contestants to successfully coordinate their expectations: those in which both superpowers recognized that they had mutually strong interests (for example, Berlin) and those in which both recognized that one side had unambiguously predominant interests (for example, Eastern Europe for the Soviet Union and Latin America for the United States). In regions where both sides had modest, disputed, or uncertain interests, rule making for conflict management did not materialize as readily.

The alliances formed as part of the Cold War of Position were located in arenas conducive to the creation of ground rules. The norms created here lacked symmetry and elegance, and they underwent slow, sporadic, and uneven growth following the failure of planned rule making at the 1945 United Nations Conference in San Francisco. Nevertheless, they helped regulate the competition, removed particular regions from the theater of superpower competition, and thereby added a modicum of order and predictability to the superpower rivalry.

Foremost among these tacit "rules of the game" were those that pertained to delineating spheres of influence and avoiding direct military confrontation. Like the Tordesillas regime between Spain and Portugal in the fifteenth century and the various nineteenth-century agreements over respective European interests in Africa and Asia, the alliances born of the Cold War of Position clarified the political landscape. They provided a "focal point solution" to pressing questions about the architecture of the bipolar system that was to be built on the ashes of the old Eurocentric balance of power (Weede, 1975: 55; Schelling, 1966: 137–138). The lines of demarcation drawn by NATO, the Warsaw Pact, and the other alliances of the Cold War of Position were simple, recognizable, conspicuous, and unambiguous. In contrast to the ill-defined configurations produced by such grandiose alliances as CENTO and SEATO, they contributed to the long peace in at least two ways.

First, clear lines of demarcation helped prevent disputes over areas of vital interest from escalating into frequent crises. Historically, conflicts that have followed in rapid succession on the heels of their predecessors have proven dangerous (Midlarsky, 1984). One such source of danger has been the tendency of national leaders to use more coercive bargaining techniques in each subsequent encounter (Leng, 1983), a tendency that has caused crises to evolve into wars (Gochman and Leng, 1983; Leng and Wheeler, 1979). Another source of danger has been the propensity for numerous distinct political stakes to become linked into a single overarching issue during a series of disputes, thereby increasing the intractability of the conflict and lessening the prospects for its amicable settlement (Mansbach and Vasquez, 1981). These linkages were evident throughout the Cold War's evolution. Where superpower spheres of influence were clear, neither side mounted a significant challenge to its rival; where they were unclear (as in the case of South Korea after Secretary of State Dean Acheson's "defensive perimeter" speech) or in decay (as in the case of Cuba between the Bay of Pigs invasion and the 1962 missile crisis), recklessness and opportunism overcame prudence and caution.

Second, as qualitatively prominent focal points for the coordination of reciprocal expectations, the lines of demarcation drawn by the alliances of the Cold War of Position provided a framework for subsequent rule making. Take, for instance, Europe, where the superpowers not only used alliances to define their own mutual relations,

> but in the process, and as a by-product of it, also established a system of relationships with and among the countries of Europe, their own allies and dependents, and those of the other. They thereby provided a solution, inadvertently, to the problem which the countries of Europe had faced and failed to master since 1890: the place of a too-powerful Germany in a European system which could not of itself preserve the independence of its members in the face of German strength. (DePorte, 1979: 116)

As described by Lord Ismay, first secretary general of NATO, the purpose of the Atlantic Alliance was "to keep the Russians out, the Americans in, and the Germans down." Not only did the Atlantic Alliance, by meeting these objectives, help allay the fears of those Western Europeans who were concerned about future German rearmament, it also furnished some of the political scaffolding that was later used to construct such agreements as the Austrian State Treaty in 1955 and the Helsinki Accords in 1975.

In summary, the history of alliances during the Cold War casts doubt about their direct influence on the preservation of great-power peace. Logically, if both rigid and fluid alliances existed alongside peaceful great-power relations, then full credit for the absence of war cannot be assigned to the alliance structures that materialized. Nevertheless, the alliances of position had an indirect impact on reducing the probability of war by providing clear, conspicuous lines of demarcation around which international norms could arise to coordinate the contestants' expectations.

Did Preparations for War Keep the Peace?

Many people interpret the events leading to the end of the Cold War as proof that American military superiority accounted for the implosion of the Soviet Empire. Their view springs from the belief that the United States spent the Soviet Union into submission. By engaging Moscow in a prohibitively costly arms race, so this reasoning goes, the United States was able to deter Soviet aggression and draw Moscow into an economic competition it could not sustain. Facing an unmatchable arsenal, Mikhail Gorbachev had no alternative but to accept imperial devolution. This assertion, frequently voiced by former Secretary of Defense Caspar Weinberger (1990), rests on the dubious premise that a "willingness to spend enough and deploy enough [produced] the right sort of perception in the minds of Soviet leaders" (Barnet, 1987: 78). Though the estimated $10 trillion spent to contain the Soviet Union during the Cold War was "enough to buy everything in the United States except the land" (Sagan, 1992: 24), the price is claimed to have been modest, given the substantial geopolitical return on the investment.

Peace through Strength

At the heart of arguments crediting military buildups with the submission of dangerous rivals is the assumption that commitments are challenged when states appear irresolute and lack the capability to defend them. Behind this assumption is a set of beliefs about the importance of closing windows of vulnerability and negotiating from a position of strength. Allegedly, the language of military might is the only language aggressive opponents understand. Vacillation encourages intransigence, while military might provokes earnest efforts to bargain. Applying these beliefs to the Soviet Union at the end of World War II, President Truman (1955: 552) predicted that "unless Russia is faced with an iron fist and strong language, another war is in the making." His secretary of state, James F. Byrnes, concurred: "The only way to negotiate with the Russians is to hit them hard" (cited in Paterson, 1978: 314). Similarly, Secretary of State Dean Acheson (1969: 275, 728) noted that whenever firm diplomacy shows the Soviets that their position is untenable, "they hastily abandon it." Perseverance, he continued, "is the only avenue to success."

Similar beliefs were expressed by Ronald Reagan in his presidential campaign against Jimmy Carter, when the former averred that "more nations can back themselves into trouble through retreat and appeasement than by standing up for what they believe" (*New York Times*, January 29, 1980). A decade later, George Bush emphasized the same beliefs: "There are few lessons so clear in history as this: only the combination of conventional forces and nuclear forces have ensured this long peace in Europe." Similarly, Reagan's military adviser Richard Perle (1991: 33, 35; also 1992) declared that "those who argued for the buildup of American military capabilities contributed mightily to the position of strength that eventually led the Soviet leadership to choose a less bellicose, less menacing approach to international politics." Claiming that "We're witnessing the rewards of the Reagan policy of firmness," Perle asserted that had the West succumbed "to the siren call" of the pacifists, this "would surely have kept the Cold War going or even allowed the Soviet bloc to win it."

This thesis is disarmingly attractive because it must be acknowledged that the postwar peace unfolded alongside a massive weapons-building program in the United States that was accompanied by the vertical and horizontal proliferation of weapons throughout the globe. Because a direct correlation appears extant, many have been quick to assume that American military expenditures and superpower peace are causally linked (Waltz, 1992a; Mearsheimer, 1992b). Those who contend that the buildup of American military capabilities brought the Cold War to an end draw inspiration from the oft-cited maxim: "If you want peace, prepare for war." Speaking before the National Press Club on October 27, 1988, Colin L. Powell, assistant to the president for national security affairs, exemplified this point of view when he declared: "A side that sees an easy victory will go after it." "Nations don't cause wars inadvertently by accumulating the military strength to deter them," agreed Patrick Glynn (1990: 60); "nations cause wars by failing to match or exceed a rising power's capabilities and resolve."

From Absolute Security to Absolute Insecurity

Yet the policy of peace through strength is not beyond reproach. Given that the international system lacks a central governing body capable of enforcing the laws established among its sovereign members, states often rely on self-help to guard their security. But increases in security for one state may be perceived as decreasing security for the others, with the result that every competitor becomes locked into an upward spiral of countermeasures that jeopardize the security of all. Sir Edward Grey summarized this *security dilemma* in the following way:

> The increase of armaments, that is intended in each nation to produce consciousness of strength, and a sense of security, does not produce these effects. On the contrary, it produces a consciousness of the strength of other nations and a sense of fear. Fear begets suspicion and distrust and evil imaginings of all sorts, til each government feels it would be criminal and a betrayal of its own country not to take every precaution, while every government regards every precaution of the other government as evidence of hostile intent. (Grey, 1925: 92)

If this is so, then we need to consider the following alternative to the orthodox view about the pacifying effects of weapons: "Security based on strength is a mirage; if one side feels safe from attack, the other will feel at the mercy of the enemy" (Aron, 1965: 212). Absolute security for one state implies absolute insecurity for its rivals (Kissinger, 1973: 2), with the result that "defensive measures only breed more dangerous countermeasures to nullify them" (Wildavsky, 1989: A16).

Looking at the Cold War from this alternative perspective, massive peace-time preparations for war may have bred a spiraling arms race that inhibited the growth of nonmilitary means of dispute settlement and misdirected scarce resources away from programs designed to combat poverty, inequality, and environmental degradation (Johansen, 1991: 235–240; 1995). The Reagan military spending binge left the United States so debt-ridden and economically prostrate that its victory in the Cold War may be Pyrrhic rather than absolute. According to this view, there is little foundation for the assertion that America's buildup preserved superpower peace and forced a Soviet retreat in Europe, Afghanistan, and elsewhere, since rapproachment with the West "was only achievable *after* the leadership change in the Soviet Union" that brought Gorbachev into power, not as a result of tough bargaining strategies and a massive arms buildup (Risse-Kappen, 1991: 163).

Did Nuclear Deterrence Keep the Peace?

Of the three most frequently voiced explanations of the sources of the long postwar peace, the proposition that nuclear deterrence prevented war is by far the most popular. Many proponents of this view embrace Winston Churchill's observation in 1953 that in a nuclear armed world "safety [would] be the sturdy child of terror and survival the twin brother of annihilation." For example, Arthur Schlesinger, Jr. (1992a: A10) was one among many who echoed Churchill by attributing the avoidance of superpower war since 1945 to the existence of nuclear weapons. The "Nobel Peace Prize," he quipped, "should have gone to the atomic bomb."

Peace through Peril

At the heart of deterrence theory is the assumption that nuclear weapons are so devastating that they make war an irrational choice. So long as one communicates a credible threat to retaliate against an aggressor and one possesses the capacity to punish him with unacceptably high costs even after absorbing a first strike, adversaries allegedly will be dissuaded from attacking. When both sides in an enduring rivalry can mutually assure each other's destruction, the terror of utter devastation preserves peace between them.

In contrast to the Clausewitzian view that war is a political instrument that can be used to attain foreign policy goals, students of deterrence hold that nothing can be gained by waging nuclear war. The frightening costs of nuclear war simply outweigh any conceivable benefits. In the words of Nikita Khrushchev: "If you reach for the push button, you reach for suicide" (cited in Brodie, 1973: 375). Under this condition, peace will prevail.

Weighing the Impact of Nuclear Deterrence

As plausible as this explanation of the long peace sounds, it begs the question of what would have happened after World War II had nuclear weapons not existed (Nye, 1989). John Vasquez (1991: 207) illustrates the difficulty in explaining why something does not occur by telling the story of a boy in Brooklyn who ran out of his house every afternoon waving his arms. After observing this behavior for several days, a curious neighbor asked, "Why do you run down the street like that at the same time every day?" The little boy replied, "To keep the elephants away." "But there are no elephants in Brooklyn," insisted the neighbor. "See, it works!" declared the boy. We may laugh at the youngster, writes Vasquez, because we know that even if there were elephants in Brooklyn they would not be frightened off by someone running wildly down the street at exactly the same time every day. But when we fear something that we do not understand, he continues, if authority figures claim their actions will prevent it from occurring, we want to believe them.

It is premature to conclude that the threat of nuclear annihilation alone caused superpower disputes to be resolved by means short of war. At least six reasons can be advanced that should caution us to suspend judgment.

First, we lack direct evidence to support the claim that nuclear weapons deterred an attack by either side against the other since neither Washington nor Moscow ever stood on the verge of launching a premeditated strike on the other's homeland.[3]

Second, indirect evidence that has been obtained by testing expectations deduced from deterrence theory is equally inconclusive. Contrary to what might be expected, "nuclear nations have not *consistently* prevented opponents from attaining contested policy objectives" (Kugler, 1984: 478–479).

Third, it is difficult to separate out any independent effect produced by nuclear weapons since they have been coincidental with other factors that may have played a major role in preventing a Soviet–American war, including the absence of a superpower dispute involving contiguous territory, satisfaction with the status quo, and memory of the horrors of World War II (Mueller, 1989).

Fourth, despite numerous predictions over the centuries that one new weapon or another would bring an end to war, the creation of extremely destructive new weapons alone has never deterred war (Luard, 1986: 396).

---

3. Many analysts distinguish between crisis stability and general stability. From their perspective, nuclear weapons (and formal military alliances, for that matter) may not have been crucial to crisis stability, but they helped provide general stability by preventing many potential war-threatening crises from developing in the first place.

Fifth, contrary to the assertion that the specter of nuclear devastation raised the provocation threshold high enough to prevent war from erupting under conditions that would have produced war in the past, it could be argued with equal cogency that nuclear weapons exacerbated tensions and impeded "the demilitarization of international relations" (Arbatov, 1990: 50). This is because nuclear weapons did not eliminate the need for allies in order to compensate for military inferiority, but instead accelerated the search by the great powers for allies to enhance their sense of security, resulting in an East–West conflict that grew in intensity and geographical scope.

Finally, given the awesome destructive capabilities of nuclear weapons, there is a tendency to equate a great power's possession of nuclear weapons with an automatic ability to deter potential aggressors and exercise influence on the world's stage. But this ascribed effect is easily exaggerated. "The discussion of military instruments of power, especially the role of nuclear weapons, needs to be carefully nuanced" since, as Bruce Russett (1989: 177–178) explains, "nuclear weapons remain most useful," but only "for the purpose for which they are least needed, and have always been least needed: deterrence of nuclear or convention- al attack on the home territory of a superpower." Neither superpower really ever had a need to fear such a deliberate, unprovoked attack. Hence,

> the primary purpose of superpower nuclear weapons—extended deterrence—has always been of somewhat doubtful utility, and . . . the doubts have grown sub- stantially, and with good reason, over the past two decades. Concurrent with the military situation, international norms have evolved to reinforce the unusability of nuclear weapons. Their unusability has meant that the role of nuclear weapons in reinforcing hierarchies of central power (hegemony), whether globally, within alliances, or within states, has declined. . . . (Russett, 1989: 177)

To say that nuclear weapons *by themselves* did not secure the long postwar peace, however, is not to say they had no impact. As newly released documents from the Cuban missile crisis illustrate, fear of virtual extermination had a sobering effect on those looking into the nuclear abyss. Nuclear weapons pro- vided an incentive for leaders in the Kremlin and the White House to treat each other with caution and to establish a set of informal, normative rules that would regulate their competition. Just as the alliances that were formed as part of the Cold War of Position led to the formation of tacit rules of prudence regarding spheres of superpower influence, the environment of mutual assured destruction prompted Moscow and Washington to establish implicit rules that encouraged both sides to avoid direct military confrontations, to maintain a sharp distinction between conventional and nuclear weapons, and to use the latter only as a last resort.

COLD WAR MYTHS AND DANGEROUS EXTRAPOLATIONS

Emerging from World War II with unrivaled power, the United States set out, in Harry S Truman's words, "to run the world the way the world ought to be run." The results of America's attempt at global management were not always medicinal, despite the best of intentions. Yet many people cling to the belief that a network of collective defense alliances, high military expenditures, and nuclear deterrence were responsible for the great-power peace and the end of the Cold War.

This set of beliefs exaggerates the extent of U.S. power in managing world order and underestimates the contribution to peace made by other nations. As shown in Box 2.2, it also neglects a variety of plausible, rival explanations for the long peace and the Cold War's end.

The sources of the long peace and the reasons for the end of the Cold War are not as simple as many policymakers insist. "The Cold War's end was a baby that arrived unexpectedly, but a long line of those claiming paternity has quickly formed," observe Daniel Deudney and G. John Ikenberry (1992: 125). Parenthood is hard to establish, for the absence of great-power war since 1945 probably resulted not from a single seed but from multiple sources. Historians and social scientists have yet to perform an adequate autopsy of the Cold War, which will identify the relative weight of both the external sources of this conflict's death emphasized by realists and the internal sources that others cite (see Kegley, 1994). Until that analytic task is completed, it would be prudent to resist jumping to immediate conclusions about the processes by which great-power rivalries can be managed without warfare. More specifically, the claims that (1) alliances deterred warfare, (2) preparations for war preserved peace, or (3) nuclear weapons made war obsolete rest on rather dubious premises that mask the compound, interactive effects among these influences that more reasonably, collectively produced the outcome that "caught most everyone, particularly hardliners, by surprise" (Deudney and Ikenberry, 1992: 124).

In summary, this chapter outlines the prevalent interpretations of why great-power war did not occur in the second half of the twentieth century. Even though the factors that produced this long period of peace among the most powerful states in the international system leave many suspended questions, many policymakers today operate as if they fully understand the answers. To the extent that their untested speculations remain an entrenched dogma, there is risk that policymakers will act on misleading but seductive historical lessons and continue "to see the world in terms of the 1947 mindset" (Iklé, 1990: 14). "As if stupefied by the pace of events," warns Stanley Hoffmann (1989: 85), "many members of the American foreign policy establishment [seem to cling] to the remains of an obsolete strategy and [appear] incapable of defining a new one." There is a risk that they—and leaders of the other great powers as well— will remain captives of the thinking that emanated from the period of Cold War bipolarity and fail to fashion strategies that confront the realities of an incipient new multipolar world.

There are many reasons to believe that as bipolarity gives way to multipolarity, new approaches founded on more sophisticated images of the infrastructure of great-power peace will be required. The post–Cold War environment is likely to be quite unlike the phase of history we have just left

BOX 2.2
RIVAL IMAGES OF THE CAUSES OF COMMUNISM'S
COLLAPSE AND THE COLD WAR'S END

Postulated Cause	Proposition
Economic Mismanagement	"No other industrialized state in the world [than the Soviet Union] for so long spent so much of its national wealth on armaments and military forces. Soviet militarism, in harness with communism, destroyed the Soviet economy and thus hastened the self-destruction of the Soviet empire." —Former U.S. Undersecretary of Defense Fred Charles Iklé (1991–1992: 28)
The Economic Burdens of Arms Competition	"Gorbachev's cooperative initiatives toward the United States came at a time when the Soviet leadership no longer believed that it was riding the wave of an inevitable Communist triumph in its competition with the West and when the current and potential costs of that competition were weighing heavily on a struggling Soviet economy." —Martin Patchen (1990: 33)
	"In the case of the Cold War's miraculous dissolution, Bush mistook his great good fortune for greatness itself. His vanity was that of the heir who claims his trust fund as a credit to his own initiative. In fact, with the Soviet Union on the verge of destruction, Gorbachev ended the Cold War because he could not afford to do otherwise." —David Remnick (1993: 105)
	"Ultimately, the Soviet Union collapsed under the weight of its efforts to keep up and the U.S. emerged from the 1980s as not only a superpower, but the only superpower." —George Melloan (1993: A17)
The Ideological Appeal of Liberal Democracy	"Many of the demonstrators . . . who sought to reject communist rule looked to the American system for inspiration. But the source of that inspiration was America's reputation as a haven for the values of limited government, not Washington's

(continued)

BOX 2.2
(CONTINUED)

Postulated Cause	Proposition
	$300 billion-a-year military budget and its network of global military bases." —Ted Galen Carpenter (1991: 37–38)
Tough Bargaining	"Ronald Reagan won the Cold War by being tough on the communists. . . . It was only after three to four years of unremittingly tough policies under Reagan . . . that the desired sea-change in Soviet leadership opinion took place." —Patrick Glynn (1993b: 172)
Russia's Response to the United States and Its Allies	"Russia did not lose the Cold War. The Communists did. The U.S. and our allies deserve great credit for maintaining the military and economic power to resist and turn back the Soviet aggression. A democratic Russia deserves credit for delivering the knockout blow to Communism in its motherland." —Richard Nixon (1993: A17)
Media Publicity of Soviet Moral Weakness	"It was the moral reassessment of the seventy-odd years of this socialist experiment that shook the nation, not Ronald Reagan's Star Wars. It was the flood of publications of the Soviet Union's human rights record and its tremendous distortions of moral and ethical principles that discredited the system, especially when introduced into the everyday lives of its individual citizens through the popular media. This is what focused the drive for change and first made people vote against representatives of the morally corrupt old political elite. . . ." —Vladimir Benevolenski and Andrei Kortunov (1993: 100)
	"The demise of communism was accompanied by what I believe was more than a political revolt. It was also a revolt of the soul against the soullessness of communism. And a revolt of the soul is often followed by spiritual enlightenment and the reemergence of a new and higher moral imperative." —Philip Dimitrov (1992: A10)

(continued)

BOX 2.2
(CONTINUED)

Postulated Cause	Proposition
Communism's Impracticality	"Given communism's inherent unworkability and the valiant resistance it engendered among its victims . . . the Soviet empire was doomed in the long run." —Arthur Schlesinger, Jr. (1992b: A10)
	"The Soviets lost the Cold War because of the rot of the Communist system far more than [the United States] won it by the policy of containing Soviet power." —Leslie Gelb (1992: A27)
Poverty	"It was the squalor, more than the terror, that really eroded the faith [in Communism]." —Ernest Gellner (1992: 41)
Domestic Dissatisfaction	"Some conservatives argue that the Reagan defense buildup forced Gorbachev to change his policies. And, clearly, the Soviets were concerned about having to compete with U.S. technological superiority. But it seems likely that internal pressures played as much, if not more, of a role in convincing the Soviet leader to agree to measures that cut his country's firepower more than they cut U.S. strength." —Carl P. Leubsdorf (1991: D3)

(see Box 2.3). Accordingly, the policies and practices that kept the peace during the Cold War may not have the same stabilizing influence in the new world order and could even prove dysfunctional.

Although global conditions have changed as the world evolves into a new multipolar distribution of power, we face the prospect that foreign policies based on ingrained practices may persist. Not only do the lessons of history that inform these past practices rest on weak foundations, but as products of a bipolar world they may have even less relevance in a multipolar future. What is needed "is some new, imaginative thinking . . . and not a mere projection of yesterday's role and policy" (Kristol, 1990: A6). Our need for better under-

BOX 2.3
STRUCTURAL CONSEQUENCES OF THE END
OF COLD WAR BIPOLARITY

"The collapse of the former Soviet Union means that the tight power distribution of the Cold War has once again been replaced by a loose distribution. . . . Now, because no state is on the verge of military dominance (not even the United States), all states are once again free to engage in conflicts that were formerly suppressed, while uncertainty has increased about how states define their basic interests and therefore about who will ally with whom in future conflicts. Other things being equal, therefore, one could infer that the probability of war among the major states has increased."

—R. Harrison Wagner (1993: 106)

"Divergent perceptions of national interests in a world with fewer constraints on action by national governments will encourage individualism and opportunism that will threaten historic friendships and alliances."

—W. Y. Smith (1992: 274–275)

"The end of the Cold War will mean a loosening of bipolarity even if it does not mean . . . a world of five or more roughly equal major powers. The delegitimation of nuclear weapons and the increasing constraints on their deployment and potential use could increase the probability of conventional war. . . . The end of the Cold War . . . does not mean the end of the struggle for power and influence. . . . It could mean the end of the Long Peace."

—Samuel P. Huntington (1989: 5, 6)

standing of the determinants of great-power peace has increased, not declined. "Today's leadership," warned Bill Clinton in August 1992 before the Los Angeles World Affairs Council, "is rudderless, reactive, and erratic. It is time for leadership that is strategic, vigorous, and grounded in American values." Much of the world would agree, and it is waiting.

To grasp the strategies that the United States and the other great powers might forge to deal with the new realities of a twenty-first century multipolar world, we will examine in Chapter 3 the characteristics of such a multipolar system and the attributes that distinguish it from the former bipolar system.

· 3 ·

MUST WE FEAR A MULTIPOLAR FUTURE?

Today, a generation raised in the shadows of the Cold War assumes new responsibilities in a world warmed by the sunshine of freedom but threatened by ancient hatreds and new plagues. . . . Profound and powerful forces are shaking and remaking our world, and the urgent question of our time is whether we can make change our friend and not our enemy.

—PRESIDENT BILL CLINTON,
Inaugural Address, 1993

After 1945, the United States found itself in an extraordinary situation. Although, in Winston Churchill's words, the "hot rake of war" had deeply scarred the other great powers, the United States stood in a preponderant military and economic position. Not only was it the lone nation with atomic weapons, but the U.S. economy accounted for roughly half the combined gross national product (GNP) of the world's nations. The United States was not just stronger than anybody—it was stronger than everybody.

This immediate postwar distribution of power was short-lived, however. The rapid recovery of the Soviet Union introduced a new power configuration into world affairs. The Soviets broke the American monopoly of atomic weapons in 1949 and exploded a thermonuclear device in 1953, less than a year after the United States. Their achievement solidified a bipolar distribution of power and led onlookers to ask whether a system dominated by two superpowers would be more stable than the multipolar systems of old. Political realists, in particular, took up the question of how this structural change would affect the operation of balance-of-power politics.

REALIST THEORY, MULTIPOLARITY, AND THE POST–COLD WAR WORLD

Political realism has a long, distinguished history that dates back to the writings of Thucydides in ancient Greece and Kautilya in India. International politics, according to realists, is a ceaseless and repetitive struggle for power that occurs among territorially organized entities. Regardless of what might be the ultimate aim of a nation's foreign policy, power will be sought as a means for attaining that end (Morgenthau, 1985: 5). Prudent leaders, they argue, will carefully weigh the perceived costs, risks, and benefits of alternative strategies with an eye toward marshaling the wherewithal needed to ensure security and advance national interests. From the realist point of view, security is a function of power, and power is primarily a function of military strength. Those who depreciate the ubiquity of the struggle for power are dismissed as being utopians.

From Classical Realism to Neorealism

Although those who call themselves realists concur that statesmen act in terms of interest defined as power, they disagree over why foreign policy is formulated in the brooding shadow of violence. Classical realists blame human imperfections. Echoing Spinoza, they point to an ongoing conflict between passion and reason; furthermore, in the tradition of St. Augustine, they warn that materialism and vanity enable passion to overwhelm reason. In short, classical realists paint a dualistic portrait of human nature where the forces of light and darkness perpetually vie for control (Niebuhr, 1940: 157). For them, power politics is a byproduct of the struggle for domination among competing egos.

Rather than asserting that the vicissitudes of human nature cause international life to be, in the words of Thomas Hobbes, "nasty, brutish and short," a variant of realism blames the anarchic structure of the international system. Foreign policy, argue these *neo*realists, unfolds in an environment that lacks a central arbiter. States are sovereign: They have supreme power over their territory and populace, and no higher authority stands above them wielding the legitimacy and coercive capability required to undertake the extractive, regulative, and distributive functions that governments normally perform in domestic political systems. Given the absence of a central arbiter to which states can turn to resolve disputes, retaliatory self-help becomes the court of last appeal for punishing the perpetrator of any alleged transgression. Like the participants in Jean-Jacques Rousseau's allegory of the Stag Hunt, members of the international system engage in defensive noncooperation. Varying in strength and uncertain of one another's intentions, they arm for the sake of security.

Thus, from the perspective of neorealism, the very structure of the system leads even well-intentioned leaders to be suspicious and hedge their bets by practicing power politics. It requires that they remain ever mindful of their position within the global hierarchy and maintain a wide margin of safety when calculating their military needs. War occurs frequently in this system of mistrust and ever-present rivalry, and the most that prudent statesmen can do is postpone its outbreak and reduce its destructiveness. According to this version of realpolitik, the distribution of military might among the great powers plays an influential role in determining the length of time between the wars for domination that great powers are expected to wage.

This image is directly relevant to the prospects for peace today, with our primary concern being whether the great powers can manage an emergent multipolar distribution of power in a way that controls its dangers. Let us take a closer look at the reasons why realists view the prospect of a new multipolar era with such alarm.

Neorealist Criticisms of Multipolarity

For the neorealist, a multipolar distribution of power similar to the classical European balance-of-power system best describes the international system of the immediate future. Such a system would revolve around, say, five great-power competitors occupying positions of approximate parity, and, if the historical analogy holds, the equilibrating mechanisms of the system would be grounded in the logic of realpolitik, with ideology a distinctly secondary concern. Alliance formation and dissolution would be frequent as each state struggles for advantage while trying to counterbalance the military might of any aspiring hegemon. At the same time, contenders for global preeminence would fear the power accumulation of challengers and seek to protect themselves from domination by struggling to attain a position of preponderance.

Neorealists insist that multipolar systems are to be feared because they are structurally unstable. To back this claim, they advance what might be called an *argument from caution*: The bipolar world that emerged after World War II was stable because the heightened tension accompanying a great-power duopoly encouraged the bloc leaders to exercise care, to assume greater responsibility for their actions, and to restrain the crisis-provoking, aggressive actions of their subordinate allies (Waltz, 1964). Ironically, stability resulted from threats that often reached the brink of war. Under such stark conditions, the superpowers had incentives to prevent minor conflicts from escalating into a military maelstrom that could engulf the entire world.

Several other attempts have been made to support the proposition that a bipolar system is more stable and peaceful than a multipolar system. A standard justification consists of an *argument from probability*: Unlike in a multipolar environment, where any combination of major and minor powers may wage war, within a bipolar system only one great-power dyad exists across which war might occur; hence system-destabilizing war is less likely due to the fewer possibilities for its onset. Perhaps the best illustration of this argument can be seen in the contention that so long as there are "only two great powers, like two big battleships clumsily and cautiously circling each other, confrontations—or accidents—[are] easier to avoid." Once "the global lake [is] more crowded with ships of varying sizes, fueled by different ambitions and piloted with different degrees of navigation skill, the odds of collisions become far greater" (House, 1989: A10).

The third effort to ground the assertion that bipolarity is more peaceful than multipolarity rests on an *argument from certainty*: The clear, unambiguous nature of bipolarity dampens the chances of underestimating the strength or resolve of one's adversary; hence war is less likely to occur due to miscalculation. Conversely, two general kinds of miscalculation are said to happen during periods in which resources are evenly divided among three or more dominant great powers. On the one hand, states that believe their security is intertwined with the survival of others and perceive that advantages lie with offensive action may chain themselves to reckless allies, only to be pulled toward war if any of their partners stumble into hostilities. On the other hand, states that perceive defensive advantages may not align with others soon enough because of a propensity to pass the buck, trying to ride free on the actions of third parties (Christensen and Snyder, 1990:140–147). Insofar as the dominant states in a bipolar world are not dependent upon their smaller allies for survival, and since their minions cannot confront the opposing superpower alone, miscalculations due to chain-ganging or buck-passing will not occur.

A fourth opinion favoring bipolarity draws upon on an *argument from equality*: A system composed of two preponderant powers does not breed extreme inequalities; hence it will tend to have great long-run stability. Under conditions of scarcity, multipolarity engenders serious inequalities in resources among the most advantaged and disadvantaged great powers. Since these inequalities lead to envy, political intrigue, and contentious efforts to redress perceived imbalances, state systems consisting of three or more poles will experience instability unless some form of compensation is available to avoid conflict (Midlarsky, 1988: 66–67; 1993: 174).

Finally, the last way advocates of bipolarity have sought to advance their claim about the structural preconditions for peace is through an *argument from simplicity*: The uncomplicated edifice of bipolarity makes it easier to establish the game rules that facilitate reaching international accords; hence war is less likely since these rules and accords help regularize behavior and institutionalize cooperation. As Robert J. Lieber (1991: 269) asserts, "the prospects for cooperation appear to erode as the number of players increases." The diffusion of power among multiple, contending states raises unprecedented obstacles to establishing and maintaining order. Alignments ebb and flow as each player in the game becomes more assertive, independent, and distrustful of multilateral and collective problem solving. Fears of defection from commitments rise, with the result that national leaders operating within a multipolar milieu increasingly find it difficult to distinguish ally from adversary (Oye, 1986: 18–20).

In summary, neorealists perceive the kaleidoscope of contending powers associated with multipolarity to be disruptive and dangerous and conclude that more will be demanded of the great powers as their capabilities become more diffused and equally distributed than in the simpler bipolar period. This prediction has been expressed vociferously by John J. Mearsheimer (1990a and

1990b), who was among the first to anticipate the ensuing post–Cold War disruptions and to predict, on the basis of a structural realist argument, why future disruptions and even another great-power war were likely to follow as the alleged constraints of bipolarity gave way to a multipolar free-for-all contest for supremacy. Other voices too have suggested that "stability decreases as the system complexity increases" (Saperstein, 1991: 68), giving more credence to this grim prophecy.

Constructing three scenarios of Europe's multipolar future, Mearsheimer argued that if (1) nuclear weapons are removed from Europe, (2) a nuclear-free zone is created in Central Europe, or (3) nuclear weapons proliferate on the Continent, the probable outcome will be the same: War will eventually erupt. Even under a more optimistic fourth scenario—limited, well-managed proliferation—Europe would not be as stable as it had been under Cold War bipolarity. By implication, the other regions of the globe would also become increasingly vulnerable to warfare as power spreads from the two centers that formerly monopolized it during the Cold War.

The two world wars, Mearsheimer contends, did not extinguish the appetites of states for war. Europe, and the great powers, enjoyed peace for almost half a century due to three principal reasons: bipolarity, a rough equality in the distribution of power between the superpowers, and the restraining influence of nuclear weapons. If these restraints are lifted and the world reverts to multipolarity, Mearsheimer predicted, a new era of turbulence will follow. Whereas some analysts feel that economic interdependence will induce stability (and peace will be strengthened further because liberal democracies rarely wage war against one another), Mearsheimer predicted that these theories are not applicable to the emergent multipolar world because

> . . . the prospects for major crises and war in Europe [and elsewhere] are likely to increase markedly if the Cold War ends. . . . This pessimistic conclusion rests on the argument that the distribution and character of military power are the root causes of war and peace. . . . The departure of the superpowers from Central Europe [would] transform Europe from a bipolar to a multipolar system. . . . (Mearsheimer, 1990a: 6, 7, 52)

Thus, according to the neorealist version of history, the paradox of bipolarity was that, amid endemic threats, major war between the great powers did not occur. The ceaseless competition and enormous destructive power in the hands of the contestants allegedly produced stability. Emerging from this chain of reasoning is the conclusion that the compelling security threats of bipolar confrontation were pacifying and that the two militarily strongest great powers had an interest that they and others did not appreciate, namely, an interest in perpetuating the Cold War order. From this inference neorealists conclude that the transition to a multipolar world will bring with it a new wave of conflict and aggression.

Arguments in Support of Multipolarity

Notwithstanding these gloomy pronouncements, many theorists believe that neorealist pessimism springs from unwarranted assumptions and that under the proper conditions and adaptive foreign policy responses to them, multipolar systems, not bipolar ones, can produce relatively greater stability (for example, Gulick, 1955: 9; Hoffmann, 1978: 12).

One common approach to supporting this claim entails an *argument from flexibility*: In a multipolar world of ever-shifting alliances and counteralliances, the crusading zeal and cut-throat competition inherent in a two-power standoff are replaced by a process of political give-and-take; hence war is less likely because inflammatory issues can be sidestepped, deflected, or postponed. The shifting equilibrium of forces in a multipolar balance of power encourages conciliation. Anyone is a potential partner; no one is an implacable enemy. But in the rigid bipolar Cold War system that emerged in the 1950s, some of this was lost, as the two superpowers behaved like a pair of boxers in a narrow alley, where they could

> advance and meet in what is likely to be combat, or retreat and allow the other side to advance into what to them is precious ground. Those manifold and variegated maneuvers through which the masters of the [multipolar] balance of power tried either to stave off armed conflicts altogether or at least to make them brief and decisive yet limited in scope . . . [became during Cold War bipolarity things of the past]. With them [went] into oblivion the peculiar finesse and subtlety of mind, the calculating and versatile intelligence and bold yet circumspect decisions, which were required from players in that game. (Morgenthau, 1985: 378–379)

In short, disputes are less prone to move toward bloodshed in a multipolar system because states do not envision one another as mortal enemies. The gains made by one state are not automatically seen as losses by the others.

A second approach to backing claims made on behalf of the stability of multipolar systems involves an *argument from interaction opportunity*: As more states ascend to great-power status, the number, range, and diversity of mutually beneficial trade-offs among them rise; hence the prospects for armed conflict decline. According to Karl W. Deutsch and J. David Singer (1964), any upswing in trade-offs increases the possibility for stabilizing interactions. With any number of powerful states interacting on multiple issues, each dyadic relationship will contain elements of cooperation in one issue-area or another. Competitors in any given arena may be partners somewhere else. The greater the number of essential actors involved in these compensatory trade-offs, the better the chances of maneuvering among contending parties and of preventing future disputes by establishing buffer zones in areas of potential friction (Kaplan, 1957: 130).

The third way support is given to claims about the stability of multipolarity is through an *argument from attention*: As the number of great powers increases, the share of attention that any state devotes to any other will fall; hence the potential for conflicts to escalate will also drop since states must focus considerable attention on one another in order to become hostile enough to contemplate war. Two examples illustrate this tendency, alliance formation and arms acquisition. Within a fluid multipolar system, the coupling or decoupling of any two states would be a common occurrence and less threatening to the security of others than in the taut, uncompromising world of bipolar antagonism where both great powers are preoccupied with every change in political allegiance. Likewise, weapons accumulation by any single actor in a multipolar system would not necessarily trigger the arms race so characteristic of bipolar rivalry because marginal increases by a combination of like-minded states could easily offset any attempt by a single country to obtain a military advantage (Deutsch and Singer, 1964).

The final approach to upholding the merits of multipolarity relies on an *argument from risk aversion*: The larger the number of major powers, the greater the difficulty of appraising relative capabilities and predicting possible alignments; hence war is less likely within a multipolar system because national leaders are not apt to risk military confrontations so long as they harbor grave doubts about the strength and composition of their opposition. Without a clear way to gauge the probability of success on the battlefield, they will negotiate rather than fight. Uncertainty, in other words, has a "restraining effect upon the nations actively engaged in the struggle for power" (Morgenthau, 1985: 361).

In summary, advocates of bipolarity assert that a world containing two centers of power that are significantly stronger than the next tier of states will be stable because the heightened tension accompanying a great-power duopoly encourages the bloc leaders to exercise caution, to assume greater responsibility for their actions, and to restrain the crisis-provoking, aggressive actions of their subordinate allies. Conversely, those favoring multipolarity believe that the parity of a great-power oligopoly will be stable because a rise in interaction opportunities and a diminution in the share of attention that can be allocated among many potential adversaries reduce the rigidity of conflicts. In rebuttal, the former submit that because of its ambiguous nature, multipolarity will promote war through miscalculation. The latter retort that bipolarity, lacking flexibility and suppleness, will deteriorate into a struggle for supremacy.

Although the conventional wisdom holds that "the international environment of the next several decades is likely to be characterized by a further diffusion of power and the continued devolution of the bipolar structure" (Working Group on U.S.–Soviet Policy, 1987: 14), does such a transition create special dangers? As shown above, no consensus exists among international relations theorists on the answer to this question. We simply do not have a solid basis for accepting the dire predictions of the neorealists.

How, then, are we to judge whether a new multipolar period presages great-power war or peace? George Santayana's famous dictum that "those who cannot remember the past are condemned to repeat it" suggests the need to examine previous multipolar periods for clues. An inspection of that historical record will be undertaken in Part II (Chapters 4, 5, and 6), where we shall search for the factors that individually or in combination have promoted great-power peace in previous multipolar environments.

Such a quest for the underpinnings of multipolar peace begs a question, however: What is it about multipolar systems that we should investigate? Fortunately, several comprehensive empirical surveys based on sophisticated statistical data analysis have been conducted on variations in global power distributions, and they provide valuable evidence on the dimensions of multipolar systems most worthy of our attention.

THE GEOMETRY OF MULTIPOLAR SYSTEMS

According to these empirical studies, the presence or absence of multipolarity, *by itself*, does not raise or lower the likelihood of war. Ted Hopf (1991 and 1993), for example, found that the instability between 1495 and 1559 was not related to changes in polarity. Similarly, after analyzing data on the capabilities of individual major powers and their coalitions, Bruce Bueno de Mesquita (1981a: 564) found no relationship between the distribution of power and war during the post–Napoleonic Era. Charles Ostrom and John Aldrich (1978: 765) also failed to discover a significant relationship between the number of prominent great powers and the probability of war.

In contrast to the gloomy predictions voiced by neorealists, the historical evidence generated by these studies suggests that multipolar systems do not produce, in every circumstance, great-power antagonism and war. The probability of war is not altered merely by the emergence of more than two centers of power within the international system. Indeed, the evidence indicates that "bipolarity can, at times, be just as destabilizing as multipolarity" (Thompson, 1988: 220).[1]

Commentators who assert that multipolar systems are inherently unstable are prone to confuse instabilities that threaten state sovereignty with those that pertain to the constant maneuvering by great powers for relative advantage (Niou and Ordeshook, 1990: 1230). Hence, a direct relationship between multipolarity and war cannot be safely drawn; the relationship is more complicated because it is influenced by other factors. Indeed, we have strong reasons to assume that it is only when multipolarity is *combined with other systemic conditions* that global instabilities may be exacerbated. Therefore we need to

---

1. Among the examples of unstable bipolar systems that could be cited are the rivalries between Rome and Carthage in antiquity and between the Hapsburgs and Valois in the sixteenth century.

probe deeper to uncover the specific conditions that cause multipolar systems to degenerate into war, as well as those conditions under which they tend to remain peaceful.

Again, previous research provides guidance as to where our historical investigation should be directed. Consider a hypothetical state system with ten members. As Figure 3.1 shows, the movement back and forth between multipolarity, bipolarity, and unipolarity in this or any other state system is a manifestation of the more general process of capability concentration and deconcentration. Within our hypothetical system, a unipolar concentration of capabilities would entail one preponderant state and nine minor powers; a bipolar system would contain two dominant states and eight minor powers; and the multipolar part of this capability distribution continuum would include several possibilities. One form of multipolarity would consist of three roughly equal great powers and seven lesser powers, another would contain four great powers and six lesser powers, still another would encompass five great powers, and so on until the distribution of capabilities was diffused among ten approximately equal competitors. Thus the first dimension that we can use to differentiate between different types of multipolar systems is their *size*, that is, the number of great powers who possess approximately equal capabilities.

A second dimension used to distinguish among different types of multipolarity is the degree to which alliances are polarized into rigid blocs. Whereas polarity pertains to the distribution of power, *polarization* refers to the propensity of countries to cluster in alliance around the most powerful states. Thus a system with multiple power centers can be said to be moving toward a greater degree of polarization if its members gradually form two separate blocs whose interac-

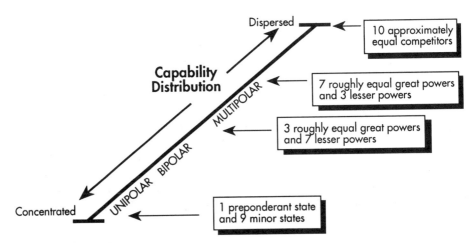

FIGURE 3.1 Polarity and the Distribution of Capabilities in a Hypothetical Ten-Member State System.

tions with others are characterized by increasing levels of conflict while the interactions among themselves become more cooperative (Rapkin, Thompson, and Christopherson, 1979).

The third dimension is the degree to which prevailing international norms support a permissive rather than a restrictive *normative order*. The expectations of proper action expressed by international norms define the "cultural climate" within which great-power interaction takes place. At any time this rudimentary political culture communicates prevailing opinions about acceptable patterns of state behavior. Whereas a permissive normative order advances rules that accept the use of force as an instrument of statecraft and allow nations to repudiate agreements whenever they wish to free themselves from treaty obligations, a restrictive order encompasses rules that limit force, uphold the sanctity of treaties, and promote the development of rules governing the spatial limits of state authority.

Taking these three dimensions together, we can say that multipolar systems differ according to the number of great powers that they contain, whether their alliances are polarized or not, and whether the content of prevailing international norms supports a permissive or a restrictive code of international conduct. By using these three dimensions, we can describe different *types* of multipolar systems, some of which may be more war prone than others.

The cube shown in Figure 3.2 provides a three-dimensional representation of these systemic conditions. Imagine that the dark plane intersects the cube within the multipolar sector of the capability distribution axis at a system size of five great powers.[2] As such, it would portray the analytical field on which we could locate the different types of five-power multipolar systems. For instance, the upper-left-hand corner of the plane depicts a multipolar system that is characterized by highly flexible alliances and a normative climate that limits the use of force and supports the inviolability of commitments. Within this particular "ideal type" multipolar system, coalitions would frequently shift among the multiple contending great powers. But while any particular combination of these states would be as probable as any other combination, once an alliance treaty was signed, the parties would not abrogate the agreement prior to the expiration date unless it was done by mutual consent.

---

2. One could construct other planes to cross the capability distribution axis at three, four, six, or more great powers. In every one of these hypothetical multipolar systems, the distribution of capabilities among the great powers would be roughly equal, but the size of each system would vary.

Of course it is also possible to have different levels of capability concentration for two multipolar systems of the same size (Mansfield, 1993: 112–113). A multipolar system with ten states could be composed of five minor powers and five roughly equal great powers, or it could have five great powers that are not equal in their capabilities. The critical factor in labeling the latter system "multipolar" would be that any variation in capabilities not be so large as to make one or two of these five unequal great powers *significantly* stronger than the others. If that occurred, the system would possess either a unipolar (one dominant state) or bipolar (two dominant states) structure.

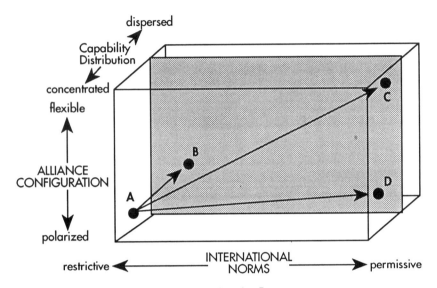

FIGURE 3.2. Three Paths to Alternative Multipolar Futures.

Point **A** in Figure 3.2 depicts the structure of the bipolar Cold War international system. Capabilities were concentrated in the hands of two superpowers, alliances were polarized into adversarial blocs, and both superpowers found their interests served by promoting norms that circumscribed the use of force, prohibited the desertion of an ally from its bloc commitments, and supported clear lines of demarcation around spheres of influence.

Points **B**, **C**, and **D** on the dark intersecting plane represent three possible multipolar futures, each of which has different implications for the construction of a stable post–Cold War world order. At point **B**, capabilities would be dispersed among several major powers in a pattern of approximate parity, alliances would retain a moderate degree of flexibility, and those pacts that form would be backed by normative rules supportive of binding agreements, limits on the use of force, and the nonviolability of boundaries. Point **C** represents a different form of multipolarity. As alliance flexibility reached its maximum and prevailing norms encouraged national leaders to disregard their commitments at will, uncertainties about who might be in league with whom, who might renege on their agreements, and who might subsequently join forces could engender massive insecurity. Point **D** presents yet another form of multipolarity, one in which bloc leaders in a highly polarized environment would face the disquieting prospect of obstreperous allies backing out of their pledges at the very time that they were most needed.

Regardless of the specific path that leads us to some multipolar future, the purpose of the cube in Figure 3.2 is to challenge images of multipolarity that do not discriminate among different types of multipolar state systems. Any one of several types of multipolarity could emerge over the next few decades, depending on the policies adopted by the great powers. Some types will be more prone to instability than others. Because it is the *type* of multipolar future that counts, not the existence of multipolarity *sui generis*, we can enhance the prospects for peace by proposing policies that steer us toward the more stable types of multipolarity.

MULTIPOLAR SYSTEMS IN HISTORY

This recommendation takes us, inescapably, to consideration of multipolar systems in the past. As shown in Table 3.1, previous multipolar state systems can be found in a variety of cultural and historical settings. Sometimes they experienced incessant violence, such as the Chinese endured during the troubled "Epoch of Warring States" (403–221 B.C.E.) and the Maya suffered after 761 C.E. At other times, conflict was managed. Bound together by trade and a common culture, interstate interactions in premodern multipolar systems did

TABLE 3.1
Examples of Premodern Multipolar Systems

System	Domain	Composition
Sumerian	First half of third millennium B.C.E. in Mesopotamia, ending with conquest by Sargon I of Agade	Politically autonomous but economically interdependent city-states, including Ur, Lagash, Nippur, Eridu, and Kish
Chinese	Spring and Autumn through the Warring States periods of Chou dynasty, 771–221 B.C.E.	Kingdoms and feudal principalities, including Ch'u, Ch'in, Han, Wei, and Ch'i
Indic	Period extending from 150 C.E. to the defeat of the Western Saka dynasty by Yajna Satakarni at the end of the century	Regional empires, including Gandhara, Surashtra, and Mulaka
Greek	Period extending from defeat of Persians in 478 B.C.E. until 446 B.C.E.	City-states, including Athens, Sparta, Corinth, Corcyra, and Thebes
Maya	Period extending from 250 to 800 C.E.	City-states, including Tikal, Uaxactum, Dos Pillas, Aguateca, and Tamarindito
Italian	Fifteenth century, ending with French invasion in 1494	City-states, including Venice, Florence, Milan, Naples, and the papal states

not always resemble a Hobbesian state of nature. In Sumeria, for example, a single city was accorded the authority to arbitrate disputes between other cities and to keep the use of force within certain limits. The ancient Greeks possessed an elaborate code of conduct covering neutrality and the peaceful resolution of disputes.[3] Renaissance Italians developed a network of permanent embassies, alliances aimed at counterbalancing the power of opportunistic states, and, following the Peace of Lodi in 1454, a rudimentary collective security organization known as the Most Holy League. Although these mechanisms did not always preserve peace, they made international political life something less than a war "of every man, against every man."

The Rise of the Modern State System

Not only did multipolarity exist in the ancient and Renaissance worlds, it also surfaced during several periods in modern history. A comparison of these periods will provide insight into the conditions under which a multipolar future may either become stable or disintegrate.

Scholars generally date the origins of the modern world at the close of the fifteenth century (see Map 3.1). This was a time when a group of so-called "New Monarchs" in Europe expanded their armed forces, curbed civil strife, increased state revenues through taxation, and limited the influence of feudal nobles. Leaders such as Henry VII (1485–1509) of the Tudor line in England and Louis XI (1461–1483) of the Valois in France exemplified these trends. By defining themselves as sovereigns who possessed the authority to enact and enforce law over everyone residing within their territorial boundaries, they departed from the medieval conception of suzerainty and laid the foundation for national states.

Concurrent with the internal consolidation of power across Europe was the emergence of a new system of states. Throughout the Middle Ages, Europeans thought of themselves as part of an all-pervading Christian commonwealth, despite living in a galaxy of separate political jurisdictions. To be sure, strong local ties accompanied this sense of belonging to Christendom, but a well-defined sense of nationalism was absent. The salient divisions for most people were horizontal strata: the nobility, from kings to knights; the clergy; the burghers, engaged in manufacturing and trade; and the peasants, toiling on the land. Even royal families, like the Hohenstaufen and the Plantagenets, did not

---

3. We agree with W. R. Connor (1991: 55) that bipolarity is an "inadequate characterization" of the Greek city-state system prior to the Peloponnesian War. Given that Corcyra was one of the leading naval powers of the day, Thebes was a major land power, and significant capabilities were held by the city-states of *Magna Graecia* on Sicily, it would seem more appropriate to describe the system as having a multipolar distribution of power but a set of alliances that were polarized around Athens and Sparta. As we have stressed throughout this chapter, polarity and polarization are two separate structural dimensions of the state system.

MAP 3.1. Europe at the End of the Fifteenth Century.

think of themselves as being limited to a particular nation. With the rise of strong, centralized governments, however, the horizontal structure of medieval Christendom was gradually replaced by a vertical structure of competitive, independent states (Watson, 1992: 138–144).

Far-reaching changes accompanied the rise of these states. New methods in mining and metallurgy, new means of finance, and new techniques of warfare added to their strength. Improvements in navigation and shipbuilding facilitated transoceanic expansion and ultimately led to the globalization of international politics. The end of the fifteenth century thus marked the dawn of the modern international system.

Born in the vortex of European state building and stimulated by a dramatic upsurge in economic growth, the system gradually grew far beyond its European core. This transformation has been called as dramatic as "the crystallization of a liquid" or "the changing of a gear" (Mattingly, 1971: 122). While the processes behind it may have taken centuries to develop, they matured at "a quite definite moment," in much the same way that "water gathers in the basin of a fountain until, at a particular moment, the basin is filled and the water overflows into a second, surrounding basin" (Dehio, 1962: 23).

Six Periods of Multipolarity

Table 3.2 lists six periods in the history of the modern state system when, we submit, the strongest evidence can be found for postulating that multipolar distributions of power existed.[4] They will provide the basis for the comparative analyses presented in the next three chapters. The size of the state system during all six periods was approximately equal, as measured by the number of great powers that held a vast proportion of military capabilities at the time. Although power was not concentrated in the hands of a single state, power disparities underwent changes over time, so that within the constant setting of a stratified hierarchy, the gaps separating the contestants continuously widened and narrowed.

Table 3.3 summarizes some of the conspicuous ways in which these periods of multipolarity differed and presents, for purposes of subsequent interpretation, our reading of the historical record. Among the differences one could identify, we posit that five are especially important. First, cycles of expansion and contraction in the world *economy* were not uniform, with some periods experiencing both upswings and downturns and others suffering only economic stagnation.

Second, the type of *governments* that managed the great powers changed. The farther back in time we travel, the greater the authority and control of rulers over their countries' policies. During the first four multipolar periods, all the great-power governments were highly centralized, with monarchs ruling their countries without meaningful input from the citizenry. They were "closed" governments, unrestrained by the need to make foreign policy decisions with an eye to public approval. It is only in the final two multipolar periods that democratic governance becomes a factor. Yet this development cannot be dismissed, for as governments became more "open" or representative, the choices about war and peace were demonstrably different. As we shall

---

4. This periodization does not dismiss the controversies that underlie the continuing disagreement among historians over precisely when multipolarity existed. We are well aware that, as Joseph Nogee's (1975: 1204) survey of the literature on international systems demonstrates, "There is no agreement within the discipline on what kind of international structure prevails, when it came into existence, or what preceded it." Nowhere is this more evident than in the debates surrounding the dating of multipolar periods. Scholars often differ on the appropriate benchmarks because "when the end of one phase is usually but the preliminary to the onset of the next it is easy to mistake the onset of another phase for the beginning of an entirely new departure" (Hinsley, 1963: 153). As a result of these conceptual difficulties, the periodization used here rests not on unanimity but on our judgment of what the accumulated historical evidence suggests.

TABLE 3.2
Multipolarity in the Modern World

Period	Onset Events	Great Powers	Termination Events
1495–1521	Treaty of Tordesillas (1493) French invasion of Italy (1494)	France, England, Austrian Habsburgs until 1519, and Spain until 1519 (thereafter United Habsburg entity), Ottoman Empire, Portugal	Conflict between Francis I of France and Charles V (Habsburgs)—First War of Charles V (1521)
1604–1618	Peace of Vervins (1598) War of the Armada (1585–1604)	France, England, Austria, Spain, Ottoman Empire, The Netherlands beginning in 1609, Sweden beginning in 1617	Thirty Years' War (1618–1648)
1648–1702	Peace of Westphalia (1648): treaties of Münster and Osnabrück	France, England, Austrian Habsburgs, Spain, Ottoman Empire until 1699, The Netherlands, Sweden	War of Spanish Succession (1702)
1713–1792	Treaty of Utrecht (1713) Treaty of Rastadt (1714)	France, Great Britain, Austrian Habsburgs, Spain, Sweden until 1721, Russia from 1721, Prussia from 1740	French Revolutionary Wars (1792–1802)
1815–1914	Napoleonic Wars (1803–1815) and Congress of Vienna (1815): Treaty of Chaumont (1814), Treaties of Paris (1814, 1815), Quadruple Alliance (1815)	France, Great Britain, Austria-Hungary, Russia, Prussia/Germany, Italy from 1861, United States from 1898, Japan from 1905	World War I (1914–1918)
1919–1939	Treaty of Versailles (1919)	France, Great Britain, Soviet Union, Germany, Italy, United States, Japan	World War II (1939–1945)

TABLE 3.3
A Comparison of Six Multipolar Periods

Multipolar Period	Economic Cycle(s)*	Similarity of Governments	Domestic Stability of Great Powers		Ideological Consensus	Influence of Nationalism
			Level	Source		
1495–1521	Stagnation: 1495–1508 Expansion: 1509–1521	Very High	High	Hereditary elite	High	Low
1604–1618	Stagnation	Very High	Declining	Religious strife	Low	Low
1648–1702	Stagnation: 1648–1688 Expansion: 1689–1704	High	Moderate	Constitutional reforms	High	Low
1713–1792	Expansion: 1713–1719 Stagnation: 1720–1746 Expansion: 1747–1761 Stagnation: 1762–1789 Expansion: 1790–1792	High	High but declining	Rise of popular participation	High	Low but rising steadily
1815–1914	Stagnation: 1815–1847 Expansion: 1848–1871 Stagnation: 1872–1892 Expansion: 1893–1914	Moderate	High except at mid-century	Insurrection	High but eroding	Moderate but rising rapidly
1919–1939	Stagnation	Low	Low	Leadership changes	Low	High

*Source: Terrence K. Hopkins, Immanuel Wallerstein, and Associates, "Cyclical Rhythms and Secular Trends of the Capitalist World-Economy," in Terrence K. Hopkins, Immanuel Wallerstein, and Associates, eds., World-System Analysis: Theory and Methodology (Beverly Hills: Sage, 1982a), p. 118.

see in subsequent chapters, the type of governments managing foreign policy makes a difference in the dynamics of multipolar systems. Of 116 major wars between 1789 and 1941, "no wars have been fought between independent nations with elective governments" (Babst, 1964: 10). Democracies have dealt with conflicts against other democracies by methods other than war (Doyle, 1995; Maoz and Abdolali, 1989). This does not mean, obviously, that democracies never experience war; they fight as often as do other types of states but rarely, if ever, against each other, presumably because the political culture of democratic states promotes pacific methods of conflict resolution and institutional procedures place constraints on the policy choices of national leaders (Morgan and Schwebach, 1992; Gleditsch, 1992; Ray, 1994a; Small and Singer, 1976).

A great power's level of *domestic stability* also influences its external conduct, and the amount of civil strife has varied from one period to the next. There is reason to believe that leaders sometimes wage war abroad because they assume that national cohesion will rise when an external threat exists and that they can manage domestic unrest by initiating foreign adventures. This so-called "diversionary theory of war" assumes that armed conflict is a last chance for states riddled with domestic strife to overcome internal antagonisms (Simmel, 1956; Jensen, 1982; Levy, 1989b). For example, Article 6 of the French Constitution in 1791 renounced "war for purpose of conquest," yet external war was nonetheless waged "solely to divert from social problems" (Albert Soboul, cited in Rothenberg, 1988: 207). Similarly, "Hitler also used an aggressive foreign policy to consolidate his internal political position" (Levy, 1988: 94).

Fourth, the periods listed in Table 3.3 differed with regard to the *ideological and philosophical views* rulers held about the purpose of government and appropriate goals of their foreign policy. Here a long-term erosion of consensus is evident, as the solidarity that once united great-power heads of state has decayed over time. Ideological disagreement has led to the pursuit of disparate goals: Where once great-power foreign policy was directed almost exclusively to the expansion of state power and territory, the view that foreign policy should promote certain ideological beliefs has taken root, undermining the capacity of great powers to resolve their differences and collectively coordinate their policies to deal with common problems. When the great powers united in their ideological opposition to a particular movement, as the conservative heads of state were at the Congress of Vienna in their dread of revolution, they have been more successful at containing the rivalries among themselves.

Finally (but not exhaustively), *nationalism* has influenced these six periods in different ways. Nationalism did not become a powerful force until the late eighteenth century. But ever since, it has been an increasingly potent determinant of great-power conduct. As an attitude of mind, nationalism presents the world with a psychological orientation radically different from the ideas that preoccupied rulers in earlier multipolar eras.

It is a predisposition to pay far more attention to messages about one's own people, or to messages from its members, than to messages from or about any other people. At the same time, it is a desire to have one's own people get any and all values that are available. The extreme nationalist wants his people to have all the power, all the wealth, and all the well-being for which there is any competition. He wants his people to command all the respect and deference from others; he tends to claim all rectitude and virtue for it, as well as all enlightenment and skill; and he gives it a monopoly of his affection. In short, he totally identifies himself with his nation. Though he may be willing to sacrifice himself for it, his nationalism is a form of egotism written large. . . . [The growth of nationalism] has altered the world in many ways. Nationalism has not only increased the number of countries on the face of the earth, it has helped to diminish the number of its inhabitants. All major wars in the twentieth century have been fought in its name. . . . (Deutsch, 1974: 124–125)

In summary, these six multipolar periods differed in terms of economic conditions, types of ruling governments, the degree of civil strife, prevailing ideologies, and popular loyalty. While these differences underscore the point made in Chapter 1 that no multipolar periods are the same, this does not prevent us from searching for common behavior patterns, which may reveal why previous multipolar periods degenerated into war.

Knowing what caused the onset of war in the past will assist us in developing prudent foreign policies for the multipolar future we may soon face. By comparing multipolar systems according to their size, degree of polarization, and prevailing norms, the chapters in Part II will explore whether variations in the *type* of multipolarity affect the probability of war, as potentially influenced by the differences we have just described. In accordance with the three-dimensional framework discussed above, each chapter will focus on a different set of systemic conditions that, on the basis of the existing empirical evidence, we postulate will affect the stability of multipolar distributions of power. Chapter 4 discusses whether the number of great powers or movement in their rankings makes a multipolar system war prone. Chapter 5 examines the ramifications of alliance polarization for multipolar systems. In Chapter 6, we investigate the impact of restrictive versus permissive normative orders.

After drawing conclusions on how these three sets of conditions affected the stability of historical multipolar systems, we turn our attention in Part III to outlining the most viable paths to peace in a twenty-first century multipolar world.

PART II
Understanding the Past

. 4 .

POLARITY AND UNCERTAINTY

We talk of the ancien regime *as though there reigned then a divine stability. In fact Powers ran up and down the scale with dizzy rapidity. Of the Powers indisputably ranked among the Great at the Congress of Westphalia in 1648, three—Sweden, Holland, Spain—ceased to be Great and one—Poland—ceased to exist, before the close of the eighteenth century; their place was taken by Russia and Prussia, two states hardly within notice a hundred years before. There was no such whirligig of fortune during the nineteenth century, despite its supposedly revolutionary character. The Great Powers who launched the First World War in 1914 were Great Powers who had made up the Congress of Vienna in 1814.*

—A. J. P. TAYLOR, 1954

The key to grasping the future is to recognize that "international relations continues to be a recurring struggle for wealth and power. . . ." (Gilpin, 1981: 7). The dramatic changes since the end of the Cold War notwithstanding, the ageless contest for advantage will remain the international system's primary fact of life into the twenty-first century, especially if a new multipolar system emerges.

To understand what might develop as the twentieth century ends, we need first to investigate the rise and fall of the great powers and the consequences of changes in their rank in previous multipolar systems. The purpose of this chapter is to review the historical evidence on shifts in the composition and size of the great-power club. In the previous chapter, we identified three dimensions along which all multipolar systems could be classified—size, degree of polarization, and the extent to which prevailing international norms support a permissive or restrictive code of great-power conduct. The chapters in Part II will focus on each of these dimensions in succession, comparing six previous multipolar systems since 1495.

DOES THE NUMBER OF GREAT-POWER COMPETITORS MATTER?

A common metaphor for great-power politics is the movement of balls on a billiards table. It is widely used because states routinely define their relationships with one another in terms of their position with respect to others, and they are sensitive to the speed and force with which others move. The logic of realpolitik argues that the probability of collision increases as the number of units increases. System size is assumed to make a difference in the degree to which great-power interactions are conflictual or calm. But is this assumption warranted? Does the number of great-power competitors matter? And if so, how? With what consequences?

In addressing these questions, we will use the definition proposed in Chapter 1 and elaborated upon in Chapter 3. Recall from those chapters that multipolarity is defined as a circumstance in which roughly equivalent capabilities are possessed by three or more great powers. Polarity is not equivalent to the number of great powers; it is a measure of the distribution of capabilities among the great powers. The number of great powers pertains to the *size* of the system (Levy, 1985: 47). Thus multipolar systems may include three, four, or even more great powers, each approximately equal to one another.

Does the size of a multipolar system affect its stability? A reasonable argument can be made on behalf of different figures. For example, R. Harrison Wagner (1986: 575) argues that multipolar systems with three great-power contestants are the most stable, whereas Arthur Lee Burns (1964: 508) disagrees, maintaining that "the most stable arrangement would seem to be a world of five or some greater odd number of powers, independent and of approximately equal strength."

Let us compare the number of great powers that existed, according to our interpretation of the record, in each of the six historical periods of multipolarity described in the last chapter. The states that achieved great-power status in these multipolar periods are listed in Table 4.1.[1] The chronology documents

---

1. Keep in mind that there is no agreed-upon definition of "great power" and "there are problems with evaluating the consequences of particular criteria, such as population, size, military force, princely rank or role as a diplomatic focus" (Black, 1990: 198–199). Note also that our focus is on nation-states. Yet the further back in time we travel, the more misleading this semantic convention becomes. The dynasties that ruled in the sixteenth century were less states than members of an hereditary nobility that intermarried and ruled without concern for the welfare of the people whose destinies they controlled. For example, the Austrian Habsburgs were more a dynasty than a state, "closely related to the Spanish Habsburgs [that] ruled a collection of territories that are collectively, though somewhat inaccurately, referred to as Austria." Similarly, the Turkish or Ottoman Empire was less a state than "an Islamic monarchy based at Constantinople, that also ruled Egypt, the Near East and the northern shores of the Black Sea, including the Crimea" (Black, 1990: 2).

These entities create confusion, but historians have nonetheless made for analytic convenience the practice of describing them as great powers, despite the differences between them and the modern sovereign nation-state. The list in Table 4.1 summarizes the views of diplomatic historians

TABLE 4.1
Great-Power Contenders in Six Multipolar Periods

Multipolar Period	Great Powers	Number
1495–1521	England, France, Austrian Habsburgs until 1519 and Spain until 1519 (thereafter United Habsburg entity), Ottoman Empire, Portugal	6
1604–1618	Austria, England, France, The Netherlands beginning in 1609, Ottoman Empire, Spain, Sweden beginning in 1617	7
1648–1702	Austrian Habsburgs, England, France, The Netherlands, Ottoman Empire until 1699, Spain, Sweden	7
1713–1792	Austrian Habsburgs, Great Britain, France, Prussia from 1740, Russia from 1721, Spain, Sweden until 1721	7
1815–1914	Austria-Hungary, France, Great Britain, Italy from 1861, Japan from 1905, Prussia/Germany, United States from 1898, Russia	8
1919–1939	France, Great Britain, Germany, Italy, Japan, Soviet Union, United States	7

how membership has expanded over time from its European core to gradually encompass increasingly distant geographical regions transcending the Atlantic (the United States) and the Pacific (Japan) oceans. It displays how changes have occurred in the composition of the great powers in different multipolar periods, but also how continuities are evident across the last five hundred years as some pairs of states have engaged in "enduring rivalries" (Goertz and Diehl, 1993), resuming their disputes with each other in successive multipolar periods (Gochman and Maoz, 1984).

Inspection of this record suggests no consistent pattern of covariation between the number of great powers and the ultimate outcome of each previous multipower system, as each eventually culminated in a "hegemonic" war where two or more great powers crossed swords in their efforts to dominate the system.[2] There appears to be no direct relationship between a multipolar sys-

---

and social scientists who, while they base their assessments on different criteria, nevertheless generally agree on the population of countries that were great powers during the post-1495 period.

2. "Confusion," warns Charles F. Doran (1991: 118), can arise "because of the ambiguity of the term 'hegemony.' Hegemony is actually a very old concept taken from the Greek notion of ruler and associated with the modern ideas of both leadership and dominance. In nineteenth century diplomatic parlance, it means attempted preponderance of one or more of the great powers by

tem's size and its duration. As we will see in subsequent chapters, other factors mediate the linkage between the number of poles and the system's stability and duration.

What is clear is that the identity of the great powers has undergone substantial modification over the past five centuries. Some once-great powers (Austria-Hungary, Sweden, Portugal) have fallen out of membership in the category of great powers. Others (the United States) have catapulted from relative obscurity to the pinnacle of power. And still others (Germany, Japan) have declined but, phoenix-like, have now reentered the charmed circle. Consider the changes that occurred in the composition of the great powers prior to 1800 as an illustration:

> By the last quarter of the 18th Century . . . the Western State System comprised five major Powers on the European Continent, a large number of minor Powers, and a new State across the Atlantic, born of European colonialism. Of the States which might have been described as Great Powers in 1648, England, France, and Austria retained their former position. Spain had fallen to the rank of a second-rate Power, in spite of the vast colonies which she still held in the Americas and the East Indies. Holland and Portugal likewise retained extensive overseas possessions, but they had long since passed the halcyon days when they could cope with other Powers as equals. Following the failure of France to establish her supremacy over the Continent, the new State of Prussia, founded on the Mark of Brandenburg, had emerged in Central Europe as the dynastic creation of a line of able kings. In the east, the Tsardom of Muscovy had extended its power over a vast domain. Under Peter the Great (1682–1725), Russia became partly "Westernized" and made itself a member of the European System. Under Catherine the Great (1762–96) it became a Great Power. Its expansion pushed the Swedes from the eastern shores of the Baltic and the Turks from the northern shores of the Black Sea. The Ottoman Empire was already in decay. The end of Poland brought the enlarged States of Russia, Prussia, and Austria into closer relations with one another. The petty States of Italy and Germany remained pawns among their greater neighbors. The first great struggle for overseas empire was ended. The Powers had achieved an equilibrium which seemed reasonably permanent and stable. (Schuman, 1969: 79)

System Size and Interaction Opportunities

As the number of roughly equal great powers increases, the number of interaction opportunities among them also increases. As we discussed in Chapter 3, one school of thought maintains that multipolar systems composed of a large

---

military force, threatening the very sovereignty and political integrity of the nation-state. In the recent international political economy, it means the dominance by the leading capitalist economy or of the 'core state' in the system." We use the term consistent with both the military and economic meanings.

number of great powers are more stable than smaller systems because everyone has a larger number of possible partners for interaction. This diffuses and reduces the intensity of conflict since "the increase in the number of independent actors diminishes the share [of attention] that any nation can allocate to any other single actor" (Deutsch and Singer, 1964: 400). In addition, increased system size produces more cross-cutting loyalties, which may dispel the temptations to move against a state that has lent support in the past and from whom future backing may be needed. Moreover, larger multipolar systems may be less prone to war because a multitude of autonomous actors makes possible more potential allies for coalitions to counter any single great power aiming for hegemonic superiority.

According to a second school of thought, however, increases in the size of a multipolar system may be destabilizing since there will be greater opportunity for intersecting claims and conflicts of interest (Miller, 1992: 8–9; see also Miller, 1994). Just as the number of automobiles converging at an intersection will make for complicated interactions and increased traffic will raise the likelihood of collision, so will the number of great-power contenders shape the system's pattern of interaction. As interaction opportunities increase due to the larger membership in the great-power club, so this argument goes, there is greater propensity for the competitors "either to overreact to external threats, as was the case on the eve of World War I, or to underreact, as was the case in the late 1930s" (Miller, 1992: 25). Behavior allegedly becomes less predictable, and as a consequence disputes and war become more likely.

System Size and Uncertainty

The size of the great-power system may matter in at least one other respect: It is regarded by all observers as a source of uncertainty. Uncertainty is a property of every multipolar system because it is always exceedingly difficult for great powers to measure and compare their power and assess the intentions of their peers. To some, uncertainty breeds caution and constrains the great-power contest, as each great power navigates the churning sea of world politics ever mindful of the risks of collision with many others; to others, it creates a condition for increased contact, contest, and conflict. Karen A. Rasler and William R. Thompson explain these contending positions:

> If decision makers have difficulty interpreting the hierarchical pecking order and the probable behavior of other states, uncertainty is greater than when they have fewer difficulties reading their structural environment. However, opinions are divided on whether uncertainty itself is beneficial or dangerous. If one contends, as proponents of predominance are said to do, that wars are the product of misperceptions and that uncertainty increases the probability of misperception, increased uncertainty renders war more probable. But if one argues, along the lines said to be favored by proponents of parity, instead that ambiguity tends to

restrain decision makers, increased uncertainty should lead to less rather than more war. (Rasler and Thompson, 1992: 3)

Table 4.2 summarizes data on the incidence of bilateral or dyadic wars between pairs of great powers in our six multipolar systems. It suggests that as the number of great powers in a multipolar system changes, the frequency of war between pairs of them will also change, but not necessarily in a consistent pattern of covariation. The largest multipolar system (1815–1914) was the longest lasting and among the least prone to experience great-power wars. The smallest system, with the shortest duration (1495–1521), experienced five great-power wars. Intermediate were multipolar periods with numerous power centers and episodic eruptions of great-power aggression. In short, the number of great-power competitors may matter, but not decisively. The association is too weak to draw the conclusion that historical upswings in the use of force were the product of more great powers in the system. As we shall see, other factors affect the relationship, so that it would be inaccurate to posit the existence of a direct relationship between the size of the great-power system and the stability of multipolarity.

What is more compelling is the likelihood that the emergence of a dominant state relative to the other great powers that challenge its position will provoke changes in the incidence of great-power wars. The question remains, however, whether those wars occur when a dominant power's strength is rising or when it is in a period of decline.

DOES THE STABILITY OF THE GREAT-POWER HIERARCHY MATTER?

Realist theory holds that rank and relative capabilities are important determinants of the degree of conflict and cooperation in great-power relations. National leaders throughout history have made energetic efforts to estimate where their state's capability ranks against their rivals. They are acutely attentive to *power transitions*, especially if they believe their state's position is rising or falling relative to the others (Doran, 1991). Their concern is justified because "actual power ratios and trends in power ratios are never fully visible to the participants [and] each party must make complex calculations based on its *perceptions* of present factors and trends and its *expectations* of future states of being" (Rosen, 1970: 229). That concern is normally high, because each great power is understandably fearful that a rival's expanding power will increase its own vulnerability. Sometimes this concern is exaggerated, almost paranoid. When convinced that other great powers are intent upon reducing his or her state to a second-rate status, a leader can easily feel compelled to strive by whatever means necessary to prevent that outcome. Hitler, Richard J. Barnet (1977: 14–15) observes, in 1928 warned that Germany must move quickly to prevent becoming "a second Holland or a second Switzerland" because "with the American Union a new power of such dimensions has come into being as

TABLE 4.2
Wars in Six Multipolar Periods

Multipolar Period	Largest Number of Great-Power Poles	Wars between Great-Power Rivals	Other Wars
1495–1521	6	War of the League of Venice (1495) Neapolitan War (1501) War of the Holy League (1511) Austro–Turkish War (1512) Second Milanese War (1515)	Polish–Turkish War (1497) Venetian–Turkish War (1499) First Milanese War (1499) War of the Cambrian League (1508) Scottish War (1513)
1604–1618	7	Spanish–Turkish War (1610) Spanish–Turkish War (1618) Thirty Years' War–Bohemian (1618)	Austro–Venetian War (1615) Spanish–Savoian War (1615) Spanish–Venetian War (1617) Polish–Turkish War (1618)
1648–1702	7	Franco–Spanish War (1648) Anglo–Dutch Naval War (1652) Great Northern War (1654) English–Spanish War (1656) Ottoman War (1657) Anglo–Dutch Naval War (1665) Devolutionary War (1667) Dutch Wars of Louis XIV (1672) Ottoman War (1682) Franco–Spanish War (1683) War of the League of Augsburg (1688) Second Northern War (1700)	Spanish–Portuguese War (1642–1668) Turkish–Venetian War (1645–1664) Scottish War (1650) Dutch–Portuguese War (1657) Sweden–Bremen War (1665) Turkish–Polish War (1672) Russo-Turkish War (1677)

(*continued*)

TABLE 4.2 (Continued)

Multipolar Period	Largest Number of Great-Power Poles	Wars between Great-Power Rivals	Other Wars
1713–1792	7	Second Northern War (1700–1721) War of the Quadruple Alliance (1718) British–Spanish War (1726) War of Polish Succession (1733) War of the Austrian Succession (1739) Seven Years' War (1755) War of the Bavarian Succession (1778) War of the American Revolution (1778)	Ottoman War (1716) Ottoman War (1736) Russo–Swedish War (1741) Russo–Turkish War (1768) Confederation of Bar (1768) Ottoman War (1787) Russo–Swedish War (1788)
1815–1914	8	Crimean War (1853) War of Italian Unification (1859) Austro–Prussian War (1866) Franco–Prussian War (1870)	Neapolitan War (1815) Franco–Spanish War (1823) Navarino Bay (1827) Russo–Turkish War (1828) Austro–Sardinian War (1848) First Schleswig–Holstein War (1849) Roman Republic War (1849) Anglo–Persian War (1856) Franco–Mexican War (1862) Second Schleswig–Holstein War (1864) Russo–Turkish War (1877) Sino–French War (1884) Russo–Japanese War (1904) Italo–Turkish War (1911)

(continued)

TABLE 4.2 (Continued)

Multipolar Period	Largest Number of Great-Power Poles	Wars between Great-Power Rivals	Other Wars
1919–1939	7	Russian Civil War (1918–1921) Russo-Japanese War (1939)	Manchurian War (1931) Italo–Ethiopian War (1935) Sino–Japanese War (1937) Russo–Finnish War (1939)

Source: Jack S. Levy, *War in the Modern Great Power System, 1495–1975* (Lexington, Ken.: The University Press of Kentucky, 1983), pp. 70–73.

threatens to upset the whole former power and order of rank of the states."

Hence, because "multipolar systems engender serious inequalities" and the prospects for survival or supremacy will change "in response to changes in [the great powers'] equality" (Midlarsky, 1988: 66, 67), rapid changes in the rank order of states can easily create anxiety. The historical record of these changes (see Table 4.3) suggests that this apprehension is warranted.

Multipolar systems are comprised of near equals, but not absolute equals. Some states have more power than others, and the differences among them have tended to change over time. Great powers customarily struggle for power—not always for its own sake, but more commonly to obtain *relative advantage* over their nearest rivals. As Joseph M. Grieco explains,

> [R]ealists find that the major goal of states in any relationship is not to attain the highest possible individual gain or payoff. Instead, *the fundamental goal of states in any relationship is to prevent others from achieving advances in their relative capabilities.* . . . In addition, realists find that defensive state positionality and the relative gains problem for cooperation essentially reflect the persistence of uncertainty in international relations. States are uncertain about one another's future *intentions*; thus, they pay close attention to how cooperation might affect relative *capabilities* in the future. This uncertainty results from the inability of states to predict or readily to control the future leadership or interests of partners. (Grieco, 1988: 498, 500)

The search for national "competitive advantage" (Porter, 1990) bred by this drive and fear has routinely resulted in shifts in the positions of the contenders, but the process is even more complicated than outlined here. The dynamic that animates the rise and fall of the great powers is influenced by other factors, four

TABLE 4.3
Rank Disequilibria in Multipolar Systems

Multipolar Period	System Size		Stability of Relative Rank	Frequency of Status Disruptions	Major Contenders	Dominant Power	Hegemonic Aspirant
	High	Low					
1495–1521	6	3	High after 1501, until 1519	High	France, Spain, England, Portugal, Austrian Habsburgs, Ottoman Empire	Charles V's Spain	Francis I's France
1604–1618	7	3	Low until 1615	High	Spain, England, Netherlands, Sweden, Austria, France, Ottoman Empire	France	Hapsburg Spain
1648–1702	7	3	Moderate until 1690	High	France, Netherlands, England, Austrian Habsburgs, Ottoman Empire, Spain, Sweden	France	Louis XIV's France
1713–1792	7	3	Low until 1740	Moderate	Great Britain, France, Prussia, Spain, Austrian Habsburgs, Russia, Sweden	Great Britain	Napoleon's France
1815–1914	8	3	High except 1860–1870 and after 1890	Low until 1860	Great Britain, France, Russia, Prussia-Germany, Italy, Austria-Hungary, Japan, United States	Great Britain	Germany
1919–1939	7	3	Low	Low until 1930	United States, Great Britain, Soviet Union, Germany, Japan, France, Italy	United States	Hitler's Germany

of which are regarded in the literature as especially potent: war, uneven growth, long economic cycles, and imperial overstretch.

War

When a great power goes to war, either against another great power or against a subordinate state, resources are redistributed. Territory often changes hands, and both victors and vanquished come out of the experience with an altered power base. Peter the Great's defeat of Sweden in 1709—"the beginning of the end of her great-power status" (Dehio, 1962: 105)—is but one example of the pronounced tendency for wars to change the pecking order of those at the top. Some challengers gain and others lose, which is why great-power wars "punctuate the periodic major redistribution of power" (Thompson, 1992: 127).

Inspection of the list of states that have achieved great-power status shows that membership in this exclusive club is hardly a guarantee of either external peace or domestic tranquility. Wars, whether fought for aggrandizement or to prevent subjugation, have cost several countries their status as great powers: The Austro–Hungarian, Ottoman, German, and Russian empires dissolved in the flames of World War I, and Germany, Japan, and Italy sacrificed their standing with the Second World War. In addition, many great powers lost ground as a result of their bellicose adventures. Following the Napoleonic Era, for example, "when a major power initiated war against another major power, the initiator was victorious in only 3 of 9 such wars, or 33 percent" (Small and Singer, 1982: 195). More commonly, great powers have initiated wars against weaker nations (Gochman and Maoz, 1984: 597) and, not surprisingly, increased their capabilities and sometimes their territory as a result of their victories over these minor powers.

Not to be overlooked is the impact of *civil war* or internal rebellion as another powerful factor affecting relative rank. Revolutions from within have often weakened and destroyed a great power's capability to compete on the international stage. For example, consider the corrosive effects of the constitutional crises that swept England between the onset of civil war in 1642 and the restoration of Charles II in 1660. That traumatic episode cost Britain dearly: The English subsequently failed "to defeat the Dutch in the Second and Third Anglo–Dutch wars (1665–7, 1672–4) and had watched with concern the French advance under Louis XIV into the Spanish Netherlands" (Black, 1990: xiv).

Arguably, civil war also affected the status of the United States. Some historians classify the United States as a great power as early as 1815 after the Louisiana Purchase broadened its territory, population, and resources. Others (Geller, 1988: 374) disagree, contending that America's devastating Civil War (1860–1865) delayed the rise of the United States to great-power status until the 1890s. The Russian Revolution in 1917 similarly limited that country's capabilities for many years. Hence, both international war and civil war have profoundly affected the rank of the great powers.

Uneven Growth

Shifts in the balance of power also are caused by the fact that the economies of the great powers expand at different rates. During no previous multipolar period have the leading powers' economies grown at the same pace; their growth rates have been affected by waves in the global economy—swings between expansion and contraction and cycles of boom and bust. Over the long run, these shifts in the rank of the great powers' relative wealth have precipitated alterations in their political and military relations, sometimes converting formerly cooperative trade partnerships into conflictual security rivalries (Sayrs, 1993). (As will be seen in Part III, the shifting economic fortunes of the great powers in the post–Cold War era threaten to once again disrupt their presently cordial military relations in the next millennium, raising anew the specter of multipolar instability and even warfare, despite the fact that the probability of interstate warfare among the great powers is very remote at the moment.)

In general, the pace of the great powers' relative economic growth has historically been determined primarily by two internal or domestic influences. The first cause of uneven growth has been "the technological and organizational breakthroughs which bring greater advantage to one society than to another. For example, the coming of the long-range gunned sailing ship and the rise of the Atlantic trades after 1500 was not *uniformly* beneficial to all the [great powers] of Europe" (Kennedy, 1987: xv–xvi). The second has sprung from the innovations and technological advantages that advanced learning made possible for those who invested in the education of their citizens. Great universities and centers of learning facilitated industrialization, and "differential industrialization is the key to understanding shifts in power" (Organski, 1968: 345–346).

Internal development has propelled some powers to the top of the global hierarchy and left others behind. But uneven growth alone is a necessary but not sufficient condition. Other theories, as noted below, expand the radius of explanation to encircle additional factors.

Long Economic Cycles

The economic foundations of political power are, in the long run, critically important determinants of changes in the great powers' pecking order. Economic growth provides the resources from which military might is forged. To identify which states rise to prominence and which states do not, some analysts have theorized that several processes within the modern world system are cyclical and unfold through a series of distinct phases. Immanuel Wallerstein (1974, 1979, 1980), for example, maintains that cyclical processes have had a major impact on the capitalist world-economy. For Wallerstein, a world-economy is an interregional network with a single division of labor but with multiple polities and cultures. The capitalist world-economy, which emerged in fifteenth-century Europe and ultimately expanded to encompass the entire globe, contains three structural positions: a *core* (strong, well-integrated states whose economic activities are diversified and capital-intensive), a *periphery* (areas lacking strong state machinery and engaged in producing relatively few unfinished goods by unskilled, low-wage labor), and a *semiperiphery* (states embodying elements of both core and peripheral production).

Within the core of economic great powers, a state may rise to hegemonic status by achieving productive, commercial, and financial superiority over its rivals. However, hegemony is difficult to maintain: The diffusion of technological innovations and the flow of capital to competitors, plus the massive costs of maintaining global order, combine to break the hegemon's market advantage in production.

Following the failure of the house of Habsburg to establish a world-empire under Charles V, Wallerstein asserts that the capitalist world-economy experi- a succession of four-phased cycles of hegemony/rivalry, which appear to be closely tied to several other rhythmic movements, most notably paired Kondra-tieff waves of economic expansion and stagnation in the core and periphery.[3] Wallerstein's four phases are outlined below:

- *Ascending hegemony* is a period of economic expansion and severe competition among core rivals in which the properties of multipolar politics are most in evidence.
- *Hegemonic victory* is a time of contraction that marks the emergence of a hegemon, as well as the movement of high-wage commodity production from periphery to semiperiphery and core areas. When this occurs, the ascendant power is not confronted by serious challenges from rivals, and thus the behaviors characteristic of multipolar periods are less evident.
- During the *hegemonic maturity* phase that follows, economic expansion returns as the new hegemon formally establishes its superiority in indus-trial production, agriculture, commerce, and financial resources.
- Finally, in the *declining hegemony* phase, the costs of preserving hegemo-ny and the diffusion of economic capabilities to challengers combine with

---

3. During the early 1920s, Nikolai Kondratieff published several studies of long waves in price and industrial production cycles. These waves of approximately fifty-year duration contained phases of economic expansion (A-phases) and contraction (B-phases), which have been linked to war (Goldstein, 1985), power transition (Väyrynen, 1983; Geller, 1993), and cycles of colonialism, tariffs/free trade, and industrial firm expansion/merger (Bergesen, 1981; Bergesen and Schoen-berg, 1980).

the contraction of the world-economy to prepare the battleground for a return to multipolar competition.

At this last phase of the cycle, the conflict between the hegemon and its potential successors, which historically has been associated with every multipolar system, grows in intensity as the number of great-power rivals increases and the duration of their rivalry lengthens (Hopkins, Wallerstein, and Associates, 1982a: 113–116).

Looked at as a long-term process unfolding over centuries, the great powers are thus pitched up and down by the economic currents of the time, with the macroeconomic processes of the world economy influencing their composition, rank, and conduct while they compete as participants in a multipolar arena. From the vantage point of this theoretical framework, the fate and fortune of previous hegemonic leaders (the Netherlands, 1625–1675; Great Britain, 1763–1815 and 1850–1873; and the United States, 1945–1965) have been determined by forces beyond their direct control. Like a cork in a stream, a great power's ultimate position and its territorial expansion and contraction are not products exclusively of its own practices and policies. More accurately, innovations in economic methods affect each great power's relative productivity, profits, trade balance, and, ultimately, position in the hierarchy.

Mercantilism and Imperialism

Many long-cycle theorists link these structural periodicities in the capitalist world-economy to cycles of imperialism and colonial expansion. European empire building began during the sixteenth and seventeenth centuries when Spain, Portugal, the Netherlands, Great Britain, and France used their military power to derive profits from overseas commerce. Innovations in a variety of sciences made the adventures of European explorers possible. Merchants followed in their wake, seizing the opportunities to profit from their government's exploits to expand their wealth and power by financing trade derived from political control of overseas territories (Cohen, 1973).

Mercantilism emerged as a philosophy prescribing governmental regulation of economic life to protect each nation's merchants and manufacturers from foreign competition and thereby increase the state's power. It sought to advance "the nation's position in the world economy" through "economic activity [that] necessarily involved conflict as one country's gain required another's loss" (Horne, 1987: 335–336). As such, mercantilism became an economic strategy for imperial expansion.[4]

Based on the belief that state power derived from the amount of gold and

---

4. The concept of "imperialism" is used to "refer to a world system of political domination or economic exploitation, to a policy of defending or expanding an empire, to an ideology which supports imperial ambitions (the original sense of the word), or even to individual acts of aggression. All of these different usages refer to different aspects of a complex historical process, culminating early this century, in which a few countries came to dominate most of the world, either by direct conquest or by less formal military and economic pressures" (Brewer, 1987: 238).

silver stockpiled, the European great powers sought a favorable balance of trade to acquire the treasured bullion. In 1664, Thomas Mun put forth this strategy in *England's Treasure by Foreign Trade*, arguing "The ordinary means to increase our wealth and treasure is by foreign trade, wherein we must observe this rule: to sell more to strangers yearly than we consume of theirs in value" (cited in Horne, 1987: 335). Colonies were crucial in this regard because they limited commercial competition in new markets and guaranteed access to sources of cheap materials (Cohen, 1973).

By the end of the eighteenth century, the European powers had stretched their economic empires across much of the world (see Map 4.1), and national trade followed the flag. But as the costs of administering territories overseas mounted, colonies became less profitable. Partially in reaction, Britain acquiesced to the independence of its thirteen North American colonies in 1776, and Spain grudgingly consented to the independence of most of its possessions in South America early in the nineteenth century. Between 1775 and 1825, ninety-five colonial relationships ended (Bergesen and Schoenberg, 1980: 236). "In this sense, Empires do not *fall*; they *fall apart*, usually very slowly, though sometimes remarkably quickly" (Puchala, 1992: 12).

With the breakup of colonial empires, faith in the mercantilist philosophy that had sustained classical imperialism diminished. In its place, a system of free international trade consistent with the precepts advocated by Adam Smith in *The Wealth of Nations* became the dominant philosophy. European powers continued to hold numerous colonies, but the prevailing sentiment was now more anti- than pro-imperial, at least until the last part of the nineteenth century.

European Imperialism Redux

Beginning in the 1870s and extending until the outbreak of World War I, another wave of imperialism swept the world as the European great powers, and later the United States and Japan, colonized new territories at a rate nearly four times faster than during the first wave of colonial expansion (Bergesen and Schoenberg, 1980). By 1914, just seven European powers (Belgium, Britain, France, Germany, Italy, Portugal, and Spain) controlled nearly all of Africa. In all of the Far East and the Pacific, only China, Japan, and Siam (Thailand) remained outside the direct control of Europe or the United States. China, however, was divided into spheres of influence for commercial exploitation by the great powers, and Japanese imperialism led to the acquisition of Formosa (Taiwan) and Korea. Elsewhere, the ascendant United States acquired Puerto Rico, Cuba, and the Philippines from Spain, leased the Panama Canal Zone "in perpetuity," and extended its imperial reach over Hawaii (see Map 4.2).

The nineteenth century witnessed the emergence of Great Britain as Europe's preponderant state. Between 1815 and 1900, the island nation gained control of no less than 44 percent and as much as 68.9 percent of the total economic capabilities held by all the major powers (Spiezio, 1990: 175). By 1900 its

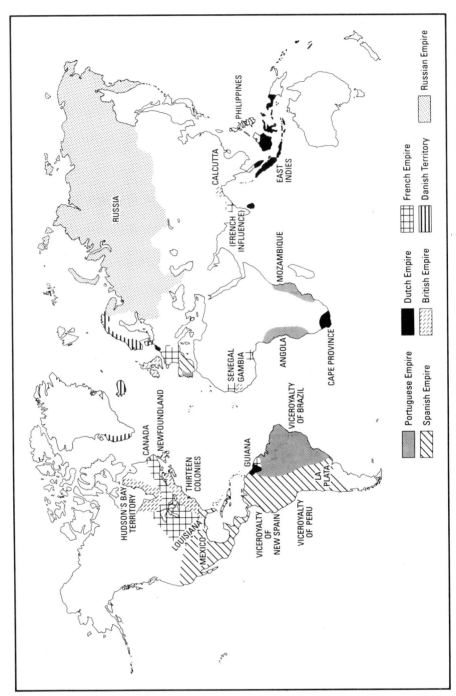

RUSSIA

PHILIPPINES

CALCUTTA

(FRENCH INFLUENCE)

EAST INDIES

MOZAMBIQUE

ANGOLA

CAPE PROVINCE

SENEGAL
GAMBIA

CANADA

NEWFOUNDLAND

HUDSON'S BAY TERRITORY

THIRTEEN COLONIES

LOUISIANA

MEXICO

GUIANA

VICEROYALTY OF BRAZIL

VICEROYALTY OF NEW SPAIN

VICEROYALTY OF PERU

LA PLATA

Portuguese Empire

Spanish Empire

Dutch Empire

British Empire

French Empire

Danish Territory

Russian Empire

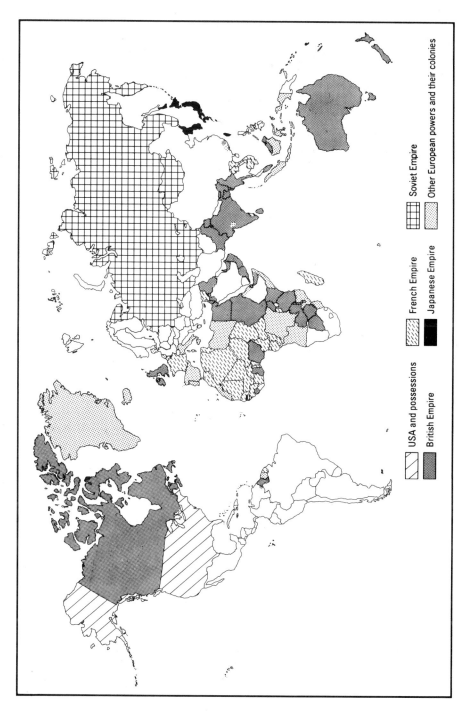

MAP 4.2. Imperial Control of the World following World War I.

Legend:

- USA and possessions
- British Empire
- French Empire
- Japanese Empire
- Soviet Empire
- Other European powers and their colonies

realm included one-fifth of the earth's land area and as much as one-quarter of its population (Cohen, 1973: 30). It was an empire on which the sun never set.

In contrast with imperialism in the sixteenth and seventeenth centuries, the imperial powers engaged in extraordinary competition in the late nineteenth century. Colonies symbolized national power and prestige, and the great powers' struggle to acquire them in the twilight of this multipolar period was unrestrained.

As the new leader politically and economically, Great Britain became the chief exponent of free international trade, from which it could benefit the most. By the 1890s, however, Britain's superiority began to slip, with its share of great-power economic capability sliding from 47.9 percent in 1890 to 13.5 percent when World War I broke out (Spiezio, 1990: 175). At this phase, Germany emerged on the European continent as a powerful industrial nation, as did the United States in the Western Hemisphere. Accordingly, Britain's imperialism represented an attempt to maintain its privileged position in the international division of labor in the face of growing competition from Germany and the United States, the newly emerging core states.

Imperial Overstretch

A fourth potential cause of great-power decline can be traced to the costly effort to remain at the the top of the international hierarchy. Maintaining top-dog status requires extraordinary resources. "The problem in defense spending," former U.S. President Dwight Eisenhower once observed, "is to figure how far you should go without destroying from within what you are trying to defend from without." In expressing this view, he echoed the belief of his predecessor Harry S Truman, who commented that "all through history it's the nations that have given the most to the generals and the least to the people that have been the first to fall."

The problem of a gap between external commitments and internal resources has faced every previous great power over the past five centuries. Great powers frequently reach beyong their grasp. In 1557, for example, "not only the Habsburgs but also the French crown . . . had to declare bankruptcy" (Kennedy, 1987: 57). Once-mighty great powers have all eventually fallen, not always by defeat in battle, but paradoxically by the weight of their own strength. Commitments abroad have eroded economic strength at home.

Paul Kennedy (1987) coined the term "imperial overstretch" to describe this phenomenon. In his opinion, if

> too large a proportion of the state's resources is diverted from wealth creation and allocated instead to military purposes, then that is likely to lead to a weakening of national power over the longer term. In the same way, if a state overextends itself strategically—by, say, the conquest of extensive territories or the waging of costly wars—it runs the risk that the potential benefits from external expansion may be

outweighed by the great expense of it all—a dilemma which becomes acute if the nation concerned has entered a period of relative economic decline. The history of the rise and later fall of the leading countries in the Great Power system since the advance of western Europe in the sixteenth century—that is, of nations such as Spain, the Netherlands, France, the British Empire, and currently the United States—shows a very significant correlation *over the longer term* between declining productive and revenue-raising capacities on the one hand and military strength on the other. (Kennedy, 1987: xvi)

Evidence supports this interpretation, showing that "when undertaking a major war, the participants exhaust their resources and inflate their currency, which tends to inaugurate a long stagnation period" (Boswell, Sweat, and Brueggemann, 1989: 13). Great powers have repeatedly burdened themselves with military expenses that retarded their long-term economic growth and, ultimately, destroyed their national wealth and hastened their international demise. Perhaps this explanation of national decline is what Napoleon Bonaparte had in mind when in 1805 he wrote that "all empires die of indigestion."

POLARITY, POWER TRANSITIONS, AND PEACE

At some point, the distribution of capabilities among great-power rivals begins to change. When this happens, the ascending state and the declining state may perceive threats from each other and square off (Organski and Kugler, 1980). As Daniel Geller summarizes,

The general argument holds that a hierarchy of power supports the international order at any given time. Both the rules of the system and the division of values reflect the interests of the dominant state and its allies. However, the power relations among states are not permanent, and differential or uneven national growth rates ensure that the international distribution of power will shift and undermine the foundations of the order. Hence, a growing disjuncture between a changing power distribution and the hierarchy of prestige produces a disequilibrium that, if uncorrected, results in crisis. In this way, shifts in power relations favoring challenger states rather than the dominant nation create the necessary conditions for war. The work of this set of scholars suggests that great power wars are produced by *unstable* power balances—war occurs when a dominant nation finds its advantage in relative capabilities eroding due to the rising power trajectory of a challenger. Whether presented in the form of hegemonic stability (Gilpin), long-cycles (Modelski), or power transition (Organski)—all of these theories see a mechanism for war in the operation of dynamic power balances which lead away from preponderance and toward equality. (Geller, 1993: 175)

In essence, this theory assumes that the dominant nation is "more satisfied with the existing international order than any other since it is to a large extent *its* international order" (Organski, 1968: 366). As Donald J. Puchala (1992: 11) observes, "World economic 'playing fields' are always tilted to the advantage of dominant political actors, *because these actors do everything they possibly can to tilt them.*" Conversely, challenging great powers are dissatisfied with their position, and, as their power increases, they may go to war to achieve the status they feel they deserve.

> If the challenger's internal and external capabilities are increasing slowly, there is a greater likelihood that the problems arising from a great power's catching up with its rival can be resolved without resort to military conflict. However, if the challenger's capabilities are increasing rapidly, then both the dominant power and the challenger are caught unprepared for the resulting shift in the international power order. The fast-growing challenger alters the existing international power order, and this attempt will lead the fast-growing great power to attack the dominant nation. (Kim, 1992: 157)

Ascending great powers often hope to achieve through force the recognition and status that their new-formed muscles permit them. On the other hand, established powers may employ force to arrest their relative decline. Thus, when advancing and retreating states seek to cope with changes in their relative power and the difference in power between them declines, war becomes more likely: "The aggressor will come from a small group of dissatisfied strong countries; and it is the weaker, rather than the stronger, power that is most likely to be the aggressor" (Organski and Kugler, 1980: 19). According to A. F. K. Organski,

> It might be expected, that a wise challenger, growing in power through internal development, would wait to threaten the existing international order until it was as powerful as the dominant nation . . . , for surely it would seem foolish to attack while weaker than the enemy. If this expectation were correct, the risk of war would be greatest when the two opposing camps were almost equal in power, and if war broke out before this point, it would take the form of a preventive war launched by the dominant nation to destroy a competitor before it became strong enough to upset the existing international order. In fact, however, this is not what has happened in recent history. Germany, Italy and Japan attacked the dominant nation and its allies long before they equalled them in power, and the attack was launched by the challengers, not by the dominant camp. (Organski, 1968: 371)

Surprisingly, it is the weaker of the great powers that tend to initiate great-power wars. According to one study, second-ranking nations historically have had the highest relative rate of war initiation, whereas the set of first-ranking nations has had the lowest war initiation rate (Bremer, 1980: 69; also see Maoz, 1982: 160). The chances of the starter being victorious is shrinking, however (Wang and Ray, 1991: 14).

Preliminary evidence suggests that wars in a multipolar environment may be different than those characteristic of periods when one state stands at the pinnacle of world power. As John Vasquez summarizes the findings:

> Scientific research has shown that sometimes a balance in the system . . . is associated with peace and at other times with war . . . which suggests that the relationship is random. In fact, it can be argued that neither a balance of power nor a preponderance of power is associated with peace, but rather each is associated with different types of war! From this perspective, the balance of power has been associated with total wars like the Peloponnesian War, the Punic Wars, the Thirty Years' War, the Napoleonic Wars, and the First and Second World Wars. These were wars of rivalry among relative equals. Conversely, a preponderance of power has been associated with imperial wars of conquest. A balance of power may prevent the latter wars in the short run, but in so doing often produces conditions that lead to wars between rivals. (Vasquez, 1992: 852)

The proposition that different types of warfare are associated with different polarity structures has been advanced by theorists who focus on cycles of world leadership (Modelski, 1974, 1978, 1987; Thompson, 1983, 1986, 1988). According to their interpretation of the historical record, the modern world system has experienced a succession of four-phased cycles of capability concentration/deconcentration. The first of these phases, *global war*, involves a devastating struggle among great powers that ends with a single dominant state emerging as the provider of the public good of security and manager of international economic relations. During this *world power* phase, the system's distribution of military and economic capabilities is highly concentrated. Over time, however, memories of war and reconstruction fade, competitors emerge, and the policies of the dominant state come under attack. This *delegitimation* phase is followed by a phase of *deconcentration*, where the dominant state loses its preponderant position, and the distribution of capabilities within the system gradually becomes more diffuse. As this movement toward parity continues, rivalries intensify and eventually erupt into another global war, thereby completing the cycle.

Recent research has shown that during periods of high capability concentration, preponderant states tend to intervene militarily into the civil wars of their neighbors in an effort to preserve the international order they helped create. In other words, the world power phase of the concentration/deconcentration cycle is highly prone to internationalized civil wars (Raymond and Kegley, 1987: 495). These interventions are less frequent during the delegitimation and deconcentration phases, possibly because declining powers attempt to arrest further slippage by avoiding military interventions that might become costly, protracted conflicts. Although a declining great power may continue other forms of intervention, fear of having its strength sapped by overextended commitments could lead it to eschew the quagmire of a potentially long, bloody, civil war far from home.

To summarize, multipolar systems with their ever-shifting balance-of-power dynamics are highly turbulent. Resource scarcity may be a key factor in creating turmoil because multipolarity typically engenders serious inequalities among system members (Midlarsky, 1988: 48–62). Over time these inequalities have often led to envy, political intrigue, and movement up and down the global hierarchy where the power trajectories of ascendant states overtake those of their declining rivals, especially in periods in which global economic growth is relatively stagnant (Midlarsky, 1993). The ceaseless movement of states on the vertical axis of the global power hierarchy combines in a multipolar environment with incessant maneuvering for allies on the horizontal axis of balance-of-power politics (Doran, 1991). As a result, crises are common (Brecher, James, and Wilkenfeld, 1990: 72), third parties do not enjoy high rates of success in resolving the issues that divide disputants (Raymond, 1980: 98), and wars erupt with alarming regularity (Haas, 1970: 121; also Wayman, 1985: 131–133; Thompson, 1988: 220).

As we have seen in this chapter, the tumult of multipolar systems is not mitigated by changes in system size. Yet there may be other systemic conditions that combine with multipolar distributions of power to dampen the prospects for war, especially wars of rivalry between equals. Are there structural conditions that lower the probability of war in multipolar systems? Alternatively, do certain conditions make war more likely? The answers to these questions may illuminate potential paths to peace should a multipolar future materialize early in the next century.

As noted in Chapter 3, the degree of alliance flexibility is one possible factor that affects the stability of multipolar systems. "Power transition theorists generally overlook alliance formation as an important means of augmenting power" when nations are caught up in the shifting tides of historical change (Kim, 1992: 155). So it is to that neglected component of multipolar state systems that we turn in the next chapter.

· 5 ·

POLARIZATION AND ESCALATION

There is no such thing as a little *war for a great nation.*
—ARTHUR WELLESLEY,
DUKE OF WELLINGTON, 1838

No account of the stability of multipolar systems can ignore the critical function performed by alliance formation and dissolution. Throughout history, great powers have been obsessed with the power of their rivals. One way to deal with increases in a rival's power is to acquire arms; another approach is to recruit allies. "Whenever in recorded history a system of multiple sovereignty has existed, some of the sovereign units when involved in conflicts with others have entered into alliances" (Wolfers, 1968: 269). For this reason, we turn now to the powerful influence that alliances exert on great-power behavior in multipolar periods. After beginning with a few definitional preliminaries and a summary of alliance theory, the chapter will examine the impact of alliance polarization on the stability of multipolar systems.

ALLIANCES AND ALIGNMENT IN WORLD POLITICS

States are said to *align* themselves with one another when they adopt a common stance toward some shared national security problem (Teune and Synnestvedt, 1965). In contrast, an *alliance* is produced when their tacit agreement to cooperate is made explicit through a written treaty. Alliances, in other words, are formal agreements between sovereign states "for the putative purpose of coordinating their behavior in the event of certain specified contingencies of a military nature" (Bueno de Mesquita and Singer, 1973: 241). The degree of coordination may range from a detailed list of military forces that will be furnished by each party under certain conditions (for example, the Little Entente of 1920) to a guarantee of neutrality in the event that an alliance member is attacked (for example, the 1887 Russo–German Reinsurance Treaty) or to the broader requirement of consultation should a military conflict erupt (for example, the *Dreikaiserbund*). The target of the accord may be implicit or may be identified as a single country, a group of states, or a geographic region that the agreement covers. The duration of the accord may be limited to a relatively short period of time or forged to last indefinitely.[1] Designed to serve convergent security interests, alliances result from the purposeful choices by two or more states to specify "the conditions under which they will or will not employ military force" (Russett, 1974: 301).

Just as alliances differ according to the scope, target, and duration of their accords, they also differ according to their purpose (Moul, 1988: 252). One way to classify these goals is to differentiate between *wartime alliances*, whose members join together to fight some third party, and three types of alliances that typically are formed in peacetime: (1) *defense pacts*, where the signatory parties agree to intervene militarily in the event of an attack on one of their numbers; (2) *nonaggression agreements*, in which the parties pledge to remain neutral should one of them become involved in a war; and (3) *ententes*, which require consultations if one of the signatories is attacked (Singer and Small, 1966). Clearly, the nature of each of these kinds of alliance goals varies, as do the prospects for compliance with their treaty provisions. Defense pacts, for example, place more demands on the signatories than do the vague understandings found in ententes. As a result, they are entered into more reluctantly and entail greater incentives for defection when changes occur in the conditions that existed at the time of their formation. Why then are great powers willing to ignore these risks and tie their fate to the compliance of an ally in time of need?

WHY GREAT POWERS FORGE ALLIANCES

Explanations for why states voluntarily reach agreements to combine capabilities for joint action are often couched in terms of gaining "coldly calculated advantages" (Jordan and Taylor, 1984: 474). Because the advantages are am-

---

1. International law distinguishes between temporary and perpetual treaty provisions, with pacts *in perpetuiate* referring to the "many such treaties in which the obvious intention is to establish a permanent state of things" (Brierly, 1955: 256). This concept of perpetuity is illustrated by the 1373 Treaty of Friendship and Peace between Portugal and Great Britain, which stated that "there shall be from this day forward . . . true, faithful, constant, mutual, and perpetual friendship . . . and that as true and faithful friends we shall henceforth, reciprocally, be friends to friends and enemies to enemies, and stand, assist, maintain, and uphold each other mutually, by sea and by land, against all men that may live or die." On October 12, 1943, Winston Churchill declared in a speech to the House of Commons that "this treaty was reinforced in various forms by Treaties of 1386, 1643, 1654, 1660, 1661, 1703, and 1815, and in a secret declaration of 1899. . . . The validity of the Old Treaties was recognized—in the Treaties of Arbitration concluded with Portugal in 1904 and 1914. . . . This engagement has lasted now for nearly six hundred years. . . . I have now to announce its latest application."

biguous, decisions to ally are usually made cautiously after careful consideration of their opportunities and dangers.

When making their calculations, most leaders have sought to serve that nebulous standard known as "national interest." Rarely have they built military partnerships just to express friendship or ideological affiliation. Instead, they forged alliances when (1) the perceived benefits have exceeded the costs and (2) the costs were politically sustainable. To put it another way, regardless of the risk-taking propensity of its leadership, a great power is likely to "shun alliances if it is believed it is strong enough to hold its own unaided or that the burden of commitment resulting from the alliance is likely to outweigh the advantages to be expected" (Morgenthau, 1985: 201). This pattern is supported by historical evidence showing that "potential alliances which fail to increase both partners' security levels [have] almost never [formed]" (Altfeld, 1984: 538).

THE AMBIVALENT REALPOLITIK IMAGE OF ALLIANCES

Discussions about alliances are informed almost exclusively by realpolitik, the dominant world view held by great-power decision makers (Vasquez, 1993). Although evidence shows "that so-called 'realpolitik' considerations of security are crucial to alliance formation decisions" (Lalman and Newman, 1991: 251), realpolitik is "marked by disagreements on the conditions under which [alliances] are likely to form, the kinds of alliances most likely to be effective and cohesive, and the effects of alliances on the international system" (Thies, 1991: 336). Thus, realpolitik may be the most compelling theory of alliances discussed within the halls of government, but the realist perspective displays many internecine quarrels, and realist theories defy easy characterization.

Realist theorizing takes as its point of departure the premise that security is a function of power, power is a function of military capabilities, and the purpose of foreign policy is to increase power. Alliances are an economical means of increasing power in that they enable the costs of defense to be shared with others. This advantage might lead great-power leaders to the conclusion that alliances should be the preferred method for obtaining security, but they also identify important disadvantages. While great powers facing dangerous rivals may have their reasons to recruit allies, they also have incentives to "go it alone" in order to escape entrapment, abandonment, or betrayal. Inspection of the historical record therefore must proceed with recognition that policymakers in previous multipolar systems were divided about the virtues and vices of alliances (see Box 5.1).

To untangle the trade-offs associated with alliances, the diversity of realpolitik thought must be described. During previous multipolar periods, three divergent schools of thought have struggled for acceptance. The first image holds that alliances are basically *beneficial* because of their capacity to enhance

BOX 5.1
ALLIANCES DENOUNCED AND DEFENDED IN SIX MULTIPOLAR PERIODS

Alliances Denounced   **Alliances Defended**

1495–1521

"You plainly see that hitherto nothing has been effectively done towards permanent peace by treaties. . . . Now is the time to pursue different measures. . . ."

—Desiderius Erasmus, 1517

"[Venice successfully] had often changed friendship according to the condition of the time and affairs, maintaining the constant aim to keep their forces as equally balanced as they could [with their rivals] so that they should both be weakened by their contention with one another."

—Paolo Paruta, 1521

1604–1618

"An ambassador is an honest man, sent to lie abroad for the good of his country."

—Sir Henry Wotton, English ambassador to Venice, 1604

"Warfare today is not a question of brute strength . . . but rather of winning and losing friends. . . ."

—Count Gondomar, Spanish ambassador to London, 1618

1648–1702

"If one shall speak the truth quite frankly, treaties are concluded from the beginning with this mental reservation. All the beautiful provisions about alliances, affirmations of friendship and the promises to great advantages, do only mean according to the experience of centuries, as understood by the two signatories, that they want to abstain from armed encroachments and from public enmities. Secret violation of the treaties which are not visible to the public are expected. . . ."

—Louis XIV, 1668

"Defensive alliances are . . . just and necessary when they are in reality intended to prevent an exorbitant power, such as might be in a condition to subdue all."

—François Fénelon, 1700

(continued)

BOX 5.1
(CONTINUED)
1713–1792

"It is a maxim founded on the universal experience of mankind that no nation is to be trusted farther than it is bound by its interest."

—George Washington, 1778

"The use of alliances . . . has in the last age been too much experienced to be contested. It is by leagues, well concerted and strictly observed, that the weak are defended against the strong, that bounds are set to the turbulence of ambition, that the torrent of power is restrained, and empires preserved from those inundations of war that, in former times, laid the world in ruins. By alliances . . . the equipoise of power is maintained, and those alarms and apprehensions avoided, which must arise from vicissitudes of empire and the fluctuations of perpetual contest. . . ."

—Sir Robert Walpole, 1741

1815–1914

"We shall not seek the alliance of kings, nor delude ourselves with any idea of maintaining our liberty by diplomatic arts or treaties. . . ."

—Guiseppe Mazzini, 1832

"When any one state menaces the independence of any other, . . . that other ought to call in the aid of its allies, or to contract alliances for its protection. . . ."

—Lord Henry Brougham, 1857

1919–1939

"A treaty rests and must rest . . . upon moral obligation. No doubt a great power . . . can cast aside a moral obligation if it sees fit and escape from the performance of the duty which it promises. The pathway of dishonor is always open."

—U.S. Sen. Henry Cabot Lodge, 1919

"How else are we going to marshal adequate and if possible overwhelming forces against brazen, unprovoked aggression, except by a grand alliance of peace-seeking peoples under the authority of an august international body?"

—Winston Churchill, 1937

security. The second maintains that the costs of alliances usually outweigh the benefits and that, because alliances are generally *risky*, they should be eschewed except when a clear danger is present. The third image holds alliances in contempt, arguing that they have proven so *destructive* that prudent statesmen should avoid them.

Alliances as Beneficial

According to the logic of realpolitik, the absence of a central authority to settle interstate disputes makes preparations for war necessary. This creates a threat system where, as Sir James Macintosh described it in 1815, "mutual jealousy [makes] every great Power the opponent of the dangerous ambition of every other" (cited in Gulick, 1955: 54). Within such an environment, leaders are advised to form coalitions for several reasons. First and foremost, realists perceive alliances as a means of self-protection "in order to balance against *threats*" (Walt, 1992a: 190). The defensive alliance network that Bismarck wove in central Europe during the 1880s followed this approach to preventing war by ensuring that any aggressor would confront multiple adversaries. Hence, realists stress that alliances are war-preventing instruments: "International trouble-makers are likely to be deterred much more effectively by superior power than by merely equal power" (Claude, 1989: 80), and alliances are useful for attaining this superiority.

Second, alliances are sometimes used as a method of national self-aggrandizement to maximize predatory power. For example, the alliances of the Thirty Years' War led by France and Sweden, and by Austria, promoted imperialist ambitions (Morgenthau, 1985). By combining power, an alliance can serve as a "latent war community, based on mutual cooperation" (Osgood, 1968: 19; see also Beer, 1970). "It is the existence of an enemy that gives rise to the need for allies, and it is for the advantageous conduct of fighting that alliances are formed" (Rosen, 1970: 215). The Hitler–Mussolini "Pact of Steel" provides an example. As Hitler in 1925 wrote in *Mein Kampf*, "Any alliance whose purpose is not the intention to wage war is senseless and useless."

Third, relatively weak states join alliances and exploit them as arrangements of expedience. By bandwagoning, "states tend to ally *with* the strongest or most threatening state" (Walt, 1992a: 190; also Christensen and Snyder, 1990) in order to reduce the threat to their survival, and these strong states recruit and support such clients in order to prevent their alignment with any counter-coalition. "Nothing weakens enemy strength more," one realist (Hartmann, 1983: 327) avers, "than detaching, or exploiting the detachment of, the enemy's allies." Bandwagoning occurred prior to World War I, when some states rushed into the arms of others to gain protection and to share in the potential spoils of war. The same phenomenon was evident in other multipolar periods when war erupted. At these times "ambivalent powers will always band-wagon" (Brawley, 1990: 22) by siding with the hegemon, as Spain did between 1688 and 1713 when it allied with Holland in the War of the League of Augsburg but allied with France in the War of Spanish Succession, and as Prussia did when it allied with the Holy Roman Empire.

What these examples highlight is that great powers have often constructed alliances for narrow, opportunistic reasons by bandwagoning with the principal threat to peace rather than allying against a rival that attacked someone else. Self-interest is the motive when states ally with aggressors, "as England and Sweden did with expansionist France in 1672, . . . as France did with aggressive Prussia in 1740; and as Russia and France did with revanchist Austria in 1750" (Luard, 1987: 295). Alliances in this sense are sometimes used to acquire power to be used in later struggles with rivals.

Fourth, alliances reduce costs by spreading them among several partners, and they provide benefits that cannot be obtained unilaterally. Aside from the common benefit of security, which accrues as a "public good" to all members, alliances can also bestow a "private" benefit by increasing the military capability of certain states. By joining with France in 1921, for example, Poland was able to supplement its capabilities by gaining access to large supplies of war material for equipping its army. Even a preeminent power like imperial Great Britain could enhance its position by aligning with distant nations so as to acquire support facilities from which it could project its power.

Fifth, great powers with allies may gain increased influence over other countries' foreign-policy decisions. Alliances furnish a medium for exerting leverage over partners. Normally we think of this leverage in terms of the alliance leader influencing its smaller partners. However, the influence can flow in the opposite direction as well: "Bargaining power accrues not necessarily to the party possessing superior resources generally, but to the party which possesses issue-specific resources, is able to communicate its resolve clearly and convincingly, and is able to exploit asymmetries in its relations with another state" (Jönsson, 1981: 256). These commitments clarify expectations and relationships and help to avoid the "rigidity of strategy" that often accompanies "flexibility of alignment" (Waltz, 1979: 169).

Sixth, alliances afford a leader an opportunity to shore up his or her standing at home. Leaders sometimes join alliances to gain status, economic assistance, or a legitimizing ideology.

Finally, "Alliances have been regarded by realists as essential for the balance of power and *eo ipso* as stabilizing" (Møller, 1992: 51). It is through shifting alliances that an aspiring hegemon may be prevented from achieving universal dominance. This function was implanted in the conceptual underpinnings of great-power peace in the seventeenth century, when a hegemonic aspirant such as France under Louis XIV and, later, Napoleon could be held in check by a coalition of the other threatened great powers. As George Liska (1962: 12) states, alliances are "typically against, and only derivatively for, someone or something." From this perspective, necessity drives alliance formation. The adages that alliances should be "marriages of convenience" and that "politics makes strange bedfellows" capture the realpolitik view that only collective interests should justify the banding of states together in a common cause.

> In a multipolar balance-of-power system (characterized by the distribution of capabilities among a number of comparable, if not equal, actors), shifting align-ments are the central mechanism in the preservation of equilibrium. . . . Both peacetime alliances and arms races function to deter expansion or attack by rivals; should deterrence fail, wartime coalitions and violence attempt to prevent domination by the enemy. (Aliano, 1978: 206)

Together with these purposes, realism also advances principles about the dissolution of alliances. In general, the realist credo holds that the only good alliance is one that can be easily dissolved when the threat to the security of its members recedes. When an alliance no longer serves the military purpose for which it was originally constructed, it should be dismantled. Loyalty to allies is not held in high regard, and alliances should be terminated when the need for them vanishes.[2]

Alliances as Risky

It is always uncertain whether an alliance will serve the purposes for which it was originally created, and uncertainty invariably increases the longer an alli-ance remains in force (Lissitzyn, 1967). Hence, the preeminent risk inhibiting the decision to ally resides in the chance that an alliance treaty will bind one's state to a commitment that later ceases to remain in its interest. Alliances are a rudimentary means of "fate control," and, as realists routinely warn, many have sown the seeds of undesirable, "fateful" consequences for their members.

> Take, for example, the Franco-Prussian War in 1870. France lost that war badly, and one reason for that loss was that France did not receive help from its potential allies. The leaders of France, in the months leading up to the war, believed that Austria-Hungary, or perhaps Italy, might come to their aid if France became involved in a conflict with Prussia. But when the time came, France found itself

---

2. Realism makes public and private morality separate realms and argues that ethics should play a subordinate role in the affairs of states. As Thomas Hobbes wrote in 1651, "Force and fraud are in war the cardinal virtues." Cardinal Richelieu expressed a similar opinion when he noted in 1640 that "One may employ everything against one's enemies." This contrasts sharply with private morality where, for example, lovers may swear in their marriage vows to love each other, in sickness and in health, for better or for worse, till death do them part. Realpolitik rejects such a code of conduct for states, counseling instead that alliance commitments should be honored only when a military partnership enhances a state's strategic situation.

alone. Both Austria and Italy left the French to their sad fate. (Ray, 1992: 395; also Howard, 1961)

Many other examples can be provided of states that have escaped from their prior alliance agreements by claiming that national interests overrode their obligations. For instance, the Ottoman Empire used this defense when it withdrew from the 1913 Treaty of London and severed its ties with the Allied Balkan Powers. When the danger of abiding by promises increases, as they usually do on the eve of war, fears that an ally may desert or negotiate a separate peace intensify. Such fears were captured by the words of the Viennese courtier Questenburg, who lamented in April 1631 when the Papacy withdrew assistance after Sweden conquered Frankfurt, "We cry 'Help, Help,' but there is nobody there" (cited in Parker, 1987: 130).

Accordingly, many statesmen have been wary of entrusting their country's security to the pledges of others and have followed George Washington's advice in 1796 to "steer clear of permanent alliances" because whereas a state "may safely trust to temporary alliances for extraordinary emergencies" it is an "illusion . . . to expect or calculate upon real favors from nation to nation." By tying their state to another, leaders may find that future foreign policies can be held hostage. George F. Kennan summarizes this apprehension:

> The relations among nations, in this imperfect world, constitute a fluid substance, always in motion, changing subtly from day to day in ways that are difficult to detect from the myopia of the passing moment, and even difficult to discern from the perspective of the future one. The situation at one particular time is never quite the same as the situation of five years later—indeed it is sometimes very significantly different, even though the stages by which this change came about are seldom visible at the given moment. This is why wise and experienced statesmen usually shy away from commitments likely to constitute limitations on a government's behavior at unknown dates in the future in the face of unpredictable situations. This is also a reason why agreements long in process of negotiations, particularly when negotiated in great secrecy, run the risk of being somewhat out of date before they are ever completed. (Kennan, 1984: 238)

Hence, even though alliances provide advantages, binding one's state to another reduces freedom of maneuver by requiring conformity with certain contractual stipulations. This is a great liability in multipolar systems where "statesmen must be able to act quickly and expertly in cutting encumbering ties or making new ones as balance necessities dictate" (Gulick, 1955: 67). Agreements to ally are risky because they reduce mobility of action, making great powers dependent on their allies' compliance and diminishing their latitude of choice and sovereign independence.

Though inertia may prolong the life of an alliance, the usefulness of any alliance is destined to diminish when the common external threat that brought the coalition into being recedes (Wolfers, 1962: 29). Since time will erode the

---

BOX 5.2
THE FRAGILITY OF ALLIANCES

"Any coalition is a precarious thing, for it rests upon the effective suppression of divisive tendencies. . . . Things can change. Where the peril is simple to comprehend and substantially equal in danger to all the vital interests of all the members of the bloc, the coalition is extremely hard to dissolve. But these circumstances are rarely all present over a long period of time. . . ."
—Frederick H. Hartmann (1983: 325)

"Alliances . . . are frequently uncertain in actual operation, since they are dependent upon political considerations of the individual nations. The defection of Italy from the Triple Alliance in 1915 and the disintegration system of alliances between 1935 and 1939 illustrate this weakness. . . ."
—Hans J. Morgenthau (1985: 213)

---

degree to which allies feel obligated to abide by the provisions of their agreements, disputes about duties invariably arise as new circumstances provoke controversies related to the meaning of a treaty's wording (see Box 5.2). In essence, alliances are inherently fragile. As one policymaker has noted, there are distinct seasons to the life of every alliance:

> Almost by definition alliances have a limited life cycle. . . . National objectives change, the threat which made it worthwhile to subordinate some national interests to the evolution of a collaborative policy changes also, and the strains of alliance become too great to bear. For though alliance has been an essential device of international politics for nearly three thousand years, it is bound to develop internal strains once the period of clear and present danger is past, since it must involve a relationship between strong and less strong powers, restricting the freedom of both without giving either a decisive influence upon the policy of the other. (Buchan, 1965: 295)

To realists, therefore, statesmen should not take a fixed position on a temporary convergence of national interests. An alliance is valued only as an instrument for dealing with *immediate* threats; cementing security relationships in treaties of alliance is not intrinsically beneficial since the result of an alliance is "like a house built by a host of jealous carpenters with no boss and with many different plans for the design of the building" (Gulick, 1955: 86). Thus, many leaders have concluded that alliances should be formed only for very limited and specific purposes. They also have maintained that when the conditions that make alliances useful erode, they should be dissolved, before the costs of adherence become too burdensome. To realists, this principle is all but sacrosanct;

since future conditions can never be known at the time an agreement is negotiated, realists routinely counsel respect for the concept of *raison d'état*—the classic escape clause by which the repudiation of prior commitments can be justified by citing the exigencies of a particular situation.

In summary, this line of realpolitik reasoning suggests that great powers should avoid alliances, enter into them only to meet immediate threats to their security, and defect when national self-interests are jeopardized. When the going gets tough, national interests may dictate the search for allies; but when allies constrain, alliance ties should be severed promptly.

Alliances as Destructive

Beyond the fact that alliances reduce great powers' capacity to act autonomously in pursuit of their national interests, realists depict two other, even more troublesome potential dangers. First, rather than deterring war through the operation of the balance of power, alliances may enable aggressive great powers to combine resources in order to overturn the status quo through offensive wars. Imperial powers, this line of reasoning continues, can act more aggressively than they otherwise would when they can count on their allies' assistance. Second, even though alliances are often formed to preserve the balance of power, alliance aggregation frequently has had the opposite effect, converting local disputes into larger conflicts. If, as Franklin D. Roosevelt observed in 1935, "war is a contagion," then one reason for its spread is the existence of alliances that pull countries into armed conflicts that they might otherwise have avoided.

Several propositions are associated with the claim that alliances expand war. Foremost is the prediction that, rather than functioning as a means of defense against adversaries, alliances threaten enemies and thereby provoke counter-alliances, with the result that the security of *both* coalitions are reduced. One coalition's search for security increases the insecurity of its adversaries. "The principle of 'My ally, right or wrong' is one that cuts both ways; it can be reassuring as a guarantee for oneself but alarming as a liability to help others" (Hudson, 1968: 179). Vigorous support for an ally in a crisis elevates tensions:

> . . . peacetime alliances may occur in order to reduce the insecurity of anarchy or reduce armament costs [but] they will tend to create relations of enmity as well as alignment. Even if the initial alliance is not dictated at a specific opponent, other states will perceive it as a threat and begin to behave as enemies, perhaps by forming a counter-alliance. Not only will alliances identify friends and foes, they will also create interests consistent with such relations. (Snyder, 1990: 108)

Designed initially to balance threats and counter inequalities of strength, alliances unleash "a reactive process, with one state creating or entering an alliance because of what another state has done" (Vasquez, 1990: 2). In this sense, the level of alliances operates as a thermometer of war fever. When taken to the extreme, alliance formation may produce polarized blocs of mutual animosity that can increase the likelihood of war. Alliances "reveal any added support that a state may have, and the amount of support that a potential belligerent may need. . . . The reduction of uncertainty brought about by such information may be all that is needed to facilitate an aggressor's desire to attack another state" (Bueno de Mesquita, 1981b: 151). This was demonstrated by the Molotov–Ribbentrop Pact of 1939 between the Soviet Union and Nazi Germany, which paved the way for the German attack of Poland and the Soviet attack on Finland and the Baltic states. In short, alliances may encourage aggression by enhancing the confidence of an expansionist power.

Related to this drawback is the equally troublesome prospect that alliances will widen an ongoing war by drawing third parties into the dispute. When states join forces, the conflict of one member becomes the conflict of its partners; "at worst, the polarized situation can result in the very thing that the original alliance was designed to avoid—an enemy attack" (Ray, 1992: 394). As George Washington warned in his Farewell Address (1796), alliances are entangling because they require members to come to each other's aid and thereby become involved in conflicts that they might have otherwise avoided.

The warning that alliances expand war is grounded in evidence that wars between states without allies are less likely to draw others into it than are disputes between states tied to allies (Siverson and King, 1979; also Oren, 1990). Inasmuch as great powers with allies have a more difficult time avoiding being "dragged into a war even when they should not" (Vasquez, 1990: 4; also Siverson and King, 1980; Midlarsky, 1989), realist fear of alliances is not without foundation. Consider the origin of World War II and its expansion. The surprise attack at Pearl Harbor on December 7, 1941, was partly undertaken because of Japan's knowledge that Germany and Italy also had promised to declare war on the United States, which they did in conformity with their agreement on December 11.

Still another potential destabilizing effect of alliance formation relates to the necessity for states to control the behavior of their own allies once they join forces. This manifests itself in two ways. To begin with, intra-alliance relations must be managed to deter each member from taking action against its enemies that might threaten the security of the rest. In other words, allies must be restrained; if they are not, their wars will become their allies' wars. If the commitment to an ally is valued above the need to avoid antagonism with an enemy, the scope of war will expand rather than contract. Leaders fearful of going it alone may abide by their commitments even at the risk of becoming involved in a war they did not choose.

Beyond this danger, prudent statesmen must also consider the possibility that today's ally might become tomorrow's enemy. Realist theory holds that because all states are natural enemies and there are no permanent friends or adversaries, war *between* allies is always possible. According to one review of the historical record, "Wars between allies are common, three times greater than would be expected by chance: More than 25 percent of coalition partners eventually go to war against each other" (Russett and Starr, 1989: 95). The German attack on Poland in 1939 in violation of the German–Polish neutrality pact of 1934 and the Italian invasion of Albania in 1939 in violation of the Italian–Albanian defense pact of 1927 both illustrate that alliances may not deter one member from attacking another.

If we extrapolate from this line of reasoning, we would expect to find that the greater the proportion of states joining alliances, the greater will be both the number of participants in the wars that occur and the magnitude of the fighting. This "contagion" thesis posits that alliances spread wars: As the number of alliances increases, the number of belligerents will increase and the number of major powers involved in war will expand because alliances drag powerful states into the wars of their weaker confederates. As John Vasquez summarizes,

> The chances of an allied major state staying out of a war are not very good. . . . Indeed, the evidence [between 1815 and 1945] indicates that major states within the central system herald their wars by alliances. For example, all of Austria-Hungary's, Prussia/Germany's, and Russia's wars (seven, seven, and eight wars, respectively) are preceded by alliances. All but one of Britain's four wars . . . , six of France's nine wars, eight of Italy's eleven wars, and five of Japan's seven wars are preceded by alliances. (Vasquez, 1993: 159–160)

On balance, then, the realist vision of the benefits and costs of alliance formation is ambivalent. Both positive and negative consequences are foreseen when great powers join forces (see Table 5.1). However, if we put the divergent components of this vision together, it is clear that realism emphasizes the "risky" properties of alliances over their "beneficial" attributes. Alliances have proven prudent under some conditions and counterproductive under others. What they become depends on the extent to which they evolve into rigid structures that entrap members and provoke nonmembers. To explore this proposition further, we next examine the impact of alliance polarization on the stability of multipolar systems.

THE CONSEQUENCES OF POLARIZED ALLIANCES

When the distribution of capabilities among the great powers is not examined in isolation, but combined with other systemic conditions, a more complex picture of the sources of stability and instability in multipolar periods emerges. The influence of alliance polarization as a potential mediating variable in the polarity–war relationship is of particular importance because multipolar contests appear to be shaped by the prevailing configuration of great-power alliances (Liska, 1962). A multipolar distribution of power across three or more states may set the stage for a widespread war, but the clustering of powerful

TABLE 5.1
The Benefits and Costs of Alliances in Multipolar Systems

Benefits	Costs
▪ Friendship develops among otherwise potential rivals	▪ Counteralliances form
▪ Predictability increases and uncertainty declines	▪ Flexibility declines as options are foreclosed
▪ Relationships clarify	▪ Bargaining power diminishes
▪ Military capabilities increase	▪ Adversaries provoked to increase arms
▪ The pace of arms races slows	▪ Weaker states accelerate preparations for war
▪ The fear of attack declines	▪ Rivals' insecurities heighten
▪ Nonmilitary collaborative endeavors increase	▪ Others excluded from participation in allies' cooperative ventures
▪ Expansionist members of the alliance are constrained	▪ Members become entrapped in disputes with their allies' enemies
▪ Allies' resolve and confidence strengthen	▪ Great powers divided into adversarial blocs
▪ Capabilities of rival coalitions are balanced	▪ Motives for a preemptive first strike increase

states into two rigid, hostile, and relatively equal coalitions seems to be the key factor in determining whether such a war will occur (Wayman, 1985).

Polarization

Recall that whereas polarity is defined by the distribution of power among the members of the state system, polarization refers to the propensity of actors to cluster around the most powerful states. This occurs through alliances. Thus a system with multiple power centers can be said to be moving toward a greater degree of polarization if its members gradually form separate countervailing blocs (Hart, 1985: 25).

Polarization transforms the environment within which great powers compete. Through alliance formation, the distribution of capabilities becomes aggregated into a bloc of military might larger than would have been the case had each ally relied only on its own arsenals. The balance of power is thus modified when two or more great powers unite to forge a coalition. The degree to which an alliance merges these states into larger, more powerful clusters affects the security calculations of both members and nonmembers alike.

Figure 5.1 portrays the principles underlying this conception of polarization. Note how in the left column five independent great powers stand alone, untied to each other and in potential opposition. Note also how their military capa-

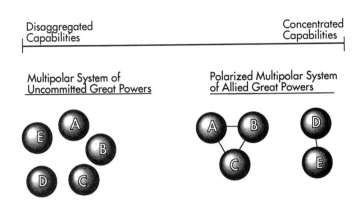

FIGURE 5.1. Alliances, Polarization, and the Aggregation of Capabilities.

bilities (depicted by the area encompassed by each circle) are similar, with only modest disparities in their force levels. This distribution represents an extreme—the maximum dispersion in the distribution of power, in which each great power comprises an independent actor. When blocs form, however, a configuration like that pictured in the right column can emerge. Such a polarized multipolar system would aggregate capabilities between three powers that have one alliance and a counteralliance composed of two other great powers. Needless to say, a range of alternate configurations is possible beyond the single three-against-two alliance structure presented here. But the key point is that when alliances come into being, the state system can take on a character radically different from what would exist had countries remained uncommitted and nonaligned. As Box 5.3 shows, whether this is beneficial or not remains a matter of debate.

Polarization in History

To reduce the scope of disagreement about the effect of alliance polarization, we need to examine the degree of polarization that existed in the six previous multipolar periods being compared. Unanimous agreement among historians and quantitatively oriented social scientists about the precise level of polarization in these periods does not exist. Fortunately, the investigations of these analysts have converged on agreement about the general level of polarization in each and whether the trend was moving toward greater or less polarization when each period neared its conclusion. Table 5.2 summarizes this information.

The bases for these characterizations rest on observations of the nature of the alliances that formed in each period. Table 5.3 presents an inventory of these alliances in the six multipolar systems under examination.

BOX 5.3
ALLIANCES AND GLOBAL STABILITY: CURE OR CURSE?

Alliances and Global Stability

"Force of arms is not the only expedient by which we may guard against a formidable power. . . . The most effective is a confederacy of the less powerful sovereigns who, by the coalition of strength, became able to hold the balance against that potentate whose power excites their alarms. Let them be firm and faithful in their alliance; and their union will prove the safety of each."

—Emerich de Vattel, 1758 (in Luard, 1992: 392–393)

"[In] international affairs, payoffs often come to stable alliances; and statesmen do much to maintain these alliances."

—Bernhardt Lieberman (1968: 371)

"Alliances are a necessary function of the balance of power operating in a multiple state system."

—Hans J. Morgenthau (1959: 185)

Alliances and Global Instability

"A tight system with many alliances, members, and minor powers allied to major powers is very likely to have many powers actively engaged in wars."

—Michael Haas (1970: 114)

"One might question whether . . . a security alliance really provides security [since] security alliances, because of their threatening character, increase tensions in the international system. . . ."

—David J. Finlay and Thomas Hover, Jr. (1975: 319)

"The grouping of states in permanent alliances which are committed to act together . . . would tend to . . . decrease stability."

—Quincy Wright (1965: 122)

"In a multipolar system . . . the value of [an] alliance must be discounted by the probability that it will trigger a counteralliance, provoke the adversary to greater hostility, or increase the hostility of some other state that is friendly to the adversary."

—Glenn H. Snyder (1990: 107, 111)

"Nations that are fond of the status quo are not immune from war with each other. Allies are more likely to be satisfied with the status quo between them than they are other states. This fondness, however, is not a guarantee of peaceful relations."

—Bruce Bueno de Mesquita and David Lalman (1992: 166)

TABLE 5.2
Polarization in Six Multipolar Periods: Characteristics and Trends

Multipolar Period	Level of Polarization	Trends in Power Concentration*
1495–1521	Low	Stable
1604–1618	Low but rising	Rising
1648–1702	Declining	Rising
1713–1792	Moderate	Rising
1815–1914	Low but rising after 1870	Decreasing 1815–1829, rising 1830–1869, declining thereafter
1919–1939	High	Rising 1919–1929, decreasing thereafter

*Measures after 1815 based on Geller (1992a: 276).

This inventory confirms what analysts of great-power relations generally report: Alliances regularly appear when military and economic capabilities are divided among more than two great powers in a setting of approximate parity. In no multipower system has a unilateral, defiantly independent policy response by the great powers remained the norm. Sooner or later great powers have found incentives to combine resources, despite the fears and dangers posed.

Moreover, we note another continuity. At the start of each multipolar era the new security environment has usually been cloudy, and this has made it difficult to define where the interests of two or more great powers most converge. Yet, as each multipolar period evolved, the great powers engaged in an active competition to acquire allies. Indeed, as each period neared its conclusion, alliance formation became increasingly energetic. To illustrate this characteristic, let us look at four representative multipolar periods when alliance formation was the chief characteristic of the great-power game.

The 1495–1521 Multipolar System
In the system that developed in the waning days of Renaissance Italy, "No overriding body of law existed. . . . At the time of the [Holy Roman] Empire's decay and the Papacy's waning strength," observes Ludwig Dehio (1962: 24), "there arose among the political units a lawless and pitiless struggle which saw the emergence of Caesarean tyrants. This frightful process of selection gave birth to five major states, which, unable to destroy one another, had to reconcile themselves to one another's existence in a condition of equilibrium."

TABLE 5.3
Alliance Aggregation in Multipolar Periods: Representative Great-Power Coalitions

Multipolar Period	Great-Power Defensive and Neutrality Alliances*	Other Alliances
1495–1521	France–Spain–Emperor (League of Cambrai) (1508) France–England (1518)	France–Venice (1498) France–Swiss Confederation (1499) France–Swiss Confederation (Perpetual Alliance) (1516)
1604–1618	France–England—Netherlands (1608)	France–Savoy (1610)
1648–1702	France–Netherlands (1662) France—England (1667) France–England–Netherlands (Triple Alliance) (1668) Austrian Habsburgs–Spain–Sweden–Venice–Poland–Bavaria–Saxony–Palatinate–Savoy (League of Augsburg) (1686)	Sweden–Brandenburg (Treaty of Konigsburg) (1656) France–German Princes (League of the Rhine) (1658) Austrian Habsburgs–Brandenburg (1672)
1713–1792	Britain–Austria–Netherlands (Barrier Treaty) (1715) Britain–France–Netherlands–Austria (Quadruple Alliance) (1718) Britain–Sweden (1720) Britain–France–Spain (1721) Britain–France–Prussia–Netherlands (Treaty of Hanover) (1725) Britain–France–Spain–Netherlands (Treaty of Seville) (1729) Britain–Austria–Netherlands (1731) Britain–Russia (Subsidy Treaty) (1755) France–Austria (First Treaty of Versailles) (1756) Britain–Prussia (Treaty of Westminister) (1756) Austria–Russia (1781) Britain–Prussia–Netherlands (Triple Alliance) (1788) Austria–Prussia (1792)	Austria–Spain (1725) Prussia–Saxony–Hanover–Brunswick–Mainz–Hesse Cassel–Baden–Mecklenburg–Anhalt–Thuringianlands (League of German Princes) (1785)

(*continued*)

TABLE 5.3 (Continued)

Multipolar Period	Great-Power Defensive and Neutrality Alliances*	Other Alliances
1815–1914	Austria–Prussia–Baden–Bavaria–Hesse Electoral–Hesse Grand Ducal–Saxony–Wurttemberg–Hanover (1818)	Russia–Turkey (1833–1840)
	Britain–Austria–Prussia–Russia–France (Quadruple Alliance) (1818)	Austria–Modena (1847–1859)
		Austria–Parma (1851–1859)
		France–Sardinia (1859)
		Prussia–Baden (1866)
	Britain–France (1841)	Prussia–Wurttemberg (1866–1870)
	Portugal–Spain (1834–1846)	Prussia–Bavaria (1866–1870)
	Britain–Austria–Prussia–Russia–Turkey (1840)	Britain–Turkey (1878–1880)
		Austria–Serbia (1881–1895)
	Mecklenburg–Schwerin (1843)	Russia–China (1896–1902)
	Germany–Russia (1873–1881)	Britain–Portugal (1899–1947)
	Austria–Russia (1877–1878)	Britain–Japan (1902–1921)
	Germany–Austria (1789–1918)	
	Germany–Austria–Russia (Three Emperors' League) (1881–1887)	
	Germany–Austria–Italy (Triple Alliance) (1882–1914)	
	Germany–Austria–Romania (1882–1914)	
	Germany–Russia (Reinsurance Treaty) (1887–1890)	
	Austria–Italy–Spain (1887–1895)	
	Germany–Austria–Italy (1887–1914)	
	France–Russia (1892–1914)	
	France–Italy (1902–1914)	
1919–1939	Germany–USSR (1926–1936)	France–Belgium (1920–1936)
	France–USSR (1932–1939)	France–Poland (1921–1939)
	USSR–Italy (1933–1941)	Italy–Yugoslavia (1924–1927)
	Germany–Italy (1939–1943)	France–Czechoslovakia (1925–1939)
	Germany–USSR (1939–1941)	USSR–Turkey (1925–1939)
		France–Romania (1926–1940)
		USSR–Afghanistan (1926)
		USSR–Lithuania (1926–1940)
		Italy–Albania (1927–1939)
		France–Yugoslavia (1927–1939)
		Italy–Hungary (1927–1943)
		USSR–Persia (1927–1939)

(continued)

TABLE 5.3 (Continued)

Multipolar Period	Great-Power Defensive and Neutrality Alliances*	Other Alliances
		Italy–Turkey (1928–1939)
		Italy–Greece (1928–1938)
		France–Turkey (1930–1939)
		Britain–Iraq (1932–1956)
		USSR–Finland (1932–1939)
		USSR–Latvia (1932–1940)
		USSR–Estonia (1932–1940)
		USSR–Poland (1932–1939)
		Germany–Poland (1934–1939)
		USSR–Czechoslovakia (1935–1939)
		USSR–Mongolia (1936)
		Britain–Egypt (1936–1951)
		Italy–Yugoslavia (1937–1939)
		USSR–China (1937–1945)
		Britain–Poland (1939)
		Germany–Denmark (1939–1940)
		Germany–Estonia (1939–1940)
		Germany–Latvia (1939–1940)

Source: Inventory provided by Jack S. Levy, based on operational criteria described in Levy, "Alliance Formation and War Behavior," *Journal of Conflict Resolution* 25 (December 1981): 581–613.
*Two or more great powers

That equilibrium in the chaotic multipolar period after 1495 was achieved through alliance formation. A modicum of stability resulted from shifting coalition formation against whichever of the major powers threatened to consume the others:

> The Papacy, a weak state especially vulnerable to domination by the powerful, played a prominent part in bringing such combinations about. Pope Alexander VI mobilized the most powerful states of Europe (the [Austrian] emperor, Spain, Venice and Milan) to join in ejecting Charles VIII from Italy after his conquest of Naples in 1494; Julius II organised the League of Cambrai to drive Venice from northern Italy in 1508; the same pope created the Holy League to drive France from Milan in 1511–12; while the treaty of Mechlin created a still larger alliance against the French in 1513. From that point on, during the great duel between the Hapsburgs and the Valois, such powers as England, Venice, Genoa, and the Papacy shifted alliance regularly to create leagues against the main threat to peace: joining Charles against Francis in 1520 after the latter had conquered

Milan; and joining Francis against Charles (in the League of Cognac) after the latter's triumph at Pavia (Henry VIII made war against France in 1512–13); joining with France in planning war against the Hapsburgs in 1515. . . . Even the Turks and the Scandinavian powers were occasionally brought in to maintain the balance. . . . (Luard, 1987: 282)

This early multipolar period founded on constant maneuvering succeeded in avoiding imperial subjugation in large part because flexible coalitions emerged to balance and deter the hegemonic ascendance of any single power.

The most persistent threat to establish hegemony over the system arose from France and its adventures in Italy. These gambits were repeatedly blocked by various coalitions; and there was great variety, not rigidity, in the composition of alliances.

When Charles VIII invaded Italy in 1494, he was met by the League of Venice, comprising Spain, the Papacy, Austria, and Venice. By the end of 1495, Charles was forced to retreat across the Alps. After Venice defeated Austria in Venezia-Giulia and Friulia and appeared to be making a bid for the domination of a substantial piece of the Italian peninsula, the League of Cambrai was formed in 1508 to counter this effort. It consisted of the Papacy, Austria, France, and Spain, indicative of just how flexible alignments were in the period. (Hopf, 1991: 487)

Hence, we witness in the birth of the modern state system's first multipolar era an uneasy stability resulting from constantly shifting alliances and counter-alliances designed to balance the power of whatever state or coalition most threatened to dominate the other. Florence and Venice, for example, forged a temporary alliance to war against Milan when they were threatened by its power; "however, as the power of Milan was whittled away, Venice's relative power position was augmented. Gauging Venice to be the new threat to her security, Florence defected from the alliance and joined forces with her former enemy to thwart the aggrandizement of her former partner" (Aliano, 1978: 196). In this manner, between 1495 and 1521 fluid alliances contributed to the five great-power wars but prevented any single great power from vanquishing the others.

The 1713–1792 Multipolar System

The same maneuvering was also evident after the Treaty of Utrecht (1713) restored peace, implanted the balance of power as a formal concept to regulate great-power rivalry, and set the stage for renewed efforts to prevent dominance by any particular power through formation of countervailing alliances. The Treaty of Utrecht asserted boldly the belief that the balance of power was "the best and most solid foundation of . . . a lasting general concord [among states]." The great powers enthusiastically acted on this conviction, as the 1713–1792 multipolar period was an era in which the fluid balance of power became accepted as the overarching principle to guide the great powers' alliance behavior.

By doing so, it was inevitable that they would change sides, desert old alliances, and form new ones whenever it seemed to them that the balance of power had been disturbed and that a realignment of forces was needed to reestablish it. In that period, foreign policy was indeed a sport of kings, not to be taken more seriously than games and gambles, played for strictly limited stakes, and utterly devoid of transcendent principles of any kind. Since such was the nature of international politics, what looks in retrospect like treachery and immorality was then little more than an elegant maneuver, a daring piece of strategy, or a finely contrived tactical movement, all executed according to the rules of the game, which all players recognized as binding. The balance of power of that period was amoral rather than immoral. The technical rules of the art of politics were its only standard. Its flexibility, which was its peculiar merit from the technical point of view, was the result of imperviousness to moral considerations, such as good faith and loyalty, a moral deficiency that to us seems deserving of reproach. (Morgenthau, 1985: 210)

Alliances formed rapidly, for both aggressive purposes and to prevent hegemonic subjugation.

The many coalition wars that filled the period between the Treaty of Utrecht of 1713 and the first partition of Poland of 1772 all attempted to maintain the balance that the Treaty of Utrecht had established and that the decline of Swedish power as well as the rise of Prussian, Russian, and British strength tended to disturb. The frequent changes in the alignments, even while war was in progress . . . have made the eighteenth century appear to be particularly unprincipled and devoid of moral considerations. . . . Yet the period in which that foreign policy flourished was the golden age of the balance of power in theory as well as in practice. (Morgenthau, 1985: 209)

The great powers entered into and broke alliances repeatedly in their effort to contain hegemonic pursuits. Consider, for example, the fluidity of one of this multipolar period's phases:

Back in Frederick the Great's time the shifts were even more bewildering. During the last three years of the Seven Years' War (1756–1763) George II of England had been aiding Frederick of Prussia with subsidies. But following George II's death, the new king, George III, although fighting a common enemy, ceased subsidizing the Prussian armies (1760). Frederick the Great's position was greatly weakened and his back to the wall when Czarina Elizabeth of Russia died (January 5, 1762). The new czar, Peter III, an admirer of Frederick's military talents, concluded peace with Prussia in March. Then in May Prussia and Russia became allies. But in July Catherine II deposed Peter and recalled Russian troops from Frederick's army! Early the next year (1763) the Treaty of Paris restored peace between England and France and Spain; five days later the Treaty of Hubertusburg ended the war between Austria and Prussia. (Hartmann, 1983: 329)

From this operation of countervailing coalitions and realignments, no great power succeeded in achieving hegemony. The fluid balance-of-power structure eventually rigidified, however, and terminated in 1792 in a colossal great-power struggle.

Since the new multipolar system that began in 1815 is uniformly regarded by diplomatic historians as a classic example of the balance-of-power process, examination of this period also can provide insight into the impact of alliance polarization on the stability of multipolar systems.

The 1815–1914 Multipolar System

In the aftermath of Napoleon's defeat, the allied victors meeting at the Congress of Vienna sought to manage great-power relations and avoid another systemwide war. Great Britain, the world leader at the beginning of this multipolar period, promoted a set of rules for the preservation of the balance of power that encouraged coalition adjustments and flexibility in alignments. These rules would also permit Great Britain to play the foreign-policy role of a "balancer" to offset any new threat by a powerful coalition to gain preponderance.

The Concert system worked for three decades. Then the revolutions that swept Europe in 1848 and the four great-power wars that occurred thereafter (the Crimean, Austro-Italian/Sardinian, Austro-Prussian, and Franco-Prussian) drastically altered the European balance of power and restored enthusiasm for alliances as a way of preventing future conflicts. The apparent harmony at the 1856 Congress of Paris and the conferences in London (1850, 1864, 1867), Paris (1858, 1860, 1869), and Vienna (1853, 1855) notwithstanding, the great powers began to challenge the precepts of the Concert of Europe. As Great Britain's influence began to wane and new rivals such as Prussia emerged to challenge its supremacy, the great powers increasingly sought allies to buttress their security and returned to the balance of power to keep the peace.

As always, these changes in approach were influenced by rapid changes in the distribution of power. The 1854–1856 Crimean War witnessed a coalition of France, Great Britain, and Turkey defeat Russia and thereby preserve the balance of power within the Balkans. With the subsequent decline of Russian power and the concomitant rise of German influence, the emerging new balance generated still greater enthusiasm for alliances. "The *diplomatic* history of the Great Powers for the decade or so after 1871 was one of a search for stability" (Kennedy, 1987: 188), and that search led to the construction of an intricate network of alliance systems, built on the expectation that if attacked, timely assistance from allies would be forthcoming. The Prussian victory over France "encouraged statesmen to scramble to line up allies in advance of the next war" (Christensen and Snyder, 1990: 148). Bismarck's readiness to weld together both a "conservative triple alliance" of the monarchies in Eastern Europe with the formation of the Three Emperors' League and the Dual Alliance between Germany and Austria was indicative of the race that commenced. The complex interlocking alliances fabricated after 1874 assumed greater symbolic importance than those formed in the preceding phase of this post-1815 multipolar period (McGowan and Rood, 1975: 866).

The cooperation expected to result from these alliances did not materialize, however, and a number of them underwent rapid disintegration, particularly in the volatile environment after 1885 when alliance formation was so frenetic. As alliances dissolved, a series of secret agreements were negotiated between the conflicting parties, such as Germany's and Austria-Hungary's pledge to assist Romania against a Russian attack and Bismarck's Reinsurance Treaty with Russia in 1887. In the fluid system of alignments that developed, many followed Bismarck's preference for short-term commitments and hidden agreements designed for rather limited ends—reassuring nervous friends and isolating enemies.

As a result, by the 1880s the great powers sought to contain their feuds by constructing a complex network of cross-cutting coalitions, based on the hope that the system would "not degenerate into chaos perhaps because the enemy of a friend was often a friend" (McDonald and Rosecrance, 1985: 80). Thus, the years following the wars of European unification witnessed a prolonged period of growing acceptance of alliances alongside a growing willingness of the great powers to abandon their allies:

> We might say that [the 1815–1878] period marked the heyday of the balance of power. Defense pacts among central system members were few (6) and brief (average duration 4.3 years), and they were by and large entered into in response to a given potential disturbance of the Concert and its settlement. More interesting, perhaps, was the lateral mobility of the major powers. For example, England left the Quadruple Alliance in 1840 in order to join the conservative courts against French ambitions in the Middle East; Austria broke away from the Holy Alliance in 1853 and lined up with France and England against her traditional ally, the Czar; and both Austria and Germany effectively destroyed the Three Emperors' League . . . by failing to support Russia after her victory over Turkey, lining up with France and England at the Berlin Conference. In all of these cases, the powers maintained their new commitments just long enough to counter the perceived threat to the European state system, and then return to the more flexible entente arrangements with their traditional and 'natural' allies. . . .
>
> If the 1815–78 period can be characterized as the prime of the balance of power mechanism, the next forty years clearly mark its passage into atrophy. Though less than two-thirds as long, the years between 1879 and 1919 saw twice as many nation months of war and more than ten times as many battle deaths due to such armed conflict. Conceivably there is some causal relationship between these outcomes and the sharp changes in alliance activity. (Singer and Small, 1966)

Recall here the turbulence, especially between 1879 and 1919, and the change in alliance practices that characterized the period and ultimately led to the counterpoised blocs on the eve of World War I:

Where . . . the process [of alliance aggregation] is carried through to its logical conclusion by involving all the great powers in two rival blocs, the war, if and when it comes, will be a general war. To illustrate, there had often been friction in Europe after 1870. In 1886–1888 there had been danger of war between Russia and Austria-Hungary. In 1875 and then again in 1885 and 1898, Russia and Great Britain had approached conflict. The same was true of Germany and France in 1857, 1887, and 1905; and of England and France in 1898. But whereas before the Algeciras Conference of 1906 (by which time rival blocs had begun to take definite shape) the two rivals had usually been reconciled by a united Europe intervening as umpire, after 1906 the great powers themselves took sides even where they were not directly involved. . . . Before 1906 the local balances were the focuses of tension; after that time all the powers mentioned had actively entered into one overall alignment system. As a result, there were no unilateralist great powers left in Europe after 1906. (Schuman, 1969: 321)

The product was disappointing, however. By 1914, "the European state system was virtually honeycombed with formal alliances" (Ray, 1992: 397), and when a minor conflict broke out between Austria and Serbia, the entire system erupted into history's most destructive war. Despite the promises of alliances, hopes in their ability to protect were dashed; the aggregation of capabilities through polarized blocs that set the Triple Alliance against the Triple Entente (see Map 5.1) was fuel on the fire. The unanticipated and catastrophic First World War threw into question the wisdom of the alliance strategies that had been pursued.

The 1919–1939 Multipolar System

The multipolar period following the First World War again was a time in which the great powers intensely assessed the costs and benefits of alliances, which were alternately chastised as a source of war or praised as an instrument for its prevention. The bargaining of the day was dominated by the effort to reconcile these contending propositions.

After the war, boundary changes created a new distribution of power in Europe (see Map 5.2). To avoid the problems inherent in the old balance-of-power structure with its entangling alliances perceived to encourage rather than to deter conflict, the victors at Versailles turned a critical eye on alliances and sought to design a system that would rest on collective security and a rule of law. Condemning secret diplomacy, Woodrow Wilson led the reformers in prescribing a new regime of "open covenants, openly arrived at." In many respects, the year 1919 appeared to represent a turning point in images of alliance politics, as the League of Nations, depicted by Sir Edward Grey as an institution of members "binding themselves to side against any Power which broke a treaty" (Link, 1965: 94), marked a fundamental departure in the great powers' thinking.

But enthusiasm over the new order dissipated rapidly. Rather than fleeing from alliances perceived to be potentially entangling, after World War I the great powers promptly reversed course and combined forces enthusiastically.

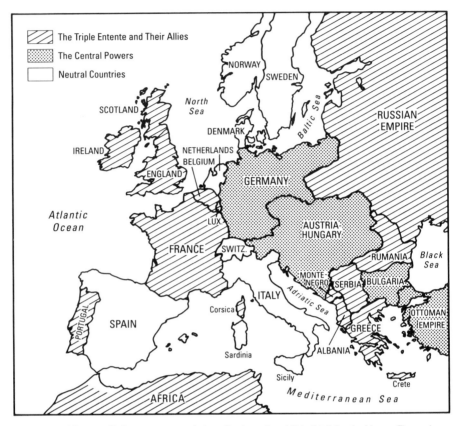

MAP 5.1. Alliance Polarization and the Outbreak of World War I. *Note:* Though a member of the German alliance system, Italy remained neutral when World War I erupted and joined the anti-German coalition in 1915. *Source:* Based on Gérard Chaliand and Jean-Pierre Rageau, *Strategic Atlas: Comparative Geopolitics of the World's Powers,* 3rd ed. (New York: Harper Perennial, 1992), p. 44.

Alliance formation in the early 1920s became frenetic and reached unprecedented proportions. In fact, the frequency with which states entered into formal alliance caused the period from 1923 to 1933 to be labeled "the era of pacts" (Langsam, 1954: 79). A review of the open alliances forged between the wars (see Figure 5.2) reveals the strong preference to enhance security through the recruitment of allies and to give far less faith to collective security.

In the period after the First World War, "the principle of the balance of power was supposed to have been superseded by the League-of-Nations principle of collective security," but in fact stood "under the sign of the balance of power by alliances and counteralliances":

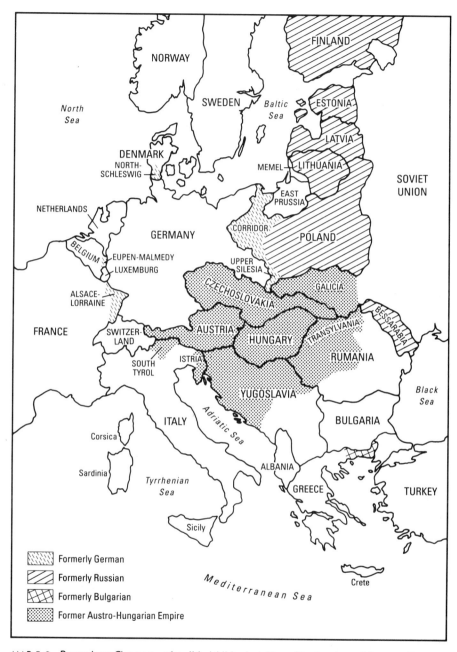

MAP 5.2. Boundary Changes after World War I: A New Distribution of Power. *Source:* Based on William R. Keylor, *The Twentieth-Century World: An International History,* 2nd ed. (New York: Oxford University Press, 1992), p. 93.

After the First World War, France maintained permanent alliances with Poland, Czechoslovakia, Yugoslavia and Rumania and, in 1935, concluded an alliance—which was, however, not implemented—with the Soviet Union. This policy can be understood as a kind of preventive balance-of-power policy which anticipated Germany's comeback and attempted to maintain the status quo of Versailles in the face of such an eventuality. On the other hand, the formation in 1936 of an alliance between Germany, Italy and Japan, called the Axis, was intended as a counterweight against the alliance between France and the Eastern European

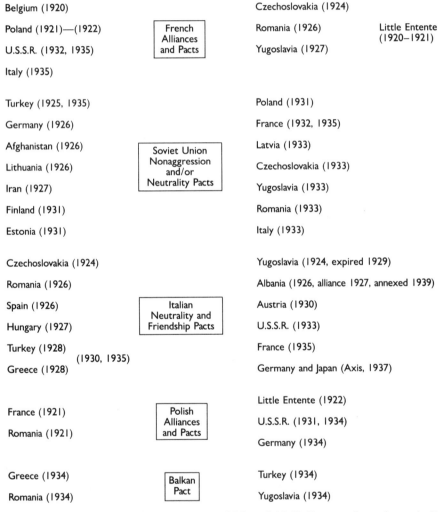

FIGURE 5.2. Alliances and Pacts between 1920 and 1940. Dates in Parentheses Indicate the Year in Which Treaties Were Signed. *Source:* Derived from Walter Cunsuello Langsam, *The World Since 1919* (New York: Macmillan, 1954), p. 92.

nations, which would at the same time neutralize the Soviet Union. (Morgenthau, 1985: 212)

Although the magnitude of alliances in this multipolar period is impressive, it may underrepresent the actual frequency of alliance formation. It is important not to overlook the unknown number of secret alliances that undoubtedly were arranged during this phase, contrary to Article 18 of the League Covenant that required all treaties of alliance to be publicly announced and registered. Regardless of the measure used, the rate at which states formed formal alliances with one another rose steadily between 1920 and 1940, with the percentage of nations involved in alliances expanding from 10 percent in 1920 to nearly 80 percent in 1940 (Singer and Small, 1966: 13; Gurr, 1972: 144).

Even though the interwar period represented an age of alliance politics, it was not a time in which the struggle between great powers was peaceful. By 1938, when Germany had forged a coalition with Italy and Japan to pursue world domination, the stage was set for Germany's annexation of the Sudetenland in Czechoslovakia (see Map 5.3) and other aggressive moves that soon culminated in World War II.

GREAT-POWER COALITIONS AND ESCALATION TO WAR

Is there a pattern to alliance aggregation in the six post-1495 multipolar systems? The number of great-power alliances has varied, as have the cross-cutting bonds within each successive phase. Although we can observe a consistent increase in the number of bilateral and multilateral ties that were forged in each, the density resulting from this thicket of coalitions has been dissimilar. So, too, has been the degree to which realignments, defections, and shifts between and among allies have occurred.

Still, looked at over time, a long-term secular trend is discernible:

Where alliances [in earlier multipolar systems] were concluded most frequently at or near the onset of or during wars, the contemporary trend is toward more and more permanent types of arrangements concluded far in advance of war. Where once alliances were never made decades in advance and a fairly general European war might begin with one or more great powers uncommitted and with the others concluding hasty and temporary alliances, it is more and more the trend today for all the great nations to take part in coalitions at a time when war has not broken out and is still fairly distant. They also tend to remain on the same side *during* a war, whereas shifts of powers to the other side were not at all rare in former times. . . . There has been a . . . growth in the permanence, inclusiveness, and duration of alliances. (Hartmann, 1983: 329)

MAP 5.3. Europe in 1938. *Source:* Based on John M. Rothgeb, Jr., *Defining Power: Influence and Force in the Contemporary International System* (New York: St. Martin's Press, 1992), p. 30.

Lacking suppleness and encouraging a zero-sum outlook, a polarized configuration of power has usually proven hazardous because its attendant structural rigidity reduces the number of potential alternative allies and thereby decreases the chances of cross-cutting rather than overlapping cleavages among competitors. In the absence of a tangle of divided loyalties, polarization may focus adversaries' attention on a single threat, thus making it more likely that minor disagreements will become magnified into larger tests of will.

Numerous studies have sought to uncover the effects of systemic polarization, with many strongly supporting the conclusion suggested by the comparisons given in Table 5.2, namely, that polarized configurations of power tend to be unstable. Once formed, adversarial coalitions and their augmented capabilities have heightened tensions. As Walter Lippmann (1943: 106) warned, when the great powers combine their forces but "the alliance is inadequate because there is an opposing alliance of approximately equal strength, the stage is set for a world war." Rising polarization, like that evident on the eve of World War I when alliances of approximately equal capability stood in grim opposition, has regularly resulted in great-power wars (Bueno de Mesquita, 1978: 241–267; Organski and Kugler, 1980: 54; Kim, 1989: 269). Alliances "not only fail to prevent wars, but by making wars spread, they encourage dangerous, complex wars [with many participants]. . . . All other factors being equal, increasing polarization of blocs [also] makes for longer wars. . . ." (Vasquez, 1987: 121–122, 132).

However, the actual historical relationship could be more complicated than this characterization implies because the existing evidence "suggests that alliances are a key factor in wars expanding, but they are not the only factor" (Vasquez, 1990: 5). Polarized blocs in multipolar systems may be war prone, but very high levels of alliance flexibility also have proven to be destabilizing. Thus, the relationship between alliance flexibility and war appears to be U-shaped: The incidence of war is high when alliances are either rigidly polarized or so fluid as to appear chaotic to those responsible for crafting foreign policy. In contrast, when alliance flexibility is moderate, warfare among the powerful remains relatively low (Kegley and Raymond, 1990; Wallace, 1973). In other words, if some degree of maneuvering is left open for the great powers to form new partnerships as conditions warrant, they are better able to avoid warfare.

This conclusion suggests that the presence or absence of multipolarity, *by itself*, will not raise or lower the likelihood of great-power wars in the twenty-first century. The historical record reveals another, more complicated pattern: Alliances can weaken the prospects for a multipolar peace if they combine capabilities in a highly polarized manner, or if they become so diffuse that it is difficult to ascertain who is in league with whom from one issue to the next. On the other hand, alliances can contribute to the chances of achieving peace in a multipolar world if they retain a modest amount of flexibility.

Multipolar distributions of power thus combine with different alliance configurations to produce some systemic structures that are more stable than others (Wayman, 1985). As pointed out in Chapter 3, an additional condition that mediates the relationship between polarity and war is the extent to which the state system is enveloped within a permissive or a restrictive normative order.[3] It is one thing to be able to switch alliance partners in a multipolar system regardless of ideological affinities or personal ties; it is quite another to do so prior to the expiration of one's current treaty agreements. Whether allies can be counted on to comply with promissory obligations is critical in estimating the potential impact of alliances. Even a multipolar system containing a moderate degree of alliance flexibility can still become unstable if prevailing international norms permit great powers to use force as an instrument of foreign policy, allow them to disregard their treaty commitments as they please, and do not place parameters around the geographical scope of their competition.

In the next chapter we examine the role of these "rules of the game" in fostering great-power cooperation by comparing how permissive and restrictive normative orders affect the stability of multipolar systems.

3. The importance of a restrictive normative order can be seen in the discussion of the long peace in Chapter 2. Although the Cold War era was highly polarized and therefore potentially dangerous, the development of international norms that coordinated expectations regarding spheres of influence and the use of force helped prevent the outbreak of war between the superpowers. While these tacit rules of prudence were not the only contributors to the long great-power peace following World War II, their impact was significant. It is unlikely that the rules of the game under a more permissive normative order would have done as much to help dampen the threat of war.

· 6 ·

INTERNATIONAL NORMS AND GREAT-POWER COOPERATION

In every treaty, insert a clause which can easily be violated, so that the entire agreement can be broken in case the interests of the State make it expedient to do so.

—LOUIS XIV,
KING OF FRANCE, 1668

Our attempt to discover the keys to great power peace by comparing previous multipolar systems has thus far revealed two noteworthy patterns. First, the longevity of these systems varied widely: Some lasted for many decades; others ended abruptly. Second, although contending great powers sought security through arms and allies, neither consistently prevented the outbreak of war. Indeed, each successive system-dismantling war became more destructive than the last.

To understand the prospects for preserving great-power peace in a new multipolar system, we need to refine our understanding of the factors that affected the stability of previous multipolar systems. In the last chapter we examined the problem of alliance polarization. In this chapter we turn our attention to those international norms that influence great-power behavior within and between these blocs. Many scholars overlook international norms and concentrate on those concrete properties of alliances that are most amenable to observation and measurement: the number of alliances within the international system, the number of poles around which they are clustered, and the tightness and discreteness of the clusters. But in order to predict the consequences of those structural configurations generated by alliance bonds, the reliability of alliance commitments must also be examined (Sullivan and Siverson, 1981: 18). The same alliance networks can produce different international outcomes if the great powers hold an elastic versus a binding attitude toward their obligation to abide by treaty commitments. To better predict the aggregate consequences of alliance polarization, therefore, we need to pay attention to prevailing normative rules of great-power conduct.

THE NORMATIVE CONTEXT OF GREAT-POWER INTERACTIONS

Norms are "generalized formulations—more or less explicit—of expectations of proper action by differentiated units in relatively specific situations" (Parsons, 1961: 120). The expectations expressed by international norms pertain to the proper action of nation-states. That is, norms communicate injunctions that prescribe certain actions but proscribe others. Throughout history, great powers have tried to establish normative rules to add a modicum of predictability to their relations, recognizing that "order in any society is maintained not merely by a sense of common interests in creating order or avoiding disorder, but by rules that spell out the kind of behavior that is orderly" (Bull, 1977: 54).

Any account of the influence of international norms on world politics must acknowledge that the rules of the system are made *by* the great powers and *for* their benefit. The rules to which the powerful willingly agree are those that serve their interests. They are designed to maintain the great-power hierarchy (Friedheim, 1968) and to benefit the strong at the expense of the weak (Galtung, 1969). Rule enforcement is left "to the vicissitudes of the distribution of power between the violator of the law and the victim of the violation." This, as Hans J. Morgenthau (1985: 312) concludes, "makes it easy for the strong both to violate the law and to enforce it, and consequently puts the rights of the weak in jeopardy."

Yet international law is not violated more frequently than domestic law (Joyner, 1992) because even the most powerful states recognize the advantages of self-restraint. Countries that opportunistically break the rules suffer long-term costs for their behavior: Their prestige and influence will diminish, other states will be reluctant to trust them as allies, and retaliation by the victims of their transgression may someday occur. For these reasons, even at the highest realm of great-power interactions, statesmen have "nearly always [perceived] themselves as constrained by principles, norms, and rules that prescribe and proscribe varieties of behavior" (Puchala and Hopkins, 1983: 86). Indeed, "all groups of nations in regular contact," as Evan Luard's (1976: 61) research on historical multistate systems shows, "have in practice adopted certain rules defining conduct which could usually be expected among their members."

This is not to say that international norms remain constant over time nor does it mean that the degree of consensus about them never changes. Norm formation occurs in a political environment. Any state "interested in a new rule of customary law must take action that violates existing law and they must encourage others to do the same" (Charney, 1986: 914). The reason is simple: When a form of behavior becomes widespread, rules *of* behavior tend over time to be converted into rules *for* behavior (Hoffmann, 1971: 35).

Legal theorists disagree, however, over the structural conditions that are most conducive to this happening. A review of the scholarly literature reveals two schools of thought. As depicted in Figure 6.1, one school has its roots in hegemonic stability theory (Model I), the other in balance-of-power theory

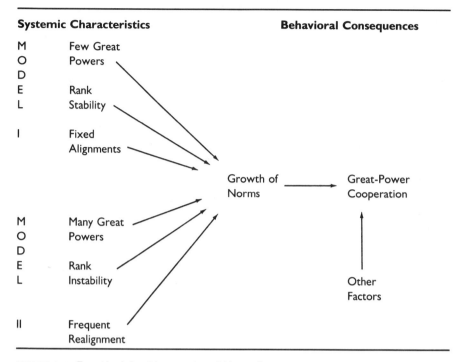

FIGURE 6.1. Two Models of International Norm Formation.

(Model II). Whereas Model I contends that high, stable levels of capability concentration are conducive to the development of international norms (see Gilpin, 1981: 35; Keohane, 1980: 132), Model II asserts that legal norms flourish during periods when national capabilities are dispersed, when the rank order of states is in flux, and when frequent changes occur in alliance partnerships. As Nicholas Spykman (cited in Perkins, 1981: 26) postulates, "An equilibrium of forces inherently unstable, always shifting, always changing . . . encourages cooperation, conciliation, and the growth of law. . . ." (also see Oppenheim, 1928; Lauterpacht, 1933; and Hoffmann, 1961: 214–215). Thus both models of norm formation focus on the structural attributes of the international system and conceptualize norms as intervening variables in a causal chain linking that structure to the behavior of the great powers. But they differ in their image of those specific structural conditions under which norms will develop the strength needed to regulate great-power behavior.

Preliminary research on this question indicates that different norms generally arise under the conditions outlined in Model I as opposed to those in Model II. In other words, a small multipolar system with a fixed hierarchy of states and few changes in alliance partners would likely witness the rise of norms quite different from those found in a larger multipolar system characterized by high levels of rank mobility and alliance flexibility. To illustrate this point, we will examine normative rules that (1) pertain to the use of force, the *ultima ratio* in world politics, (2) bear upon the sanctity of agreements, and (3) attempt to confine the geographical scope of great-power competition.

The Legal Control of Warfare

To many observers of great-power politics, international law appears to perpetuate a competitive laissez-faire arena in which restraints on the powerful are weak or nonexistent (Toynbee, 1967; Lawrence, 1915). This situation prompted Clement Attlee's well-known complaint that "the root of the trouble in today's world" is that "we believe in the complete, or almost complete, right of every nation to do what it chooses."

What the former British prime minister identified as the fundamental problem of international law was that it often embodies the values of a *permissive normative order*. As pointed out in Chapter 3, at any given time the prevailing "rules of the game" within the state system may range from permissive to restrictive. A permissive normative order contains rules that give national leaders considerable latitude to use force in the name of state security, no matter how repugnant such uses might seem in the light of those moral dictates that guide the behavior of people in their private, interpersonal lives. Unburdened by these moral considerations, leaders are allowed to do whatever must be done to protect the state and advance its position within the global hierarchy.

By way of contrast, a *restrictive normative order* contains a set of rules that give national leaders far less leeway in using force. Specific criteria exist on *when* it is appropriate to wage war and *how* to fight. Many of these guidelines were developed in the seventeenth century by Hugo Grotius and others, as adapted from the fifth-century writings of St. Augustine. Among the guidelines that typify restrictive normative orders are just cause (acting in self-defense), right intention (fighting to gain peace rather than because of a love of violence or hatred of the enemy), immediacy (facing imminent danger), last resort (all other means of conflict resolution have been tried), discrimination (respect for the principle of noncombatant immunity), proportionality (the good achieved must outweigh the harm that is done), and responsibility (the decision must be made by a competent authority who is accountable to judicial review).

Throughout the history of the modern state system, international law has changed in response to changing global conditions. The laws of war, for example, "were extremely permissive" in the early seventeenth century and at the end of the eighteenth century "did not seek to infringe the right of states to undertake war" (Bull, 1968: 58, 54). As Figure 6.2 reveals, since 1815 there has been a gradual but steady increase in the international community's dis-

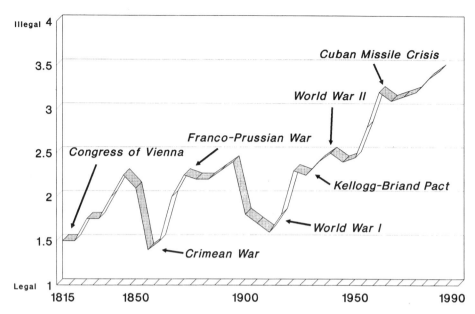

FIGURE 6.2. The Legal Prohibition of War. *Source:* Transnational Rules Indicators Project (TRIP), as described by Charles W. Kegley, Jr., and Gregory A. Raymond, *When Trust Breaks Down* (Columbia, S.C.: University of South Carolina Press, 1990).

avowal of war as a legitimate tool of foreign policy.[1] Following World War I, in particular, the great powers began to withhold their previous support of the legal right to use force. A new mood crystallized, and in response the Covenant of the League of Nations, which was incorporated as Part I of the Treaty of Versailles in 1919, implemented a new security regime. Articles 11 to 17 stipulated that in no case could a state resort to war until three months after a

1. The data on changing attitudes toward the legality of war were taken from a content analysis of 244 authoritative legal treatises from the post–Napoleonic period that was conducted under the auspices of the Transnational Rules Indicators Project (TRIP). The criteria used to select the treatises for content analysis were whether a work had gone through multiple revised editions or had been identified as authoritative by either independent scholarship (for example, listed in the Association of Law Schools' bibliography of international law texts) or a recognized legal body such as the World Court (see Kegley and Raymond, 1990).

The purpose was to determine the kind of behavior that the authors perceived as legally permissible at the time they were writing. That is to say, the analysis focused on what norm the publicists actually observed rather than on the norm they thought members of the international community ought to follow. Each treatise was coded on a four-point scale, where a score of 1 was given if a publicist observed that war was considered an acceptable tool of foreign policy, a score of 4 was given if war was thought to be an illegitimate tool, and intermediate scores were given to positions arrayed in between these two extremes. Once every treatise in a particular half-decade was coded, the mean for that period was recorded.

judicial determination by the League had elapsed. They also contained provisions subjecting any member "who committed an act of war against another member to sanctions."

Another step was taken in 1928 when the United States and France signed the Kellogg-Briand Pact, which culminated in the Treaty Providing for the Renunciation of War as an Instrument of National Policy. The prohibition was reaffirmed in the 1933 Anti-War Treaty of Rio de Janeiro and in the Nuremberg war crimes trials at the end of World War II. Both of these spoke of war as "the supreme international crime."

The United Nations Charter (Article 2) subsequently expanded the prohibition by unequivocally outlawing both the threat and initiation of war. At the same time, Article 39 gave the international community the right to determine "the existence of any threat to the peace, breach of the peace or act of aggression," and Article 42 authorized the Security Council "to take such action . . . as may be necessary to maintain or restore international peace and security."

The normative order providing support for the international legal system has thus grown increasingly restrictive. Legal injunctions limit the once-accepted right of states to resort to war and, consequently, modify the political culture in which great powers compete. Indeed, this shift from a permissive to a restrictive normative order represents a cultural watershed. In the multipolar epochs in which they lived, Spain's Philip II, France's Louis XIV, and Prussia's Frederick the Great could unabashedly praise warfare as an effective and legal method to expand their country's power, and few monarchs objected. Territorial conquest was regarded as a legitimate and accepted practice. But as each general war became more destructive, revulsion replaced praise, and acceptance of expansionist policies to establish hegemony waned. To be sure, normative approval of power politics and territorial conquest did not decay abruptly. But by gradually accepting a restrictive interpretation of when it is permissible to resort to war, the great powers have fundamentally altered the rules for competition. To the extent that they continue to support a restrictive normative order, great-power competition in a new post–Cold War multipolar system will not resemble the aggressive behavior that has characterized every previous multipolar era.

Adherence to Agreements

Beyond communicating modal patterns of belief about how force ought to be used in particular situations, the normative order that exists at any given time also stipulates how promissory obligations should be interpreted. States symbolize their acceptance of responsibilities by vowing to adhere to a treaty's provisions, but conformity with the terms of a treaty can erode if conditions change after the original agreement is signed. Because defection is always a tempting response when the incentives for compliance diminish, disputes often arise over the performance of the parties' promises. Within a hierarchical political system, such disputes are adjudicated by a central authority. However, within an anarchical political system they frequently are avenged through reprisals. It is for this reason that Arthur Lee Burns (1968: 3) defines the key difference between domestic and international politics as residing in the latter's "scarcity or ineffectiveness of fiats meant to bind its agents jointly."

Two opposing commitment norms have competed for acceptance throughout the history of the modern state system. One norm is associated with restrictive orders insofar as it dictates that treaties create binding contractual obligations between the signatory parties. The other norm is characteristic of permissive orders since it claims that changed conditions allow for the unilateral termination of an agreement prior to its established expiration date. Let us briefly describe each norm in turn.

Agreements Are Binding

The first of these two contrasting norms of promissory obligation is *pacta sunt servanda* (agreements are binding). The roots of this norm can be traced back to antiquity (Wehberg, 1959: 775), and references to its role in preserving peace can be found in the writings of such noted legal publicists as Vitoria, Suarez, Pufendorf, and van Bynkershoek. Its primary purpose is to promote shared expectations that treaty commitments will be honored in good faith. When agreements are routinely kept, states have greater confidence in the behavior of others. Honoring agreements enhances credibility and promotes predictability; a habit of breaking them results in uncertainty, miscalculations, and a greater likelihood of war.

Statesmen appreciate this norm and recognize that uncertainty about alliance guarantees can weaken the resolve of partners. Consider French behavior when Germany warned that its interests in Morocco had been ignored during the formation of the 1904 Anglo–French *Entente Cordiale*. Confident of British support, French Foreign Minister Delcassé recommended resisting Berlin's pressure. However, the remainder of the cabinet lacked confidence in their new ally's commitments and therefore acquiesced to German demands. Had the great powers at the time been more likely to adhere to agreements, perhaps another outcome would have resulted. "One powerful and trustworthy ally is worth a dozen feeble and fickle allies" (Schuman, 1969: 277).

Doubts about the reliability of great-power commitments can also lead to miscalculations, such as those made by key officials in Wilhelmian Germany regarding the possibility of detaching members from rival alliances. Thinking that states would "bandwagon" with the strongest great power, many Germans expected demonstrations of their capabilities to attract nonaligned states into an alliance with Berlin while simultaneously pressuring those aligned with adversaries to abandon their commitments. Gottlieb von Jagow, state secretary of the German Foreign Ministry, and Admiral Alfred von Tirpitz, for instance, assumed incorrectly that preponderant German strength would force the British to renege on their obligations to France. Similar erroneous thinking led German Chancellor von Bethmann-Hollweg to assume that an Austrian attack on Serbia might shatter Franco–Russian ties by forcing one of them to back out of pledges regarding the Balkans (Van Evera, 1985: 88).

In sum, arguments that stress the merits of binding commitments contend that (1) flexible conceptions of treaty commitments foster uncertainty; (2) uncertainty breeds miscalculation; (3) miscalculation increases the likelihood of war; therefore (4) great powers should support restrictive normative orders containing rules that uphold the sanctity of treaty commitments.

Agreements Can Be Broken

The norm *pacta sunt servanda* defines commitments in nonsituational terms: Governments are obligated to abide by their promises even at the expense of immediate gain. In contrast, the norm *rebus sic stantibus* (by reason of changed conditions) defines commitments in situational terms: Whether governments fulfill an agreement is contingent on whether it serves national interests at the moment. To be sure, most leaders customarily have voiced respect for preserving alliances despite the erosion of their utility (Rothstein, 1968: 119). But when the costs of honoring commitments increase due to incompatibilities born of changing international conditions, the temptation to rescind one's promises becomes powerful. As Machiavelli in 1513 asserted, "a sagacious prince . . . cannot and should not fulfill his pledges when their observance is contrary to his interest, and when the causes which induced him to pledge his faith no longer exist."

Because future conditions can never be known when the provisions of an agreement are negotiated, great powers frequently invoke *rebus sic stantibis* as an "escape clause" to justify policy reversals. Interpreted in its most narrow sense, *rebus sic stantibus* allows a state to terminate an agreement unilaterally only if a fundamental change has patently occurred in those circumstances that existed at the signing of the agreement. In its broadest sense, it allows unilateral termination if one party merely claims a treaty is injurious to the so-called "fundamental rights of necessity" possessed by every state. Of course, the content of these self-defined rights may be defined so widely that they include almost any justification. When incorporated into the provisions of an alliance treaty, *rebus sic stantibus* preserves tremendous freedom of maneuver for each member, especially if the broader interpretation is accepted. Agreements under this norm are not inviolable; they can be unilaterally rescinded to free allies from their stipulations.

Those who support a permissive normative order with its elastic interpretation of promissory obligations contend that flexibility restrains great-power impulsiveness. If the leaders of great powers are unsure about their allies' loyalty, they will be hesitant to engage an opponent. Uncertainty, in other words, induces restraint and thereby decreases the probability of war.

It is also claimed that a norm facilitating the disavowal of commitments will reduce the incidence with which states are pulled into conflicts they could otherwise avoid. For example, in October 1913 the Russians called upon France to support their protest of General Liman von Sanders's appointment to command the army corps in Constantinople, an appointment that had been made as part of Germany's effort to modernize the Turkish army. Although the French proclaimed loyalty to their alliance with Russia, they avoided becoming involved by making their response contingent on British action, which was unlikely since London had similar connections with the Turkish navy. The alliance norms of the time made this argument more acceptable than would have been the case if rigid adherence to alliance agreements had been strenuously supported.

Clearly, a flexible interpretation of obligation gives decision makers considerable latitude in adapting to changing circumstances. It allows them to keep options open, as the Italians did in 1902, when despite membership in the Triple Alliance they secretly assured France of their neutrality should the latter find itself in a war with Germany. Moreover, the need for such latitude could be justified by appealing not just to national interest, but also to prevailing diplomatic mores. Thus when Lord Salisbury (quoted in Williamson, 1969: 21) declared, "Our treaty obligations will follow from our national inclinations and will not precede them," his pronouncement was not regarded as unacceptably defiant by the standards of the day.

Finally, advocates of a loose conception of promissory obligation point out that flexibility enables third parties to play the role of the "keeper of the balance" between antagonists. Take, for instance, French foreign policy in the mid-seventeenth century. Although Louis XIV had an alliance with the Dutch and provided them with troops, he concluded a secret agreement with Charles II of England in 1667 under which he promised to withhold naval assistance from the Dutch (Friedrich and Blitzer, 1957: 177).

In a normative environment condoning rapid alliance formation and dissolution, deterrence results from uncertainties about who is in league with whom, who might unilaterally terminate an alliance treaty prior to its expiration, and who will subsequently join forces with whom. So long as the lines between associate and adversary are shifting and unclear, and as room is left open for neutrals to maneuver between them, disputes may be less apt to escalate to catastrophic wars.

Binding versus Elastic Conceptions of Commitments

Pacta sunt servanda and *rebus sic stantibus* need not be considered mutually exclusive (Kunz, 1945: 190; Lissitzyn, 1967: 922); however, the two norms frequently have been treated as opposites, particularly by strident advocates of the broader interpretation of *rebus sic stantibus* (David, 1975: 83). Consequently, during most periods international law has drawn a sharp distinction: "Treaties either were binding or were not binding at all" (Gould, 1957: 57).

The expectations of proper action expressed by international norms define the cultural climate within which great-power interaction takes place. At any time, this rudimentary political culture has placed more or less stress on the permissibility of different kinds of great-power behavior. By emphasizing binding commitments, the climate encourages long-lasting alliances. But by emphasizing an elastic interpretation of action over the restrictive view that great-power activity should be constrained, the cultural climate facilitates flexibility, freedom of maneuver, and swift realignments. Once a particular norm gains wide acceptance throughout international society, even great powers cannot escape having their states' subsequent behavior shaped by the climate of opinion. "Rule changes may make an alliance more (or less) attractive to one (or more) of its members. Evolving rules also can catalyze the formation of new alliances in response to newly perceived problems. Rule changes affect the way actual and potential alliance partners perceive their objectives, and hence . . . have an impact on alliance dynamics" (Brecher and James, 1986: 53).

Figure 6.3 describes recent changes in the perceived relative importance of these two injunctions regarding treaty commitments.[2] The trend line shows that in the aftermath of the Napoleonic Wars, considerable emphasis was placed on norms stressing flexible interpretations of treaty commitments. However, binding conceptions subsequently gained strength prior to the outbreak of the Wars of European Unification between 1854 and 1870, whereupon they underwent a very gradual erosion as flexible alliance norms received support once again in the period preceding the First World War.

Following the end of that cataclysmic war, the perceived importance of flexible alliance commitments momentarily increased, but beginning in the 1920s a vigorous emphasis on binding alliance obligations took root and accelerated rapidly. This support remained intense and stabilized at the conclusion of World War II, although normative support for the sanctity of treaties began to show signs of incipient decay in the 1980s. In view of research findings indicating that the magnitude and severity of war increase when alliance com-

---

2. As in the case of the trend line reported in Figure 6.2, TRIP data were used to create this graph of changes in the content of commitment norms (see footnote 1). Each legal treatise was coded according to whether existing legal norms were seen by the author as supporting or rejecting a binding interpretation of treaty obligations. Once every treatise in a particular half-decade was coded, a summary index of commitment was calculated by means of the following formula: (the percentage of authors who perceived legal norms supporting a binding interpretation of treaty obligation) − (the percentage of authors who perceived norms supporting a flexible interpretation of treaty obligation) / 100. The resulting index ranged from +1.00 (commitments are binding) to −1.00 (commitments may be terminated unilaterally), with intermediate positions arrayed in between and a perfect balance (0.00) indicating that neither *pacta sunt servanda* nor *rebus sic stantibus* was dominant during the half-decade in question.

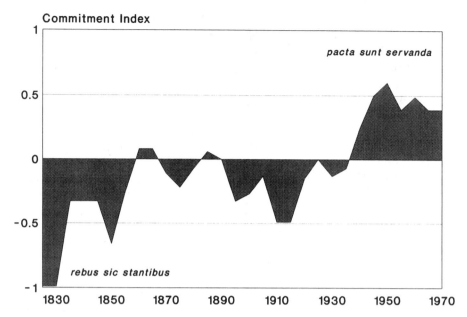

FIGURE 6.3. The Transformation of Alliance Norms. After Kegley and Raymond (1990).

mitments are not considered binding (Kegley and Raymond, 1990), any continuation of this decay in restrictive commitment norms will not augur well for the immediate future.[3]

Borders and Boundaries

Since antiquity, great powers have collided over territorial questions. At times, they have sought to preserve peace by accepting rules to limit the geographical scope of their competition. Such rules were inspired by the recognition that barriers designed to restrict encroaching rivals could help coordinate great-power expectations around simple, unambiguous, and prominent lines of demarcation.

3. Although allies are more likely to assist one another than states that are not allied (Singer and Small, 1968), the historical record of assistance is hardly comforting for those considering an alliance agreement. Of 177 alliance war-performance opportunities between 1816 and 1965, only 27 percent were fulfilled in accordance with treaty commitments, 61 percent were met with abstentions, and 12 percent actually involved allies fighting each other (Sabrosky, 1980b: 177). While alliance members tend to stand together in wartime rather than fight one another, when commitments are not considered binding, they often have stood aside when a partner has become embroiled in an armed conflict.

Whether tacit or embodied in a formal treaty, there are several variations on these kinds of rules. States may unilaterally declare a *cordon sanitaire*, or quarantine line, to protect an area from the imperialist expansion of others. Or, more typically, they may divide territory into *spheres of influence*, where each power exercises dominant influence in its designated area and the others acquiesce in exchange for their right to manage affairs in their own (Modelski, 1972: 116). Finally, they may establish a *condominium* that involves joint rule over a particular territory.

Closely related to these rules of territorial demarcation are *neutrality* norms, whose origin has been traced back to the ancient Greek city-state system. Modern laws of neutrality have been supported by the great powers to keep third parties outside the arena of conflict. This support derived, in part, from a recognition that neutralized buffer states would separate potential belligerents. Moreover, if other states were not obliged to judge the legitimacy of a conflict between any two great powers, it was felt that war would not spread since bystanders were insulated from hostilities by their steadfast impartiality.

In some respects, the effort to establish and enforce the *nonintervention* principle as a norm of conduct represents another mode of encapsulating great-power rivalry. When the Habsburg drive for hegemonic control was repelled after the Thirty Years' War, the great powers at Westphalia sought to contain religious and ideological conflict by prohibiting great-power interference in each other's domestic affairs. By making sovereignty sacrosanct, an effort was made to preserve the independence of territorial nation-states and the authority of the leaders who ruled them. It has been undermined in recent years, however, by increasing interdependence and a concomitant blurring of the boundaries between domestic and foreign economic policy. Moreover, alongside the rise of international commerce and communication, the great powers have steadily increased their ability to penetrate borders and intrude into others, so that the violation of nonintervention has increased as it has become less visible and less militarily overt.

To review, restrictive orders contain international norms that establish demarcation lines, support the inviolability of neutral territory, and uphold the principle of nonintervention. The less the support for these kinds of rules of the game, the more permissive the normative order.

NORMATIVE CONSTRAINTS ON GREAT-POWER RIVALRY?

In spite of their ability to flout international law, the great powers often have accepted rules that regulate their conduct. Though claiming the prerogative to push and shove lesser-rank states, they have nonetheless sought to establish rules that would help prevent their struggles with one another from boiling over into system-disrupting wars. As might be expected, support for rules of this sort has increased in the aftermath of hegemonic wars. To illustrate the tendency of great powers to craft such rules following a system-transforming war, let us briefly examine the European great-power system that emerged after the Napoleonic Wars.

The Concert of Europe

Napoleon's defeat at Waterloo in 1815 concluded a period that had seen Europe battered for almost a quarter century and left over two and a half million combatants dead. When measured by battle deaths per population, the toll exceeded that of all wars fought during the preceding three centuries (Levy, 1983: 58).

The post–Napoleonic Era was a period in which the great powers achieved unusually high agreement about the rules to govern their relations. Napoleon's quest for empire challenged not only the existing distribution of power on the European continent, but also the Westphalian self-help system of legitimized competition among sovereign great-power equals (Murphy, 1982; Gross, 1969). But with the defeat of Napoleon came the defeat of his vision: "When the Congress of Vienna cleaned up after the Napoleonic Wars in 1815, its participants were careful to restore the pre-Napoleonic map of Europe so that the game of nation-state coexistence in accordance with laissez-faire rules could be played again" (Miller, 1985: 31).

The new normative order accepted conflict as a natural component of interstate interaction. The great powers operated from the assumption that disputes would arise just as naturally as friction results from objects in contact. In order to compete, they reserved for themselves the freedom to vie with one another through military action. However, they also "agreed to observe certain rules between themselves" (Clark, 1966: 23) to reduce the incentives for initiating war and to contain its spread.

Three months after Waterloo, Austria, Prussia, and Russia signed the Treaty of the Holy Alliance in which they vowed to "remain united by the bonds of a true and indissoluble fraternity" and "on all occasions and in all places, lend each other aid and assistance." Less than a month later, they concluded a Quadruple Alliance with Great Britain to renew the pledges of cooperation against French aggression that all four had previously made in the Treaty of Chaumont. In addition, they resolved to hold periodic congresses "for the purpose of consulting upon their common interests." Equally noteworthy, they allowed the defeated power, France, which had tried to establish universal dominion, to play a role as an equal power in the peace-maintaining process. Rather than excluding France from participation and imposing a harsh peace settlement, the great powers welcomed French reentry into the great-power consortium as a full-fledged member (see Map 6.1). France, many assumed,

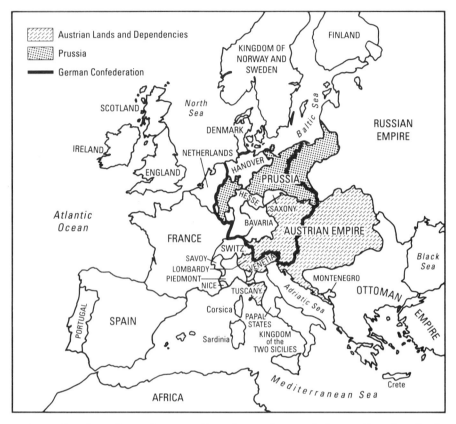

MAP 6.1. The Great-Power European State System Restored. *Source:* Based on Frederick L. Schuman, *International Politics* (New York: McGraw-Hill, 1969), p. 85.

would be needed to help police the new order, and its exclusion, partition, or forced demise could plant the seed for a subsequent war.[4]

The Concert created by these agreements sought to coordinate great-power relations. Consensus was achieved through a shared fear of war and revolution and propelled by a common desire to act collectively to combat their occurrence. The latter, in particular, was driven by the changes unleashed after the French and American revolutions. Nationalism arose as a major force and

4. In 1919 this enlightened policy was not practiced, with disastrous consequences as Germany rearmed, in Hitler's words, to "fight for the reparation of an injustice imposed on us" and to recover by force its place in the sun (cited in Luard, 1987: 367). The security regime created after World War I thus ignored Woodrow Wilson's plea that "It must be a peace without victory. . . . Only a peace between equals can last."

rationalized the struggle for independence by separatist groups. The consequences for the heads of great-power states were profound:

> Decision makers no longer felt more loyalty to each other than to their own
> people. Fewer social and cultural ties united decision makers of different coun-
> tries, and correspondingly more social and cultural ties grew between each coun-
> try's decision makers and its general populace. The willingness to use more force
> and less restraint against other states increased as members of the system became
> geographically dispersed and culturally heterogeneous. Increases in speed of
> transportation and communication [after 1815] did more to tie nations together
> internally than it did in promoting cooperation among states. Xenophobia, the
> fear and hatred of foreign states, became a force . . . in almost every state. Where
> [before the French and American revolutions] the classical decision maker had
> difficulty in engendering patriotism among nations, the decision maker [after
> them] had difficulty in controlling patriotism in order to follow a flexible foreign
> policy. (Coplin, 1971: 305)

From this setting emerged a regime that assumed a different outlook on the
use of force than had existed prior to the onset of the Napoleonic Wars.
Intervention, for instance, was uncommon in the eighteenth century, but since
Revolutionary France had overturned the constitutions of conservative states,
reactionary statesmen such as Austria's Foreign Minister Metternich now proclaimed the right to use forcible methods to suppress revolutionary uprisings
(Hoffmann, 1961: 218; Rosecrance, 1963: 29). Bound together in a common
cause to combat rebellion from within, the great powers experimented with
collective action. For example, at the Congress of Aix-la-Chapelle in 1818 Tsar
Alexander I of Russia proposed an alliance to intervene on behalf of rulers who
were threatened by revolutionary insurrection. At each successive congress (see
Table 6.1), proposals were advanced to coordinate a collective great-power
response to the threat of the moment, be it insurrection or the expanding
strength of an aspiring hegemon.

However, great-power unanimity proved to be elusive. While the British
were willing to help the three Eastern monarchies stem military aggression
aimed at upsetting the post-Napoleonic balance of power, they did not counte-
nance interventions to prop up tottering autocrats. For example, Foreign Minister Castlereagh refused Metternich's invitation in 1819 to approve the Carlsbad Decrees and in 1829 rejected the Protocol of Troppau. In the first instance,
the burning of conservative books and the murder of a conservative journalist
by members of the German nationalist student movement prompted Metternich to convene a meeting of the larger German states at Carlsbad, where he
coerced those leaders to promulgate measures he had drafted in order to suppress liberal nationalist ideas (Nicolson, 1946: 265). In the second instance,
revolts in Spain and Naples led the three Eastern courts to agree at the Congress of Troppau that force could be used against states "which have undergone
in their internal structure an alteration brought about by revolt, whose conse-

TABLE 6.1
Major Great-Power Conferences in the Concert of Europe

Meeting Date(s)	Location	Issues on Agenda
1814–1815	Vienna and Paris	Peace treaty, Quadruple Alliance
1818	Aix-la-Chapelle	France, Quadruple Alliance
1820	Troppau	Naples revolution
1821	Laibach	Naples revolution
1822	Verona	Italy, Spain, "the Eastern question"
1830–1832	London	Belgian independence
1831–1832	Rome	Papal States government
1835	Münchengratz	Reactivate Holy Alliance
1838–1839	London	Belgium (implementation of Treaty of London)
1839	Vienna	Egyptian insurrection
1840–1841	London	Egypt and the Straits
1850–1852	London	Schleswig-Holstein
1853	Vienna	Turkey
1855	Vienna	Crimean War settlement
1856	Paris	Crimean War peace treaty
1858	Paris	The Principalities (implementation of Paris treaty)
1860–1861	Paris	Syrian revolution
1864	London	Schleswig-Holstein, the Ionian Islands
1866	Paris	Navigation on the Danube
1867	London	Luxembourg
1869	Paris	Cretan revolution

quences may be dangerous to other states." Although Castlereagh was sympathetic to the fears held by his counterparts across the Channel and supported their right to undertake action in self-defense, he resisted use of the great-power congress system to regulate other states' domestic affairs. Castlereagh, observed the Austrian ambassador in London, "is like a great lover of music who is at Church; he wishes to applaud but he dares not" (cited in Kissinger, 1973: 275).

Despite British refusal to police sociopolitical upheaval, Austria, Prussia, and Russia were determined to support rules to prevent revolution. Therefore, at the 1821 Congress of Laibach the three conservative powers sanctioned Austria's intervention into Naples and Piedmont to suppress liberal revolts, and the following year at Verona agreed to a French proposal to crush rebels in Spain.

Still, popular attacks on absolute monarchy continued. On July 29, 1830, after an unsuccessful attempt to exert royal control over the French press and legislature, Charles X lost his throne to Louis Philippe, who had fought in the republican army of 1792. Shock waves from the French Revolution of 1830 reverberated across the Continent: The Belgians revolted against King William I of Holland; the Polish Diet declared their country independent of Russian rule; and the rulers of Brunswick, Hesse-Cassel, and Saxony were forced to abdicate their thrones. In response, the Austrian and Russian emperors and the Crown Prince of Prussia met at Münchengratz in 1833 to reaffirm the Holy Alliance, voice support for collective great-power cooperation, and exercise the declared right to use force to contain civil rebellion.

The right to intervene in lesser powers' internal affairs was also rationalized by goals other than the conservative purpose of preserving monarchies and the status quo. Under Castlereagh's successor, George Canning, the threat of British sea power was used to support the independence movement in Spanish America; later, under Lord Palmerston, the British supported constitutionalist causes in Spain and Portugal. Intervention and forcible procedures, in other words, also had become tools of liberal statecraft, as progressive thinkers like Stratford de Redcliffe and John Stuart Mill advocated their use to engender democratic reform abroad and liberate repressed peoples (Holbraad, 1970: 162–165). The definition of legitimate uses of force was thus broadened to accommodate intervention for whatever goal, liberal or conservative, a great power chose to pursue.

The Disintegration of the Concert

A story is told of Metternich watching an eclipse of the sun from the garden of his castle on the Rhine. According to Koppel Pinson (1966: 56), "A great sense of relief came over him when the moon finally completed its path across the sun and the temporary darkness was dispelled. There was 'order' again in the world." The restoration of order preoccupied great-power leaders from the Congress of Vienna to Metternich's exile in the midst of the Revolution of 1848. Toward that end, the security regime that evolved from the Concert of Europe promoted rules to maintain internal stability and great-power peace.

Though Britain's insular position sometimes led it to disagree with the continental monarchies over these rules, at critical junctures the great powers were able to agree upon a normative framework that prevented serious disputes from escalating into wars. When peace was threatened by the 1830 uprising in Belgium, the great powers were able to resolve their differences despite King William's plea to the conservative states for help, a plea which threatened to expand to war when Russia responded with an offer of 60,000 troops to assist in restoring him to his throne.

The fragile consensus underlying the Vienna settlement managed to persist for three decades with important adaptations, but the regime was eventually challenged and ultimately collapsed. The revolutions that swept Europe in 1848 undermined both the governments and the rules for international conduct that the great powers had advocated.

Crisis exerts pressure for legal reform, and the historical watershed of 1848 witnessed vigorous efforts to formulate new rules with which to regulate the violence that had been unleashed. This push reached its zenith with the outbreak of the Crimean War in 1854, but failed to culminate in great-power agreement on a new security regime.

The two decades following the decay of the Concert of Europe were dominated by a mood of realism, an insistence on stripping away illusion and seeing life as it was depicted in Courbet's paintings, Dickens's novels, and Ibsen's dramas. Among statesmen, this intellectual climate elevated the concepts of power and national interest far above the old ideal of a common European interest. Instead of promoting collective action, it led the great powers to return to short-term countervailing alliances, whose purpose was to ensure another state's neutrality during a projected war against some third party (Hinsley, 1963: 238). Thus force continued to be an instrument of state policy, but the conciliatory milieu that had constrained great-power behavior dissipated. The climate of normative opinion after 1848 was significantly different from that of the previous three decades.

What were the consequences of the erosion of the Concert of Europe? Table 6.2 compares the number of crises and uses of force that occurred from the Congress of Vienna to 1848 with the figures covering the period from 1849 until the rise of the new Bismarckian order in 1870. The 1816 to 1848 period experienced roughly the same number of serious interstate disputes as did the 1849 to 1870 period, but in the earlier period there were fewer disputes among great powers and none escalated to wars. This seems especially remarkable given the greater frequency of interventions and reciprocated military actions during the reign of the Concert system.

In contrast, during the period of the Concert's decline, the propensity of disputes to escalate to war was not contained. Four wars erupted among the great-powers: the Crimean (1854), Austro-Italian/Sardinian (1859), Austro-Prussian (1866), and Franco-Prussian (1870). Moreover, these wars drastically altered the European balance of power. Ties between the Habsburgs and Romanovs were severely strained by rivalry over the Danubian Principalities; Austria's defeats at Magenta, Solferino, and Königgratz ended its influence over German and Italian affairs; and the newly unified German Empire emerged as the dominant military power on the Continent.

In sum, the ostensible harmony at the congresses in London (1850, 1864, 1867), Paris (1856, 1858, 1860, 1869), and Vienna (1853, 1855) masked the unraveling of the post-Napoleonic security regime. The conservative solidarity that provided the normative support for the Concert system had collapsed. By the end of the Crimean War, no major power remained committed to preserving the rules emanating from the Vienna settlement. On the contrary, men like Bismarck, Cavour, and Napoleon III actively sought to replace the agreement of the great powers to act in concert—and the constraints those rules imposed—

TABLE 6.2
A Comparison of Uses of Force, 1816–1848 and 1849–1870

Variable	1816–1848 Period	1849–1870 Period	Data Source
Frequency of militarized disputes involving European states	29	31	Gochman and Maoz (1984)
Frequency of threats in European international conflicts[a]	2	10	Siverson and Tennefoss (1982)
Frequency of unreciprocated military action in European international conflicts[a]	5	7	Siverson and Tennefoss (1982)
Frequency of reciprocated military action in European international conflicts[a]	5	0	Siverson and Tennefoss (1982)
Frequency of serious disputes among European major powers	5	12	Wallace (1979)
Percentage of serious European great-power disputes escalating to war	0	50	Wallace (1979)
Frequency of great-power interventions into European civil wars	18	9	Wright (1965)
Frequency of large-scale great-power interventions into European civil wars[b]	4	0	Small and Singer (1982)

[a]Only events with one or more great-power participants counted.
[b]Defined as direct foreign military participation of such a magnitude that either 1000 troops were committed to the combat zone or 100 battle deaths were sustained.

with a new regime that permitted each to act unilaterally and freely in pursuit of its own perceived self-interests.

Great-Power Consensus and War Prevention

The formation and decay of the Concert of Europe suggest that the maintenance of a security regime supported by the great powers is critical to the preservation of peace. Furthermore, that support is difficult to obtain without a

shared sense of threat. A great-power consensus about the normative foundations of an international security regime may not be sufficient for its successful
operation, but warfare cannot be effectively brought under normative control
in the absence of agreement on rules governing use of force.

While it appears that we can extract some potential lessons from the nineteenth century about the normative foundations of a multipolar peace (see Box
6.1), we must exercise caution and remember that the Concert of Europe
operated within the confines of an unusually high level of shared great-power
values and a limited geographical space. Moreover, it was composed of a
modest number of approximately equal military powers reacting to one of the
most destructive wars in history. We have highlighted the post–Napoleonic Era
precisely because these conditions made it, in theory, one in which international norms were most likely to exert a constraint on the recourse to war. If
sanctioned rules could not contain violence in this relatively auspicious environment, then the prospects for norms to inhibit violence in less favorable
circumstances would indeed seem remote.

THE NORMATIVE FOUNDATIONS OF MULTIPOLAR PEACE

When great powers agree to limitations on (1) their use of force, (2) their freedom
to disregard their treaty commitments, and (3) the geostrategic boundaries of
their competition, a *restrictive* normative order exists. When few constraints-
apply in these three areas, a *permissive* order exists. The difference between these
two orientations is captured by the policy prescriptions in Box 6.2 (page 142).

As can be seen in Table 6.3, different sets of international norms reflect
contrasting assumptions about the nature of the state system. Norms communicate images of how the rivalry among the strongest states ought to be conducted. In effect, they "determine not only the type of response chosen for
particular situations, but the entire range of situations demanding such a response" (Luard, 1992: 319).

If the past is to provide lessons for the future, we need to reach conclusions
about which of these orders has been most conducive to stability in previous
multipolar systems. Is global stability fostered under a permissive order prescribing no obligation on the part of great powers other than pursuit of their
national interests, so that a fluid balance-of-power system can contain the
rivalry? Or, will a permissive order make war more probable? Some clues are
provided by Table 6.4 (page 145).

Rules cannot regulate if they are not recognized. Although the level of support for international norms has been inconsistent, there has been a tendency
for support to be strong at the beginning of each multipolar phase, when
painful memories of the last great-power war were fresh; but, at the end of these
periods, when the trauma of the past is forgotten, great-power consensus has
declined. In short, perception of threat has been conducive to consensus about

---

BOX 6.1
GREAT-POWER CONSENSUS, NORM FORMATION, AND WAR PREVENTION IN MULTIPOLAR SYSTEMS: PRINCIPLES SUGGESTED BY THE 1816–1848 AND 1849–1870 PERIODS

1. At the close of periods of relatively high instability, the great powers are apt to pay increased attention to the creation of rules designed to regulate the uses of force.
2. These periods of turmoil tend to breed consensus about the nature of a security regime among the most powerful states in the system.
3. The maintenance of this great-power consensus about these rules is critical to their efficacy, and the prospects for peace are best enhanced when great-power consensus:
   - places emphasis on norms regarding war;
   - recognizes the legitimacy of certain uses of force for certain purposes;
   - delineates legal criteria for defining the conditions under which forcible procedures are regarded permissible;
   - permits freedom of action but obligates the great powers to consult with one another and take collective action to uphold agreements; and
   - allows defeated hegemonic aspirant to remain in the system as an equal power and participant in order to deter any potential recidivism inspired by resentment of postwar punishment.
4. However, great-power consensus is often fragile and tends to erode over time; unanimity is particularly ephemeral in the absence of recurrent threats to the great powers' common interests, which serve to arouse their awareness of the dangers posed and their need for a collective response.
5. The outbreak of great-power disputes escalating to war tends to generate renewed consensus on the need for, and emphasis on, the creation of norms designed to constrain conflict.
6. Although a great-power consensus on the normative rules of a security regime can reduce the probability that disputes will escalate into war, such a consensus is unlikely to increase the prospects for freedom, justice, or self-determination within and between the other states in the system.

---

the norms needed to regulate great-power relationships and to avoid a general war. Conversely, when those fears have receded, so has the restraining influence of a normative consensus.

Are the relaxation of attention to great-power rules and justification of unregulated competition instrumental in the collapse of multipolar systems?

BOX 6.2
THE QUEST FOR MULTIPOLAR PEACE: TWO VISIONS OF THE PREFERRED RULES OF THE GAME

The Freedom of Sovereign Choice Is Sacred

"A prudent leader ought not to keep his word when by so doing it would be against his interest."

—Niccolò Machiavelli, 1513

"[The Utopians] never enter any alliance with any other state. They think leagues are useless things, and reckon that if the common ties of human nature do not knit men together the faith of promises will have no great effect on them."

—Thomas More, 1516

"Such are the great powers of Europe. You will need cleverness, flexibility, a capacity for intrigue and substantial 'expenditure' to take advantage of them, and to get them to assist (without noticing it) in the achievement of your goals."

—Frederick the Great, 1768

"In the intercourse between nations, we are apt to lay too much weight upon the formality of treaties and compacts. We do not act much more wisely when we trust to the interests of men as guarantees of their engagements. . . . Men are not tied to one another by papers and seals."

—Edmund Burke, 1796

"Governments keep their promises only when they are forced or when it is to their advantage to do so."

—Napoleon Bonaparte, 1817

"It is not usual for England to enter into engagements with reference to causes which have not actually arisen, or which are not immediately in prospect; and this for a plain reason. . . . Parliament might probably not approve of an engagement which should bind England prospectively to take up arms in a contingency which could not yet be foreseen."

—British Foreign Secretary Lord Palmerston, 1830

"Hope nothing from foreign governments. They will never be really willing to aid you until you have shown that you are strong enough to conquer without them."

—Giuseppe Mazzini, 1840

"In wartime, truth is so precious that she should always be attended by a bodyguard of lies."

—Winston Churchill, 1943

(continued)

BOX 6.2
(CONTINUED)

Agreements to Constrain Great-Power Choice Should Be Honored

"Kings should be very careful with regard to the treaties they conclude, but having concluded them they should observe them religiously."
—Cardinal Richelieu, 1641

"A skillful negotiator ought never to found the success of his negotiations on false promises and on breach of faith. It is an error to believe . . . that an able minister ought to be a great master in the art of deceit."
—François de Callières, 1716

"Let [states] be firm and faithful in their alliances and their union will prove the safety of each."
—Emerich de Vattel, 1758

"It is an essential principle of the Law of Nations that no power can free itself from the engagements of a treaty, nor modify its terms except with the assent of the contracting parties."
—The Treaty of London, 1919

"Observance of understandings, agreements, and treaties between nations constitutes the foundation of international order. . . . There is no task more urgent than that of remaking the basis of trusted agreement between nations. . . . It is to the interest of everyone that there be an end of treaties broken by arbitrary unilateral action."
—U.S. Secretary of State Cordell Hull, 1936

"Every treaty in force is binding upon the parties and must be performed in good faith."
—The Vienna Convention on the Law of Treaties, 1969

Must fears grow for restraint to be exercised? The record discloses quite different conclusions about the *type* of rules that were reached in the six multipolar periods. For example, a laissez-faire conception consistent with the flexibility and freedom of action that the balance of power would seem to demand prevailed during most of the early periods of multipolarity. A more restrictive consensus emerged during the eighteenth-century Age of Reason, in the immediate aftermath of the Napoleonic Wars, and following the First World War.

TABLE 6.3
Attributes of Two Normative Orders

Permissive Order	Restrictive Order
Great-Power Rules	
• The use of force to expand power is condoned	• The right to use force is limited
• Treaty agreements can be broken if violation advances national interests	• Alignment agreements are perceived binding
• A great power's military reach can extend as far as its resources permit	• Great-power competition is confined to specified territorial boundaries
• The great powers are to compete unconstrained by commitments to consult and act in concert	• The great powers are to coordinate their policies, communicate, and agree to act in concert to regulate common problems
Rationale for the Rules	
• The competition for power is stabilizing	• Order results from restraints on freedom and competition
• The balance of power preserves peace	• Cooperation and collective action preserve peace
• Self-help measures are the only safe strategy for defense	• Allies sharing defense burdens can strengthen national security
• Agreements reduce the capacity to adapt to changing circumstances	• Agreements can limit the potential issues in conflict
• Adherence to binding agreements diminishes flexibility	• Compliance with agreements increases predictability and order
• Confrontation is endemic and serves to preserve an equilibrium	• Commitments to a code of conduct prevents great-power confrontation

Since these multipolar periods all ended in devastating wars, many people believe that "foreign policy should be based on national power and interest, rather than abstract moralistic principles. . . ." (Dougherty and Pfaltzgraff, 1990: 111).

Yet we submit that normative restraints matter. According to Henry A. Kissinger (1979: 232): "If history teaches us anything it is that there can be no peace without equilibrium and no justice without restraint." As for restraint, he felt it critical to recognize that "All nations, adversaries and friends alike, must have a stake in preserving the international system. They must feel that their principles are being respected and their national interests secured. They must, in short, see positive incentives for keeping the peace, not just the dangers of breaking it" (Kissinger, 1979: 55).

During periods when those positive incentives supported a restrictive nor-

TABLE 6.4
The Culture Context of Six Multipolar Periods

Multipolar Period	Normative Culture	Degree of Great-Power Ideological Consensus	Acceptance of War	Support for Binding Treaties	Sphere-of-Influence Regime?	Degree of Great-Power Commitment to Coordination
1495–1521	Permissive	Moderate	High	Low	Yes	Low
1604–1618	Permissive	Low	High	Low	No	Low
1648–1702	Permissive	High	High but declining	Low but rising	Yes	Low
1713–1792	Restrictive	High	Moderate	Low/steady	No	Moderate
1815–1914	Increasingly restrictive	High	High but declining	Low but rising rapidly	Yes	High but declining
1919–1939	Restrictive	Low	Declining rapidly	Modest but increasing	No	Moderate but declining

mative order, maneuvering for power continued but its boundaries were fenced in by rules of prudence. This thesis is advanced by Hans J. Morgenthau (1985), regarded as the intellectual godfather of modern realist theorizing. He believed that the moral consensus that existed prior to the First World War exerted a potent restraining influence on the great powers' use of force and maintained that it is the absence of such rules that has made great-power relations so barbaric in the twentieth century. The danger today is that "no international moral consensus exists in sufficient depth and strength to sustain a comprehensive and binding international community" (Schlesinger, 1986: 73), and "in the last analysis . . . states are still above the law" (Hoffmann, 1971: 41). Consequently, great-power peace is more precarious than when a shared culture restrained the frequency and brutality of war.

To sum up, several different types of multipolar systems have existed since the modern state system took shape at the end of the fifteenth century. One way to distinguish among these forms of multipolarity is to sort them out according to their size, degree of polarization, and the degree to which prevailing international norms support a permissive rather than a restrictive normative order.

In Chapter 4 we considered a multipolar system's size, defined by the number of great powers that possess approximately equal capabilities. Great-power policymakers in multipolar systems of every size face a security dilemma, which they can either address alone or in concert. If they choose to act in tandem with the other great powers, the alliances they form can affect system stability. As a result, in Chapter 5 we focused on what tends to happen in multipolar systems when alliances become polarized into rigid blocs. Nations in alliances continually face questions about the extent of their obligation to uphold commitments when changing international conditions make it expedient to repudiate prior promises. In this chapter we investigated the international norms that great powers may promote to regulate their conduct and the conditions under which these rules of prudence may contribute to system stability.

Whereas system size does not appear to have had a significant impact on the stability of previous multipolar systems, polarized alliances and the existence of a permissive normative order seem to be related to the least stable forms of multipolarity. If the international system continues to move toward true multipolarity during the remainder of this century, it would behoove today's statesmen to do what is possible to create the least war-prone types of multipolarity. Several possible routes to a peaceful multipolar future stand before them. In the next four chapters we will analyze the costs, benefits, and trade-offs that are associated with each of these contending paths to peace.

PART III
Choices for the Future

· 7 ·

PATHS TO PEACE

Very deep reaches of policy exist in the pages of history, much oftener than in real life: nations, like the individuals of which they are composed, act generally either from passion, or from contingent circumstances; seldom from long foresight and prescribed system.

—WILLIAM EDEN, 1779

"Peace hath her victories no less renowned than war," wrote John Milton at the conclusion of the Thirty Years' War. But given that states exist under a condition of anarchy where no higher authority is empowered to prevent the mighty from imposing their will over others, how can we achieve these victories? The question has haunted men and women of goodwill throughout the history of the state system.

National leaders with blueprints in mind for a new post–Cold War order face the same task today that confronted the peacemakers assembled at Münster and Osnabrück over three centuries ago—discovering the path to lasting peace in a multipolar system. As we have seen in the previous three chapters, multipolar systems are not all alike; they vary according to size, the degree to which states ally for the purpose of combined action and these alliances become polarized into rigid blocs, and the extent to which prevailing norms restrict the use of force and the repudiation of treaties. Furthermore, some types of multipolar systems are more war prone than others. In view of these findings, the path to a multipolar peace is likely to be the one that leads us to the most stable type of multipolarity, namely, a system that is neither polarized nor governed by permissive international norms. What security policies should the great powers undertake in order to avoid the twin dangers of alliance polarization and a permissive normative order?

Although the outlines of the new post–Cold War era have not yet taken on clear definition, national security remains the primary concern of every leader. Without a means of defense, national values cannot be realized. Hence no country debates the merits of security, but they all debate the *methods* by which it is guaranteed. For this reason discourse about national security continues to pivot on questions of strategy. From the weakest, most vulnerable state to the strongest at the top of the global pyramid of power, national leaders agonize over how they might best achieve the goal of self-preservation.

International circumstances limit the range of choice for even the strongest nations. In particular, the global distribution of power "spell[s] out the menu of choice that [is] available to policymakers" (Holsti, 1991a: 87). Debates about the relative advantages and disadvantages of any national strategy are constricted by a state's position in the global hierarchy. Foreign policymakers must adopt policies for achieving peace ever cognizant that "the structure of the balance of power and the rules of the international system shape the options that are open to decision makers, occasionally in decisive ways" (Pelz, 1991: 49).

To argue that national security policies should and do evolve in response to changes in the international distribution of power contradicts the strong evidence that leaders are often reluctant to initiate radical changes in their foreign policies. More typically, foreign policy is governed by inertia and momentum; it is highly resistant to adaptive change except under the most intense pressure (see Holsti, 1982; Kegley and Wittkopf, 1991). The reason is not difficult to identify. Attachment to an ideology contributes to policy continuity, but beyond this the task of rethinking national purpose and building a national consensus in support of revising an established policy is not a challenge leaders welcome, primarily because a domestic political price is paid by leaders bold enough to try redirecting policy. Such changes inevitably threaten entrenched domestic constituencies who have a stake in the preservation of existing policies. Incentives for continuity usually far outweigh the rewards for reorienting a state's foreign policy posture, which is why at major historic watersheds a propensity to concoct new rationales for existing policies and practices is often evident.

Yet countries do change their foreign policy course, sometimes dramatically. These redefinitions of national security goals and strategies occur most often in periods of high turbulence. Rapid global changes, such as those that usually follow the end of major hegemonic wars, can free a state from the paralyzing grip of the past and force it to reappraise national purpose. When the distribution of global power is undergoing a fundamental restructuring, national security policy is most susceptible to revision. A transformation, for example, from a unipolar to a bipolar system or from a bipolar to a multipolar system often will be closely associated with shifts in the strategies for peace fashioned by the leading contenders for power.

Such a shift occurred after the Second World War, when the United States jettisoned its isolationist tradition and pursued a globalist national security policy dedicated to the mission of preserving world order. History is replete with similar shifts, demonstrating that the paths to peace each great power follows can also change in response to new conditions.

In this chapter we will explore the primary paths that the great powers have traveled since the advent of the modern state system, as well as what paths they perceive to be available in a new post–Cold War multipolar system.

THE RANGE OF GREAT-POWER CHOICE IN A MULTIPOLAR SYSTEM

Since the demise of the Soviet Union and the Warsaw Pact in 1991, consensus about the policies that should govern great-power relationships in the emerging multipolar system has yet to crystallize. In contemplating the possibilities, there is little that is novel. The options are defined by logical categories that are timeless and have retained their relevance across the ages. Security strategies fall into a discrete number of categories, each of which has become more or less practical, prudent, or problematic for each great power depending on the particular time and circumstance. For tomorrow's multipolar world, as for the multistate systems of old, the choices are defined along unchanging dimensions.

In tracing these basic categories of potential response, we begin by assuming that great powers are, by definition, predisposed to involvement in the management of world affairs. Isolationism, or what Arnold Wolfers (1962) aptly termed the "role of indifference" to international issues, has rarely been an attractive response for these states. Those at the top of the global hierarchy are engaged by the very weight of their power. They can escape this national "role" (Holsti, 1970; Walker, 1987) only with great difficulty and at great cost, and usually only in the short run. Active internationalism goes with a position of privilege and power.

But the *extent* of a great power's preferred involvement with others can be subject to wide variation. Accordingly, we can array the range of great-power choice on a hypothetical continuum comprised of four options (see Figure 7.1), keeping in mind that these categories are neither exhaustive nor mutually exclusive and that in practice great powers have relied on various combinations of them as their interests have dictated.

At one end of the continuum is a *unilateral* conception of a great power's

| Unilateralism | Specialized Relationships | A Concert of Powers | Collective Security |

FIGURE 7.1. Strategies for Preserving Peace among Equal Centers of Power.

role in international affairs. This preference for acting alone stems from a great power's self-confident sense of independent strength. It may manifest itself in isolationism, in an attempt to exert hegemonic leadership, or in efforts to play the role of a "balancer" who skillfully backs one side or another in a dispute, but only when necessary to maintain a military equilibrium between the disputants so as to prevent the domination of any power over the rest.

Positioned next to the unilateral orientation is the cultivation of a *specialized relationship* with another great power, similar to the kind built between Great Britain and the United States after World War II. Once again, there are several variants of this strategy, ranging from informal understandings between states to formal alliances.

A third option is construction of a great-power *concert*, designed to manage the international system jointly and prevent disputes among the leading states from escalating to war. The Concert of Europe at its apex between 1815 and 1822 is the epitome of this path to peace.

Finally, at the far end of the continuum, the great powers may choose to unite with the lesser powers in constructing a true system of *collective security*. The principles rationalizing formation of the League of Nations in 1919 exemplify this approach to peace under conditions of multipolarity.

This typology simplifies the complexity of choice. The categories are Weberian "ideal types" that for heuristic purposes exaggerate differences between the classifications and minimize the differences within them. As such, they organize our thoughts about the four strategic options that great powers may draw from to build a "new world order."

To illustrate the advantages of such a typology, consider the degree of collaboration to which this simple classification draws attention. As depicted in Figure 7.2, a multipolar world in which every great power practiced unilateralism would require the least amount of mutual consultation and provide the greatest amount of flexibility. While this might make a "go it alone" strategy attractive, the laissez-faire environment that unilateralism creates would have few restraints on aggression, free-riding, or exploitation.

In contrast, a system dominated by specialized great-power relationships would build greater reliability and predictability into international interactions. Yet it too has drawbacks. Though this configuration fosters an element of policy coordination between allies that might otherwise be lacking, the capacity for rapid realignment would be sacrificed.

The maximum degree of collaboration among the great powers occurs in a concert arrangement, but it excludes lesser powers; concerts can thus accentuate latent fears those weak states on the periphery of the system might harbor about their domination by the strong. Collective security, the fourth option, admits the weaker states to full participation with the great powers in managing global affairs. However, it suffers from the limitation that large, diverse organizations are often slow to respond to festering international problems.

Though elementary, the above typology delineates the basic paths to a multi-

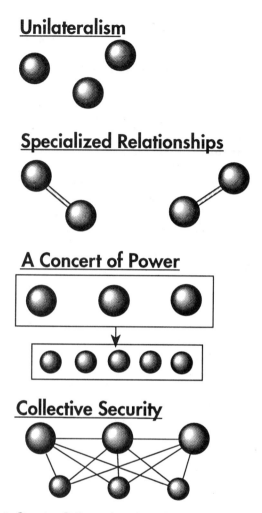

FIGURE 7.2. Picturing Different Levels of Great-Power Collaboration.

polar peace. To make this classification more concrete, let us flesh out the theoretical skeleton. In the following sections, we trace the ideas historically associated with each of these four postulated paths to peace.

Unilateralism

A preference for preserving autonomy in international affairs is rooted in the folklore that surrounds statecraft. Autonomy implies freedom, and national leaders treasure the freedom to do what they deem necessary to protect the state. International law makes the independence of states, and the right for the state to advance its interests without interference, the core principles of its very foundation. In many capital cities around the world, sovereignty and *raison d'état* are thought to justify a state's right to take any action, including war, to preserve itself. No state, especially not a great power, would sacrifice its freedom of action in a manner that would compromise national security. International law realistically stops short of such demands.

Great powers are usually able to prevail in tests of strength with smaller states. Yet they also try to act as they please in relations with one another and to obtain relative advantage over their rivals (Grieco, 1988). This quest for maximum freedom and superior power compared to that possessed by their allies and adversaries becomes readily apparent when one observes great-power behavior under conditions of multipolarity. Indeed, many slogans voiced by leaders of great powers in multipolar systems express the preference for autonomous action. The adages "avoid entangling alliances," "maximize one's alternatives," and "trust another no further than one's interests" echo the dictum of Lord Palmerston who advocated in 1848 that the policy of Great Britain should be to "have no eternal allies and . . . no perpetual enemies. [Britain's] interests are eternal and perpetual, and these interests it is our duty to follow." Additionally, unilateral policy responses subscribe to the realist prescriptions to "never put yourself in a position from which you cannot retreat without losing face and from which you cannot advance without grave risks" and to "never allow a weak ally to make decisions for you" (Morgenthau, 1985: 589).

Unilateralism incorporates these notions, as it appeals not to isolating a great power from international affairs so much as it does to preventing dependency. In the classic balance-of-power system, this role was customarily played by a "balancer," which stood on the sidelines, positioned to enter the fray by defending the actor or coalition most in danger of falling to an aspiring hegemon. The roles of a "neutral" or a "nonaligned" state also derive from the desire to preserve flexibility and to avoid commitments that might entrap one in the conflicts of others.

Incentives for Unilateralism in a Balance of Power

Balance-of-power theory justifies unilateralism. Conceived as a mechanism to deter the outbreak of a general war, the balancing mechanism was envisioned by the policymakers and publicists who popularized it as a formula for preserving peace. The willingness of one or more great powers to remain independent is indispensable for the balance to function properly. Balance-of-power theory assumes that each great-power contender will practice flexibility of alignment and maximize its freedom of maneuver, honoring one rule above all: Seek power and check the military power of every other competitor in order to frustrate expansionist ambitions. Morton Kaplan described the "essential rules" of behavior in an effective balance-of-power regime by noting that in it each great power was obligated to

> (1) increase capabilities but negotiate rather than fight; (2) fight rather than fail to increase capabilities; (3) stop fighting rather than eliminate an essential actor; (4) oppose any coalition or single actor which tends to assume a position of predominance within the system; (5) constrain actors who subscribe to supranational organizational principles; and (6) permit defeated or constrained essential national actors to reenter the system as acceptable role partners. (Kaplan, 1957: 23)

According to these rules, competition in a multipolar world is proper because it leads to the equalization of capabilities among the great powers. The problem of arms races is dealt with in a way that preserves the problem, for weapons and war are ways of measuring national strength and a means for redistributing power while perpetuating the basic features of the system itself. As a path to peace, unilateralism—if practiced by each and every rival—is advocated as the best approach to preventing any from gaining predominance over all.

> In contrast to collective security, which calls upon states to abandon such 'natural' habits as forming alliances and discriminating between threats that have a direct and those that have a remote impact and to adopt the view that their own safety can be secured only if they give priority to world order, balance of power treats world order as a happy by-product of the urge of states to defend their own security, individually or in combination with allies. (Claude, 1989: 83)

Many advise that in a new multipolar system this policy, designed to preserve a great power's latitude for choice, remains the most prudent and advantageous one. In a system where ideology matters less than clashing economic interests and ominous military capabilities, remaining unattached is a tempting path to follow.

Unilateralism and the Quest for Hegemonic Rule

Another facet of unilateralism is illustrated by the contention of "hegemonic stability theory" (Kindleberger, 1973) that a single dominant power provides the best promise for peace by possessing sufficient power to police the entire system. According to this variant of unilateralism, a division of power among the major contenders is dangerous, whereas a concentration of power into the hands of a single leader is medicinal for the system as a whole.

Of course, the wisdom or folly of this contention depends on the goals to which such a leader aspires. If it rules by force and, maintaining that what is good for the hegemon is good for the rest, intervenes in other countries to police the system, then the security and welfare of all others will be put at risk. Conversely, if a preponderant power practices benevolent rule, then a protracted peace through unilateral regulation may indeed materialize. Realism dismisses this expectation, given the propensity of hegemonic rulers to lose sight of their original objectives and to put their national self-interests ahead of the collective interest of the international community (see Gilpin, 1981). On the eve of the twenty-first century, the form of unilateralism practiced—assuming that one or more of the great powers attempts to go it alone—will make a critical difference for the ultimate stability of the system.

Specialized Relationships

Independence has its advantages, but as it also has substantial costs, not everyone agrees with the above reasoning. Going it alone can maximize freedom, but it can leave a state exposed. Unilateralism requires self-reliance; it necessitates drawing on one's own resources, without the benefit of help from others. Placing trust in the goodwill and faithful performance of promises is risky, but the alternative can be even more risky, especially in the absence of a clear-cut superiority in military strength. As a result, great powers sometimes reject unilateral self-help and autarky in favor of cultivating a specialized relationship with another great power. Three varieties of specialized relationships are common: alignment, entente, and condominium.

Alignment

Bilateral relationships can either culminate in formal alliances or remain loosely defined informal friendships, with the degree of potential coordination subject to wide variation. But whatever form such collaborative, partner-specific great-power alignments may take, the motive underlying this kind of specialized relationship is the same: mutual protection against aggression from a great-power rival or coalition and formation of a common front on global issues where the partners' interests converge.

Entente

An entente represents an alternative kind of specialized relationship through which such mutual protection and joint lobbying might be achieved, especially in the case of multiple threats from other great powers. Such quasi-alliances assume a harmony of core interests among their members, strengthened by their common concerns over other great powers or coalitions. Joined by shared fears of a mutual adversary, the two powers agree to consult with one another in the event of certain contingencies.

Ententes have many precursors and vary between public pledges of cooperation at one extreme to secret commitments of friendship and mutual support at the other. The Anglo–French Entente of 1904 illustrates the functions of an entente. It was negotiated secretly by two friendly governments in the pre–World War I crisis atmosphere to assure their cooperation without arousing

German alarm or public opposition. The accord preserved the good relations between the two countries without incurring the risks and obligations that a mutual defense treaty would have entailed. For Britain's part, the Anglo–French Entente accommodated English attraction to its "splendid isolation" tradition while providing a means to restrain French policy and to prevent Britain's becoming isolated against Germany (Williamson, 1969).

Condominium

A third form of specialized relationship is a condominium, or joint great-power rule over one or more geographic regions. Historically, condominiums have been formed to administer territories whose ownership has been in dispute, as in the cases of the Falkland Islands, Northern Ireland, or the Anglo–Egyptian Condominium over the Sudan between 1899 and 1955.[1] But the model has often been suggested for application as an appropriate form of global management by dominant great powers. Recently, for example, a former U.S. undersecretary has advocated creation of a Russo–American security condominium (Iklé, 1991–1992), and U.S. Secretary of Defense Les Aspin proposed in June 1993 to "create a new security system" by training U.S. and Russian troops for joint peacekeeping operations.

A Concert of Power

Beyond forming special bilateral partnerships with certain states, great powers have the option of establishing a multilateral relationship with all of their peers at the top of the global hierarchy so as to promote their mutual interests. These great-power concerts help control rivalries among the mighty and provide a vehicle for enforcing peace among the remaining states whose conflicts and civil wars could draw the great powers into combat. The expectation driving efforts to organize concerts is that regular great-power consultation and consensus building will produce multilateral decision making on divisive issues. Compromise and conciliation, rather than the thrust and parry of unbridled competition, would yield outcomes acceptable to all of the great powers.

Concerts enjoy a long history. In the fourteenth century, for example, Pierre Dubois proposed a congress of the reigning princes in Europe to manage political affairs on the Continent. He felt that it was possible to police aggression by waging preventive war. Any aggressor would "be subdued by an international army formed from the troops of all the confederate states" (cited in Possony, 1946: 916).

The idea behind a concert is "rule by a central coalition" among the great

---

1. Condominial relationships date back to antiquity. George Liska (1967: 13–14) has identified such arrangements between Egypt and the Hatti in 1278 B.C.E., and later between the Babylonians and the Medes, and between the Romans and the Macedonians in Illyria.

powers, a scheme "fundamentally different from that of the balance of power" (Rosecrance, 1992: 65, 72). It is predicated on the belief that the leading centers of power will see their interests advanced by renunciating territorial expansion and collaborating to contain conflict from escalating to war in the regions under their mutual jurisdiction. Although it is assumed that the great powers share a common outlook, concerts still allow "for subtle jockeying and competition to take place among them. Power politics is not completely eliminated; members may turn to internal mobilization and coalition formation to pursue divergent interests. But the cooperative framework of a concert, and its members' concern about preserving peace, prevent such balancing from escalating to overt hostility and conflict" (Kupchan and Kupchan, 1992: 253).

As mentioned previously, the Concert of Europe that commenced with the Congress of Vienna in 1815 exemplifies this path to peace.[2] It was "an exclusive club for great powers, whose members were self-appointed" (Claude, 1964: 21). Hence the organization fell short of a true collective security system, which is the logical extension of the premises and principles on which a great-power concert is based.

Collective Security

At the conclusion of long, grinding wars, victorious allies frequently are aware of how close cooperation facilitated their victory. Such a recognition has usually stimulated negotiations about how to continue the wartime collaboration through some broader institutional framework that would include lesser-rank countries as well. Collective security comprises this fourth and most ambitious of our alternative paths to peace. As one study describes the ideas underlying the concept,

> Collective security is based on the principle that peace is indivisible: therefore, a threat to the peace anywhere is of *common concern* to the entire international community (as that is defined at any particular moment), which must agree *in advance* both *to react* against such a threat and *how* to react against it.
>
> In a very simple kind of way, collective security may be seen as an effort to transfer to the international scene the "one for all and all for one" concept which guided Alexandre Dumas' d'Artagnan and his three doughty Musketeer friends. (Finkelstein and Finkelstein, 1966: 1)

Many aver that collective security did not gain recognition as an approach to peace until the League of Nations. But this belief is mistaken.

---

2. A more recent example of an attempt to create a great-power concert can be found in Franklin Roosevelt's so-called four policemen plan. As Roosevelt saw it, the United States, Great Britain, the Soviet Union, and China could form a security directorate after World War II. In what he called his "Great Design," these four policemen would work together to counter any threats to peace in the postwar world.

We are accustomed to thinking of collective security as a comparatively modern development, dating mainly from the League of Nations and including the United Nations. But it is worth pointing out that the concept itself is of ancient origin. Thus, for example, the oath taken by the Greek city-states which belonged to the ancient Amphictyonic League provided an obligation not to destroy any city of the Amphictyons, "nor cut off their streams, in war or peace, and if any should do so, they would march against him, and destroy his cities, and should any pillage the property of the god, or be privy to or plan anything against what was in his temple at Delphi, they would take vengeance against him with hand and foot, and all their might." Interesting practical developments took place also in the Middle Ages and during the nineteenth century. And there has been throughout modern history an abundance of plans and schemes designed to achieve the major goal of collective security: the preservation of the peace through common, predetermined, collective action. (Finkelstein and Finkelstein, 1966: 2)

Two additional examples of early forerunners of contemporary proposals for collective security illustrate the historic roots of this strategy. The first is found in the eleventh century, when

the participants of the synod of Bruges in 1038 swore to take military measures against violators of ecclesiastic peace laws. Under the energetic leadership of Archbishop Aimon of Bruges several punitive expeditions were carried out against rebellious knights; the Archbishop may, in fact, be considered as the earliest predecessor of the commander of a modern international armed force. Priests in large numbers fought in his peace enforcement army to safeguard the inherent justice and the disinterested nature of the intervention. (Possony, 1946: 912)

The second example occurred four centuries later, when in 1462

. . . George Podebrad, King of Bohemia, under the influence of the otherwise obscure pamphletist Antonius Marinus, proposed the establishment of a European league. The nucleus of this league was to be an alliance against the Turks between France under Louis XI, Venice and Bohemia. (Constantinople had fallen nine years earlier.) The suggested treaty authorized sanctions against the aggressor; the victim of aggression was to be helped by all members of the confederation, which was to assume the initiative to settle disputes even among states not belonging to it. Article VI stipulated the outlawing of any individual who disturbed the peace; every aggressor was to be punished as a 'violator of general peace.' The right to declare war was no longer to be exercised by individual states, but devolved upon the confederation as a whole. (Possony, 1946: 914)

As portrayed in Figure 7.2, collective security is a comprehensive system of international security that by design encompasses the full participation of *every* state to assure the independence of all. Collective security requires the complete collaboration of the great powers, for without their cooperation an organization composed of small and middle-rank states would lack the means for effective action. The key is universal and obligatory participation: To deter war, an aggressor would need to be faced by the united opposition of the entire international community. Collective security is designed to protect both the weak and the strong, inspired by the conviction that in a multipolar system the victimization of the former would ultimately undermine the security of the latter.

Collective security and collective defense are sometimes confused, as is the relationship of both to the balance of power. According to most observers, collective security has a more inclusive membership with a less specific mission. However, the precise meaning of collective security remains a subject of debate (see Box 7.1), and, as a consequence, has

> . . . largely lost its clarity and specificity. New wine has been mixed with the old in the semantic bottle whose label has come to be prized for its own sake, diluting the flavor of the original vintage. Collective security has been appropriated as an honorific designation for virtually any and all multilateral activities that statesmen or scholars may regard, or wish to have regarded, as conducive to peace and order. In a particularly ironic twist of fate, the label has been applied to alliances, bilateral or multilateral, by their champions—in flagrant disregard of the fact that the notion of a collective security system was originally developed in reaction against and in the hope of providing a substitute for the traditional system of competing alliances. (Claude, 1964: 247)

For our purposes, we will adhere to this interpretation: As a path to peace, collective security is distinct from collective defense treaties because the latter are designed to meet a common danger from a specific enemy, defined in advance. Most typically, collective defense agreements are organized on a regional or bloc basis against a particular threat. During the Cold War, NATO, the Warsaw Pact, the Baghdad Pact, and the Rio Pact were representative. These kinds of defense treaties did not require great-power unanimity; in fact, they often would pit one great-power alliance against another. In contrast, in our conception a collective security regime has a broader mandate obligating *all* states, big and small, to combine capabilities against *any* nation that illegally breaks the peace. This more stringent expectation assumes that all states, including those not immediately threatened or distant from the danger, will honor their pledge to participate in sanctions against the aggressor. As one authority describes it,

> The rock bottom principle upon which collective security is founded provides that an attack on any one state will be regarded as an attack on all states. It finds its measure in the simple doctrine of one for all and all for one. War anywhere . . . is the concern of every state.
> Self-help and neutrality, it should be obvious, are the exact antithesis of such a theory. States under an order of neutrality are impartial when conflict breaks out, give their blessings to combatants to fight it out, and defer judgment regarding the

BOX 7.1
COLLECTIVE SECURITY: AN ALTERNATIVE TO THE BALANCE OF POWER, OR A PROPERTY OF AN ENDEMIC BALANCING PROCESS?

"'Collective security,' far from being alien to the 'age-old tradition of the balance of power,' not only derives from the latter, but also must be regarded as the logical end point of the balance-of-power system, the ideal toward which it has been moving, slowly and haltingly, for several hundred years. This contention leads to the hypothesis that the League of Nations and the United Nations, when considered as instruments for maintaining the 'continued co-existence of governments in contact with one another,' were merely further refinements in balance practice—namely, organizations representing a worldwide state system of sovereign, independent, and armed states, intent on preserving their security and independence and prepared to use an automatic coalition to prevent the dangerous expansion of any member state. . . . At bottom, the collective security of 1919 or 1945 was merely an elaboration and refinement of the coalition equilibrium of 1815, just as the latter was an elaboration and refinement of the alliance balance. . . ."

—Edward V. Gulick (1955: 307–308)

". . . Policies of balance of power naturally lead to policies of collective security which become institutionalized through common organs, procedures, and rules of law to assure that aggression will be always confronted by insuperable force. International organization to promote collective security is, therefore, only a planned development of the natural tendency of balance of power policies. It is the natural tendency of states, when faced by an emergency, to gang up against the aggressor who, if successful against his first victim, will eventually turn on the others. Collective security seeks to supplement this natural tendency by positive obligations and convenient agencies and procedures to enlist common action. . . ."

—Quincy Wright (1955: 204)

"Perhaps the most useful service a student can do himself in attempting to study great power co-operation in the years immediately after the Napoleonic Wars is to dismiss from his mind altogether the notion that there ever was such a thing as a Congress System. He may then have some chance of realizing that although there were Congresses after 1815 there was little that was systematic about them. There was no agreement between the powers as to what Congresses were for, and there was no permanent organization for international co-operation such as was set up after each of the two German wars of the twentieth century. Like so many of the 'systems' in history, the Congress System is an invention of historians."

—L. C. B. Seaman (1963: 10)

justice or injustice of the cause involved. Self-help in the past was often "help yourself" so far as the great powers were concerned; they enforced their own rights and more besides. In the eighteenth and nineteenth centuries this system was fashionable and wars, although not eliminated, were localized whenever possible. In a more integrated world environment, a conflict anywhere has some effect on conditions of peace everywhere. A disturbance at one point upsets the equilibrium at all other points, and the adjustment of a single conflict restores the foundations of harmony at other points throughout the world. (Thompson, 1953: 755)

COMPARING STRATEGIES FOR PEACE

The four strategies presented above can overlap. As already noted and further illuminated in Box 7.1, some theorists link collective security to a balance-of-power system. The convergence between collective security and the balance of power emanates from the fact that a collective security mechanism cannot effectively operate without the participation and support of the great powers. Despite the coordination and cooperation that collective security is designed to foster, some level of maneuvering is to be expected as the great powers jockey to balance potential rivals. Accordingly, collective security may belie its name and mask the great-power intrigue that cannot be extinguished by decrees pledging their consent to the charter of some international organization.

What, then, is the critical difference between collective security and the balance of power? It resides not in the extent of great-power participation, which is constantly at play, or in the balancing motives that animate their response to the threat posed by another great power's rising military capabilities. It resides, rather, in the degree to which great and lesser powers are willing to institutionalize their political and military collaboration. Collective security is predicated on the assumption that war can be avoided by aggregating superior power and that rational actors confronting an expansionist power will form a countercoalition to deter the threat of aggression. "In this respect," notes Inis Claude (1964: 250), collective security "is fundamentally similar to a balance of power system involving defensive alliances. However, . . . collective security is basically different from the system of policy which it was explicitly designed to replace." Collective security was conceived as an improvement on the balance of power because it incorporated a consultive mechanism to promote consensus. As U.S. Secretary of State James F. Byrnes (1947: 70) summarized it, collective security "would facilitate agreement among the major powers and at the same time provide the smaller states with ample opportunities to express their views." Collective security thus can be seen as a more inclusive form of a concert, which in turn is more inclusive still than a bilateral special relationship.

The essential ingredients here are the level and pattern of agreement among the players. What elevates a collective security system above the collisions of

TABLE 7.1
The Relationship between Security Systems and Cohesion at Different Levels
of International Stratification

Security System	Great Powers	Subordinate Powers
Unilateral Balance of Power	Divided	Divided
Specialized Relationships	Divided	United
Great-Power Concert	United	Divided
Collective Security	United	United

interest in balance-of-power politics is that within a collective security system, coordination supersedes contestation. Table 7.1 summarizes the following four types of security strategies that generally develop when different combinations of unity and disunity exist:

- If disunity appears among the great powers and among subordinate states, a unilateral struggle for survival by all actors in accordance with balance-of-power precepts will be common.
- If the great powers are divided and lesser powers are united, the former will tend to form specialized relationships while the latter will attempt to isolate themselves from great-power struggles through nonalignment and neutrality, all the while calling for initiatives to redistribute power and alleviate the exploitation of the weak by the strong.
- When the great powers are united but the smaller states are not, concerts will tend to form.
- Finally, whenever both great and lesser-rank powers are united, efforts to construct collective security organizations can be expected.

As conveyed in Chapters 4–6, no single consistent pattern appears in the rules and regimes that victorious great powers have endorsed at the conclusion of past hegemonic wars. Each of the four discrete strategies identified here has gained the favor of some great power at one time or another, but none has commanded lasting allegiance, which points to the limitations of any single plan. Each strategy has compelling reasons for its adoption (see Box 7.2), in part because there exists an inherent tension behind the incompatible needs for both unilateral independence and multilateral collaboration.

The divisions in today's policy debate echo debates from the distant past. The answers were unclear then and remain so as we end this century. Given the trade-offs associated with each strategy, we should not be surprised to hear voices advocating and criticizing all of them.

What policies have the best prospect of preserving peace in the new millennium? The three remaining chapters look more closely at the options now being

BOX 7.2
RESPONDING TO MULTIPOLARITY: REASON AND
RATIONALE FOR FOUR RIVAL GREAT-POWER STRATEGIES

Unilateralism

"The nation which indulges toward another a habitual hatred or a habitual fondness is in some degree a slave. It is a slave to its animosity or to its affection, either of which is sufficient to lead it astray from its duty and its interest."

—George Washington, 1796

"I hold with respect to alliances, that . . . a Power [is] sufficiently strong, sufficiently powerful, to steer her own course, and not to tie [itself] as an appendage to the policy of any other Government."

—British Foreign Secretary Lord Palmerston, 1848

Specialized Relationships

"Great as is the influence and power of Britain, she cannot afford to follow, for any length of time, a self-isolating policy."

—William Ewart Gladstone, 1850

"The greatest security against war in any part of the world . . . would be the close collaboration of the British Empire with the United States of America. The combined powers . . . would be a sanction that no power on earth however strong dare face."

—Lord Baldwin, 1935

Concert

"Neither the Balance of Power nor Treaties are sufficient to maintain Peace; the only way is by a European Union."

—Abbé de Saint-Pierre, 1713

"I am proposing that all nations henceforth avoid entangling alliances which would draw them into competition of power. . . . There is no entangling alliance in a concert of power. When all unite to act in the same sense and with the same purpose, all act in the common interest and are free to live their own lives under a common protection."

—Woodrow Wilson, 1917

Collective Security

"History shows that the danger threatening the independence of this or that nation has generally arisen, at least in part, out of the momentary predomi-

(continued)

BOX 7.2
(CONTINUED)

nance of a neighboring State at once militarily powerful, economically efficient, and ambitious to extend its frontiers or spread its influence. . . . The only check on the abuse of political predominance derived from such a position has always consisted in the opposition of an equally formidable rival, or of a combination of several countries forming leagues of defence."

—Sir Eyre Crowe, 1907

"It would be a master stroke if those Great Powers honestly bent on peace would form a league of peace, not only to keep the peace among themselves, but to prevent, by force, if necessary, its being broken by others. . . . Power to command peace throughout the world could best be assured by some combination between those great nations which sincerely desire peace and have no thought themselves of committing aggressions."

—Theodore Roosevelt, 1910

considered by the United States and other great powers. We begin in Chapter 8 with an analysis of the advantages and drawbacks of a unilateralist strategy. In Chapter 9 we turn our attention to exploring the efficacy of the bilateral strategy of special relationships. Finally, in Chapter 10 we examine the prospects for a multilateral strategy that would entail creating a new, concert-based collective security regime.

· 8 ·

THE UNITED STATES: RECLUSE, LEADER, OR BALANCER?

Today, as an old order passes, the new world is more free but less stable. Communism's collapse has called forth old animosities and new dangers. Clearly, America must continue to lead the world we did so much to make.

—PRESIDENT BILL CLINTON, INAUGURAL ADDRESS, 1993

In retrospect, the simplicity of the bipolar era had a certain appeal: Germany, Europe, even the world were neatly divided. Stability existed within and between the Eastern and Western blocs. Now that the Cold War is over, these simplifying realities have given way to a confusing global landscape. The end of the Cold War can be likened (Kielinger, 1990) to waking up from a long sleep—with a headache!

In this chapter, we will look at the implications of an emerging post–Cold War multipolar system primarily from the perspective of the world's leading military power, the United States, and focus on the unilateral approach to peace. Then, in Chapters 9 and 10, we will consider the other strategies presented in Chapter 7, special relationships and collective security through a great-power concert, and evaluate their potential for success against the backdrop of the historical patterns that characterized the six previous multipolar periods described in Chapters 3–6.

Let us begin by considering the U.S. view of Europe. The diplomatic agenda on the Continent is much more crowded than in the recent past. Public support for integration has faltered amid growing concern over the influence of Germany, the costs entailed in widening the European Community, the spread of ethnic hatred and violence, and the revival of European nationalism and reemergence of wars of national consolidation (Maynes, 1993: 11).

The Europe on the horizon is profoundly different from the one we have known during the past fifty years. Many of the international political and economic solutions of that era have become today's problems. For example, the

European Community that united Europe in the Cold War era now divides it into a peninsula of prosperity jutting out from a mainland of economic decay. Prior to 1989 NATO simplified West European security; now it complicates pan-European security. Weakening and ultimately crippling the Soviet Union was the western Cold Warriors' singular aim; strengthening Russia and the former Soviet satellites is the more complex challenge today.

For central and eastern Europeans, single-party governments and centrally planned economies have been exchanged for political pluralism and market economies. The COMECON countries' strategy of avoiding close economic relations with the West has been replaced by efforts to increase economic contact and to receive development assistance. The might of the Soviet Union was the solution for Warsaw Pact governments' security problems, and the Warsaw Pact was part of the solution for the Soviet Union's security problems. Today the Warsaw Pact is defunct and its former members represent potential security threats to one another. Throughout the Continent virulent ethnic hatreds long contained by the threat of great-power intervention have reappeared and are wreaking havoc. In this chaotic setting, the United States is challenged by the difficulty of playing a constructive role in world affairs that avoids the extremes of interference and indifference.

But it is not just Europe that is changing. Consider the rest of the world, where the turmoil and disorder are equally unsettling. Questions abound over the future stability of Korea, Cambodia, the Middle East, and sub-Saharan Africa; famine and despair reign in much of what was once called the Third World. Given that the post–Cold War world looks like a political minefield, many speculate (see Box 8.1) that a new multipolar world—if it truly does emerge—will be fraught with peril, even while it may hold promise.

CONSTRAINTS ON U.S. POLICY OPTIONS

Although the United States now stands at the apex of the global pyramid of power, the pyramid has begun to crumble. Superior military power no longer seems to translate into a capacity to exercise proportionate political influence, and "the high defense burden has caused some economic damage, and gives an advantage to commercial rivals like Japan and Germany" (Kennedy, 1993a: 42). Paradoxically, Washington may be more constrained today than it was when the perceived danger of communist expansionism existed.

The current period of unchallenged U.S. military strength may be a temporary phase that will yield to a new multipolar system. In the past, the advent of multipolarity stimulated repositioning. If three or more approximately equal centers of power emerge, we can expect these states to readjust their alignments and change the course of their national security policies to accomodate shifts in the hierarchy of world power.

The advent of a new multipolar world presages a new balance-of-power

BOX 8.1
GRAVE NEW WORLD? THE PERILS AND PROMISE
OF MULTIPOLARITY

Perils

"We are . . . returning to a more traditional and complicated time of multipolarity, with a growing number of countries increasingly able to affect the course of events despite the wishes of the superpowers. . . . The issue . . . is how well the United States accomplishes the transition from overwhelming predominance to a position more akin to a 'first among equals' status, and how well America's partners—Japan and Western Europe—adapt to their newfound importance. The change will not be easy for any of the players, as such shifts in power relationships have never been easy. . . . What we have to understand is that the post-war era, in which the U.S. and the Soviet Union dominated world events and set the agenda for their respective alliances, is over."

—U.S. Secretary of State Lawrence Eagleburger (1989: 244–245)

"Just as the hegemonic role of the United States was one of the necessary conditions for the unprecedently high levels of economic integration and political coordination that characterized the international system (outside the Soviet hegemony) during the post-war period, so the waning power and influence of the United States in the present period are in part responsible for the system's gradually declining integration and coordination."

—Theodore Geiger (1988: xii)

"History suggests that there is considerable risk of conflict, which may even spill over from the economic sphere to create or intensify political rivalries. Such a pattern contributed to the breakdown of global order prior to 1914 and again in the interwar period."

—C. Fred Bergsten (1990: 96)

"Not since the Napoleonic upheavals (if not the Peace of Westphalia in 1648) have the rights of states, people and governments been so unclear. . . . New vacuums are setting off new conflicts. Old problems are being solved, begetting new ones. The result of this process is a global law-and-order deficit that is straining the capacity of existing and emerging security institutions."

—Chester A. Crocker (1993: 23)

Promise

"It [will] be a better and safer world if we have a strong healthy United States, Europe, Soviet Union, China and Japan, each balancing the other."

—Richard M. Nixon, 1971 (cited in Nye, 1990: 235)

(continued)

BOX 8.1
(CONTINUED)

"The post—Cold War world is in many ways a safer world."
—U.S. Secretary of Defense Dick Cheney (1993: 1)

"The emerging multipolar configuration of power may be somewhat less stable than the old bipolar nuclear stalemate but . . . this should not in itself foster major conflicts involving the great powers."
—Jack Snyder (1992: 260)

"The decline of [U.S.] hegemony does not necessarily sound cooperation's death knell."
—Robert O. Keohane (1984: 9)

---

system. The United States faces growing competition from Germany, Japan and China on the economic front and from Russia on the military front. Should these challengers continue to narrow their disparity of resources with the United States, it will set the stage for a world altogether different from the one we have come to know (see Map 8.1). "We may simply see the emergence of a five-way balance of power rotating around the United States, Europe, Japan, China, and what remains of the Soviet Union" (Alperovitz and Bird, 1992: 207–208). "For diplomatic purposes," notes Henry A. Kissinger (1993: 1), "there are no longer two superpowers, but five or six more or less equal power centres. . . . The United States is militarily the strongest, but the circumstances in which its military power is relevant are diminishing." The problem, Kissinger points out, resides in the fact that "the United States has very little experience with a world that consists of many powers and which it can neither dominate nor from which it can simply withdraw in isolation."

Before considering the likely U.S. policy response to a twenty-first century multipolar system, a review of the genesis of this likely distribution of global power is in order. We need to consider the seeds from which this future might spring, as well as the form such a world would take if this scenario comes to pass. Here, two corollary propositions command wide attention: (1) The United States is a hegemon in decline, and (2) other great powers are moving into position to challenge its leadership.

A Declining Hegemon?

More than half a century ago, Walter Lippmann (1943: 9) observed that "foreign policy consists of bringing into balance . . . the nation's commitments and the nation's power." During the preceding half-century, the "Lippmann gap"

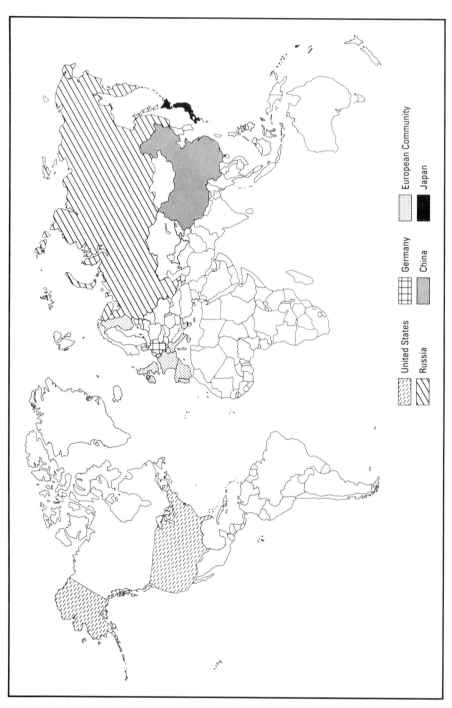

MAP 8.1. Emerging Centers of Power in a New Multipolar System.

Legend:
- United States
- Russia
- Germany
- China
- European Community
- Japan

between commitments and power has gained increasing importance on the American national agenda. To those who doubt the uniqueness of the United States and believe that it faces the same kinds of problems as other states, the central question is how to balance external activities with what the country can afford. Whereas symptoms of the erosion of U.S. power are evident, there also is evidence that the U.S. position has not waned. "Given the size and complexity of the American economy, it is impossible to categorize it as either hopelessly weak or immensely strong; it is a mixture of strengths and weaknesses" (Kennedy, 1993a: 43). As a result, the debate between declinists and their critics is intense (see Box 8.2).[1] At the heart of this debate is a difference of opinion about the sources of national power.

Money Matters

Early in the atomic age, most students of international affairs, awed by the destructive potential of nuclear weapons, stressed the military foundations of national power. As the Cold War evolved, the limits of military force became more evident. The states with the largest arsenals did not always get their way; sometimes they lost in conflicts with militarily weaker states. Vietnam and Afghanistan, for example, prevailed over their vastly superior adversaries, the United States and the Soviet Union, respectively. For most Americans, the war in Vietnam "provided a useful and sobering reminder that a vast superiority in military hardware and economic productivity will not always and automatically translate into military effectiveness" (Kennedy, 1987: 405).

Concomitant with the realization of limits to military power, attention shifted to the importance of economic power (see Knorr, 1973). Japanese and German economic ascendance demonstrated that building trade, rather than weapons, provided an effective strategy for gaining international prominence (see Rosecrance, 1986). Awareness of the economic foundations of great-power strength was heightened by Paul Kennedy's (1987) widely read comparative historical analysis *The Rise and Fall of the Great Powers*:

> Although the United States is at present still in a class of its own economically and perhaps even militarily, it cannot avoid confronting the two great tests which challenge the longevity of every major power that occupies the 'number one' position in world affairs: whether it can preserve a reasonable balance between the nation's perceived defense requirements and the means it possesses to maintain those commitments; and whether . . . it can preserve the technological and

---

1. Contrasting conclusions about the alleged decline of American hegemony are presented in Burman (1991), Kennedy (1987 and 1993b), Lepgold (1990), Nau (1990), Rosecrance (1990), Russett (1985), and Strange (1987). Much of the debate is clouded by differences over conceptualization and measurement. As Samuel Huntington (1988–1989: 84) sees it: "If 'hegemony' means having 40 percent or more of world economic activity . . . American hegemony disappeared long ago. If hegemony means producing 20 to 25 percent of the world product and twice as much as any individual country, American hegemony looks quite secure."

BOX 8.2
THE UNITED STATES: A HEGEMON IN DECLINE?

Portents of Decline

"The decline, and ultimately the fall, of the American Empire is the basic political fact of the present period in world history."
—Walter Russell Mead (1987: 10)

"If security concerns continue to decline in importance, the bargaining power of the United States . . . will steadily decrease. . . . Even a dominant economic power like the United States finds that its fate is increasingly in the hands of others."
—Charles William Maynes (1993: 20, 22)

"In statistical economic terms . . . the picture is unequivocal. The USA has experienced a relative decline and this has been accentuated by the concomitant loss of its hegemonic privileges in the world financial system."
—Stephen Burman (1991: 71)

"From every standpoint the United States confronts a unique challenge. . . . Beginning in the 1990s and for the first time in their history, Americans face a gloomier economic prospect than did their parents. . . . Overall, it appears that the American dream of unfolding opportunity is being transformed into one of shrinking horizons."
—Richard Rosecrance (1990: 7)

"We're weak in the world."
—Bill Clinton (cited in Levinson, 1992: 44)

Portents of Continuing Primacy

"[The United States is the] one first-rate power [with] no prospect in the immediate future of any power to rival it. . . . It is the only country with the military, diplomatic, political, and economic assets to be a decisive player in any conflict in whatever part of the world it chooses to involve itself."
—Charles Krauthammer (1991: 24)

"U.S. based companies are competitive, even triumphant, in several sectors with a 'future.' The Americans have overcome rivals both blessed and cursed with more active government involvement in their affairs. . . ."
—Tim W. Ferguson (1993: A15)

"Far from becoming a geopolitical dinosaur, [the United States is] uniquely placed to point the way toward a better world order."
—Chester A. Crocker (1993: 23)

"American power does not represent just another cycle in the rise and fall of great powers. . . . America's purposes are more widely shared in the world today than they were in 1947 or 1967. Accordingly, to influence this world, America does not need as much power as it did 20 or 40 years ago. It can maintain its leadership by being more of a global pope than a global power, supporting basic political values . . . less by its military legions than by its diplomacy and domestic example."
—Henry R. Nau (1990: 5, 11)

economic bases of its power from relative erosion in the face of ever-shifting patterns of global production. (Kennedy, 1987: 514–515)

Indeed, the rise of the United States to great-power status can be attributed to the principle that economic growth is a primary determinant of political status. "The basis of the American Empire after 1945 was economic. The military might that seems so awesome [was] not the result of superior valor or intelligence, but of wealth. America rose to power not because it overpowered the rest of the world, but because the rest of the world exhausted itself" (Mead, 1987: 54). In the long run, economic strength has proven the most influential source of a great power's rise to military and political prominence, and economic weakness has been a potent cause of its decline.[2] This principle was emphasized by Bill Clinton in his race for the presidency: "We cannot choose," he said, "between international engagement and domestic reconstruction. These are two sides of the same coin" (cited in Brademas, 1992: 10).

The importance of the economic dimension of national power speaks to the widespread concern about an uncomfortable statistic: America's economic position relative to others, as measured by its proportion of world domestic product, has steadily eroded since its zenith at the end of World War II (see Figure 8.1). Should this and several other troubling social trends continue, they will constrain the leadership role of the United States in world affairs, inhibiting America's capacity to exercise influence as a new multipolar world takes shape. As a recent study by the Brookings Institution concluded, the United States is faltering: "Beneficiary for decades of a system of free trade, it now quakes before economic competition" (Aaron, 1990: 1). "An American collapse to second-rank status will not be for foreign but for domestic reasons . . . [including] America's low savings rate, poor educational system, stagnant productivity, and declining work habits" (Krauthammer, 1991: 26). "The enemy is not at the gate," warns William Hyland (1991: 6); "it may already be inside."

The security system of the next century is likely to rest on economic foundations, and here the United States is unprepared (Sandholtz et al., 1992). "Both necessarily and by inclination, a focus on and expansion of the U.S. economy will be the basis for much foreign policy decisionmaking" (Howell, 1993: 45). With communism dead, the game of great-power competition now centers on rivalries of capitalists versus capitalists and their race to become a role model.

The rise of economic rivals to the United States bodes more than a long-run reduction of U.S. political influence in the world. The diffusion of wealth also promises to intensify great-power political competition. Throughout modern history hegemonic powers achieved their prominent positions because they

---

2. Jean-Baptiste Colbert, the chief minister of King Louis XIV of France during the late seventeenth century, stressed the connection between economic and military power. Paraphrasing Cicero, he remarked that "trade is the source of finance and finance is the vital nerve of war" (cited in Moravcsik, 1992: 27).

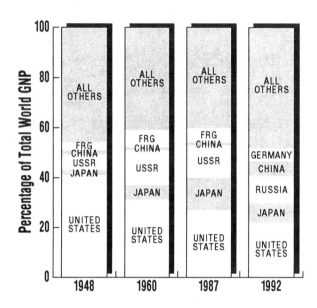

FIGURE 8.1. The Rise and Fall of the Great Powers' Financial Fortunes. *Sources:* Sivard (1991: 51–52); Van Evera (1992b); *The Economist,* May 15, 1993, p. 83.

were strong financially, and their economic resources were the means by which they acquired military muscle. "The sinews of war," remarked one eighteenth-century commentator, "depend more on gold than on steel" (cited in Mor-avcsik, 1992: 27). When economic power spreads to other countries, the diffusion of military and political power is not far behind. Wealth confers an ability to control others in ways that the mere possession of military power does not. Changes in comparative *economic* advantage presage long-term changes in comparative *political* advantage.

This historical pattern is fundamental to understanding the geostrategic landscape of a new multipolar system. "In the race ahead, one of the three great economic powers is apt to pull ahead of the other two. . . . Whichever pulls ahead is apt to stay ahead" (Lester Thurow, cited in Levinson, 1992: 44). To the extent that the United States finds itself on the verge of being surpassed by Germany, Japan, or China political and even military rivalry can be expected to follow. In short, support for free trade will most likely decline with the onset of multipolarity (Gowa, 1989).

Does Military Muscle Still Matter?

As important as economic growth is for obtaining and retaining great-power status, when competition has turned to conflict it has been military power that has mattered most. Because economic rivalry can lead to war, great powers throughout history have found it prudent to use their wealth to prepare for war. Indeed, leaders in Washington, Moscow, Tokyo, Beijing, Brussels, and Berlin continue to ascribe great importance to military force; and, as in previous multipolar periods, they operate from the realpolitik conviction that military might is necessary for defense, influence, and status.

With the collapse of the Soviet Union, the United States holds a position of military supremacy. Yet this does not automatically mean that the United States can get its way in world affairs. "In plain terms, America can no longer do whatever it wants even if it is the only superpower" (Hyland, 1993: 27). The power to destroy does not necessarily translate into a power to persuade. "Military prowess is a poor predictor of the outcomes in the economic and transnational layers of current world politics. The United States is better placed with a more diversified portfolio of power resources than any other country, but the new world order will not be an era of American hegemony" (Nye, 1992b: 88). What we see unfolding before our eyes is the high probability of not just the emergence of a new multipolar phase of history, but also the advent of a system in which traditional ways of thinking about power have changed.

Rising Rivals?

In thinking about the future of the United States and the other great powers, it would be well to heed the following advice regarding the ephemeral character of empires:

> When discussing the rise and fall of empires, it is as well to mark closely their rate of growth, avoiding the temptation to telescope time and discover too early signs of greatness in a state which we know will one day be great, or to predict too early the collapse of an empire which we know will one day cease to be. The life-span of empires cannot be plotted by events, only by careful diagnosis and auscultation— and as in medicine there is always room for error. (Braudel, 1973: 66)

As discussed in Chapter 1, the key to minimizing error when predicting the character of a new distribution of power is to remember that power is *relative*. The absolute economic or military power of a state is meaningless by itself; it only has relevance in relation to the power of the other states with which it must contend. Thus, the shape of a twenty-first century multipolar system will be determined by the trends within each major state relative to the others, as well as by the changes in the international environment that collectively influence the capacity of every great power to exploit its sources of power.

Even though it is not clear which distribution of power will develop as the national attributes of the major contenders undergo change, it is clear that disparities in capabilities (see Tables 8.1 and 8.2) will eventually separate the ascending (Germany, Japan, and China) and descending (Russia) rivals relative to the

TABLE 8.1

Profiling the Great-Power Hierarchy, 1992: The Resources, World Rank, and Share of Global-Power Resources of the Major Contenders

	United States	Russia	Japan	Germany[a]	European Community	China
Size						
Population (in millions 1990)	249.2	147.4	123.51	77.6	327.6	1,139.1
(World rank)	(4)	(7)	(8)	(12)		(1)
Territory (sq km)	9,372,614	17,075,400	377,708	357,039	2,253,720.7	9,561,000
(World rank)	(4)	(1)	(60)	(61)	(13)	(3)
Wealth						
GDP (1992 $ in billions)	5,446	1,466[b]	3,141	1,486	5,089.4[c]	416
(World rank)	(1)	(3)	(2)	(4)		(10)
GDP/capita (1992 $)	21,700	4,003[b]	25,430	19,530	14,243[c]	370
(World rank)	(9)	(45)	(5)	(13)		(123)
Total industrial output (1987 $ in billions)	1,495	485[b]	1,156	495		201
(World rank)	(1)	(4)	(2)	(3)		(8)
Total exports (1992 $ in billions, fob)	393	109.2[b]	280.4	396.7	1,125.9	61.3
% of world total	12.5%	3.6%	7.9%	11.2%	37%	1.4%
(World rank)	(1)	(10)	(3)	(2)		(19)

Military Might

	(1)	(2)	(3)	(4)	(5)	(6)
Nuclear arsenals						
ICBMs deployed	2,370	5,575[b]				
SLBMs deployed	3,840	2,696[b]				
# of warheads (1992)						175
1989 Military expenditures ($ in thousands)	304,000[b]		28,410	33,600	149,985	22,330
(World rank)	(1)		(6)	(5)		(7)
Personnel 1991 (in thousands)	3,700[b]		247	503	2,702	3,903
(World rank)	(2)		(27)	(14)		(1)
1989 Military expenditures ($ in thousands)	304,000					
(World rank)	(2)					
Personnel 1991 (in thousands)	2,241					
(World rank)	(3)					

Sources: U.S. Arms Control and Disarmament Agency (1992), World Bank (1993), *The Economist* (1992), *Basic Statistics of the European Community* (1991), *1989 International Trade Statistics Yearbook*, the Arms Control Association.

[a] Figures are for the Federal Republic of Germany.
[b] Figures are for the Commonwealth of Independent States.
[c] Figures are for 1989.

TABLE 8.2

A Distribution of Power in Transition? Trends in the Relative Power of the Strongest Players*

Source of Power	United States	Russia	European Community	Germany	Japan	China
Tangible						
Basic resources	Strong	Strong	Strong	Strong	Medium	Strong
Military	Strong	Strong	Medium	Weak	Medium	Medium
Economic	Medium	Weak	Strong	Strong	Strong	Strong
Science/technology/education	Strong	Strong	Strong	Strong	Strong	Weak
Population/territorial size	Strong	Strong	Strong	Weak	Weak	Strong
Intangible						
National cohesion	Strong	Weak	Weak	Strong	Strong	Weak
Domestic stability	Medium	Weak	Strong	Medium	Strong	Weak
International prestige	Strong	Weak	Strong	Medium	Medium	Medium
Support of allies	Medium	Medium	Medium	Medium	Weak	Weak

Source: Categorizations modified from typology suggested by Joseph S. Nye, Jr., *Bound to Lead: The Changing Nature of American Power* (New York: Basic Books, 1990), p. 174.

United States. If prevailing trends persist (see Kennedy, 1993b, for a comprehensive comparison), the gap between the great powers in the next century is likely to narrow, and a truly multipolar system composed of five or six approximately equal centers of power will emerge. The world will pass through a fundamental restructuring or redistribution of global power and create an environment in which the rules for world competition will be fundamentally altered.

Table 8.3 lists the most noteworthy global trends that will modify the environment in which these rising and falling great powers will interact. Many countervailing integrative and disintegrative processes are currently unfolding, each of which will pull the great powers into different kinds of relationships,

TABLE 8.3
Stability in a Multipolar System? Forecasting Some Conditioning Trends

Stabilizing Developments	Problematic Developments	Destabilizing Developments
■ Increasingly restrictive normative culture	■ Dispersion of military capabilities	■ Accelerating pace of change
■ Prohibition of war	■ Binding nature of agreements	■ Collapsing clarity of spheres of influence
■ Inviolability of national borders	■ Fragility of fledgling democracies	■ Lack of buffer states around Russia
■ Expansion of capitalism throughout the entire world economy	■ Lack of guarantees of rights of national minorities	■ Horizontal proliferation of weapons to new states
■ Acceleration of democratization	■ Cohesion of alliances	■ Vertical weapons proliferation if nuclear powers expand their existing arsenals
■ Rising support for United Nations	■ Absence of great-power ideological consensus	■ Expanding arms trade
■ Progress toward arms control and disarmament agreements	■ Political unification of Europe	■ Chronic domestic instability
■ Growth of regimes to protect the environment and regulate transnationally dispersed disease	■ Membership and stability of great-power hierarchy	■ Religious and cultural clash of civilizations
■ Instantaneous great-power communication	■ Response to power transitions	■ Rise of hypernationalist-driven separatist revolts and civil wars
	■ Intensifying interdependence	■ Potential fragmentation of Russia and/or return of praetorian practices with failure of democratic reforms
		■ Emergence of trade blocs
		■ Rise of protective barriers to trade
		■ Widening gap between North and South

some cooperative and some conflictual. These processes will shape the range of great-power choice and, in turn, affect the *type* of multipolar system that develops.

SETTING U.S. PRIORITIES

Having claimed credit for "winning" the Cold War, U.S. policymakers now confront the equally daunting task of managing the peace. Out of the crucible of a bloodless but triumphant war has come disillusionment. Building constructive relations among all the emerging great powers is a formidable challenge, one that is exacerbated by the simultaneous existence of military and economic competition. Because the issues and the hierarchy of power are different on each of these playing fields, solutions on one level are likely to pose problems on the other, and vice versa. Policy coordination is further complicated by the probability that America's military allies may be its most contentious economic competitors. This, in fact, may best explain why "Clinton's America gives the impression of pursuing multilateralism in security and political matters while increasingly pursuing unilateralism in economic and trade matters" (Hoagland, 1993: 14A). All told, U.S. decision makers must calibrate their foreign policies in an environment where "permanent interests are less clearly defined and more difficult to discern" (James Schlesinger, 1993: 27).

Given this challenge, in which direction might the United States turn? No strict guidelines yet discipline the strategy and tactics in such a two-level game because the post–World War II foreign policy consensus about America's global purpose in the world has splintered (see Wittkopf, 1990), and there exists no singular threat around which the American people can rivet their attention and allocate their support. Bereft of a shared vision, U.S. leaders are intellectually unarmed, with no simple organizing principle on hand to structure their foreign-policy initiatives.

Classifying the Range of American Choices

As in 1823 when the Monroe Doctrine sought to position U.S. foreign policy toward the post–Napoleonic European balance-of-power system, so today the United States must define the kind of role it will play in the fluid, uncertain environment of multipolarity. The questions, then as now, revolve around whether the United States should be involved in matters that lie beyond its borders and, if so, to what extent.

At present, "The United States has no broad international strategy. Rather, it pursues a collection of policies; some are left over from the Cold War, and some are relatively new" (Hyland, 1993: 25). U.S. policymakers are likely to set priorities and attempt to craft a coherent policy by pursuing a strategy that

- promotes American power, position, and primacy in order to enhance the capacity of the United States to exercise influence abroad;
- preserves global stability in order to foster a free market environment conducive to prosperity and the realization of American economic interests;
- advances the core liberal principles of democracy, human rights, and international law;
- provides a security arrangement that encourages arms reduction, inhibits rearmament, and reduces the risks of accidental war; and
- establishes a crisis-prevention regime to lower the chances that diplomatic crises will inflame smoldering interstate rivalries and internal rebellions.

In crafting such a policy, U.S. policymakers will have to choose from the same four strategies that have been available throughout history to all great powers: (1) unilateralism, (2) cultivation of specialized alliance relationships, and multilateralism through either (3) a great-power concert or (4) a general collective security system. Unfortunately, no single strategy will provide the United States with a universally applicable course of action (Kennedy, 1987: 540). Because it is not altogether clear where America's interests lie, each of these four strategies receives both support and criticism (see Box 8.3). The costs and benefits of each strategy vary, and these variations will drive the United States from pursuit of primacy to pursuit of collective action and back again, as global circumstances change. Our focus in this chapter is on the first strategy, unilateralism.

Predicting the U.S. posture toward a new multipolar period of history is difficult. Like a pendulum, historically U.S. policy has swung periodically between internationalism and isolationism, and between cold, calculated power politics and moral idealism. For example, withdrawal from participation in world affairs, accompanied by a wave of idealistic fervor, took root after the First World War; but after the Second World War, isolationism was repudiated in favor of a global foreign policy inspired by realpolitik efforts to expand American power and influence and to assume responsibility for management of world order (Ambrose, 1992).

With the end of the Cold War, three schools of thought have begun vying to define America's role in world affairs:

> Neo-isolationists want the U.S. to deal only with threats to America's physical security, political independence, and domestic liberty. They find no such threats at present, and therefore argue that the U.S. should let other powers, and regional balances of power, take care of all the world's woes. Realists such as Henry Kissinger want the U.S. to continue to be the holder of the world balance of power, the arbiter of the main regional power groups, and the watchdog against all potential imperialistic trouble-makers. Internationalists want a greater role for multilateral institutions and more emphasis on human needs and rights, the environment and democracy. (Hoffmann, 1992b: 59)

BOX 8.3
THE UNITED STATES AND GLOBAL STABILITY:
WHICH PATHWAY?

Unilateralism

"The United States has the financial strength to sustain *individual* strands of a unilateralist and activist foreign policy. . . . However, the United States cannot afford to implement an activist policy in multiple regions on multiple issues. A continuation of the unilateralist policies of the Reagan years would accentuate relative American economic decline. Simply put, maintaining the major elements of traditional postwar policies while adding new clients and new missions may be beyond the means of the United States."

—Kenneth A. Oye (1992: 26–27)

"Unilateral measures are downright perilous. The United States cannot altogether rule out the use of threats and tit-for-tat in its efforts to open up foreign markets, but it must also recognize . . . that any unsubtle or extensive use of threats is likely to produce bitter reactions, hurtful to all parties involved."

—Raymond Vernon and Debra Spar (1989: 189)

"With benign intent, the United States has behaved, and until it is brought into a semblance of balance, will continue to behave in ways that annoy and frighten others."

—Kenneth N. Waltz (1991a: 669)

"In the post–Cold War security environment, even though we strongly prefer to act collectively with other nations to respond to security challenges, the United States must be prepared to defend its critical interests unilaterally if necessary."

—U.S. Secretary of Defense Dick Cheney (1993: 1)

"The issue is whether the United States under Bill Clinton is prepared to behave like what it is, namely, the only superpower in the world—not impulsively or aggressively, but not passively or Panglossianly either."

—*The New Republic* (January 18, 1993: 7)

Specialized Relationships

"Most foreign policy concerns could be handled locally and regionally, rather than globally. . . . Future aggression . . . will be best met by the neighboring states that understand the issues and have the most at stake."

—Doug Bandow (1992–1993: 173)

(continued)

BOX 8.3
(CONTINUED)

"[In 1989] overnight the Bush administration switched Germany for England as its 'special relationship' in Europe. . . . The alacrity of the American response can be explained only by a trilateral logic in which the United States embraces unified Germany only to constrain it and cooperates with Japan only to corral it in order to ensure that the United States remains *primus inter pares* in a new world having three poles: Washington, Berlin, and Tokyo."

—Bruce Cumings (1993: 20)

"The new international order will see many centers of power. . . . History so far has shown us only two roads to international stability: domination or equilibrium. We do not have the resources for domination, nor is such a course compatible with [U.S.] values. So we are brought back to a concept maligned in much of America's intellectual history—the balance of power."

—Henry A. Kissinger (1992: 239)

Concert

"The smaller the number of great powers, and the wider the disparities between the few most powerful states and the many others, the more likely the former are to act for the sake of the system and to participate in the management of, or interfere in the affairs of, lesser states."

—Kenneth N. Waltz (1979: 198)

"Military guarantees and alliances in 1939 did not deter war; again, they merely dragged unwilling participants into it. . . . A central coalition [of great powers] would be a much cheaper international regulatory device than either an inefficient and dilatory balance of power, or an expensive deterrence."

—Richard Rosecrance (1992: 67–68, 82)

"The ending of the Cold War has created a vacuum. This can be filled either by the UN or by self-appointed great powers. . . . [Instead] of building walls between peoples of countries, we must build bridges, firmly based on the bedrock of cooperation. . . ."

—Ingvar Carlsson (1992: 7)

Collective Security

"Multilateral action holds promise as never before. . . . There exists an opportunity to reinvent the institutions of collective security."

—Bill Clinton, 1992 (cited in Brooks, 1992: A12)

"Collective security has to be built brick by crumbling brick at the United Nations and in regional organizations. Competent international staffs like

(continued)

BOX 8.3
(CONTINUED)

NATO's have to be developed. Countries will have to earmark forces for joint action and train them together. They must also be able to take hard decisions together—or suffer the consequences. After a transition period, collective security must be truly collective."

—Leslie H. Gelb (1993a: 12A)

"The ambivalence of the United States and other major powers toward the United Nations as an instrument of collective security is reflected in the inadequacy of the tools they have given it for the task. The world organization—like its regional counterparts—simply lacks the military capacities and financial wherewithal to do its job."

—Edward C. Luck (1992–1993: 149)

Within each school of thought about America's future world role are additional cleavages. To understand the direction U.S. policy might take as policymakers redefine America's interests and assess its capabilities, we must begin by describing the divergent paths that can be followed under the guise of "going it alone."

Unilateralism represents an effort to capture a measure of independence in foreign affairs. As a general posture, it reflects a preference for autonomy in contrast to a willingness to cast one's fate with others, either through selective alliances or through multilateral institutions. Assertively self-reliant, unilateralism requires sufficient power to act without the assistance of others.

In practice, unilateralism has several faces. Each represents a different approach to maximizing one's decision-making latitude and minimizing dependence on other states. The first of these approaches is isolationism.

Isolationism

Within the American diplomatic experience, withdrawal from involvements overseas has been common. Enthusiasm for isolationism often has arisen when foreign commitments have proven costly and dangerous. At these times, a mood against interventionism and entangling alliances has surfaced, often inspired by a desire to protect American values from the sinful ways of an allegedly evil world. But isolationists have also gained converts when external threats were perceived to be low and the American populace felt secure enough to conclude that a retreat from the burdens of global activism would allow the country to attend to pressing domestic matters. The *America First* lobby's advocacy of neutrality toward Hitler's bid for control of Europe exemplified the former attitude while the isolationist sentiment that arose after World War I reflected the latter set of beliefs.

For the United States today, isolationism retains some appeal. The absence of a threat from the Soviet Union, or from an international communist movement, has reduced anxieties about external dangers and, to some segments of American opinion, made a reduction of the scale of U.S. commitments abroad and a focus on internal problems the appropriate response to the post–Cold War world. Conflict abroad, it is argued, would "best be met by the neighboring states that understand the issues and have the most at stake" (Bandow, 1992–1993: 173).

However tempting, a new cycle of isolationist withdrawal in the late 1900s appears unlikely. The future threatens to be disorderly: Regional conflict and ethnonationalistic warfare rage on nearly every continent. Moreover, the U.S. economy is tied to the financial fates of its trading partners at unprecedented levels. The sentiments expressed in Box 8.4 are indicative of the waning enthusiasm for a broad-based retreat of U.S. presence from world affairs, as it would imperil American interests in containing localized warfare and terrorism, halting nuclear proliferation, and promoting reforms in the former Soviet Union. Because these dangers are widely recognized, no mandate for isolationism has materialized. Clinton's Deputy National Security Adviser Sandy Berger correctly observed that because "it's a chaotic world . . . American leadership is not only unquestioned but actively desired by many countries" (cited in McAllister, 1993: 20).

There are strong incentives for U.S. policymakers to accept the advice President Bush offered in his valedictory foreign policy address on December 15, 1992. Bush urged Americans to reject isolationist calls to turn inward and warned that U.S. political, economic, and security interests would suffer if the United States failed to lead the world community in combating ethnic conflict, instability, and poverty: "A retreat from American leadership, from American involvement, would be a mistake for which future generations, indeed our own children, would pay dearly." Calling on the nation to remain "secure in its military, moral and economic strength," he declared, "Our choice as a people is simple: We can either shape our times, or they can shape us" (*New York Times*, December 16, 1992: A1, C18). As he elaborated at his West Point address in January 1993 before leaving office, "Sometimes a great power must act alone" (cited in Safire, 1993a: A8).

This impulse was shared by Bill Clinton, who, in his inaugural address, bemoaned the fact that America had "drifted, and that drifting has eroded our resources, fractured our economy, and shaken our confidence." But, he continued, "we can make change our friend and not our enemy. . . . America must continue to lead. . . . When our vital interests are challenged, or the will and conscience of the international community is defied, we will act—with peaceful diplomacy whenever possible, with force when necessary."

BOX 8.4
RESPONDING TO WANING HEGEMONY:
U.S. LEADERSHIP ASPIRATIONS?

"To back away from commitments is more easily said than done. In practice, the loss in prestige may actually reduce our power more than the reduced claims on our military resources enhances that power. In that may lie the supreme irony. Closing the commitments-power gap may not be possible through reduction of commitments. The United States, as a great power, has essentially taken on the task of sustaining the international order. And any abandonment of commitments is difficult to reconcile with that imposing task. The upshot is that our commitments will remain large and that our military power will remain more modest in relation to those commitments than it has been in the past. This implies a degree of risk that we must acknowledge and accept."

—James Schlesinger (*New York Times*, February 7, 1985: A14)

"History's lesson is clear. When a war-weary America withdrew from the international stage following World War I, the world spawned militarism, fascism, and aggression unchecked, plunging mankind into another devastating conflict. . . . From some quarters we hear voices sounding the retreat. We've carried the burden too long, they say, and the disappearance of the Soviet challenge means that America can withdraw from international responsibilities. . . . But let's be clear. The alternative to American leadership is not more security for our citizens but less. Not the flourishing of American principles but their isolation in a world actually hostile to them."

—George Bush (*New York Times*, December 16, 1992: 18)

"To the traditionalists, it is important that America is present, in Europe, the Pacific, and elsewhere, in order to prevent any return to the anarchic conditions of the 1930s. . . . But acting as a world leader includes the danger of becoming the world's policeman, combatting threats to 'law and order' whenever they arise, and finding ever more 'frontiers of insecurity' across the globe that require protection."

—Paul Kennedy (1993a: 42–43)

"The post-1945 order, by placing the destructive balance of power system of the pre- and inter-war years with a benign American hegemony in which such inter-state rivalry could be kept in check by U.S. power, has given this solution an extended lease on life. The question remains, of course, as to what will happen when this hegemony wanes. . . ."

—Stephen Burman (1991: 15)

Leading among Equals

Like every former hegemon since 1495, the United States is unlikely to accept willingly its descent from top-dog status. It will be inclined to maintain a leadership role, even if this entails being first among equals.

While many people would argue "that the United States should not function as [policeman to the world], almost no one agrees on precisely where the U.S. should work the beat" (Kilpatrick, 1992: 13A). A fine line exists between the aspiration to preserve world order and the aspiration to remake the world in one's self-image. The former is dedicated to managing international affairs for the benefit of the system—to assure that rivalries are subdued without recourse to the use of force, that the global political economy protects the free trade essential to economic growth, and that the rules of international law are respected.

Great powers can also lead in an imperial manner, however, by showing more interest in preserving their dominant position than in preserving peace and disseminating justice. The propensity for some states to seek universal empire is sobering, for it attests to Lord Acton's maxim that power corrupts and absolute power corrupts absolutely. From this perspective, the idea of a new world order may be "no more than a euphemism for a *pax americana*" (Burman, 1991: 188), especially if it invents "imperial alibis" (Shalom, 1993) to rationalize U.S. interventionism against tyrants and terrorists. Not even democratic powers are immune from interventionism, as John Quincy Adams warned in 1821 when he pleaded that the United States "not go abroad in search of monsters to destroy"; indeed, democracies may be especially driven by an interventionist impulse (Stedman, 1993; Doyle, 1995).

But today America looks more imperiled than imperial, unable to lead the way it once could. Its economic resources relative to the other ascending powers have declined, and should this decline persist, it portends a continuing reduction of American political clout on the world stage and a concomitant reluctance to engage in assertive interventionism to project U.S. power, promote democracy, or punish aggressors.

Yet, declining hegemons have rarely accepted their demise gracefully. Imperial Spain provides an example:

> At a time when the face of Europe was altering more rapidly than ever before, the country that had once been its leading power proved to be lacking the essential ingredient for survival—the willingness to change. . . . The ruling class of seventeenth-century Spain was too hidebound, too traditional in its attitudes and values, to adjust to the realities of a declining power. But this raises a question that goes beyond the history of Spain—a question implied . . . in those words . . . *managing decline*. How can, and should, a great power "manage decline"? (Elliott, 1991: 87–88)

That, indeed, is the question for the United States. It can lead, but not indefinitely. If history has any relevance to America's contemporary circumstances, it tells us that "hegemons typically expand more readily than they retrench" (Lepgold, 1990: 45), and when they do retreat they often engage in symbolic but self-destructive acts of intervention, a form of exhibitionism that accelerates rather than inhibits their fall (Kennedy, 1987; Hoagland, 1992). As Henry A. Kissinger frequently preached when he was U.S. secretary of state, the question was (and is) not whether the U.S. position in the great-power hierarchy would erode, but whether the United States could retard the pace of its relative decline and accommodate itself to the reality of eroding power. This dilemma helps to explain the ostensible (see Box 8.5) U.S. difficulty in defining its global mission in order to balance the quest for primacy with the need to work in conjunction with other great powers as equals.[3] President Clinton disclosed that "he grasped the dilemma when he told diplomats in one breath that he would strive 'to resolve contentious disputes and to meet the challenges of the next century,' and in the next that 'America cannot and should not bear the world's burdens alone'" (Gelb, 1993a: 12A).

How might the United States, if its relative standing continues to decline, avoid the fate to which Spain, Portugal, the Netherlands, and Great Britain all succumbed? The history of previous great powers suggests that neither isolationism nor the pursuit of hegemonic primacy are viable paths, despite their occasional triumphal moments. Between these extremes, however, lies a third unilateral avenue—standing independent, shouldering heavy burdens when necessary to deter aggression, and playing an equilibrating role in the balance-of-power process that has characterized previous periods of multipolarity.

Balancer

If the U.S. position in the great-power hierarchy continues to decline relative to others, its leadership capacity will be compromised. While the United States is not likely to be marginalized, and will operate for many decades from a strong position, others will challenge its leadership. This challenge, moreover, might not only be assertive—it could become, under strained conditions, combative.

Should a truly multipolar world develop, it is difficult to foresee how each great power's relationship with the others will evolve. Realignments are to be expected. With the probable expansion of the number of great powers to five

---

3. Symptomatic of the U.S. ambivalence in striking a balance between the need to project a military "forward presence" and honor U.S. commitments around the world on the one hand and the need to implement deep cuts in defense spending and invest in domestic economic recovery on the other was the Clinton administration's initial struggle to formulate a military strategy. The first plan proposed was referred to as "win-hold-win" because it sought to scale back America's armed forces to the level where they could no longer win two major wars at once. It in part reflected Undersecretary of State Peter Tarnoff's contention that the United States no longer possessed the necessary resources to intervene in trouble spots around the world. But in June 1993 the administration retreated from this proposal, which arguably would have greatly compromised America's role as a superpower. Instead, the Pentagon adopted a policy that would seek to retain the U.S. capacity to fight and win two major wars at once and, in so doing, to preserve the unilateral ability of a predominant power to deter aggression and respond to regional crises around the globe.

BOX 8.5
CHANGING U.S. MILITARY GOALS AND OBJECTIVES: SELECTIONS FROM TWO PENTAGON PLANNING DOCUMENTS ON POST–COLD WAR STRATEGY

Unilateral Approach (February 18, 1992)	Collective Approach (April 16, 1992)
"Our first objective is to prevent the re-emergence of a new rival, either on the territory of the former Soviet Union or elsewhere, that poses a threat on the order of that posed formerly by the Soviet Union. This is a dominant consideration underlying the new regional defense strategy and requires that we endeavor to prevent any hostile power from dominating a region whose resources would, under consolidated control, be sufficient to generate global power."	"Our most fundamental goal is to deter or defeat attack from whatever source. . . . The second goal is to strengthen and extend the system of defense arrangements that binds democratic and like-minded nations together in common defense against aggression, build habits of cooperation, avoid the renationalization of security at lower costs and with lower risks for all. Our preference for a collective response to preclude threats or, if necessary, to deal with them is a key feature of our regional defense strategy. The third goal is to preclude any hostile power from dominating a region critical to our interests, and also thereby to strengthen the barriers against the re-emergence of a global threat to the interests of the U.S. and our allies."

Source: Patrick J. Tyler, "Pentagon Drops Goal of Blocking New Superpowers," *The New York Times* (May 24, 1992), p. 14.

(and, less likely, six if other powers materialize), new cleavages will emerge and international enmity will expand as jockeying for privilege, position, and power unfolds. Indeed, a world comprised of five or more independent and approximately equal centers of power creates an enlarged global chessboard of perhaps 15 dyadic relationships—a congested landscape fraught with great potential for conflict and much confusion about the identity of friends and foes. To make the setting even more confusing, the interplay is likely to take place simultaneously on two playing fields, the first economic and the second military.

In this altered strategic setting, it could become increasingly attractive for the United States to perform the role of a "balancer," such as that played by Great Britain in various multipolar periods since the seventeenth century. Such a role would allow the United States to contribute to the maintenance of peace by joining a blocking coalition aimed at anyone threatening domination, without necessarily committing itself to the defense of any particular state.[4] This type of response represents an altogether different dimension of unilateralism than that represented by either isolationism or attempts at resurrecting hegemonic leadership. It calls for engagement, not withdrawal, but preserves the flexibility of alignment prized by great powers whenever conditions of multipolarity have materialized. It accepts a measure of responsibility for expanding the zone of order around the globe, but resists the urge to rely on "ad hoc, unilateral U.S. actions, no matter how forceful the decision or masterful the execution" (Crocker, 1993: 23). As Michael Sheehan (1989: 124) has written, a balancer "acts as a kind of safety net," generally remaining aloof from contentious issues but ever willing to shift its weight from one side of a serious dispute to another, supporting the weaker with its marginal disposable power. As a keeper of the balance, the United States would be required "to conduct foreign policy as other nations have had to conduct foreign policy throughout their history" (Henry Kissinger, cited in Melloan, 1993: A17), responding to shifts in power, not someone's ideological orientation.

Still, we must be cautious about the capacity of the United States to perform the role of a balancer, since that role requires qualities of moderation, wisdom, and self-restraint that are rare and difficult to sustain in world politics (Organski, 1968: 288). Beyond this problem, there remain the potential dangers of a return to a full-fledged balance-of-power system of counterpoised alliances. True, as Richard M. Nixon postulated in 1971, it may become "a better and safer world if we have a strong healthy United States, Europe, [a Russian successor to the] Soviet Union, China and Japan, each balancing the other." But the history of previous multipolar systems tells us that such balances of power are precarious at best. In the long run, they have degenerated into two polarized blocs, and these have served as a prelude to general war.

In the final analysis, isolationism, efforts at resurrecting hegemonic leadership, and the role of a balancer do not appear to hold much promise for the United States in a world where power has diffused among several roughly equal great powers. One alternative to acting unilaterally is joining with selected other states in a series of special relationships. In the next chapter we turn our attention toward bilateral partnerships as a possible path to peace in a multipolar future.

---

4. Here, imagine a serious dispute arising between Russia and China. In this circumstance, the United States could step into the breach as a third-party balancer to prevent one side from attempting to dominate the other.

. 9 .

A WORLD OF SPECIAL RELATIONSHIPS?

The old geopolitical order is passing from the scene and a new order is being born. That order is likely to bear little resemblance to the familiar world of the last half of the twentieth century. In the next millennium, humanity's fate will be shaped by a new set of winners and losers.

—JACQUES ATTALI, PRESIDENT OF THE
EUROPEAN BANK FOR RECONSTRUCTION
AND DEVELOPMENT, 1991

As the bipolarity of the Cold War gives way to multipolarity, it is conceivable that we will find ourselves in a world of atomized great powers, each nervously watching the other as they all unilaterally jockey for advantage. Such a system of competitive, insular states was portrayed in the previous chapter, but it is, of course, only one scenario for the future. In this chapter we examine another course of action, that of limited cooperation rather than unilateralism.

Though a few countries may succumb to unilateralism's siren call, it is possible that many will forge bilateral partnerships to attain their foreign policy goals.[1] What impact would these partnerships have on great-power politics in the early twenty-first century? Are the special relationships described in Chapter 7 a promising approach to peace? Or, will they eventually lead us to the least stable forms of multipolarity, those characterized by polarized alliances and a permissive normative order condoning a cavalier attitude toward international commitments and the use of war as an instrument of foreign policy?

---

1. In addition to the possibility that the great powers will attempt to deal with their security concerns by building bilateral partnerships, Carsten Holbraad (1984) suggests that the onset of multipolarity will lead middle powers to bypass international organizations and pursue their interests through special bilateral arrangements as well. This requires, one expert (Hoffmann, 1993b: 59) advises, that we "think harder about a world in which the main danger is no longer an apocalyptic clash between two superpowers, but an epidemic of local chaos. The Cold War seemed to underline the impotence of the small and the weak. The new world begins to look like a sorry and suicidal revenge of the weak."

The purpose of this chapter is to explore these questions. We begin by examining the consequences of Great Britain's bid to enhance national security at the onset of this century by reaching bilateral agreements with several of its rivals. Next, we assess the probability that today's great powers will adopt similar policies, offering some predictions about the consequences that would likely occur if they do. The chapter concludes with a discussion of the limitations of special relationships as a path to peace in a multipolar world with primary focus on the response of the United States, the world's only superpower at the end of the Cold War.

SPECIAL RELATIONSHIPS IN THE PAST

Perhaps the foremost historical example of a great power creating a set of special bilateral relationships to secure peace in a multipolar world was Great Britain at the beginning of the twentieth century. The case illustrates the temptations to which a predominant power is likely to succumb when its leadership is challenged and the dangers that can result when differences in the military strength of the major powers begins to narrow. It is an example that is relevant to the end of the twentieth century, as the power of the United States declines relative to other ascending powers.

British security policy traditionally had two objectives: (1) to maintain maritime supremacy in order to defend the British Isles and protect overseas commercial interests and (2) to prevent any state from achieving hegemonic control over Europe. To achieve the first objective, the British constructed a fleet that was the equal of the next two largest navies. To accomplish the second, British policymakers sought to maintain a balance of power on the Continent. "It has become almost an historical truism," Sir Eyre Crowe (1992: 473) wrote in a 1907 memorandum on British foreign policy, "to identify England's secular policy with the maintenance of this balance by throwing her weight now in this scale and now in that, but ever on the side opposed to the political dictatorship of the strongest single State or group at a given time."

By the close of the nineteenth century, however, Great Britain could not continue its traditional policy of "splendid isolation." It was, in the words of Joseph Chamberlain, the colonial secretary, a "weary Titan." The country faced stiff industrial and commercial competition from powerful rivals whose economies were growing faster than the British economy: "Whereas in 1880 the United Kingdom still contained 22.9 percent of total world manufacturing output, that figure had shrunk to 13.6 percent by 1913; and while its share of world trade was 23.2 percent in 1880, it was only 14.1 percent in 1911–1913" (Kennedy, 1987: 228).

Threats to British interests also loomed on every horizon as London began to find it difficult to afford an empire upon which the sun never set. Disputes had broken out with the United States over the border between Venezuela and

British Guiana, with the Russians over Persia and the borderlands of India, with the French at Fashoda on the upper Nile, and with Germany over southern Africa. If China and the Ottoman Empire continued to disintegrate, additional conflicts would arise. Great Britain was overextended and, as the costly Boer War (1899–1902) demonstrated, the British would either have to resuscitate their capacity to act unilaterally on the world stage or tailor their foreign policy ends to shrinking military and economic means.

One way to maintain the capacity to influence global events was to acquire allies. Although Lord Salisbury, the British prime minister, preferred to retain a "free hand" in foreign affairs and questioned the wisdom of incurring new, burdensome obligations to allies whose strategic value remained in doubt, Colonial Secretary Chamberlain argued that all of the other European great powers had made alliances and that Britain should also. He thus counseled, "As long as we keep outside these alliances, as long as we are envied by all, and as long as we have interests which at one time or another conflict with the interests of all, we are likely to be confronted at any moment with a combination of Great Powers so powerful that not even the most extreme, the most hotheaded politician would be able to contemplate it without a sense of uneasiness" (cited in Joll, 1984: 41).

By going their own way in international affairs, the British found themselves in an increasingly exposed position. Slowly and warily they began taking steps to end their isolation. Among the first steps was a rapprochement with the United States. Under the terms of the 1850 Clayton–Bulwer Treaty, Great Britain and the United States had pledged to exercise joint control over any isthmian canal linking the Atlantic and Pacific oceans through Central America. In what they saw as a major concession to Washington, the British agreed in the Hay–Pauncefote Treaty of 1900 to permit the United States to build and operate such a canal. A year later, in an effort to further improve relations between the two countries, they allowed the United States to fortify the canal. By appeasing the Americans, British policymakers hoped to dampen potential conflict with a rising great power and therein bring overseas commitments into line with available capabilities.

The next step away from isolation occurred in 1902, when Britain signed a treaty of alliance with Japan that was intended to shore up the British position in East Asia and let the Royal Navy deal with challenges elsewhere. Though supported by both the First Lord of the Admiralty and Lord Lansdowne, the foreign secretary, the cabinet entered into the agreement with reservations. The alliance seemed risky; it could entangle Britain in a war that had nothing to do with its vital interests.

Informal security understandings were an alternative to formal military alliances. They could be used to compensate for Britain's thin military coverage in a given geographic area without creating onerous commitments. Foreign policy officials believed that such bilateral arrangements might begin with a relaxation of tensions with a rival (détente) and later blossom into genuine cooperation (entente). Such was the case with the Anglo–French Entente of 1904. This agreement granted freedom of action to France in Morocco and to Britain in Egypt, settled outstanding colonial differences in places as distant as Siam and New Hebrides, and resolved questions concerning fisheries off the coast of Newfoundland. By reconciling these two inveterate rivals, the Entente Cordiale radically transformed the geopolitical landscape of the early twentieth century.

A final step away from isolationism came with the Anglo–Russian convention of 1907. The British, concerned with rising German naval expenditures and Berlin's heavy-handed behavior at the 1906 Algeciras conference on French claims in Morocco, sought to reduce friction with Russia along the central Asian boundaries of their respective empires. The Russians were of the same mind, having recently been defeated by the Japanese at the battle of Mukden and again at Tsushima Strait. As a result of this convergence of interests, Russia recognized a British sphere of influence in the south and east of Persia, and in exchange the British recognized a Russian sphere in the north. Additional agreements were reached on Afghanistan and Tibet.

In sum, the British policy of coping with relative decline in a multipolar world stands in stark contrast to the unsuccessful grand strategy of Spain during the ministry of Don Gaspar de Guzmán, known today as the Count-Duke Olivares. From 1621 until his fall from power 22 years later, Olivares opted "not to reassess and scale down Spain's traditional foreign policy objectives, but to reform and rationalize existing structures in the hope of making those objectives more attainable. Indeed, in any clash between the claims of foreign policy and the availability of resources, the predisposition was to assume that the international emergency was too great to be shirked, and that somehow or other the resources would be found" (Elliott, 1991: 96). Conversely, when the British confronted a similar situation four centuries later, they relied on a set of bilateral security arrangements with some of their long-standing great-power adversaries to prevent foreign policy commitments from outrunning resources. "At the summit," Winston Churchill would later write, "true politics and strategy are one. The maneuver which brings an ally into the field is as serviceable as that which wins a great battle. The maneuver which gains an important strategic point may be less valuable than that which placates or overawes a dangerous neutral" (cited in Cohen, 1991: 44).

Historians have yet to resolve whether Britain's effort to accommodate itself to an eroding position in the great-power hierarchy through the cultivation of special bilateral relationships postponed the outbreak of World War I or increased its probability by contributing to German fears of encirclement. In either case, most historians agree that early in the twentieth century, the great powers gravitated toward one or the other of two opposed blocs and that this became the tinderbox from which the first truly "world" war ignited. This experience thus leads us to be cautious about special relationships as a strategy for avoiding another great-power war in a multipolar twenty-first century.

SPECIAL RELATIONSHIPS IN THE FUTURE

What are the prospects at the beginning of the next century for the great powers to pursue foreign policies based on special bilateral relationships? Some observers already see a tendency toward "bilateralization" in the high politics of security (Gärtner, 1992). Is it likely that this tendency will continue? And, if so, what are the most probable combinations among the great powers?

Like Great Britain's posture at the end of the last century, the position of the United States, "though still unrivalled, has already begun eroding" (Zakaria, 1992–1993: 27). When shifts in the rankings of the great powers occur, realignments follow. Special bilateral security arrangements are attractive because they inject a modicum of predictability into the atomized dynamics of balance-of-power politics where any alignment is equally probable.

In the nascent multipolar system of the early twenty-first century, it will be exceedingly difficult to define the cleavages and coalitions that might arise. Alignments are likely to depend on the specific issue under consideration, with combinations of like-minded nations in one issue-area (for example, trade policies) being quite different from those in other issue-areas (such as military security). The very nature of multipolarity will encourage the United States to shift its support as interests and power ratios change and "to concentrate on the capabilities of [its] armed forces to meet a host of threats and not on a single threat" (Powell, 1992–1993: 40). Though as many as five great powers may exist (alongside a sixth power center if one includes a country like India), realignments spawned by any dramatic shifts in the rankings of these powers will revolve around the strongest actor, the United States (see Figure 9.1). Such

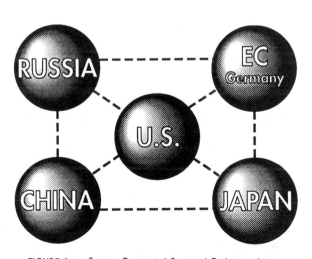

FIGURE 9.1. Some Potential Special Relationships.

a central position thus makes any U.S. effort to participate in special bilateral relationships critical to the stability of the entire international system.

Multipolar politics are even more complex and uncertain when the interplay of military and economic factors in the perceived rankings of the great powers is considered.

> A profound disparity already has defined itself between the strategic rank-order of the major powers and their economic rank-order. The strategic hierarchy for a six-power central balance would still read: the United States, Russia . . . , the European Community (or European Confederation), China, India, and Japan. The economic hierarchy would read: the European Community or Confederation (which by mid-decade may be at least 30 percent larger than the United States), the United States, Japan (by then about 70 percent the size of the U.S.), then possibly China, with India and [Russia] bringing up the rear. (Bell, 1990–1991: 38)

Simply put, the contemporary distribution of power in world politics may be said to resemble a layer cake. "The top military layer is largely unipolar, for there is no other military power comparable to the United States. The economic middle layer is tripolar [Europe, Japan, and the United States account for two-thirds of the world's product] and has been for two decades. The bottom layer of transnational interdependence shows a diffusion of power" (Nye, 1992b: 88). In this environment there are neither the stark simplicities nor the self-evident symmetries of a bipolar system, and therefore any effort to define *a priori* the kinds of partnerships that will develop is problematic. "The coming era," summarizes Robert Jervis (1992: 258), "seems odd because it is hard to locate a main axis of conflict."

Yet some clues to the immediate future can be found in emerging trends. Table 9.1 provides a matrix of bilateral great-power relationships that could appear at the turn of the century and advances some predictions about the probability of eventual conflict between any pair of actors. The likely trajectories in *economic conflict* are given in the upper-right-hand portion of the diagonal, and those in *military alliances* are positioned in the lower-left portion.

These forecasts describe two very different kinds of potential great-power relationships, with the prospect for economic rivalry and conflict generally high along with the likelihood of cross-cutting security alliances. However, inherent tensions appear between the imperatives in each sphere, as the differences in economic and military power may yield inconsistent policy postures and awkward alignments. For example, the United States, Japan, and Europe are expected to experience conflict in their commercial relations, but as liberal democracies (Doyle, 1995; Fukuyama, 1992) to cooperate in their security relations.

To fully depict the problems and prospects for the United States to function as the linchpin in a series of loosely connected special relationships, we will consider in turn each of the possible partnerships that might be formed.

TABLE 9.1
The New Great-Power Chessboard: Some Economic Rivalry and Military Alliance Possibilities

	United States	Japan	Germany	European Community	Russia	China
United States	—	H	H	H	L	M
Japan	H	—	H	H	M	M
Germany	M	L	—	—	M	L
European Community	H	L	—	—	M	L
Russia	M	L	L	M	—	H
China	M	M	L	L	M	—

Note: Lower-left matrix classifies the probability of *military alignment,* whereas upper-right matrix pictures the probability of *economic conflict,* with the symbols H = high, M = medium, and L = low signifying the likely character of the dyadic relationship that may develop in the new millennium.

Europe and the Return of History

The European Community

The passing of bipolarity unleashed two momentous but opposing forces in Europe: "the logic of economics and interdependence that spells community, and the logic of ethnicity and nationality that demands separation" (Joffe, 1992–1993: 43). Recently the forces of separation have superseded those of community; unchecked by the political straitjacket of the Cold War, the xenophobia of yesteryear has returned. From the peaceful divorce of Czechs and Slovaks to threats against minorities in Western Europe to the horrors of "ethnic cleansing" in the Balkans, ethnonationalism once again commands our attention.

Simultaneously, many Europeans have become skeptical about integration. Voters in Denmark rejected the Maastricht Treaty, and those who turned out in France supported it by only a narrow majority. Coupled with the unraveling of the European Monetary System in September 1992 and the inability of the European Community to respond effectively to fighting on its doorstep in Bosnia, the future of European unity appears uncertain. At the moment, " 'Europe' remains a purely economic and bureaucratic construction and shows few signs of becoming a nation" (Hoffmann, 1993a: 31), neither united nor possessive of a sense of confidence (Brenner, 1993; see also Ferguson, 1993).

Functionally, the European Community is not a security but a trade bloc, designed more to make business than to make peace. Some contend that the twenty-first century will belong to Europe because it is advantageously positioned, and because of this "the Europeans will write the rules for world trade and, not surprisingly, they will write rules that favor those who play the game the 'European way'" (Thurow, 1992b: 24). Given its economic advantages, Europe is likely to compete with the United States economically but continue to draw upon American military support.

As trade competition mounts, coordinated EC economic policy will present a mixed blessing for the United States. When U.S. and European interests diverge—as inevitably they will, especially on trade policy—American willingness to invest in EC security can be expected to erode. In turn, Washington's capacity to lead its traditional allies will wane. Paradoxically, the demise of the Soviet Union has diminished U.S. leverage in Europe, since American strategic weaponry is no longer needed by the Community for extended deterrence against the Soviet Union.

What seems likely is the development of a dual U.S. relationship with the European Community, with trade competition and conflict intensifying at the same time that the level of defense cooperation slowly recedes. Military conflict will not follow economic rivalry, because democracies are prone to peaceful interactions with each other (Doyle, 1995), and a U.S. commitment to European defense will continue (even if its presence on the Continent declines as does its share of the defense burden). Perhaps this scenario was what President Clinton had in mind when he stated, "I see the European Community as a positive development for peace. We seek a partnership with our allies and friends in which the U.S. remains engaged and committed to European security and the growth of a more open world economy. . . . Our tradition of military cooperation can continue in the context of NATO and of the developing European capacity for self-defense" (cited in Galo, 1992).

In the wake of the Cold War, economic issues have been elevated to "high politics." But as important as economics and interdependence may be, they do not eliminate the need to think about the conditions under which military power can and should be managed.

> As long as we live in a world of multiple sovereign political units (and economic integration in Europe and elsewhere doesn't alter this reality; it simply changes the size of the units), these conditions will have structure, and particular content. And their structure and content are going to be determined by someone or something. If we assume that states will all have the same preferences as to how to solve problems, then power may indeed be unimportant. Similarly, we need not worry about power if we assume that whose preferences prevail is unimportant. But all those who assume that the different sizes, locations, strengths, cultures, and histories of states and other units will regularly produce different preferences, some of them more desirable than others, will care deeply about power. They will care because in all negotiations not refereed by a commonly accepted authority, power will decide which preferences prevail. (Tonelson, 1993a: 73)

The question that remains in the exploration of U.S.–European relations is whether one should focus on European or German power in the early years of the twenty-first century. Can a strong Germany exist within the confines of the European Community without transforming the EC into a German-led bloc?

Germany

Now united, Germany is likely to show signs of a new assertiveness once the immense costs of reunification and rebuilding the former German Democratic Republic are digested. The challenge for Europeans will be to find a way to absorb Germany, given its size, economic strength, and geographic location, within a broad European power-sharing arrangement (Chace, 1992: 68). Germany has claimed that it wants to be an equal partner in its common European home, as indicated by Chancellor Helmut Kohl's slogan "A European Germany, not a German Europe." But according to some analysts, "Germany is too powerful to disappear into a wider European framework." It already accounts for 28 percent of the Community's gross national product, and its share of the EC budget is "three times the contribution of Great Britain and twice the amount of Great Britain and France combined." Moreover, Belgium, Britain, France, Italy, Luxembourg, the Netherlands, and Spain have linked the value of their currencies to the mark, therein giving Germany enormous leverage over interest rates and economic growth (Garten, 1992: 10).

This extraordinary economic clout assures that Germany will reign dominant within any European union, whether it is built around the federalist idea of a supranational government or some other, more modest pan-European institutional structure. In either case, "there is nothing in the European Community, on its own, to balance the power of a united Germany" (O'Brien, 1993: 17). Nor is there the prospect of a lasting external balance. "American influence in Europe is declining . . . and German influence is rising. American involvement in Europe will be thinner and weaker. Selective disengagement by both sides has already begun" (Hyland, 1993: 35).

One consequence of Germany's growing economic strength and diplomatic independence will be greater competition with the United States. Yet this is not likely to result in a renewed push to flex German military muscle. Despite the January 1993 parliamentary proposal to amend its constitution to permit German troops to take part in international peacekeeping operations, an independent German military presence on the world stage is not likely, and renewed militarism is even less so. Germany's armed forces are still deeply entrenched in and constrained by the joint command in NATO, the Western European Union, and its mutual Franco–German force structure. Also, German democratization poses a barrier to any return to militarism. Beset by a host of internal problems (including a restless right), "the notion of the new Germany embarking on a sinister power drive seems absurd, while that of a relaxed, united country able to juggle the many demands of its new political system seems unrealistic" (Kielinger and Otte, 1993: 44). Hence, economic rivalry with the United States is unlikely to culminate in military strife.

From the vantage point of the United States, the key to moderating potential conflicts lies in maintaining a partnership with Germany. As Bill Clinton stated, "For the last 40 years, West Germany has been a strong, dependable ally. Our close partnership will continue with a unified Germany. German democracy is one of the proudest accomplishments of the last half century. The more engaged we are in Europe, the more likely it is that German policies will be compatible with our own" (cited in Galo, 1992). Based on this preference, "amid all the turbulence . . . there is no real reason to think that Germany will cease being the reliable American partner it has been for the past four decades" and "if there is any 'special relationship' between the United States and a European country" then perhaps it will "be with Germany" (Kielinger and Otte, 1993: 58, 62).

In his analysis of NATO's *London Declaration on a Transformed North Atlantic Alliance*, Ambassador Henning Wegener (1990: 7) stressed that the post–Cold War "challenge is to create a continent—encompassing both the North American democracies and the [former] Soviet Union—that will increasingly derive security from peaceful cooperative interaction and the interdependence of states." But we must keep in mind that capitalist great powers are natural rivals (Hart, 1992) and that their competition can escalate in the absence of a common external enemy, especially if a new wave of mercantilism sweeps away the basis for their political collaboration. "One of the repercussions of the collapse of the bipolar order is that a post-communist Russia and a unified Germany are now, again, increasingly equals in terms of their real power and influence in international affairs" (Rusi, 1993).

As concerns over the emergence of a power vacuum in Central and Eastern Europe mount, and Germany builds bridges to Croatia, Poland, Hungary, Ukraine, and the Baltic states, the relations between the United States and Russia will be critical to a new multipolar system's stability.

Prospects for a U.S.–Russian Entente

Formerly adversaries, Russia and the United States now have incentives to become partners. As U.S. Secretary of Defense Les Aspin declared in January 1993, "the superpower rivalry is gone." For the United States, a strong bilateral partnership would reduce the chances that Russia might join forces with one of Washington's competitors, as Germany did in 1922 when it signed the Rapallo Treaty with the Soviet Union, much to the chagrin of France and Britain. For Russia, partnership with the United States could help increase the flow of technical and financial assistance needed for economic reconstruction and revitalization. For both countries, a special relationship would give their policies added weight when dealing with other nations on a range of security matters. For these reasons, scholars from East and West assert that security cannot be obtained unilaterally (see Smoke and Kortunov, 1990) and that the temptation to go it alone must be resisted. As Andrei A. Kokoshin (1989: 118) warns, if one side rejects unilateralism in favor of mutual security but "the other side behaves on the grounds of the old thinking, the result could be very devastating."

To control the impulse to act unilaterally, the United States and Russia could move toward a new collaborative partnership. While establishing an entente between these old Cold War rivals would be a delicate enterprise and might raise the specter of a superpower condominium,[2] the benefits would be profound: Rather than being marginalized in a post–Cold War order, Russia would have an important role to play in its operation and a stake in its success. In the words of former U.S. Secretary of State James Baker (1990b: 1), the opportunity to create a more secure world depends on whether the two countries "can establish an enduring improvement in [their] relations."

An entente would differ from an actual military pact insofar as it would entail a loose, ad hoc set of informal, partner-specific rules (Niou, Ordeshook, and Rose, 1989: 265–266). Partnerships of this sort have functioned well in the past when they have been made judiciously, when the obligations involved were not left open-ended, and, most important, when the members honored their word. As Peter Wallensteen's (1984) analysis of a century and a half of efforts to construct world order discloses, militarized crises and wars have decreased significantly whenever major powers have bypassed "particularistic," unilateral security policies in favor of such collaborative, partner-specific rule making.

While future interaction between the United States and Russia is unlikely to mirror the evolution of Anglo–French relations after 1904, a carefully crafted Russo–American entente anchored on the presupposition that "the security of one state is inseparably linked to the security of its neighbours" (North Atlantic Council, 1990) could underpin a series of initiatives that might guide great-power relations away from the least stable forms of multipolarity. Rather than operating from an overarching grand design, an entente would encourage Washington and Moscow to take a pragmatic, step-by-step approach to jointly resolving chronic regional conflicts, many of which were amplified by the political dynamics of the bipolar Cold War system.

By encapsulating the impulse to seek security unilaterally in a cocoon of partner-specific rules of prudence, Russia and the United States could reduce the chance that their understandings would not be repudiated when their interests diverge. Whether this is feasible will depend on many factors, including the adherence of other great powers to the same kinds of norms, continued promotion of the inviolability-of-borders principle of the Helsinki Final Act, and the

2. Although some scholars have called for a Russian–American defense "condominium" (see Iklé, 1991–1992: 29), an alliance between the system's two strongest military powers could alarm everyone else and prompt the other great powers to form a counteralliance. Russian President Boris Yeltsin seemed to recognize the dangers of alliance polarization when he announced, "We do not want axes, triangles or blocs. We would not wish for an alliance . . . to the detriment of other countries. I would call this policy the speciality of the new Russia" (*The New York Times*, January 26, 1993, p. 4).

gradual integration of Eastern European states into a pan-European security framework.

The obstacles to such an entente should not be underestimated, and they present decision makers in both countries with difficult challenges that require an agonizing reappraisal of their nations' role in world affairs. Such redirections have seldom been easy in the past.

A Russo–American bilateral entente will not eradicate the need to devise a new *global* security regime aimed at establishing fundamental deterrence in strategic weapons, nonprovocative conventional defense in Europe, and still further controls over the proliferation of chemical, biological, nuclear, and ballistic missile technologies that were achieved in recent historic agreements (for example, START II and the Paris Treaty on Conventional Armed Forces in Europe that set a precedent for the proposed Chemical Weapons Treaty). The challenge, however, will be to endow these regimes with enough resilience so their continued operation is not contingent upon the fate of any particular Russian leader or organizational arrangement between Russia and the other former Soviet republics.

The greatest obstacle to a lasting Russian contribution to international peace lies in the fear that the great-power competition that was endemic during the Cold War will resurface. Neither the singular diplomatic achievements of the 1989–1992 period nor the Russian reform experiments are irreversible. Historians could some day look back on this era as a mere interregnum, a brief, shining moment of Russian conciliation and experimentation with democratic governance that vanished before it took firm root. Dissolving an empire, building a democracy, and privatizing a command economy while holding ethnic animosities in check have put enormous pressures on a fragile government. Massive unemployment, hyperinflation, and soaring crime give demagogues on both extremes of the political spectrum an opportunity to exploit the anger of a frustrated citizenry. Neither the grim threats of economic collapse and political upheaval within a militarily powerful Russia nor the hostilities within and among many of the fifteen former republics of the Soviet Union auger well for the future. Abuse of the approximately 25 million ethnic Russians who live in other parts of the old Soviet Union could prompt Moscow to make military moves that would resurrect Western fears of Russian intentions and might.

The United States and its allies must avoid policies that would relegate the former Soviet Union to the status of a "Weimar Russia" and therein stimulate an attempt by a more intransigent leadership to reverse Soviet fortunes at a later date. "What happened in Germany after World War I ought to provide a sufficiently clear warning of the consequences that can follow when victors neglect the interests of those they have vanquished, and thereby, in the long run, neglect their own" (Gaddis, 1992c: 26). "The West must wake up," insists former President Richard Nixon (1993: A17). "Russia is the key to global security." Hence, in a post–Cold War world the chief interest of the West "may lie in the survival and successful rehabilitation of the nation that was [its] principal adversary throughout that conflict" (Gaddis, 1990: 57). Russia needs to be brought into the West's security institutions as a full-fledged, equal member. Though objections can be raised to recruiting a previous adversary into an alliance that once existed for the sole purpose of containing it, there are precedents for this kind of policy reversal that inspire confidence. Recall that

> Japan was recruited [into the Western alliance] only six years after a "shooting war," in 1951, and Germany only ten years after, in 1955, and those adversary relations had generated a lot more destruction and consequent bitterness than the Cold War. But the real parallel seems to be 1815: the recruitment of France just after the Napoleonic Wars to the status quo alliance, which became the Concert of Europe and helped keep the peace for most of the next century. (Bell, 1990–1991: 44)

In the twenty-first century, by the same logic, "the ability of the United States to preserve equilibrium in the international system [will] rest on the future health of the [former] Soviet Union" (Goldberg, 1992: 162).[3]

America in the Pacific Century

The Asian edge of the Pacific Rim also merits attention when contemplating how rules of prudence that arise in the context of bilateral partnerships can contribute to a peaceful twenty-first century. During the past decade, Asia has replaced Europe as the primary trading region for the United States, and current estimates suggest that Pacific trade will double the volume of Atlantic trade by the end of the century (Oxnam, 1992–1993: 58). Moreover, East Asia could account for roughly 50 percent of the world product (the sum of the gross national products of all states) by that time (Chace, 1992: 88).

Unlike in Europe where the last 50 years witnessed the growth of numerous multilateral institutions, East Asian security relations generally have been conducted on a bilateral basis. Given East Asia's importance and the bilateral style of its security architecture, let us broaden the analysis by bringing Japan and China into the picture.

Japan

In part because it avoided burdensome defense spending during the Cold War by standing beneath the American nuclear umbrella, Japan is now an economic giant in finance, manufacturing, and trade. "Japan's economy will be bigger

3. As one policy adviser frames the proposal from the U.S. perspective, "The American interest is not to permit either Japan or China to dominate our Asian policy. We need a balance between China and Japan, and a balance among China, Japan, and the United States. One way to achieve this is to support Russia in the Far East" (Hyland, 1993: 39).

than the U.S.'s by approximately 2030 if even the more modest target growth rates of around 3.5% occur [and] already, by most calculations, Japanese national wealth is larger than the U.S.'s on a per capita basis" (Nathan, 1993: 34). In addition, Japan is no longer a military dwarf. By the end of the 1980s, Japan was among the top seven countries in terms of military capabilities and ranked third in military expenditures. Besides producing most of its armaments domestically, Japan also supplies much of the technology used in sophisticated American weapons systems. During 1992, Japan's military force grew to 237,000 troops and its navy was the largest in the Pacific Ocean (Jacob Schlesinger, 1992: 1, 12). Japanese economic prowess, in other words, is now contributing to its military might.

To some people, all of this spells trouble, for intense U.S.–Japanese competition could mean diverging interests and a new flurry of acrimonious charges and countercharges (Prestowitz, 1989; Kester, 1991; Encarnation, 1992). Worse still, matters could escalate to military hostilities (Friedman and Le Bard, 1992)—a scenario until recently deemed highly improbable. According to this school of thought, expressed in French Foreign Minister Edith Cresson's accusation that Japan is "plotting to conquer the world" (cited in Nye, 1992–1993: 98), an upward spiral of conflict could erode the current liberal international economic regime and destroy the defense ties that were carefully nurtured after the Second World War. Throughout the Cold War, notes Kishore Mahbubani (1992: 127), "Japanese security planners did not even consider the possibility of a rupture in the U.S.–Japanese security relationship. Now they do." Rather than being allies, the United States and Japan could become rivals locked into a new Cold War that some day could become hot.

One variant of this confrontational image warns that the international system eventually will coalesce into three contending blocs: an expanded European Community, a Western Hemispheric coalition based on the North American Free Trade Area (NAFTA, composed of Canada, the United States, and Mexico), and an East Asian grouping led by Japan. In effect, the economic congealing of the East Asian region is already under way. Tokyo's regional influence is exercised through a variety of mechanisms, including loans for joint ventures, aid for infrastructure, and foreign investment. Japanese companies are constructing facilities throughout East Asia to coordinate production, assembly, and distribution. Department store chains like Yaohan and Seibu are playing a greater role in the region's retailing business, while institutions such as Sumitomo Bank and Nomura Securities are doing the same in finance (Garten, 1992: 178). Taken together, trade within Western Europe, North America, and East Asia "now accounts for almost half of world commerce" (Carnegie Endowment National Commission, 1992: 20). "Today the question is not whether these blocs will be formed," concludes a recent United Nations report (cited in Kegley and Wittkopf, 1993: 250), "but how encompassing they will be."

In the eyes of some observers, the long-range consequences of this trend toward three regional blocs are dangerous.[4] "In the twenty-first century a fierce struggle for supremacy will take place," predicts Jacques Attali (1991: 64, 67), a former adviser to French President François Mitterand. To make matters worse, this leadership struggle among the blocs will unfold against the backdrop of potential conflicts with the inhabitants of the exploited peripheral areas of the globe. "War will occur if there is no one strong enough to prevent it," Attali cautions. "We face a future in which spheres of abundance collide in a sea of instability."

This turbulent future is not preordained, however. Throughout the Cold War the United States maintained close bilateral ties with Japan, ties that can continue to bind the two countries even in the absence of a Soviet threat and despite the effort of Japan "to embark on a new Asian policy independent of the United States," inspired by the belief of the Japanese people that "their nation is in a position to lead other Asian nations" (Masaki, 1993: 1, 6). Both the United States and Japan are democracies that participate in the largest overseas commercial linkage in the world (Oxnam, 1992–1993: 67), and Japan's use of its economic power for military purposes is not predetermined, as structural realists claim (Katzenstein and Okawara, 1993). While this does not mean they will establish some form of joint governance over the future world system along the lines of Zbigniew Brzezinski's (1972) so-called "Amerrippon" condominium, it does imply that because each side has common security interests on the Korean peninsula, in Indochina, and elsewhere throughout Asia, these converging interests invite policies that work in partnership while seeking to maintain a balance of power among all the key actors in the region—including China and the Association of Southeast Asian Nations.

These common interests cannot be pursued successfully by either Washington or Tokyo alone. As I. M. Destler and Michael Nacht (1993: 307) point out, "it is hard to see any reason not to continue the mutually beneficial arrangement of the U.S.–Japan Security Treaty," though "it is easy to see large costs in breaking it off."

For the bilateral path of specialized security relationships to advance the cause of peace, several pressing challenges will have to be met. Aside from countering the prevailing zero-sum, us-versus-them mentality that is too prevalent on both sides of the Pacific, considerable effort will be needed to contain the political friction that surrounds existing and possible future economic disputes (Nye, 1992–1993: 104).

In addition, much like U.S.–Russian relations, there is a need to nest U.S.–Japanese rule making on security matters within a larger multilateral regime

4. A tripolar "balance-of-bloc system" (Masters, 1961: 782), like the one involving George Orwell's fictitious regional-states of Eurasia, Eastasia, and Oceania, could be unstable because two of the blocs would be tempted by the opportunity to gang up on the third if it was suffering through a period of decline. Postdate the title of Orwell's *1984* a few decades, suggests Strobe Talbott (1992: 46), "and the novel is a cautionary tale with a contemporary ring."

that incorporates Europe, Russia, China, and other relevant regional powers. Such a regime might develop along the lines of what Robert Scalapino (1991–1992: 38–39) calls "concentric arcs"—flexible, subregional structures that bring together the relevant parties on specific security matters. The internationalal legal system presently contains myriad linked rules that differ in content, degree of explicitness, and domain of applicability. While the center of this mosaic may contain a set of rules of conduct worked out bilaterally between any two great powers, these informal agreements and tacit understandings need to be confirmed by the other principal power centers in order to enhance the prospects for the most stable form of multipolarity.

China

"Let China sleep—for when she awakens, the world will tremble," prophesied Napoleon Bonaparte. Such an awakening is already beginning to take place and its impact is being felt globewide. China's vast resources, if developed, will place it into the orbit of great-power competition—a place already achieved if its possession of nuclear weapons is used as a criterion of great-power status. China is "a coming power" (Conable and Lampton, 1992–1993). Its economic reforms have led to a remarkable growth rate of almost ten percent annually over the past decade, and savings have been running above thirty percent of the gross national product. As a study by the Commission on Integrated Long-Term Strategy (1988) predicted, China could surpass Russia and even Japan in economic output by the year 2010 (Chace 1992: 108). To others (Weiner, 1993) this has already occurred, making China possibly "the emerging economic powerhouse of the 21st century" (Barnathan et al., 1993).

Optimistic projections notwithstanding, several obstacles could slow the pace of China's economic development. Beyond the immediate succession crisis that has spawned political infighting as the last members of the Yenan generation release the reins of power, the government in Beijing faces the prospect that its country's burgeoning population will not stop growing until the middle of the next century—an enormous problem that contributes to a host of others. As Richard Baum (1992–1993: 66) summarizes the situation, with corruption "increasing at an alarming rate," with traditional Marxist–Leninist values "failing to inspire" an increasingly alienated youth, with local governments beginning to act "in defiance of central authority," and with ethnic tensions rising, "China's future political stability and integrity are by no means assured." The ideological glue and security measures that kept otherwise dissident, distant provinces together during the Cold War have lost much of their potency, and Chinese leaders have yet to find a new unifying force to keep the country together. Neither Chinese nationalism nor rising living standards can be counted on to placate latent resentments toward Beijing and provide the divergent Chinese with a sense of common purpose. Moreover, China's economic growth has widened regional disparities and exacerbated provincial tensions rather than reduce them.

At the same time, its neighbors have become anxious as China's new wealth has been funneled into arms acquisition. China has built its military muscle rapidly by nearly doubling military expenditures between its 1988 and 1993 budgets (*New York Times*, March 17, 1993). In the mid-1990s, China had not yet resolved many of its boundary disputes with Japan, Vietnam, India, Russia, and others, and these states therefore have reasons to be wary of growing Chinese might and assertiveness.

In the meantime, "the evolution of global international politics momentarily has left U.S.–China relations in an awkward transitional stage" (Conable and Whitehead, 1993: 7). For the past twenty years, the United States has attempted to cultivate a special bilateral security relationship with China. Due to clashes over Chinese weapons sales and human rights abuses in the aftermath of the Tiananmen Square massacre, this relationship has become highly politicized, creating a "bunker mentality" among the Chinese leadership (Ross, 1993: 347). Should the relations between Washington and Beijing continue to unravel, China would then become a viable partner for Russia or Japan if either finds itself at odds with U.S. policy in the region. A Sino–Russian or Sino–Japanese alliance thus is possible if the balance-of-power game is steadfastly played in a twenty-first century multipolar world.

IMPLICATIONS FOR GREAT-POWER CHOICES

Special security partnerships have many advantages. Great Britain's use of these bilateral arrangements at the turn of the last century temporarily resolved the pressing problem of imperial overstretch and ended its long-standing and seemingly implacable rivalry with France. Yet, as the onset of World War I illustrates, special relationships also have drawbacks.

The Limitations of Special Relationships

Perhaps the most serious drawback of a network of special bilateral relationships is that they can foster a *fear of encirclement* among those who perceive themselves as the target of these actions. Consider once more our example of early twentieth-century Britain. Although London made several attempts to reach an understanding with Berlin, these efforts failed. Ultimately Britain's wide-ranging bilateral agreements contributed to German fears of being surrounded by hostile powers. As Chancellor Theobald von Bethmann Hollweg told the Reichstag on August 4, 1914, approximately seven hours after German forces crossed the Belgian frontier at Gemmerich en route to France, "hostility toward us was being nursed and chains forged for us in the East and in the West." "Where the responsibility in this greatest of all wars lies," he later added, "is quite evident to us. Outwardly responsible are the men in Russia who planned and carried into effect the general mobilization of the Russian army." But the British were responsible as well. "The London Cabinet could have made the war impossible," Bethmann Hollweg claimed, "if they had unequivocally told Petersburg that England was not willing to let a continental war of the Great Powers result from the Austro–Hungarian conflict with Serbia" (interview in Horne and Austin, 1920: 395).

In addition to fueling fears that others are teaming up against you, special relationships can *breed suspicion that one side is enjoying most of the benefits while the other is shouldering most of the burdens.* The post–World War II Anglo–American special relationship exemplifies this problem. According to Richard Neustadt (1970: 4), rarely have two governments had linkages so variegated, tight, and sustained as the United States and Great Britain had with one another in the generation after the Second World War. Yet the relationship was "special" primarily for the British insofar as it gave them the opportunity to exert private, informal influence in the highest councils of the Atlantic Alliance, even though their relative power position in the immediate postwar world had deteriorated (Hanrieder and Auton, 1980: 183). The British saw themselves as seasoned actors on the stage of high politics who could offer Washington the wisdom of experience, playing the role of "Greece" to America's "Rome" (Lieber, 1989: 6). But from the American perspective, Britain was "an ageing, self-satisfied prima donna who insisted on holding the limelight though the glory and beauty of her youth were long passed" (Northedge, 1974: 171).

Another problem associated with special relationships is the *tendency of outsiders to assume that the junior partner has the same preferences as the senior partner* and thus will not take independent action. Following the unexpected Prussian victory over Austria in the Seven Weeks' War of 1866, Otto von Bismarck, the Prussian chancellor, was careful not to humiliate the Austrians after their loss at Sadowa and crafted a lenient peace to defuse any sentiments in Vienna for a war of revenge. Bismarck's conciliatory policy succeeded: Following German unification in 1871, the diplomatic paths of Austria and the new German empire were closely intertwined. By the beginning of the twentieth century the relations between the two countries were so close that the British Foreign Office assumed that "Vienna's foreign policy was simply an extension of Berlin's" (Kahler, 1979–1980: 395). However, not only did this assumption mask policy differences between Austria and Germany, but it prevented the British from encouraging the Austrians to become more independent from Germany. This, of course, heightened British vulnerability on the eve of World War I when it had to confront the combined strength of the Triple Alliance composed of Austria, Germany, and Italy.

Special relationships also promote a politics of exclusion that can *lead to dangerously polarized forms of multipolarity.* Again, the period prior to the outbreak of World War I offers an instructive example. What began as a series of bilateral ententes pertaining to extra-European affairs gradually solidified under the pressure of crises in Morocco and the Balkans into two rigid, opposing blocs: "Once the last important European great power had made its alignments, the tension noticeably increased. There being no further allies to win . . . , it became imperative to preserve the bloc against diplomatic inroads from the opposing group" (Hartmann, 1983: 352).

Finally, as the evolution of the 1904 Anglo–French Entente displayed, special relationships can *take on a life of their own*, often growing into something quite different than what was originally envisioned by their founders. Although the British and French initially conducted ad hoc, unofficial meetings on the possibility of joint military action in the event of war with Germany, these talks gradually acquired moral force. Sir Edward Grey, the foreign secretary for the Liberal government that replaced the Conservatives shortly after the birth of the Entente Cordiale, mused that it would be "very difficult" for Britain to stay out of a war between France and Germany. The "constant and emphatic demonstrations of affection (official, naval, political, commercial and in the Press) have created in France a belief that we shall support them in war. . . . If this expectation is disappointed, the French will never forgive us. There would also I think be a general feeling that we had behaved badly and left France in the lurch" (cited in Joll, 1984: 45).

Toward the Future

To sum up, the movement from bipolarity to multipolarity promises to benefit some states and harm others. Regardless of who wins or loses, every country will be challenged. In turbulent times great powers frequently seek special bilateral arrangements to add predictability to their strategic environment and to tailor military and economic means to political ends. Such arrangements have the potential to usher in stable forms of multipolarity by creating a web of tacit, partner-specific rules supportive of a normative order that restricts the use of force and upholds the sanctity of treaty commitments. In essence, they are an antidote to the dangerous unilateralist philosophy "every state for itself."

Among the dangers of the post–Cold War world "is the fractionalization of the West, based on cultural differences and a reversion to national policies based on narrow self-interest" (Glynn, 1993a: 27). To proponents, specialized great-power relations are a partial remedy, whether they entail informal understandings or formal treaties of alliance. However, both kinds of bilateral partnerships have a common drawback: They are inherently exclusionary and potentially divisive. Any arrangement that fails to take all the great powers' security interests into account may ultimately create the very condition most responsible for making multipolar systems unstable, namely, bloc polarization. Past history proves that relying on the balance of power to provide peace in a highly polarized environment is problematic (see Box 9.1).

The vital question today is whether the United States and the other great

BOX 9.1
SPECIALIZED ALLIANCE RELATIONSHIPS AND THE BALANCE OF POWER: THE NEED FOR AN ALTERNATIVE SYSTEM

"Balance of power theory is concerned mainly with the rivalries and clashes of great powers—above all—what we have come to describe as *world wars*, the massive military conflicts that engulf and threaten to destroy the entire multistate system. It is difficult to consider world wars as anything other than catastrophic failures, total collapses, of the balance of power system. They are hardly to be classed as stabilizing manoeuvres or equilibrating processes, and one cannot take seriously any claim of maintaining international stability that does not entail the prevention of such disasters as the Napoleonic wars or World War I. Mention of those and similar disasters, however, frequently evokes the reminder that the would-be universal emperor—be it Louis XIV or Napoleon or Hitler—was defeated; in accordance with balance of power principles, a coalition arose to put down the challenger and maintain or restore the independence of the various states. In short, the system worked. Or did it? Is the criterion of the effectiveness of the balance of power that Germany lose its bid for conquest, or that it be deterred from precipitating World War I? It is not easy to justify the contention that a system for the management of international relations that failed to prevent the events of 1914–1918 deserves high marks as a guardian of stability, or order, or peace. If the balance of power system does not aim at the prevention of world war, then it aims too low; if it offers no hope of maintaining the general peace, then the quest for a better system is fully warranted."

—Inis L. Claude, Jr. (1989: 78)

"Whereas nineteenth century doctrines considered particular alliances as a normal and justifiable feature of international society, collective security must view alliances between particular states with alarm. Such particular alliances are either superfluous or dangerous; superfluous insofar as they provide a security guarantee to particular states which they already enjoy by virtue of their membership in the society of states, and dangerous insofar as they advertise the fact that those states participating in a particular community of states consider their own security of greater importance than the security of states generally."

—David C. Hendrickson (1993: 4–5)

powers should think in terms of special bilateral partnerships to guard their own national security, or whether they should aspire toward multilateral approaches to "common security" (Møller, 1992). Constructing a multilateral security regime that jettisons the push and shove of balance-of-power politics is an attractive possibility. "We will inevitably rely more and more on collective security to cope with new military challenges," predicts the Carnegie Endowment National Commission (1992: 65), "or they will not be dealt with at all."

Whether this potential path to peace will be taken by the great powers remains to be seen. Such a regime must be built by disciplined and dedicated planning; it will not develop of its own volition, or because necessity compels it. The prospects for a multilateral security regime are reduced by the danger that the "contradictions among major powers may intensify rather than diminish as they are subjected to new post–cold war challenges" (Goldberg, 1992: 161–162). As Henry A. Kissinger (1993: 1) observes, "the new world order has to find institutions and mechanisms similar to what the creators of the post–World War II international order founded in the period from 1945 to 1950. The possibilities for creativity are greater than they were then, though the beginnings of the solutions are not yet as obvious."

The promise of a multilateral regulatory mechanism, either through a new great-power concert or through a strengthened United Nations collective security system, needs to be considered. The consequences that are likely to result if the great powers take this path will be discussed in the next chapter.

· 10 ·

A CONCERT-BASED COLLECTIVE SECURITY SYSTEM?

We are now entering a different phase of the relationship of peoples and states. There is no argument for dismantling collective security. The familiar threats might reoccur.
—THE RT. HON. DOUGLAS HURD,
BRITISH FOREIGN SECRETARY, 1993

Though locked in a rivalry exacerbated by antagonistic ideologies and staggering military expenditures, the United States and the Soviet Union avoided mutual destruction. The Cold War never escalated into a fatal contest on the field of battle. Yet, as a former American foreign policymaker insists: "Nonetheless, warfare it was" (Brzezinski, 1992: 31).

"After a long war," Sir Harold Nicolson once observed, "it is impossible to make a quick peace" (cited in Beveridge, 1945: 65). In the wake of some forty-five years of protracted hostility between the United States and the Soviet Union, the construction of a durable peace may be elusive. Concepts like "Third World" and "nonalignment," which guided thinking throughout the Cold War, have lost their meaning. "Suddenly deprived of a familiar yardstick," laments Motoo Shiina (1992: 74), a former member of the Japanese House of Representatives, "the international community has lost its way. . . . Ethnic animosity, religious intolerance—these old demons, dormant during the Cold War, are back with an ominous sneer." Still more frightening is the prospect that such demons, aided by the proliferation of advanced weaponry, will cause subnational violence to spill over into other arenas.

Lurking behind many of the ethnonationalistic conflicts is a larger structural problem. The rank order of states will not rapidly crystallize into a fixed hierarchy as we move toward the millennium. States rise and fall, and they will continue to do so after the Cold War because uneven growth is an enduring feature of world politics. Shifts in the relative strength of states that harbor old grievances against their neighbors may make the future anything but orderly.

As power disperses in fits and starts to an expanding number of powerful actors on the international stage, friction and strife can be expected.

> Strategies of security through expansion make more sense in multipolar situations than in bipolar ones. In multipolarity, an expansionist power may be able to defeat its opponents piecemeal if they fail to unite because they cannot agree on who should bear the costs of resistance. At the same time, great powers in multipolarity may have strong incentives to expand to achieve autarky, since they are less likely to be self-sufficient in the resources needed for national security than are bipolar powers. (Snyder, 1991: 26)

Finding a mechanism to preserve peace in this unstable period of power shifts will be a serious challenge on the global agenda in the twenty-first century. One strategy proposed to meet this challenge is multilateralism, the focus of this chapter. In particular, we will explore the various collective approaches available for dealing with the political cleavages of the post–Cold War world and assess their potential contribution to peace in light of the characteristics that a coming multipolar system of power might assume.

Our thesis can be stated at the outset: Unilateral and bilateral approaches do not offer very promising paths to lasting great-power peace, given the tendency of previous multipolar systems to collapse when these strategies were used. Multilateral approaches provide a better solution to checking great-power competition should a truly multipolar system take shape. The question is, which multilateral approach is most likely to advance the great powers' mutual interest in preserving peace?

THE REVIVAL OF INTEREST IN COLLECTIVE SECURITY

One multilateral mechanism that has attracted considerable attention since the end of the Cold War is collective security. As discussed in Chapter 7, it is based on the notion of "one for all and all for one." If no single state is more powerful than the combination of all other states in a collective security organization, it is assumed that the membership could jointly deter—and, if necessary, defeat—an aggressor, provided that the members (1) have a common concern to maintain peace, (2) agree on who is a potential or actual threat to peace, and (3) apply prompt and powerful sanctions against the source of that threat.

Pointing to the failure of the League of Nations to deal effectively with Japan's attack on Manchuria in 1931, the Chaco War in 1932, Italy's invasion of Ethiopia in 1935, and Nazi Germany's aggression against its neighbors during the late 1930s, skeptics caution against relying on collective security. They urge policymakers to trust in their own power, not in the promises of an international organization. Collective security "assumes that every nation perceives every challenge to the international order in the same way, and is prepared to run the same risks to preserve it" (Kissinger, 1992: 239). Yet whenever such an organization has existed, some members have sought to maximize their relative gains rather than minimize their mutual losses. Thinking that they could rely on joint action to resist aggression, they reduced their own military preparedness so as to free-ride on the defense efforts of their peers. Conversely, other states have taken the opposite tack: Rather than reneging on their security pledges, they mobilized at the first hint of trouble and thus expanded what might have remained small local conflicts into larger wars. In sum, the history of collective security reveals twin deficiencies—it may "not work when needed, or . . . it would work when it should not" (Betts, 1992: 214).

Even if the post–Cold War environment is more hospitable to collective security organizations than in the past, implementing collective security will not be easy. Inis Claude uses this analogy:

> An automobile does not climb the hill just because its brake has been released, but requires a battery, fuel, and a driver intent on driving up the hill. So it is with collective security, which requires a motive force supplied by states convinced of the wisdom of, and willing to pay the price of participation in, the universal enforcement of the antiaggression rule. (Claude, 1992: 11)

A solution to this motivational problem is to create a modified version of collective security, one that is grounded in *multilateralism*, contains a *two-tiered, modular design*, and promotes the principles of *cooperative security*. A full-fledged, comprehensive, global collective security system, dedicated to containing aggression anywhere at any time, may be too ambitious and doomed to failure. But a restricted collective security mechanism might succeed if it is built on the participation of all the great powers and enjoys the support of the system's most powerful actor, the United States. One sign that this goal could materialize is found in the Clinton administration's early foreign policy pronouncements. These signaled the belief that international security is indivisible and cannot be protected "on a piecemeal, bilateral basis" (Judis, 1993: 18). As President Clinton expressed it in April 1993, "The United States has got to work through the United Nations, and all of our views may not always prevail." This posture was made concrete when the United States later announced that, as a component of its so-called "assertive multilateralism" strategy, it would support expanding the UN Security Council's permanent seats to include Japan and Germany (Bolton, 1993).

Multilateralism

In contrast to the specialized bilateral arrangements and ad hoc coalitions discussed in the previous chapter, multilateralism is a demanding organizational form that involves coordinating national policies among three or more great powers. It contains three distinguishing features: generalized principles of conduct, indivisibility, and diffuse reciprocity (Ruggie, 1992: 571).

Generalized principles of conduct are rules that specify appropriate behavior in a specific situation, without regard to individual preferences. For instance, a rule exhorting members of a collective security organization to treat an attack on a member state as equivalent to an invasion of one's homeland would not permit those belonging to that organization to respond to aggression on a case-by-case basis. *Indivisibility* pertains to the scope over which costs and benefits are spread among organization members; for example, if troubles afflict one country, there would be ramifications for its peers. Finally, *diffuse reciprocity* means that the states in question expect to benefit as a whole over the long run instead of on every issue all of the time.

A Two-Tiered, Modular Design

As noted, multilateralism rests on the belief that cooperative activities should be organized on the basis of generalized principles of conduct, indivisibility, and diffuse reciprocity for some relevant group of states (Caporaso, 1992: 603). For some, the relevant group includes *all* states. In theory, the all-inclusive nature of this type of collective security mechanism ensures that ample resources would be available for levying sanctions against an aggressor; in practice, it creates difficulties for providing a timely response to threatening situations. The experience with large-scale collective security organizations like the League of Nations and the early United Nations indicates that consensus building is usually both difficult and delayed, especially in identifying the culpable party, choosing an appropriate response, and implementing the selected course of action.

The twentieth-century history of collective security, at least until very recently, suggests that multilateralism stands a better chance of working in smaller groups. As a decision-making group's size expands, it becomes unwieldy; the complexity of negotiations increases geometrically with the addition of new members. In the words of Mancur Olson,

> Unless the number of individuals in a group is quite small, or unless there is coercion or some other special device to make individuals act in their common interest, *rational, self-interested individuals will not act to achieve their common or group interests.* In other words, even if all of the individuals in a large group are rational and self-interested, and would gain if, as a group, they acted to achieve their common interest or objective, they will still not voluntarily act to achieve that common or group interest. (Olson, 1965: 2)

This conclusion does not auger well for the successful operation of a global collective security system. It does, however, lead many analysts to conclude that a smaller security regime would be more effective than a universal, all-inclusive organization. One such alternative is a concert, an attenuated form of collective security whose smaller membership and flexible structure facilitate timely joint decision making (Kupchan and Kupchan, 1991). As outlined in Chapter 7, a concert involves mutual self-restraint and informal collaboration among the great powers. Its primary benefit is to give each great power a stake in the prevailing international order. Since the effectiveness of international sanctions "depends in part on whether the leading countries are perceived to be willing to use force should sanctions fail" (Luck, 1992–1993: 145–146), another benefit of a concert is the communication of great-power resolve to potential aggressors. In addition, a concert lessens the probability that the great powers will become polarized in rival alliances, the dangers of which are legendary (recall Chapter 5).

Although a concert of powers may avert this polarization, it has a serious drawback: Small and middle powers chafe at being excluded from decisions that affect their well-being and threaten to accelerate their subordination. Sir Shridath Ramphal (1992: 82), chairman of the West Indian Commission and former Commonwealth secretary-general, recently gave voice to this liability when he expressed his anxiety over the post–Cold War great powers acting like a "self-anointed presidium." Great-power tutelage over world affairs may not always translate into self-abnegation when the perceived interests of the powerful and powerless collide. *Who* makes security decisions, Joanne Landy (1992: 8) reminds us, "is inseparable from *what* gets decided." If the great powers act as a status quo front regulating the activities of states below them, they can be expected to make decisions that might benefit themselves at the expense of others. This would provoke not only resentment; it would also create the conditions under which disputes between the advantaged and the disadvantaged could escalate.

To cope with this problem, various scholars and statesmen have recommended creating a two-tiered, collective security arrangement that contains a modular structure. Under such a scheme, the nations at the center of policy deliberations would shift "according to the nature of the problem at hand and the moment in time" (Feinberg and Boylan, 1992: 180). Figure 10.1 depicts such a structure. States **A, B, C,** and **D** are great powers, while **w, x, y,** and **z** are small and medium powers. On the first issue, **A** and **B** would work together with **w, x,** and **y.** Alternatively, **B** and **C** would work with **y** and **z** on the second issue. Thus the system would be *concert-based*: Some great powers would play a leadership role on certain security issues, others would do so on a different set of issues. At the same time, this great-power concert would be anchored in a larger collective security framework, where small and medium powers would have a voice in pending matters if their interests were affected or if they possessed expertise in dealing with the issue in question. As such, this arrangement could provide a home for collective action against aggression that avoids the dual dangers of great-power dominance and institutional paralysis.

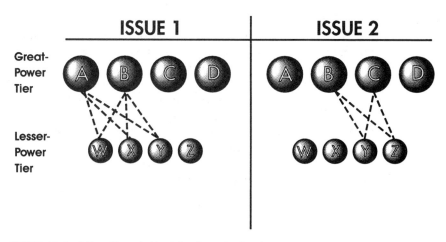

FIGURE 10.1. A Two-Tiered, Modular Security Regime.

Cooperative Security

Another recommendation for concert-based collective security is to have the entire multilateral network of large and small countries practice "cooperative security." Based on the assumption that the insecurity felt by those living in a multipolar world stems from uncertainty about the intentions of others, the idea behind cooperative security is to regulate the military capabilities and practices that give rise to these anxieties.

Four general features characterize such a cooperative security regime (Stares and Steinbruner, 1992: 224–225). The first is *offensive regulation*. By setting ceilings on the size and firepower of military forces and by establishing rules governing the density of deployment, the relocation of units, and the mobilization of reserves, it is possible to reduce the ability of one country to create a threatening offensive concentration against another, even if their total military capabilities are unequal.

The second feature is *defensive restructuring*. Military forces can be configured in many ways. Forces whose doctrine, training, and infrastructure are devised for defensive rather than offensive purposes are less threatening to other countries. While the distinction between defensive and offensive force structures is often difficult to define *a priori*, as the case of the Strategic Defense Initiative illustrates, some structures clearly reduce, if not eliminate, the use of force for offensive purposes. As such, they also dampen fears that military units could be deployed for unauthorized operations that were not a part of their designers' intentions.

Mutual transparency is the third general feature of a cooperative security regime. The greater the openness of states to inspection and exchange of data on military expenditures, weapons deployment, equipment inventories, troop maneuvers, and the like, the easier it becomes to reassure others of one's non-hostile intent. Fact-finding missions and regular meetings between senior officials can also help rivals understand the interests and concerns of the other. For these reasons, procedures for enhancing international accountability have been called "the most rational responses to the security dilemmas facing the modern great powers under the anarchic nation-state system" (Brown, 1992: 36).

The last feature of cooperative security is *functional integration*, under which security tasks would be performed by an integrated and inclusive multinational network of personnel wherever possible. These tasks may range from conducting on-site inspections to undertaking peacekeeping operations.

REQUIREMENTS FOR CONCERT-BASED COLLECTIVE SECURITY

Concert-based security regimes date back to the second millennium B.C.E., when the relations among Egypt, the Hittites, Babylonia, Elam, Mitanni, Assyria, and the Cretan Federation displayed many of the characteristics of the nineteenth-century Concert of Europe (Bozeman, 1960: 28). Though concerts have a long history, they are infrequent and short-lived. This, however, does not render them useless. The study of past concerts reveals that certain specific conditions improve their effectiveness. Let us briefly examine what some international relations theorists identify as the prerequisites for concert-based collective security to function successfully in a twenty-first century multipolar world.

For many theorists, *common threats* are the glue that holds great-power concerts together. Previous concerts formed after wars with potential hegemons or after a single, massively armed enemy appeared on the scene to threaten the existence of others. The passage of time or demise of the threat always loosened these bonds. "Friction tends to build as each state believes that it is sacrificing more for unity than are others," notes Robert Jervis (1985: 61). "Each will remember the cases in which it has been restrained, and ignore or interpret differently cases in which others believe they acted for the common good." To overcome this friction, a shared sense of common threat, either from someone bent on world domination or from a nonmilitary challenge (such as global warming) that cannot be managed unilaterally, must arise to preserve the commitment to collective action. Without a threat common to and recognized by all, the chances that great powers will show self-restraint or forgo unilateral advantages decline.

A second correlate of success is said to lie in *including defeated powers in peace settlements* (Chace, 1992: 186). At the Conference of Aix-la-Chapelle in 1818, the victorious powers agreed to admit France, the defeated former aggressor, into the Concert of Europe to give it a stake in the stability of Europe. At the 1919 Versailles Conference, the victors excluded and isolated Germany.

These episodes suggest that whenever a great power considers an international order oppressive, it will not be "the adjustment of differences within a given system which will be at issue, but the system itself" (Kissinger, 1973: 2). A dissatisfied great power lacking a voice in security matters will reject the legitimacy of the prevailing order, strive to destroy the status quo, and therein undermine a concert's capacity to act. Including a defeated or declining power as an equal and respected member of a concert can avoid this danger.

The third potential contributor to the longevity of concerts is a rough *military balance* among its members (Miller, 1992: 9). Similar remarks have been made about collective security (Claude, 1964: 234; Bennett, 1991: 131). The presence of a state that is significantly stronger than all of the other great powers allegedly reduces the effectiveness of both concerts and collective security organizations since the preponderant state would be able to withstand any pressures that the others might initiate.

A fourth factor affecting the viability of concert-based security systems is a *sense of common duty* among the great powers. Writing about the Concert of Europe, F. H. Hinsley (1963: 197) notes that the great powers, united in their revulsion of insurrection, "were prepared to waive their individual interests because it was in their individual interests to do so." To be sure, they still maneuvered for position and justified their behavior by giving their own interpretation of the Concert's informal rules. But because the great powers "were well aware of their duties as 'managers' of the balance of power" and "were conscious that there was a European interest distinct from the interests of Europe's individual states" (Mandelbaum, 1988: 13), they managed to subordinate their rivalries to the common good. Nineteenth-century diplomats recognized that effective policy coordination required continuous and forthright communication, consultation, and advance notification in order to reinforce expectations of mutual rights and joint responsibilities (Lauren, 1983: 56–57). As a protocol to the 1831 Treaty of Paris expressed it: "Each nation has its rights; but Europe too has its rights" (cited in Luard, 1992: 424).

Fifth on the list of frequently cited requirements is leadership based on a *statesmanship of self-restraint*. Here, again, the Vienna settlement provides an example. The moderate and relatively war-free international system of the post–Napoleonic Era owed much to the extraordinary diplomatic skill of prudent statesmen like Castlereagh, Metternich, and Bismarck, "who manipulated international relations within a self-imposed set of restraints against actions that could fundamentally challenge the security of any of the major states of Europe" (Brown, 1987: 145). These leaders understood that great powers must not be humiliated; neither should they be challenged on their legitimate rights and vital interests, nor have their honor impugned, nor suffer an affront to their prestige and self-esteem (Elrod, 1976: 166). During the nineteenth century, a "just" equilibrium among the contending great powers meant more than an equal distribution of capabilities; it included recognition of honor, national rights, and dignity (Schroeder, 1989: 144).

Finally, many theorists stress *flexibility* as a hallmark of effective great-power concerts. Just as a concert's small, ad hoc organization makes it more supple and resilient than highly institutionalized collective security organizations like the League of Nations, its informal processes of mutual consultation provide an "opportunity for flexibility in tailoring a solution to the special and specific requirements of the problem at hand" (Lauren, 1983: 52).

These six conditions contain lessons about the extent to which today's great powers can look to multilateral concerts as an approach for dealing with future security problems. Common threats, inclusive policies, military equilibrium, shared perceptions of duty, restrained diplomacy, and flexibility are all characteristics that history suggests prolong the life of great-power concerts.

ALTERNATIVE FRAMEWORKS FOR CONCERT-BASED COLLECTIVE SECURITY

As suggested in our introductory observations, many multilateral mechanisms are available for preserving the post–Cold War great-power peace. Seen from the perspective of the mid-1990s, the alternative frameworks on which a future concert-based collective security system might be built can be arrayed on a continuum of varying size, composition, and purpose (see Figure 10.2). At one end of the continuum is the United Nations, a multipurpose intergovernmental organization with close to universal membership. Next, moving toward the other side of the continuum, is the fifty-two-nation Conference on Security and Cooperation in Europe (CSCE), a smaller organization that possesses a far more limited mission than the United Nations. The North Atlantic Treaty Organization (NATO) and the new North Atlantic Cooperation Council (NACC), which includes the former members of the Warsaw Pact, are smaller still and also engage in a narrow range of activities. Finally, at the opposite end is the Group of Seven (G-7), composed of the world's leading industrialized countries that meet in regular summit conferences. To some extent these mechanisms overlap, though they are not necessarily incompatible.

Regardless of the ultimate organizational home for any modular multilateral form of cooperative security, the aim must be to create a "system in which every country feels protected from every other and not just from an opposing alliance" (De Michelis, 1990: 54). To explore the possibilities for accomplishing

Large				Small
Universal Membership	←———————————————→			Limited Membership
Multipurpose UN	CSCE	NATO	G-7	Single Purpose

FIGURE 10.2. Possible Locations for a Concert-Based Collective Security Regime.

this security goal in a multipolar environment, let us examine briefly the strengths and weaknesses of each of these organizations in turn.

The United Nations

After the Persian Gulf War, many people hoped that the United Nations would at long last be able "to take effective collective measures for the prevention and removal of threats to the peace" as originally proclaimed in its Charter (Article 1, paragraph 1). Political commentators spoke of bold new initiatives. No longer a victim of Cold War rivalry, the UN seemed poised to carve out an expanded role for itself.

The key to any new role resides in the Security Council. According to the UN Charter, the Security Council has "primary responsibility for the maintenance of international peace and security" (Article 24, paragraph 1). Of its fifteen members, five hold permanent seats and possess the right to veto council actions—the United States, Russia, Britain, France, and China. An artifact of the global distribution of power in the waning days of World War II, this arrangement put responsibility for preserving peace in the hands of the war's victors, whose territory (especially when their overseas possessions in their respective empires were taken into consideration) accounted for a large proportion of the earth's surface.

Although the Security Council initially fell victim to the division of these wartime allies into polarized blocs, with the end of the Cold War they once again began cooperating and thus avoided political gridlock. Of course, this harmonious veneer could fade, as great-power interests rarely converge for long in the absence of clear mutual dangers. Preventing future stalemates may prove difficult, particularly if the Security Council's permanent membership is expanded to include Germany, Japan, and such regional powers as Brazil, India, Indonesia, and Nigeria (Lewis, 1993). These countries have many divergent interests, which could easily reduce their willingness to act in concert.[1]

To complicate matters further, there is a pervasive fear among the UN's membership that the organization has become a captive of its strongest member at the moment, the United States. Although American influence is resented by many states, they still recognize the need for U.S. leadership if the United

1. In addition to proposals for expanding the permanent membership of the Security Council by adding Germany, Japan, and various other states, the argument also has been made to include major regional organizations. Writing in *The Hindu* of Madras, India, P. S. Suryanarayana (1992: 14) asserts that if regional conflicts become the primary source of instability in the future, the time is ripe for reforming the structure of the Security Council so as to better manage these disputes. Regional intergovernmental organizations, he contends, would "be able to check and balance the major powers on the question of regional conflicts." Should this occur, it would return the Security Council to the competitive push and pull of balance-of-power politics, therein diminishing the capacity of the body to perform any more effectively than it did during the Cold War.

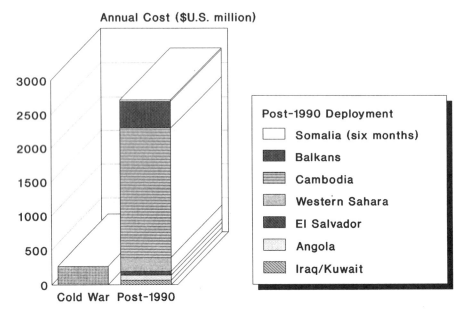

Annual Cost ($U.S. million)

Post-1990 Deployment
- Somalia (six months)
- Balkans
- Cambodia
- Western Sahara
- El Salvador
- Angola
- Iraq/Kuwait

Cold War   Post-1990

FIGURE 10.3. United Nations Peacekeeping Forces, 1993. *Sources: Washington Post,* Weekly Edition, December 7–13, 1992, p. 10; *The World in 1993*, The Economist Publications, p. 87.

Nations is to play a peacekeeping and peacemaking role. This creates a dilemma: "Without U.S. leadership and power, the United Nations lacks muscle. With it, the United Nations loses its independent identity" (Gelb, 1993b: 4).[2]

Yet enthusiasm for an invigorated United Nations continues to mount. In 1988, the Nobel Peace Prize was awarded to the UN's blue-helmeted soldiers. In the next four years, the number of peacekeeping operations undertaken equaled that of the previous four decades. As a result, by 1993 the United Nations found itself involved in peacekeeping operations across the globe. This presence not only escalated the activity—entailing the first use of force by UN peacekeepers since Korea in its Somalian operation—but also the financial costs (see Figure 10.3). In 1987, peacekeeping cost UN members $233 million in assessments; by 1992 the bill had risen more than tenfold to $2.9 billion, "of which member nations . . . contributed only $2 billion, leaving a shortfall of almost $900 million for [1993] alone" (Stedman, 1993: 10; Branigin, 1992a: 9). A larger future role for the United Nations will require even more resources—a dim prospect since the organization was still owed $1.75 billion

2. From the U.S. point of view, multilateralism is also a double-edged sword: "The danger of the 'multilateral temptation' is that [the United States] will resort to the UN reflexively. That reduces America's unilateral or non-UN options, and could even erode its sovereignty" (Bolton, 1993: A14).

in back dues in early 1993 and was under severe criticism for financial mis-management. As a result, many observers concur with former Undersecretary General Brian Urquhart's description of the United Nations as "an enormous ramshackle structure" (cited in Branigin, 1992b: 6). "Now that the UN is free to work as the Founders intended," British Foreign Minister Douglas Hurd lamented on January 27, 1993, "it is in danger of being overwhelmed by the scale of the problems."

Attempting to reform the United Nations while simultaneously coping with the exploding demand for UN peacekeepers has been described by Secretary-General Boutros Boutros-Ghali as "like trying to repair a car while you are driving at a speed of 120 miles per hour" (*Wall Street Journal*, December 17, 1992: A1). Undaunted by the difficulty of the task, he lobbied for the creation of "peace enforcement units" that would "enable the United Nations to deploy troops quickly to enforce a ceasefire by taking coercive action against either party, or both, if they violate it" (Boutros-Ghali, 1992–93: 93–94). As with UN peacekeeping forces employed during the Cold War, he recommended that these rapid deployment units be established by the voluntary contribution of member states, go into action when authorized by the Security Council, and serve under the command of the secretary-general. In contrast to traditional peacekeeping operations, however, their use could be ordered without the ex-press consent of the disputants, and they would be trained and equipped to use force if necessary.

In addition to units for enforcing ceasefire agreements, it has been suggested that the UN begin to act in accordance with its mandate under Article 43 of the UN Charter, which stipulates that all members "make available to the Security Council . . . armed forces, assistance, and facilities . . . necessary for the pur-pose of maintaining international peace and security." In the past, superpower enmity prevented such cooperation, which could again be derailed if the United States and the other great powers revert to their pre-1989 practice of treating the United Nations with ill-disguised contempt (Gregg, 1993). But if great-power harmony continues, it could facilitate the creation of a large, easily mobilized, multilateral contingency force, positioned to manage disputes in the new millennium (Rochester, 1993). Under such conditions, and given time to organize itself properly for such missions, the United Nations of the future could have the capability "not just to restore the status quo as it existed prior to a breach of the peace, but also to change the parameters of the global order to something more favorable than existed under the prior status quo" (Russett and Sutterlin, 1991: 82).[3]

3. Some commentators question the wisdom of creating such a force, preferring instead to rely on the Korean and Persian Gulf War models where ad hoc UN-sanctioned coalitions were formed. The problem with the ad hoc approach is that it may not be effective in dealing with conflicts between small, strategically unimportant countries. As Joseph Lorenz (1992: 229) points out, if such conflicts "are left to be resolved by ad hoc coalitions, they will probably not be resolved at all. That may not adversely affect the short-term interests of the major powers, but it cannot be mistaken for world order."

The Conference on Security and Cooperation in Europe

The CSCE offers a second option for a new concert-based security architecture. The Helsinki process, which originated the East–West dialogue, has established principles supportive of a two-tier formula, giving the great powers incentives to share costs and responsibilities for security without reducing the lesser powers to second-class citizens. The resistance by the smaller countries to a French proposal to create a five-power *directorate* illustrates the challenge in finding common ground among large and small countries.

Serving as an overarching umbrella, the CSCE has numerous advantages for building a concert-based collective security organization:

- It incorporates the world's two leading military powers, the United States and Russia, serving as an institutional catalyst for their continued cooperation and as a brake on any renewed rivalry.
- By including all of the EC, EFTA, former Warsaw Pact countries, and members of the Commonwealth of Independent States, it promotes the growth of a community of nations that extends across the globe from the west coast of North America to the east coast of Asia, from Vancouver to Vladivostok.
- Because the CSCE is the only forum that explicitly links political, social, and economic issues to the military aspects of security, it is considered by some (Kinkel, 1992: 4) to be "the only solution with any prospect of permanent success."
- As outlined in the Charter of Paris, the CSCE promotes democratic governance, respect for human rights, and norms of mutual respect and tolerance at a time when domestic strife and civil war are major threats to international peace.
- The CSCE facilitates linkages among many existing security institutions. For example, the CSCE zone crosses into the UN security system by virtue of the fact that four of the five permanent members of the Security Council—the United States, France, the United Kingdom, and Russia—are CSCE countries, and at least one Eastern European and one Nordic country regularly appear among the Security Council's nonpermanent members.

These advantages notwithstanding, the CSCE has not yet proven itself up to the challenges it faces. As *The German Tribune* (October 30, 1992: 2) observed, "Two years of experimenting with 'institutionalisation of the CSCE process,' with European 'crisis management' and with 'cooperative security structures' have only gone to show that the ways and means adopted are unsuitable to contain acute crises." The post–Cold War experience indicates that the CSCE must overcome some daunting institutional deficiencies if it is to provide the foundation for a concert-based collective security system. To begin with, it must find a way to reconcile the divergent interests of its large, polyglot membership. The CSCE establishes all of its policies on the basis of unanimity among the full membership, but if its security-enforcement powers are to increase, a decision-making formula accepting less than unanimous consent will be needed.

In addition, consideration must be given to transforming the CSCE from a regional security organization, however broad, to one inclusive of Japan and China. A system that does not protect all the great powers' interests by providing them with an opportunity for participation could cause a dangerous polarization in which the European and North American countries find themselves aligned against those on the Pacific Rim.

Paralleling the challenge of streamlining security decision making is the problem of empowering the organization to make a credible threat that aggression will be met by countervailing force. Those who doubt the viability of the CSCE as a host for the primary security agency of the future point to its failure to prevent or resolve the civil war in the former Yugoslavia. To be sure, the CSCE did send observers and fact-finding missions to examine the conflicts in Abkhazia, Moldovia, and Nagorno-Karabakh, but it lacked the enforcement capability to back up its initiatives.

The North Atlantic Treaty Organization

NATO represents a third possible mooring for international security. For some people, however, NATO is more an anachronism than an anchor. As discussed in Chapter 5, the utility of any alliance will diminish when the common external threat that brought it together disintegrates. Given the absence of a Soviet threat, NATO must transform its mission if it is to play a major security role in the twenty-first century.

To accomplish this task, some students of the Atlantic Alliance believe that NATO must broaden its membership to include the Eastern European countries and the successor states of the Soviet Union. To a degree, progress toward this goal is evident. Following the dissolution of the Warsaw Pact in early 1991, the North Atlantic Council's statement on Partnership with the Countries of Central and Eastern Europe asserted that the security of NATO countries was "inseparably linked to that of all other states in Europe," an assertion reiterated that August when NATO members met in Brussels. Shortly thereafter, in November 1991, proposals to institutionalize security cooperation were made at a meeting of NATO heads of state in Rome. The current North Atlantic Cooperation Council (NACC), incorporating the former members of the Warsaw Pact, represents an outgrowth of these proposals. By sponsoring regular ministerial meetings between NATO and its former adversaries, and by disbanding the pact's Nuclear Planning Group and jettisoning the use of nuclear weapons as part of its strategy (Moniac, 1992), the NACC has begun building

bridges across former Cold War borders, embracing for the first time the principle that "everything that happens anywhere in Europe is a concern for all
Europeans" (Kinkel, 1992: 6).

Yet for all the speculation about a broadened, reconfigured NATO, its future
is uncertain. NATO's impotence in dealing with the virulent conflicts within its
own region (for example, between Greece and Turkey over Cyprus and, more
tragically, the efforts of Bosnian Serbs to establish by force a Serbian republic
"cleansed" of Bosnian Muslims) has reduced confidence in the alliance's ability
to deal with the kinds of ethnonationalist clashes that are likely to pose an
enormous threat in the future. A sign of its diminishing clout in orchestrating
collective military action was given during the June 1992 meeting of NATO
foreign ministers in Oslo. Rather than assuming for itself the responsibility for
determining when peacekeeping operations were warranted, the alliance defined its mission as responding "to the international community when required . . . by making available alliance resources and expertise." By NATO's
own admission, a framework of interlocked institutions is better equipped for
dealing with the rush of ethnic rivalries and territorial disputes that have flood-
ed the international scene since the end of the Cold War.

Establishing such a framework will not be easy. Already there are signs of
friction between NATO and the Western European Union (WEU), the mechanism selected at the European Community's 1991 Maastricht summit to enhance its defense identity. While the Anglo–American position has been to
view the WEU as a bridge between NATO and an increasingly prosperous and
independent European Community, the French and the Germans have seen it as
the agent of a more militarily self-reliant Community (Kelleher, 1993: 276).
Composed of France, Germany, Great Britain, Italy, and the Benelux countries,
the WEU possesses some supranational characteristics and operates by means
of simple or weighted majorities rather than unanimity. As a result, the WEU
has been touted as a more promising security organization for the next century
than NATO (Ullman, 1991). Should the pace of European integration quicken,
NATO could rapidly lose its legitimacy on the Continent as the organizational
home for any concert-based system of collective security.

Other events could also weaken NATO's position and power. The combination of continued budget deficits in Washington and an outbreak of wrenching
trade disputes with Europe could prompt the United States to bring its troops
home, slash defense spending, and wrap itself in a protectionist cocoon. American flirtations with neoisolationism would reduce the salience of NATO on
both sides of the Atlantic and derail the efforts of those reformers who seek to
preserve the alliance by redefining its mission. The possibility that this grim
reality could easily materialize was captured by German Minister of Foreign
Affairs Klaus Kinkel (1992: 5), who warned that "It would be fatal if the
disappearance of the former common threat to the NATO partners also led in
the West to the renationalization of European security policy and a trend
towards isolationism in North America."

As pointed out in Chapter 2, NATO made an important contribution to the long post–World War II peace by providing prominent, simple, and unambiguous lines around which the superpowers coordinated their expectations and about which tacit rules of competition accumulated. And it still is, in Gregory Treverton's (1992: 110) words, "the only serious security game in town." A sense of nostalgia for NATO is understandable, especially from the United States. Nonetheless, some analysts believe that in the future "NATO will be at best a bit player" (Walker, 1991: 129). For them, NATO is a residual organization that is best suited in the aftermath of the Cold War to controlling allies rather than containing enemies. Because divisive issues undermine NATO's capacity for independent action, it appears that "we are entering the season that will decide whether NATO lives or dies" (Safire, 1993b: A21).

If NATO is to develop into a concert-based collective security organization, it must broaden its membership and the geographical definition of its responsibilities. Thus far, there is little evidence that NATO is prepared to take such a bold step away from its original mission. Its members have not been eager to bring Russia into the alliance (see Bell, 1990–1991), nor have they shown interest in incorporating Japan (or China) into an expanded security system. NATO's new Reinforcement Concept (see Ferguson, 1992) expresses satisfaction with backing the conflict-prevention operations initiated by other multilateral institutions; and its new Strategic Concept eschews leadership in favor of sharing roles, risks, and responsibilities.

In summary, NATO served its original purpose well, but now that the threat for its *raison d'être* has disappeared, NATO's relevance and legitimacy have diminished. It has not reconstituted itself to deal with either the new threats of hypernationalism and the separatist violence it spawns, or with conflict emanating from outside its traditional sphere of influence. NATO survives largely by the power of inertia and remains a symbol of division, not unity.

The Group of Seven

On November 15, 1975, at a chateau that once served as the hunting lodge of King Louis XIV, the leaders of the major Western industrialized democracies converged in the first of what was to become a series of summit meetings. The purpose of the meeting was clear: Global economic interdependence greatly increased the need for concerted political efforts to deal with transnational problems. The group included Britain, Canada, France, Germany, Italy, Japan, and the United States, and beginning with the London summit of July 1991, Moscow was accorded consulting status, leading one commentator to label the group the "G-7-1/2 directorate" (Lewis, 1991–1992). Although nonmembers look with suspicion on the Group of Seven, this loose, ad hoc organization has been suggested as the focal point for collective peacekeeping activities in the post–Cold War world (Van Evera, 1992b).

Two reasons typically support arguments promoting the Group of Seven as an updated version of the nineteenth-century Concert of Europe. The first reason is that G-7 members are democracies whose political cultures hold a common set of civic values and procedural norms. They all see politics as a non-zero-sum game; hence their policymaking processes contain a spirit of give-and-take. Compromise, the use of persuasion rather than coercion, and a reliance on legal procedures to resolve disputes are the primary means for dealing with conflict. Everyone is believed to lose if politics degenerates into violence, and this belief guides the relations among democracies in the international arena. Although democratic states have been involved in foreign conflict as frequently as nondemocratic states (Salmore and Hermann, 1969) and are only slightly less likely than nondemocratic states to initiate wars (Small and Singer, 1976; Chan, 1984; Weede, 1984; Domke, 1988), democracies almost never wage war *against one another* (Rummel, 1983; Maoz and Abdolali, 1989; Maoz and Russett, 1992; Bremer, 1992). Disputes between democracies rarely escalate to war (there are historical exceptions; see Ray, 1994) because each side respects the other's legitimacy and expects it to rely on peaceful means of conflict resolution (Doyle, 1983: 213; Doyle, 1995; Fukuyama, 1992). What is more, democracies tend to develop tacit, partner-specific norms that reinforce these expectations.

The second reason for believing that the G-7 can evolve into a new great-power concert lies in the web of economic linkages that span member states. "The natural effect of commerce," wrote Montesquieu (cited in Vernon and Kapstein, 1992: 46), "is to bring about peace." Free trade liberals such as Adam Smith, Jeremy Bentham, Richard Cobden, Herbert Spenser, and Norman Angell agreed. The presumed inverse relationship between foreign trade ties and interstate conflict is predicated on this belief: Business interests that would be harmed by the interruption of commerce are powerful enough to constrain national leaders who might otherwise use war as an instrument of foreign policy. Simply put, there are material incentives to avoid policies that will rupture profitable economic transactions. Why should any one great power attack another if its own economic welfare depends on that partner's survival and trade?

A more recent perspective on this issue stresses the pacific influence of growing economic interdependence. As states rely more on trade rather than conquest for achieving their objectives, so this school of thought reasons, they come to value their trade partners on whom their prosperity depends, and this fosters cooperation. "The growing interdependence of the world economy," notes Richard Cooper (1972: 179), "creates pressures for common policies, and hence for procedures whereby countries discuss and coordinate actions that hitherto were regarded as being of domestic concern exclusively." Hence, because the great powers have become so interdependent, many people doubt that they would militarily challenge those on whom their prosperity is contingent.

The counterpoint to this proposition lies in the economic conditions existing prior to the onset of World War I: A state system "characterized by high economic interdependence, unparalleled prosperity, and relative openness still went to war" (Kahler, 1979–1980: 393). Trade interdependence can engender irritation and disputes. Nevertheless, research on the hypothesized dampening effect of foreign commerce on international conflict supports the contention that states are less inclined to wage war on those with whom they are deeply involved in foreign trade (Domke, 1988: 137; Richardson, 1995). Of course, trading relationships involve both costs and benefits. But as postulated, the preliminary evidence indicates that the rewarding aspects of trade are associated with a decline in the intensity of hostile interactions (Gasiorowski, 1986).

To the extent that this correlation holds predictive power, it implies that the great powers' mutual economic vulnerability will mitigate disputes that might otherwise culminate in armed conflict. "It is thinkable," Harold Lasswell (1950: 252) speculated, "that men will some day face a common disaster which is capable of uniting them in concerted efforts to survive." Economic collapse would be such a disaster, and the desire to avert any interruption in trade and financial flows could become a stimulus for continued cooperation.

THE FUTURE IS NOW

As we discussed in Chapter 3, throughout history different types of multipolar systems have developed, some of which have exhibited more stability than others. Great powers facing a multipolar future have three general paths from which to choose as they contemplate how to bring about a stable form of multipolarity: They can act unilaterally; they can develop bilateral relations with one or more other states; or they can engage in multilateral collaboration with many countries. The foreign policies of most great powers contain a mix of acting single-handedly, joining with a partner, and cooperating globally. What matters is the relative emphasis placed on "going it alone" versus "going it with others" and whether joint action is defined in inclusive or exclusive terms. As we have seen in this chapter, many statesmen and scholars urge the great powers to follow the inclusive path of multilateralism. It is not a panacea for all of the world's security problems (see Box 10.1), but it offers humanity a chance to avoid those multipolar systems containing the polarized alliances and permissive norms that have proven so disruptive and destructive throughout history.[4]

The strengths and weaknesses of multilateralism were highlighted during the

---

4. This conclusion was captured by George F. Kennan (1993: 185) who observed, "[I have never been] partial to the use of multilateral channels for Cold War diplomacy; but for a country anxious to remove itself from the limelight and to give priority to its domestic challenges, the use of multilateral rather than unilateral approaches to world problems has much to recommend it."

BOX 10.1
A SKEPTICAL VIEW OF COLLECTIVE SECURITY

"It would be wrong to succumb to the fallacy of interpreting all international developments as portents of global peace. . . . It is unlikely that new collective security arrangements—directed not against a potential enemy but against any and all potential aggressors—can replace the traditional forms of armament and alliances. The history of such pacts, and most notably the League of Nations, is that they simply do not work. When the crunch comes, states either cannot agree on the definition of aggression, do not find it in their interests to oppose the aggressor, or simply do not have the stomach to use force. Collective security pacts therefore become marginal talking shops. . . .

War, and potential war, will remain a feature of international politics. Its sources will be many and changing, from ethnic animosity to irredentism, from competition for power to religious fanaticism. Its stakes will include territory (including valuable off-shore properties), water rights, and control of populations. It will result from traditional kinds of animosities, but also from the second and third order consequences of developments that are intrinsically unforeseeable. Economic depression, for instance, need not breed violence directly, but it may, as in the 1930s, abet the development of new forms of tyranny, or increase the likelihood of the resort to violence by desperate countries. . . ."

—Eliot A. Cohen (1992: 39–40)

Persian Gulf War when a multinational coalition, led by the United States and operating under the auspices of the United Nations, imposed economic sanctions against Iraq in an effort to pressure Saddam Hussein to withdraw from Kuwait, which the Iraqi military had invaded on August 2, 1990. When he refused despite the hardships caused by the sanctions, the multinational coalition forcibly liberated Kuwait. The collective international response to Iraqi aggression demonstrated the potential of multilateralism. But before we celebrate the birth of a "new world order," warns Robert Art, we should consider the possibility that the special conditions surrounding that war will rarely be present.

(1) Iraq sat quite close to the largest proven reserves of the world's oil, upon which the industrialized economies depend to a unique extent, and this led to a uniquely strong shared interest; (2) Iraq's imports and exports were easy to blockade by sea because it has only one port and only three oil pipelines to the oceans; and (3) Iraq's leader, Saddam Hussein, was widely disliked and feared because of his

grandiose ambitions and because of his ability, unless stopped, to use his oil earnings to acquire even larger military capabilities, even more chemical and biological weapons, and ultimately nuclear weapons. (Art, 1993: 116)

Because these special galvanizing conditions are unlikely to reemerge frequently, it may be far more difficult to rally the international community to respond effectively to a future crisis. Moreover, these difficulties will be multiplied if the great powers squander the unique opportunity presented to them by the end of the Cold War and fail to lay the groundwork for a new security regime.

Each of the potential foundations for a concert-based collective security regime has its own advantages and drawbacks. At the minimum, a new regime will require muscular institutions that:

- include the full participation of *all* the emergent great powers;
- encourage greater Russian–American security cooperation, while guarding against the more pressing problems created by the dissolution of the Soviet Union;
- bind Germany to the pursuit of regional and multilateral security, while protecting its security through a credible nuclear deterrence guarantee;
- foster the movement away from reliance on strictly national defense;
- cope with the security vacuum that has followed the implosion of the Warsaw Pact, as well as "spillouts" that assuredly will accompany the civil strife, ethnic rivalries, and border disputes in Eastern Europe;
- continue long-term efforts toward agreements to dismantle arms that go below START II and control the further proliferation of strategic weapons to regional powers; and
- construct rules for crisis management and design conflict-resolution mechanisms with enforcement capabilities.

No multilateral peacekeeping forces yet exist to support the norms of such a security regime. Given this problem, how might a structure for peace be created that enables the great powers to play a constructive role?

Creation of a great-power consensus about the rules for international politics has seldom proven easy and, when created, has often proven fragile. But as Chapter 6 demonstrated, the formation of great-power security regimes is not only possible, but, once formed, helps control great-power competition and warfare. History suggests that a number of preconditions must be present to entice the great powers to see their interests served by support for a regime that both regulates their competition and encourages their cooperation. Table 10.1 inventories the most important of these and presents an estimate of the extent to which these conditions are present as the twentieth century nears its end.

In addition to the fact that many of these preconditions currently exist, a number of catalysts that could accelerate the pace of great-power multilateral-

TABLE 10.1
Requirements for Great-Power Support for a Security Regime

Essential Preconditions	Extant in the mid-1990s?	Indicators
Approximately equal distribution of power	No, but developing	Converging level of the great powers' economic strength
Modest number of great powers	Yes, but probably increasing	Trend from a unipolar system dominated by the United States to an enlarged multipolar system that includes Russia, Japan, Germany, China, and perhaps the EC
Absence of a (hegemonic) power intent on universal domination	Yes	U.S. disengagement from assertive global leadership role
Benign (hegemonic) power prepared to intervene to defend the system's rules	Yes, depending on U.S. response	U.S. interventions in the Persian Gulf and Somalia
Mutual fears of commonly perceived threats	Yes	Aversion to ethnic nationalism and civil war Threat of warlord depotism Fear of rise of protective barriers to free trade Shared ecological dangers Threat of weapons proliferation and revisionist powers

ism also are present today (see Table 10.2). This mapping of the new domain for great-power interaction portrays a global system in rapid transition whose shape has not yet taken on clear definition. The many overlapping and unfolding trends listed in Tables 10.1 and 10.2 are creating a chaotic and increasingly complex environment in which the uncertainty associated with previous multipolar periods is endemic.[5] Theorists and policymakers remain divided on whether uncertainty is conducive to competition and war or to collaboration and collective management (recall Chapters 4 and 5). Which outcome will

5. Writes Immanuel Wallerstein (1993b: 4), "We have now entered into the post-American era, but also the post-liberal era. This promises to be a time of great world disorder, greater probably than the world disorder between 1914 and 1945, and far more significant in terms of maintaining the world-system as a viable structure."

TABLE 10.2

Factors and Trends Conditioning the Advent of a New Great-Power Security Regime

Promotive Catalysts	Extant in the mid-1990s?	Indicators
Common economic philosophies	Majority	Global spread of free market economies
Similar type of governments	Majority	Diffusion of democracy
Modest level of flexibility in alliances	Yes	Fragmentation of Cold War blocs, growth of new ad hoc bilateral alignments
Support for upholding treaty commitments	Declining, but slow erosion	Fragility of existing agreements in era of rapid change
Prohibition of great-power aggression	Yes	Growing sanctity of the "no first use" doctrine
Respect for territorial borders	Yes	Peaceful redrawing of boundaries through legislative procedures
Recognized great-power spheres of influence	No	Thrown into doubt with power transitions
Great-power willingness to intervene to contain violence on the periphery	Moderate but growing support for intervention	Persian Gulf and Somalia
Inclusion of all the great powers in collective security divisions	No	Partial great-power representation in peacekeeping operations

materialize at the end of this century is problematic, given these simultaneously integrating and disintegrating developments and the fact that some of the policies designed to deal with them "are flatly in conflict" (Schlesinger, 1993: 17).

Fortunately, many of the ingredients supportive of norms to regulate the competition inherent in multipolar systems are in place (see Box 10.2). In this respect, the setting for great-power relationships in the mid-1990s provides an environment conducive to the growth of great-power security regimes. On the negative side of the ledger, however, a durable commitment to concerted great-power collaboration has yet to crystallize:

BOX 10.2
FOUNDATIONS FOR A GREAT-POWER SECURITY REGIME

"Great powers have a vested interest in systemic peace. First, a general war would be ruinous for most of them. Second, stability and predictability are the foundations on which the material and moral welfare of their citizens rest. . . . [While] each great power has its own distinct interests, they all agree that a large-scale war should be prevented. . . . Of the seven [strongest great powers]—America, Japan, Germany, Russia, China, France, and England—none appears to harbor major territorial grievances; most are liberal, capitalist democracies; and none presents a radically different ideology, which would make it a 'revolutionary' state. Such revisionism as exists is limited to demands for clout in global economic affairs, international organizations, etc."

—Fareed Zakaria (1992–1993: 29–30)

"As in past ages today's concert rests on acceptance by all major powers of the same three principles: involvement of all; ideological agreement; and renunciation of war and territorial expansion, giving liberal democratic and economic development first priority. . . . All [concert] systems require the presence of a 'threat' to make them cohere. . . . Nations need to cooperate *against* something as well as *for* something. . . . Today it must be against the threat of global economic breakdown. . . . History may tell us little about the future, but it seems to indicate that a central coalition—united by economic interest in an open and growing world economy—is not doomed to fail."

—Richard Rosecrance (1992: 75, 79, 82)

There is a sharp distinction to be drawn between real and apparent multilateralism. True multilateralism involves a genuine coalition of coequal partners of comparable strength and stature—the World War II Big Three coalition, for example. What we have today is pseudo-multilateralism: a dominant great power acts essentially alone, but, embarrassed at the idea and still worshiping at the shrine of collective security, recruits a ship here, a brigade there, and blessings all around to give its unilateral actions a multilateral sheen. (Krauthammer, 1991: 25)

Thus, before assuming that truly collaborative multilateralism will materialize and endure, we must bear in mind that almost every previous multipolar system has begun with optimistic hopes for concerted great-power cooperation and ended in a costly and increasingly deadly great-power competition for predominance.

The great powers have it within their hands to chart their future. Another general war would surely end in catastrophe and perhaps the termination of mankind. "The first thing to bear in mind," George F. Kennan (1993: 212) explains, is that "in light of modern military technology, no all-out war among great influential powers (and that means all the great powers of this day) can now be other than suicidal, regardless of the formal theoretical outcome in terms of what are called victory and defeat. If war of this sort cannot be ruled out, civilization will be." This provides an awesome incentive for great-power collaboration. Hence, out of dread may arise the beginning of a new age, in which the past pattern of great-power rivalry and warfare is replaced by cooperation and peace.

But before we become euphoric over the expectation that the destructiveness of weapons will end their use, we must recall Plato's complaint more than 2,000 years ago that "only the dead have seen the end of war." It would be naive to expect that the great powers will automatically put aside their future disputes in order to advance collective interests. Instead, we should be ever mindful that "the mere fact that something is to a man's interest is no guaranty that he will be interested in it" (Burke, 1935: 55).

Some contemporary observers pessimistically assume, with Roberto Michels (1949: 40), that the "currents of history resemble successive waves. They break over the same shoal. They are ever renewed." Against this image, we can take comfort in the demonstrated capacity of nations to change their practices, reform their institutions, and inaugurate a new pattern that truly breaks with past propensities. The hard edges of history can be softened.

To use the same metaphor, successive waves breaking over a shoal can eventually erode it, thus altering the landscape and their own patterns. The great powers of the late twentieth and early twenty-first century are not doomed to repeat the failed methods of the past. They can be masters of their collective fates. Since we all will be affected by the decisions they make, we have a stake in the outcome and ample reasons to influence their plans and policies.

REFERENCES

Aaron, Henry J., ed. (1990) *Setting National Priorities: Policy for the Nineties.* Washington, D.C.: Brookings.

Acheson, Dean. (1969) *Present at the Creation.* New York: Norton.

Aliano, Richard A. (1978) *The Crime of World Power.* New York: G. P. Putnam's Sons.

Altfeld, Michael F. (1984) "The Decision to Ally: A Theory and Test," *Western Political Quarterly* 37 (December): 523–544.

Alperovitz, Gar, and Kai Bird. (1992) "The Fading of the Cold War—and the Demystification of Twentieth-Century Issues," pp. 207–216 in Michael J. Hogan, ed., *The End of the Cold War.* New York: Cambridge University Press.

Ambrose, Stephen E. (1992) *Rise to Globalism: American Foreign Policy Since 1938,* 6th ed. New York: Penguin.

Andreski, Stanislav. (1992) *Wars, Revolutions, Dictatorships.* London: Frank Cass.

Arbatov, Georgi. (1990) "Spending Too Much on the Military," *World Press Review* 37 (April): 50.

Aron, Raymond. (1974) *The Imperial Republic: The United States and the World, 1945–1973.* Cambridge, Mass.: Winthrop Publishers.

———. (1966) *Peace and War.* London: Weidenfeld and Nicolson.

———. (1965) *The Great Debate: Theories of Nuclear Strategy.* Garden City, N.Y.: Doubleday.

Arquilla, John. (1992) *Dubious Battles: Aggression, Defeat, and the International System.* Washington, D.C.: Crane Russak.

Art, Robert J. (1993) "Defense Policy," pp. 89–135 in Robert J. Art and Seyom Brown, eds., *U.S. Foreign Policy: The Search for a New Role.* New York: Macmillan.

Aspin, Les. (1992) "National Security in the 1990s: Defining a New Basis for U.S. Military Forces." Statement presented to the Atlantic Council of the United States, January 6.

Attali, Jacques. (1991) *Millennium: Winners and Losers in the Coming World Order.* Trans. by Leila Conners and Nathan Gardels. New York: Random House.

Axelrod, Robert, and Robert O. Keohane. (1986) "Achieving Cooperation Under Anarchy," pp. 226–254 in Kenneth A. Oye, ed., *Cooperation Under Anarchy.* Princeton, N.J.: Princeton University Press.

Babst, Dean V. (1964) "Elective Governments—A Force for Peace," *The Wisconsin Sociologist* 3 (No. 1): 9–14.

Bacon, Francis. (1963) [1605] *The Advancement of Learning.* Oxford: Oxford University Press.

Bailey, F. G. (1969) *Stratagems and Spoils: A Social Anthopology of Politics.* New York: Scholken.

Baker, C. Ashford. (1988) *The Ultimate Dilemma: Obligation Conflicts in Wartime.* London: University Press of America.

Baker, James A. (1990a) "From Points to Pathways of Mutual Advantage: Next Steps in Soviet–American Relations," Current Policy No. 1309. Washington, D.C.: United States Department of State, Bureau of Public Affairs, Office of Public Communication.

_____. (1990b) "Recent Developments in U.S.–Soviet Relations," Current Policy No. 1285. Washington, D.C.: United States Department of State, Bureau of Public Affairs, Office of Public Communication.

Baldwin, David A. (1989) *Paradoxes of Power.* New York: Basil Blackwell.

Bandow, Doug. (1992–1993) "Avoiding War," *Foreign Policy* 89 (Winter): 156–174.

Barnathan, Joyce, and Pete Engardio, with Lynne Curry, and Bruce Einhorn. (1993) "China: The Emerging Economic Powerhouse of the 21st Century," *Business Week* (May 17): 54–69.

Barnet, Richard J. (1990) *The Rockets' Red Glare: When America Goes to War—The Presidents and the People.* New York: Simon and Schuster.

_____. (1987) "Reflections," *The New Yorker* (March 9): 78 et passim.

_____. (1984) "The Empire Strikes Back: A Pitiful Helpless Giant Goes to War," *Progressive* 48: 16–17.

_____. (1977) *The Giants: Russia and America.* New York: Simon and Schuster.

Basic Statistics of the European Community. Comparisons with Some European Countries, Canada, the U.S.A., Japan, and the U.S.S.R. (1991) 28th ed. Luxembourg: Office for Official Publications of the European Community.

Baum, Richard. (1992–1993) "The China Syndrome: Prospects for Democracy in the Middle Kingdom," *Harvard International Review* 15 (Winter): 32–33, 66.

Beer, Francis A., ed. (1970) *Alliances: Latent War Communities in the Contemporary World.* New York: Holt, Rinehart and Winston.

Bell, Coral. (1990–1991) "Why Russia Should Join NATO," *The National Interest* 22 (Winter): 37–47.

Benevolenski, Vladimir, and Andrei Kortunov. (1993) "Ethics, Integration, and Disintegration: A Russian Perspective," *Ethics & International Affairs* 7: 97–114.

Bennett, A. LeRoy. (1991) *International Organization: Principles and Issues,* 5th ed. Englewood Cliffs, N.J.: Prentice-Hall.

Bergesen, Albert. (1981) "Long Economic Cycles and the Size of Industrial Enterprise," pp. 179–189 in Richard Rubinson, ed., *Dynamics of World Development.* Beverly Hills: Sage.

Bergesen, Albert, and Ronald Schoenberg. (1980) "Long Waves of Colonial Expansion and Contraction, 1415–1969," pp. 231–277 in Albert Bergesen, ed., *Studies of the Modern World-System.* New York: Academic Press.

Bergner, Jeffrey T. (1991) *The New Superpowers: Germany, Japan, the United States and the New World Order.* New York: St. Martin's Press.

Bergsten, C. Fred. (1990) "The World Economy After the Cold War," *Foreign Affairs* 69 (Summer): 96–112.

Betts, Richard K. (1992) "Systems for Peace or Causes of War? Collective Security, Arms Control, and the New Europe," pp. 199–237 in Sean M. Lynn-Jones and Steven E. Miller, eds., *America's Strategy in a Changing World.* Cambridge, Mass.: The MIT Press.

Beveridge, William. (1945) *The Price of Peace.* New York: Norton.

Binder, Guyora. (1988) *Treaty Conflict and Political Contradiction: The Dialectic of Duplicity.* New York: Praeger.

Black, Jeremy. (1990) *The Rise of the European Powers, 1679–1793.* London: Edward Arnold.

Bloch, Marc. (1953) [1949] *The Historian's Craft.* New York: Random House.

Bolton, John. (1993) "No Expansion for U.N. Security Council," *The Wall Street Journal* (January 26): A14.

Borrus, Michael, and John Zysman with David Bell. (1992) "Industrial Competitiveness and National Security," pp. 136–175 in Graham Allison and Gregory F. Treverton, eds., *Rethinking America's Security: Beyond Cold War to New World Order*. New York: Norton.

Boswell, Terry, Mike Sweat, and John Brueggemann. (1989) "War in the Core of the World-System: Testing the Goldstein Thesis," pp. 9–26 in Robert K. Schaeffer, ed., *War in the World-System*. Westport, Conn.: Greenwood Press.

Boutros-Ghali, Boutros. (1992–1993) "Empowering the United Nations," *Foreign Affairs* 72 (Winter): 89–102.

Bozeman, Adda B. (1960) *Politics and Culture in International History*. Princeton, N.J.: Princeton University Press.

Brademas, John. (1992) "Internationalizing Higher Education." Paper presented at the Carnegie Council on Ethics and International Affairs, New York, November 10.

Branigin, William. (1992a) "A Costly Way to Keep the Peace: Even After Decades and Billions of Dollars, U.N. Troops Are Largely Ineffective," *The Washington Post National Weekly Edition* (December 7–13): 9–10.

———. (1992b) "United Frustrations: The U.N. Is Tripping Over Its Own Bloat and Corruption," *The Washington Post National Weekly Edition* 10 (November 30–December 6): 6–7.

Braudel, Fernand. (1984) *The Perspective of the World*, Vol. 3. New York: Harper and Row.

———. (1973) *The Mediterranean and the Mediterranean World in the Age of Philip II*. New York: Harper.

Brawley, Mark R. (1990) "Challengers, Supporters and Ambivalent Powers: How Hegemony Shapes Alliance Formation and the Conduct of Major Wars." Paper presented at the Annual Meeting of the American Political Science Association, San Francisco, August 30–September 2.

Brecher, Michael, and Patrick James. (1986) *Crisis and Change in World Politics*. Boulder, Colo.: Westview.

Brecher, Michael, and Jonathan Wilkenfeld. (1991) "International Crises and Global Instability: The Myth of the 'Long Peace'," pp. 85–104 in Charles W. Kegley, Jr., ed., *The Long Postwar Peace*. New York: HarperCollins.

Brecher, Michael, Patrick James, and Jonathan Wilkenfeld. (1990) "Polarity and Stability: New Concepts, Indicators and Evidence," *International Interactions* 16 (No. 1): 49–80.

Bremer, Stuart A. (1992) "Dangerous Dyads: Conditions Affecting the Likelihood of Interstate War, 1816–1965," *Journal of Conflict Resolution* 36 (June): 309–341.

———. (1980) "National Capabilities and War Proneness," pp. 57–82 in J. David Singer, ed., *The Correlates of War II: Testing Some Realpolitik Models*. New York: Free Press.

Brenner, Michael J. (1993) "EC: Confidence Lost," *Foreign Policy* 91 (Summer): 24–43.

Brewer, Anthony. (1987) "Imperialism," pp. 238–239 in David Miller, et al., eds., *The Blackwell Encyclopaedia of Political Thought*. Oxford: Basil Blackwell.

Brierly, James Leslie. (1955) *The Law of Nations*, 5th ed. New York: Oxford University Press.

Brodie, Bernard. (1973) *War and Politics*. New York: Macmillan.

Brooks, David. (1992) "It's a Bird, It's a Plane, It's Multilateral Man!" *The Wall Street Journal* (September 12): A12.

Brown, Seyom. (1992) *International Relations in a Changing Global System: Toward a Theory of World Polity*. Boulder, Colo.: Westview.

———. (1987) *The Causes and Prevention of War*. New York: St. Martin's Press.

Brzezinski, Zbigniew. (1992) "The Cold War and Its Aftermath," *Foreign Affairs* 71 (Fall): 31–49.

———. (1972) *The Fragile Blossom: Crisis and Change in Japan*. New York: Harper and Row.

Buchan, Alastair. (1965) "Problems of an Alliance Policy: An Essay in Hindsight," pp. 293–

310 in Michael Howard, ed., *The Theory and Practice of War*. Bloomington, Ind.: Indiana University Press.

Buchanan, Patrick. (1990) "America First—and Second, and Third," *The National Interest* 19 (Spring): 77–82.

Bueno de Mesquita, Bruce. (1981a) "Risk, Power Distributions, and the Likelihood of War," *International Studies Quarterly* 25 (December): 541–568.

———. (1981b) *The War Trap*. New Haven, Conn.: Yale University Press.

———. (1978) "Systemic Polarization and the Occurrence and Duration of War," *Journal of Conflict Resolution* 22 (June): 241–267.

———. (1975) "Measuring Systemic Polarity," *Journal of Conflict Resolution* 22 (June): 187–216.

Bueno de Mesquita, Bruce, and David Lalman. (1992) *War and Reason: Domestic and International Imperatives*. New Haven, Conn.: Yale University Press.

Bueno de Mesquita, Bruce, and J. David Singer. (1973) "Alliances, Capabilities, and War: A Review and Synthesis," pp. 237–280 in Cornelius Cotter, ed., *Political Science Annual*. Vol. IV. Indianapolis: Bobbs-Merrill.

Bull, Hedley. (1977) *The Anarchical Society: A Study of Order in World Politics*. New York: Columbia University Press.

———. (1968) "The Grotian Conception of International Society," pp. 51–73 in Herbert Butterfield and Martin Wight, eds., *Diplomatic Investigations*. Cambridge, Mass.: Harvard University Press.

Bullock, Alan. (1962) *Hitler: A Study in Tyranny*. New York: Harper & Row.

Burke, Kenneth. (1935) *Permanence and Change: An Anatomy of Purpose*. New York: New Republic Books.

Burman, Stephen. (1991) *America in the Modern World: The Transcendence of United States Hegemony*. New York: St. Martin's Press.

Burns, Arthur Lee. (1968) *Of Powers and Their Politics*. Englewood Cliffs, N.J.: Prentice-Hall.

———. (1964) "From Balance to Deterrence," *World Politics* 9 (July): 494–529.

Byrnes, James F. (1947) *Speaking Frankly*. New York: Harper & Row.

Calleo, David P. (1992) "American National Interest and the New Europe: The Millennium Has Not Yet Arrived," pp. 174–190 in Charles W. Kegley, Jr., and Eugene R. Wittkopf, eds., *The Future of American Foreign Policy*. New York: St. Martin's Press.

Callières, François de. (1963) [1716] *On the Manner of Negotiating with Princes*, trans. by A. F. Whyte. South Bend, Ind.: University of Notre Dame Press.

Caporaso, James A. (1992) "International Relations Theory and Multilateralism: The Search for Foundations," *International Organization* 46 (Summer): 599–631.

Carlsson, Ingvar. (1992) "A New International Order Through the United Nations," *Security Dialogue* 23 (December): 7–11.

Carnegie Endowment National Commission. (1992) *Changing Our Ways: America and the New World*. Washington, D.C.: Brookings Institution.

Carpenter, Ted Galen. (1991) "The New World Disorder," *Foreign Policy* 84 (Fall): 24–39.

Carr, Edward H. (1939) *The Twenty-Years' Crisis, 1919–1939: An Introduction to the Study of International Relations*. London: Macmillan.

Chace, James. (1992) *The Consequences of Peace: The New Internationalism and American Foreign Policy*. New York: Oxford University Press.

Chan, Steve. (1984) "Mirror, Mirror on the Wall . . .: Are the Free Countries More Pacific?" *Journal of Conflict Resolution* 28 (December): 617–648.

Charney, Jonathan I. (1986) "The Power of the Executive Branch of the United States Government to Violate Customary International Law," *American Journal of International Law* 80 (October): 913–922.

Chase-Dunn, Christopher. (1989) *Global Formation: Structure of the World Economy*. Cambridge, Mass.: Basil Blackwell.

Cheney, Dick. (1993) *Report of the Secretary of Defense to the President and the Congress.* Washington, D.C.: U.S. Government Printing Office.

———. (1992) "Rising to the Challenge: The Right Choices for America's Defense," *Harvard International Review* 14 (Summer): 8–9, 56.

Christensen, Thomas J., and Jack Snyder. (1990) "Chain Gangs and Passed Bucks: Predicting Alliance Patterns in Multipolarity," *International Organization* 44 (Spring): 137–168.

Cicero, M. Tullius. (1913) *De Officiis.* Trans. by W. Miller. Loeb Classical Library. London: Heinemann.

Clark, G. N. (1966) "European Equilibrium in the Seventeenth Century," pp. 23–30 in Laurence W. Martin, ed., *Diplomacy in Modern European History.* New York: Macmillan.

Clark, John, and Aaron Wildavsky. (1990) *The Moral Collapse of Communism: Bland as a Cautionary Tale.* San Francisco: Institute for Contemporary Studies Press.

Claude, Inis L., Jr. (1992) "Collective Security After the Cold War," pp. 7–28 in Inis L. Claude, Jr. Sheldon Simon, and Douglas Stuart, *Collective Security in Europe and Asia.* Carlisle Barracks, Pa.: Strategic Studies Institute, U.S. Army War College.

———. (1989) "The Balance of Power Revisited," *Review of International Studies* 15 (January): 77–85.

———. (1988) *States and the Global System: Politics, Law and Organization.* New York: St. Martin's Press.

———. (1986) "The Common Defense and Great-Power Responsibilities," *Political Science Quarterly* 101 (December): 719–732.

———. (1964) *Swords into Plowshares: The Problems and Progress of International Organization.* New York: Random House.

———. (1962) *Power and International Relations.* New York: Random House.

Clinton, William Jefferson. (1993) "The Inauguration Address," *The Cincinnati Enquirer* (January 21): A4.

Cohen, Benjamin J. (1973) *The Question of Imperialism.* New York: Basic Books.

Cohen, Eliot A. (1992) "The Future of Military Power: The Continuing Utility of Force," pp. 33–40 in Charles W. Kegley, Jr., and Eugene R. Wittkopf, eds., *The Global Agenda,* 3rd ed. New York: McGraw-Hill.

———. (1991) "Churchill and Coalition Strategy in World War II," pp. 43–67 in Paul Kennedy, ed., *Grand Strategies in War and Peace.* New Haven, Conn.: Yale University Press.

Coll, Steve. (1993) "Turkey: A Modern Role for an Ancient Land?" *The Washington Post* (May 24): A13, A14.

Commission on Integrated Long-Term Strategy. (1988) *Discriminate Deterrence.* Washington, D.C.: U.S. Government Printing Office.

Conable, Barber B., Jr., and David M. Lampton. (1992–1993) "China: The Coming Power," *Foreign Affairs* 72 (Winter): 133–149.

Conable, Barber B., Jr., and John C. Whitehead. (1993) *United States and China: Relations at a Crossroads.* Washington, D.C.: The Atlantic Council of the United States.

Connor, W. R. (1991) "Polarization in Thucydides," pp. 53–69 in Richard Ned Lebow and Barry S. Strauss, eds., *Hegemonic Rivalry: From Thucydides to the Nuclear Age.* Boulder, Colo.: Westview.

Cooper, Richard N. (1972) "Economic Interdependence and Foreign Policy in the Seventies," *World Politics* 24 (January): 158–181.

Coplin, William D. (1971) *Introduction to International Politics: A Theoretical Overview.* Chicago: Markham.

———. (1966) *The Functions of International Law.* Chicago: Rand McNally.

———. (1965) "International Law and Assumptions about the State System," *World Politics* 7 (July): 615–634.

Crabb, Cecil V., Jr. (1965) *American Foreign Policy in the Nuclear Age*. New York: Harper & Row.

Crocker, Chester A. (1993) "The Law and Order Problem Goes Global," *The Washington Post National Weekly Edition* 10 (December 26, 1992–January 3): 23.

Crowe, Eyre. (1992) [1907] "The Containment of Germany," pp. 473–475 in Evan Luard, ed., *Basic Texts in International Relations*. New York: St. Martin's Press.

Cumings, Bruce. (1993) "The End of the Seventy-Years' Crisis: Trilateralism and the New World Order," pp. 9–32 in Meredith Woo-Cumings and Michael Loriaux, eds., *Past as Prelude: History in the Making of a New World Order*. Boulder, Colo.: Westview.

Dahl, Robert A. (1970) *Modern Political Analysis*, 2nd ed. Englewood Cliffs, N.J.: Prentice-Hall.

David, Arie E. (1975) *The Strategy of Treaty Termination: Lawful Breaches and Retaliations*. New Haven, Conn.: Yale University Press.

Davis, Harry R., and Robert C. Good, eds. (1960) *Reinhold Niebuhr on Politics*. New York: Charles Scribner and Sons.

De Michelis, Gianni. (1990) "Reaching Out to the East," *Foreign Policy* 79 (Summer): 45–55.

Dehio, Ludwig. (1962) *The Precarious Balance: Four Centuries of the European Power Struggle*. Trans. by Charles Fullman. New York: Alfred A. Knopf.

Deibel, Terry L. (1987) "Alliances for Containment," pp. 100–119 in Terry L. Deibel and John Lewis Gaddis, eds., *Containing the Soviet Union*. Washington, D.C.: Pergamon-Brassy's.

DePorte, A. W. (1979) *Europe Between the Superpowers*. New Haven, Conn.: Yale University Press.

Destler, I. M., and Michael Nacht. (1993) "U.S. Policy Toward Japan," pp. 289–314 in Robert J. Art and Seyom Brown, eds., *U.S. Foreign Policy: The Search for a New Role*. New York: Macmillan.

Deudney, Daniel, and G. John Ikenberry. (1992) "Who Won the Cold War?" *Foreign Policy* 87 (Summer): 123–138.

————. (1991–1992) "The International Sources of Soviet Change," *International Security* 16 (Winter): 74–118.

Deutsch, Karl W. (1978) *The Analysis of International Relations*, 2nd ed. Englewood Cliffs, N.J.: Prentice-Hall.

————. (1974) *Politics and Government*. Boston: Houghton Mifflin.

Deutsch, Karl W., and J. David Singer. (1964) "Multipolar Power Systems and International Stability," *World Politics* 16 (April): 390–406.

Dimitrov, Philip. (1992) "Freeing the Soul from Communism," *The Wall Street Journal* (March 23): A10.

Djilas, Milovan. (1961) *Conversations with Stalin*. Trans. by Michael B. Petrovich. New York: Harcourt, Brace & World.

Dockrill, Michael. (1991) *Atlas of Twentieth Century World History*. New York: Harper-Perennial.

Domke, William K. (1988) *War and the Changing Global System*. New Haven, Conn.: Yale University Press.

Doran, Charles F. (1991) *Systems in Crisis: New Imperatives of High Politics at Century's End*. New York: Cambridge University Press.

Dougherty, James E., and Robert L. Pfaltzgraff, Jr. (1990) *Contending Theories of International Relations*, 3rd ed. New York: Harper & Row.

Doyle, Michael W. (1995) "Liberalism and World Politics Revisited," forthcoming in Charles W. Kegley, Jr., ed., *Controversies in International Relations Theory: Realism and the Neoliberal Challenge*. New York: St. Martin's Press.

————. (1986a) *Empires*. Ithaca, N.Y.: Cornell University Press.

————. (1986b) "Liberalism and World Politics," *American Political Science Review* 80 (December): 1151–1169.

———. (1983) "Kant, Liberal Legacies, and Foreign Affairs," Part I, *Philosophy and Public Affairs* 12 (Summer): 205–235.

Dumas, Roland. (1992) "Time to Share the Power: Adjusting U.S. Attitudes to a Multi-polar World," *Harvard International Review* 14 (Summer): 18–20.

Duncan, George T., and Randolph M. Siverson. (1982) "Flexibility of Alliance Partner Choice in a Multipolar System," *International Studies Quarterly* 26 (December): 511–538.

Eagleburger, Lawrence S. (1989) "The 21st Century: American Foreign Policy Challenges," pp. 242–260 in Edward K. Hamilton, ed., *America's Global Interests: A New Agenda.* New York: W. W. Norton.

The Economist. (1992) *World in Figures, 1993 Edition.* London: Economist Books.

Elliott, J. H. (1991) "Managing Decline: Olivares and the Grand Strategy of Imperial Spain," pp. 87–104 in Paul Kennedy, ed., *Grand Strategies in War and Peace.* New Haven, Conn.: Yale University Press.

Elrod, Richard. (1976) "The Concert of Europe: A Fresh Look at an International System," *World Politics* 28 (January): 159–174.

Ember, Carol R., Melvin Ember, and Bruce M. Russett. (1992) "Peace Between Participatory Polities: A Cross-Cultural Test of the 'Democracies Rarely Fight Each Other' Hypothesis," *World Politics* 44 (July): 573–599.

Encarnation, Dennis J. (1992) *Rivals Beyond Trade: America Versus Japan in Global Competition.* Ithaca, N.Y.: Cornell University Press.

Encausse, Hélène Carrère. (1993) *The End of the Soviet Empire.* New York: Basic Books.

Falk, Richard A. (1980) "The Menace of the New Cycle of Interventionary Diplomacy," *Journal of Peace Research* 17 (May): 201–205.

———. (1965) "World Law and Human Conflict," pp. 227–249 in Elton B. McNeil, ed., *The Nature of Human Conflict.* Englewood Cliffs, N.J.: Prentice-Hall.

Feinberg, Richard E., and Delia M. Boylan. (1992) "Modular Multilateralism: U.S. Economic Policy Toward Southern Nations in an Age of Uneven Development," pp. 179–205 in Kenneth A. Oye, Robert J. Lieber, and Donald Rothchild, eds., *Eagle in a New World: American Grand Strategy in the Post–Cold War Era.* New York: HarperCollins.

Ferguson, Gordon. (1992) "NATO's New Concept of Reinforcement," *NATO Review* 7 (October): 31–34.

Ferguson, Tim W. (1993) "The Sounds of Eras Shifting," *The Wall Street Journal* (January 5): A15.

Filitov, Alexei. (1992) "Victory in the Postwar Era: Despite the Cold War or Because of It?" *Diplomatic History* 16 (Winter): 54–60.

Finkelstein, Marina S., and Lawrence S. Finkelstein. (1966) *Collective Security.* San Francisco: Chandler.

Finlay, David J., and Thomas Hovet, Jr. (1975) *7304: International Relations on the Planet Earth.* New York: Harper & Row.

Foreign Relations of the United States. (1946) Vol. VI. Washington, D.C.: U.S. Government Printing Office.

Friedberg, Aaron L. (1992) "Is the United States Capable of Acting Strategically?" pp. 95–111 in Charles W. Kegley, Jr., and Eugene R. Wittkopf, eds., *The Future of American Foreign Policy.* New York: St. Martin's Press.

Friedheim, Robert L. (1968) "The 'Satisfied' and 'Dissatisfied' States Negotiate International Law," pp. 68–88 in Richard A. Falk and Wolfram F. Hanrieder, eds., *International Law and Organization.* Philadelphia: J. B. Lippincott.

Friedman, George, and Meredith Le Bard. (1992) *The Coming War with Japan.* New York: St. Martin's Press.

Friedman, Julian R. (1970) "Alliance in International Politics," pp. 3–32 in Julian R. Friedman, Christopher Bladen, and Steven Rosen, eds., *Alliance in International Politics.* Boston: Allyn and Bacon.

Friedrich, Carl J., and Charles Blitzer. (1957) *The Age of Power*. Ithaca, N.Y.: Cornell University Press.

Fukuyama, Francis. (1992) *The End of History and the Last Man*. New York: Free Press.

———. (1989) "The End of History?" *The National Interest* 16 (Summer): 3–16.

Gaddis, John Lewis. (1992a) "How Relevant Was U.S. Strategy in Winning the Cold War?" Address given at the Army War College Strategy Conference, February 13, 1992. Carlisle Barracks, Pa.: Strategic Studies Institute, U.S. Army War College.

———. (1992b) "Toward the Post–Cold War World," pp. 16–32 in Charles W. Kegley, Jr., and Eugene R. Wittkopf, eds., *The Future of American Foreign Policy*. New York: St. Martin's Press.

———. (1992c) *The United States and the End of the Cold War: Implications, Reconsiderations, Provocations*. New York: Oxford University Press.

———. (1991) "Great Illusions, the Long Peace, and the Future of the International System," pp. 25–55 in Charles W. Kegley, Jr., ed., *The Long Postwar Peace*. New York: HarperCollins.

———. (1990) "Coping with Victory," *The Atlantic Monthly* 265 (May): 49–60.

———. (1986) "The Long Peace: Elements of Stability in the Postwar International System," *International Security* 10 (Spring): 92–142.

———. (1982) *Strategies of Containment: A Critical Appraisal of Postwar American National Security Policy*. New York: Oxford University Press.

Galo, Daniel P. (1992) "Interview with Bill Clinton," *Europe* (October 1).

Galtung, Johan. (1969) "Violence, Peace, and Peace Research," *Journal of Peace Research* 6 (No. 3): 167–191.

Garner, James W. (1927) "The Doctrine of Rebus Sic Stantibus and the Termination of Treaties," *American Journal of International Law* 21 (July): 509–516.

Garten, Jeffrey E. (1992) *A Cold Peace: America, Japan, Germany, and the Struggle for Supremacy*. New York: Random House.

Gärtner, Heinz. (1992) "The Future of Institutionalization: The CSCE Example," pp. 233–257 in Ian M. Cuthbertson, ed., *Redefining the CSCE: Challenges and Opportunities*. New York: Institute for East-West Studies.

Gasiorowski, Mark J. (1986) "Economic Interdependence and International Conflict: Some Cross-National Evidence," *International Studies Quarterly* 30 (March): 23–38.

Geiger, Theodore. (1988) *The Future of the International System: The United States and the World Political Economy*. Boston: Unwin Hyman.

Gelb, Leslie H. (1993a) "Lest Foreign Wars Engulf Us," *The State* (Columbia, S.C.) (January 23): 12A.

———. (1993b) "Tailoring a U.S. Role at the U.N.," *International Herald Tribune* (January 2–3): 4.

———. (1992) "Who Won the Cold War," *The New York Times* (August 22): A27.

Geller, Daniel S. (1993) "Power Differentials and War in Rival Dyads," *International Studies Quarterly* 37 (June): 173–193.

———. (1992a) "Capability Concentration, Power Transition, and War," *International Interactions* 17 (No. 3): 269–284.

———. (1992b) "Power Transition and Conflict Initiation," *Conflict Management and Peace Science* 12 (No. 1): 1–16.

———. (1988) "Power System Membership and Patterns of War," *International Political Science Review* 9 (No. 4): 365–379.

Gellner, Ernest. (1992) "The God That Paled," *The New Republic* (June 22): 40–41.

George, Alexander L. (1986) "U.S.–Soviet Global Rivalry: Norms of Competition," *Journal of Peace Research* 23 (September): 247–262.

Gilpin, Robert. (1981) *War and Change in World Politics*. Cambridge: Cambridge University Press.

Gleditsch, Nils Petter. (1992) "Democracy and Peace," *Journal of Peace Research* 29 (November): 369–376.

Glynn, Patrick. (1993a) "America's Burden," *The New Republic* 208 (January 25): 24–27.

———. (1993b) "Letter to the Editor," *Foreign Policy* 90 (Spring): 171–174.

———. (1990) "Reassessing the Lessons of Sarajevo," pp. 57–63 in Kenneth M. Jensen and Kimber M. Schraub, eds., *A Discussion of the Origins of Thinking on Arms Control: The Sarajevo Fallacy*. Washington, D.C.: U.S. Institute of Peace.

Gochman, Charles, and Russell J. Leng. (1983) "Realpolitik and the Road to War," *International Studies Quarterly* 27 (March): 97–120.

Gochman, Charles S., and Zeev Maoz. (1984) "Militarized Interstate Disputes, 1816–1976: Procedures, Patterns, and Insights," *Journal of Conflict Resolution* 28 (December): 585–616.

Goertz, Gary, and Paul F. Diehl. (1993) "Enduring Rivalries: Theoretical Constructs and Empirical Patterns," *International Studies Quarterly* 37 (June): 147–171.

Goldberg, Andrew C. (1992) "Challenges to the Post–Cold War Balance of Power," pp. 154–162 in Charles W. Kegley, Jr., and Eugene R. Wittkopf, eds., *The Future of American Foreign Policy*. New York: St. Martin's Press.

Goldstein, Joshua S. (1988) *Long Cycles: Prosperity and War in the Modern Age*. New Haven, Conn.: Yale University Press.

———. (1985) "Kondratieff Waves as War Cycles," *International Studies Quarterly* 29 (December): 411–444.

Gould, Wesley L. (1957) *An Introduction to International Law*. New York: Harper.

Gowa, Joanne. (1989) "Bipolarity, Multipolarity, and Free Trade," *American Political Science Review* 83 (December): 1245–1256.

Gregg, Robert W. (1993) *About Face?: The United States and the United Nations*. Boulder, Colo.: Lynne Rienner.

Grey, Edward. (1925) *Twenty-Five Years, 1892–1916*. New York: Frederick Stokes.

Grieco, Joseph M. (1988) "Anarchy and the Limits of Cooperation: A Realist Critique of the Newest Liberal Institutionalism," *International Organization* 42 (Summer): 485–507.

Gross, Leo. (1969) "The Peace of Westphalia, 1648–1948," pp. 25–46 in Leo Gross, ed., *International Law in the Twentieth Century*. New York: Appleton-Century-Crofts.

Gulick, Edward Vose. (1955) *Europe's Classical Balance of Power*. Ithaca, N.Y.: Cornell University Press.

Gurr, Ted Robert. (1972) *Politimetrics*. Englewood Cliffs, N.J.: Prentice-Hall.

Gwin, Catherine, and Richard E. Feinberg, eds. (1989) *Pulling Together: The International Monetary Fund in a Multipolar World*. Washington, D.C.: Overseas Development Council.

Haas, Ernst B. (1953) "The Balance of Power: Prescription, Concept or Propaganda?" *World Politics* 5 (July): 442–477.

Haas, Ernst B., and Allen S. Whiting. (1956) *Dynamics of International Relations*. New York: McGraw-Hill.

Haas, Michael. (1970) "International Subsystems: Stability and Polarity," *American Political Science Review* 64 (March): 98–123.

Hanrieder, Wolfram F., and Graeme P. Auton. (1980) *The Foreign Policies of West Germany, France, and Britain*. Englewood Cliffs, N.J.: Prentice-Hall.

Hart, Jeffrey A. (1992) *Rival Capitalists: International Competitiveness in the United States, Japan, and Western Europe*. Ithaca, N.Y.: Cornell University Press.

———. (1985) "Power and Polarity in the International System," pp. 25–40 in Alan N. Sabrosky, ed., *Polarity and War*. Boulder, Colo.: Westview.

Hartmann, Frederick H. (1983) *The Relations of Nations*, 6th ed. New York: Macmillan.

Hassner, Pierre. (1990) "Europe Beyond Partition and Unity: Disintegration or Reconstruction?" *International Affairs* 66 (July): 461–475.

Havel, Václav. (1993) "The Post-Communist Nightmare," *The New York Review of Books* 40 (May 27): 8–10.

Healy, Brian, and Arthur Stein. (1973) "The Balance of Power in International History: Theory and Reality," *Journal of Conflict Resolution* 17 (March): 33–61.

Helprin, Mark. (1991) "The Power of Russia Alone," *The Wall Street Journal* (December 27): A10.

Hemleben, Sylvester John. (1943) *Plans for World Peace through Six Centuries*. Chicago: The University of Chicago Press.

Hendrickson, David C. (1993) "The Ethics of Collective Security," *Ethics & International Affairs* 7: 1–15.

Herz, John. (1959) *International Relations in the Atomic Age*. New York: Columbia University Press.

Hinsley, F. H. (1963) *Power and the Pursuit of Peace: Theory and Practice in the History of Relations Between States*. Cambridge: Cambridge University Press.

Hoagland, Jim. (1993) "Leadership Gap Is Widening," *The State* (Columbia, S.C.) (June 15): 14A.

———. (1992) "Next President Must Not Rely on Symbolic Gestures," *The State* (Columbia, S.C.) (October 27): 8A.

Hoebel, E. Adamson. (1954) *The Law of Primitive Man*. Cambridge, Mass.: Harvard University Press.

Hoffmann, Stanley. (1993a) "Goodbye to a United Europe?" *The New York Review of Books* 40 (May 27): 27–31.

———. (1993b) "To the Editors," *The New York Review of Books* 40 (June 24): 59.

———. (1992a) "Balance, Concert, Anarchy, or None of the Above," pp. 194–220 in Gregory F. Treverton, ed., *The Shape of the New Europe*. New York: Council on Foreign Relations Press.

———. (1992b) "Bush Abroad," *New York Review of Books* 39 (November 5): 54–59.

———. (1989) "What Should We Do in the World?" *The Atlantic Monthly* 264 (October): 84–96.

———. (1978) *Primacy or World Order: American Foreign Policy Since the Cold War*. New York: McGraw-Hill.

———. (1971) "International Law and the Control of Force," pp. 34–66 in Karl Deutsch and Stanley Hoffmann, eds., *The Relevance of International Law*. Garden City, N.Y.: Doubleday-Anchor.

———. (1969) "The Study of International Law and the Theory of International Relations," pp. 150–159 in Leo Gross, ed., *International Law in the Twentieth Century*. New York: Appleton-Century-Crofts.

———. (1961) "International Systems and International Law," pp. 203–237 in Klaus Knorr and Sidney Verba, eds., *The International System: Theoretical Essays*. Princeton, N.J.: Princeton University Press.

Holbraad, Carsten. (1984) *Middle Powers in International Politics*. New York: St. Martin's Press.

———. (1970) *The Concert of Europe*. New York: Barnes and Noble.

Holmes, Jack. (1994) *Ambivalent America*. Columbia, S.C.: University of South Carolina Press, forthcoming.

Holsti, Kalevi J. (1991a) *Change in the International System*. Brookfield, Ver.: Edward Elgar.

———. (1991b) *Peace and War: Armed Conflicts and International Order, 1648–1989*. New York: Cambridge University Press.

———. (1982) *Why Nations Realign: Foreign Policy Restructuring Since World War II*. London: Allen & Unwin.

———. (1970) "National Role Conceptions in the Study of Foreign Policy," *International Studies Quarterly* 14 (September): 233–309.

Hopf, Ted. (1993) "Polarity and International Stability," *American Political Science Review* 87 (March): 177–180.

———. (1991) "Polarity, the Offense–Defense Balance, and War," *American Political Science Review* 85 (June): 475–493.

Hopkins, Terrence K., Immanuel Wallerstein, and Associates. (1982a) "Cyclical Rhythms and Secular Trends of the Capitalist World-Economy," pp. 104–120 in Terrence K. Hopkins, Immanuel Wallerstein, and Associates, eds., *World-System Analysis: Theory and Methodology.* Beverly Hills: Sage.

———. (1982b) "Patterns of Development of the Modern World-System," pp. 41–82 in Terrence K. Hopkins, Immanuel Wallerstein, and Associates, eds., *World-System Analysis: Theory and Methodology.* Beverly Hills: Sage.

Horne, Charles F., and Walter F. Austin, eds. (1920) *The Great Events of the Great War,* Vol. I. n.p.: National Alumni.

Horne, Thomas A. (1987) "Mercantilism," pp. 335–336 in David Miller et al., eds., *The Blackwell Encyclopaedia of Political Thought.* Oxford: Basil Blackwell.

Horowitz, David. (1965) *The Free World Colossus: A Critique of American Foreign Policy in the Cold War.* New York: Hill and Wang.

House, Karen Eliot. (1989) "As Power Is Dispersed Among Nations, Need for Leadership Grows," *The Wall Street Journal* (February 21): A1, A10.

Houweling, Henk, and Jan G. Siccama. (1988) "Power Transitions as a Cause of War," *Journal of Conflict Resolution* 32 (March): 87–102.

Howard, Michael. (1976) *War in European History.* Oxford: Oxford University Press.

———. (1961) *The Franco-Prussian War.* London: Davis.

Howell, Llewellyn D. (1993) "Bill Clinton and the New American Foreign Policy," *USA Today* 127 (January): 45.

Hudson, G. F. (1968) "Collective Security and Military Alliances," pp. 176–180 in Herbert Butterfield and Martin Wight, eds., *Diplomatic Investigations.* Cambridge, Mass.: Harvard University Press.

Hughes, Barry B. (1991) *Continuity and Change in World Politics.* Englewood Cliffs, N.J.: Prentice Hall.

Hunter, Robert. (1992) "The New U.S. Role in the Post–Cold War World," *The Washington Post National Weekly Edition* 10 (December 14–20): 9.

Huntington, Samuel P. (1993a) "The Clash of Civilizations?" *Foreign Affairs* 72 (Summer): 22–49.

———. (1993b) "The Coming Clash of Civilizations or, the West Against the Rest," *The New York Times* (June 6): E19.

———. (1991a) "America's Changing Strategic Interests," *Survival* 33 (January/February): 3–17.

———. (1991b) *The Third Wave: Democratization in the Late Twentieth Century.* Norman, Okla.: University of Oklahoma Press.

———. (1989) "No Exit: The Errors of Endism," *The National Interest* 17 (Fall): 3–11.

———. (1988–1989) "The U.S.—Decline or Renewal?" *Foreign Affairs* 67 (Winter): 76–96.

Hurd, Douglas. (1993) "The New Disorder." Policy Statement by the Foreign Secretary to Chatham House, January 27. New York: British Information Services.

Huth, Paul. (1988) *Extended Deterrence and the Prevention of War.* New Haven, Conn.: Yale University Press.

Huth, Paul, and Bruce Russett. (1988) "Deterrence Failure and Crisis Escalation," *International Studies Quarterly* 32 (March): 29–45.

———. (1984) "What Makes Deterrence Work? Cases from 1900 to 1980," *World Politics* 36 (December): 496–526.

Hyland, William G. (1993) "Reexamining National Strategy." Address given at the Army War College Strategy Conference, February 24–25, 1993. Carlisle Barracks, Pa.: Strategic Studies Institute, U.S. Army War College.

_____. (1991). "It's Time for Americans to Turn Inward," *International Herald Tribune* (May 20): 6.

Iklé, Fred Charles. (1991–1992) "Comrades in Arms: The Case for a Russian–American Defense Community," *The National Interest* 26 (Winter): 22–32.

_____. (1991) *Every War Must End*, 2nd ed. New York: Columbia University Press.

_____. (1990) "The Ghost in the Pentagon," *The National Interest* 19 (Spring): 13–20.

International Trade Statistics Yearbook 1989. (1991) Vol. 1: Trends by Country. New York: United Nations.

Jensen, Lloyd. (1982) *Explaining Foreign Policy.* Englewood Cliffs, N.J.: Prentice-Hall.

Jervis, Robert. (1993) "International Primacy: Is the Game Worth the Candle?" *International Security* 17 (Spring): 52–67.

_____. (1992) "A Usable Past for the Future," pp. 257–268 in Michael J. Hogan, ed., *The End of the Cold War: Its Meaning and Implications.* New York: Cambridge University Press.

_____. (1991–1992) "The Future of World Politics: Will It Resemble the Past?" *International Security* 16 (Winter): 39–73.

_____. (1991) "Will the New World Be Better?" pp. 7–19 in Robert Jervis and Seweryn Bialer, eds., *Soviet–American Relations After the Cold War.* Durham, N.C.: Duke University Press.

_____. (1985) "From Balance to Concert: A Study of International Security Cooperation," *World Politics* 38 (October): 58–79.

Jervis, Robert, and Jack Snyder. (1991) *Dominoes and Bandwagons: Strategic Beliefs and Great Power Competition in the Eurasian Rimland.* New York: Oxford University Press.

Joffe, Josef. (1992–1993) "The New Europe: Yesterday's Ghosts," *Foreign Affairs* 72 (No. 1): 29–43.

Johansen, Robert C. (1995) "Swords Into Plowshares: Can Fewer Arms Yield More Security? forthcoming in Charles W. Kegley, Jr., ed., *Controversies in International Relations Theory: Realism and the Neoliberal Challenge.* New York: St. Martin's Press.

_____. (1991) "Do Preparations for War Increase or Decrease International Security?" pp. 224–244 in Charles W. Kegley, Jr., ed., *The Long Postwar Peace.* New York: HarperCollins.

Joll, James. (1984) *The Origins of the First World War.* London: Longman.

Jönsson, Christer. (1981) "Bargaining Power: Notes on an Elusive Concept," *Cooperation and Conflict* 16 (No. 4): 249–257.

Jordan, Amos A., and William J. Taylor, Jr. (1984) *American National Security.* Baltimore: Johns Hopkins University Press.

Joyner, Christopher C. (1992) "The Reality and Relevance of International Law," pp. 202–215 in Charles W. Kegley, Jr., and Eugene R. Wittkopf, eds., *The Global Agenda*, 3rd ed. New York: McGraw-Hill.

Judis, John B. (1993) "The Foreign Unpolicy," *The New Republic* 209 (July 12): 16–20.

Kahler, Miles. (1979–1980) "Rumors of War: The 1914 Analogy," *Foreign Affairs* 57 (Winter): 374–396.

Kahn, Robert A. (1974) *A History of the Habsburg Empire, 1526–1918.* Berkeley: University of California Press.

Kaiser, David. (1990) *Politics and War: European Conflict from Philip II to Hitler.* Cambridge, Mass.: Harvard University Press.

Kaplan, Morton A. (1957) *System and Process in International Politics.* New York: Wiley.

Katzenstein, Peter J., and Nobuo Okawara. (1993) "Japan's National Security: Structures, Norms, and Policies," *International Security* 17 (Spring): 84–118.

Keal, Paul. (1983) *Unspoken Rules and Superpower Dominance*. London: Macmillan.

Kegley, Charles W., Jr., ed. (1995) *Controversies in International Relations Theory: Realism and the Neoliberal Challenge*. New York: St. Martin's Press, forthcoming.

———. (1994) "How Did the Cold War Die? Principles for an Autopsy," *Mershon International Studies Review* 1 (March): forthcoming.

———. (1993) "The Neoidealist Moment in International Studies? Realist Myths and the New International Realities," *International Studies Quarterly* 37 (June): 131–146.

———. (1992) "The New Global Order: The Power of Principle in a Pluralistic World," *Ethics & International Affairs* 6: 21–40.

———, ed. (1991) *The Long Postwar Peace: Contending Explanations and Projections*. New York: HarperCollins.

Kegley, Charles W., Jr., and Gregory A. Raymond. (1991) "Alliances and the Preservation of the Postwar Peace: Weighing the Contribution," pp. 270–289 in Charles W. Kegley, Jr., ed., *The Long Postwar Peace: Contending Explanations and Projections*. New York: HarperCollins.

———. (1990) *When Trust Breaks Down: Alliance Norms and World Politics*. Columbia, S.C.: University of South Carolina Press.

———. (1989) "Going It Alone: The Decay of Alliance Norms," *Harvard International Review* 12 (Fall): 39–43.

———. (1984) "Alliance Norms and the Management of Interstate Disputes," pp. 199–220 in J. David Singer and Richard Stoll, eds., *Quantitative Indicators in World Politics*. New York: Praeger.

———. (1982) "Alliance Norms and War: A New Piece in an Old Puzzle," *International Studies Quarterly* 26 (December): 572–595.

Kegley, Charles W., Jr., and Eugene R. Wittkopf. (1993) *World Politics: Trend and Transformation*, 4th ed. New York: St. Martin's Press.

———. (1991) *American Foreign Policy: Pattern and Process*, 4th ed. New York: St. Martin's Press.

Kelleher, Catherine McArdle. (1993) "U.S. Policy Toward Europe," pp. 270–288 in Robert J. Art and Seyom Brown, eds., *U.S. Foreign Policy: The Search for a New Role*. New York: Macmillan.

Kelsen, Hans. (1967) *The Pure Theory of Law*. Trans. by M. Knight. Berkeley: University of California Press.

———. (1945) *General Theory of Law and State*. Cambridge, Mass.: Harvard University Press.

Kennan, George F. (1993) *Around the Cragged Hill: A Personal and Political Philosophy*. New York: Norton.

———. (1989) "Just Another Great Power," *The New York Times* (April 9): 25.

———. (1984) *The Fateful Alliance: France, Russia and the Coming of the First World War*. New York: Pantheon Books.

———. (1967) *Memoirs*. Boston: Little, Brown.

Kennedy, Paul M. (1993a) "The American Prospect," *The New York Review of Books* 40 (March 4): 42–53.

———. (1993b) *Preparing for the Twenty-First Century*. New York: Random House.

———. (1992) "A Declining Empire Goes to War," pp. 344–346 in Charles W. Kegley, Jr., and Eugene R. Wittkopf, eds., *The Future of American Foreign Policy*. New York: St. Martin's Press.

———. (1987) *The Rise and Fall of the Great Powers*. New York: Random House.

———. (1980a) *The Rise of the Anglo-German Antagonism, 1860–1914*. London: Allen & Unwin.

———, ed. (1980b) *The War Plans of the Great Powers, 1880–1914*. London: Allen & Unwin.

Keohane, Robert O. (1984) *After Hegemony: Cooperation and Discord in the World Political Economy.* Princeton, N.J.: Princeton University Press.

———. (1980) "The Theory of Hegemonic Stability and Changes in International Economic Regimes, 1967–1977," pp. 131–162 in Ole R. Holsti, Randolph M. Siverson, and Alexander L. George, eds., *Change in the International System.* Boulder, Colo.: Westview.

Keohane, Robert O., and Joseph S. Nye, Jr. (1989) *Power and Interdependence: World Politics in Transition,* 2nd ed. Boston: Little, Brown.

Kester, W. Carl. (1991) *Japanese Takeovers: The Global Contest for Corporate Control.* Cambridge, Mass.: Harvard Business School Press.

Keylor, William R. (1992) *The Twentieth-Century World: An International History,* 2nd ed. New York: Oxford University Press.

Kielinger, Thomas. (1990) "Waking Up in the New Europe—With a Headache," *International Affairs* 66 (April): 249–263.

Kielinger, Thomas, and Max Otte. (1993) "Germany: The Pressured Power," *Foreign Policy* 91 (Summer): 44–62.

Kilpatrick, James J. (1992) "A Few More Things to Worry About," *The State* (Columbia, S.C.) (December 31): A13.

Kim, Woosang. (1992) "Power Transitions and Great Power War from Westphalia to Waterloo," *World Politics* 45 (October): 153–172.

———. (1989) "Power, Alliances, and Major Wars, 1816–1975," *Journal of Conflict Resolution* 33 (June): 255–273.

Kindleberger, Charles P. (1973) *The World in Depression, 1929–1939.* Berkeley: University of California Press.

Kinkel, Klaus. (1992) "NATO's Enduring Role in European Security," *NATO Review* 7 (October): 3–7.

Kiselyov, Sergei. (1993) "Nothing in Common, No Wealth," *Bulletin of the Atomic Scientists* 49 (January–February): 12–13.

Kissinger, Henry A. (1993) "World Must Tune to Post–Cold War Era," *China Daily* (January 18): 1.

———. (1992) "Balance of Power Sustained," pp. 238–248 in Graham Allison and Gregory F. Treverton, eds., *Rethinking America's Security: Beyond Cold War to New World Order.* New York: W. W. Norton.

———. (1979) *White House Years.* Boston: Little, Brown.

———. (1973) *A World Restored: Metternich, Castlereagh and the Problem of Peace, 1812–22.* Boston: Houghton Mifflin.

Klare, Michael T. (1993) "The Next Great Arms Race," *Foreign Affairs* 72 (Summer): 136–152.

Knorr, Klaus. (1973) *Power and Wealth: The Political Economy of International Power.* New York: Basic Books.

———. (1970) *Military Power and Potential.* Lexington, Mass.: D.C. Heath.

Kober, Stanley. (1993) "Revolutions Gone Bad," *Foreign Policy* 91 (Summer): 63–83.

Kokoshin, Andrey A. (1989) "Gorbachev's Force Reductions and the Restructuring of Soviet Forces," Hearings Before the Defense Policy Panel of the Committee on Armed Services, U.S. Congress, House of Representatives, 101st Cong., 1st sess. Washington, D.C.: U.S. Government Printing Office.

Krauthammer, Charles. (1991) "The Unipolar Moment," *Foreign Affairs* 70 (No. 1): 23–33.

———. (1989–1990) "Universal Dominance: Toward a Unipolar World," *The National Interest* 18 (Winter): 46–49.

Kristol, Irving. (1990) "The Map of the World Has Changed," *The Wall Street Journal* (January 3): A6.

Krugman, Paul. (1990) *The Age of Diminished Expectations: U.S. Economic Policy in the 1990's.* Cambridge, Mass.: M.I.T. Press.

Kugler, Jacek. (1984) "Terror Without Deterrence: Reassessing the Role of Nuclear Weapons," *Journal of Conflict Resolution* 28 (September): 470–506.

Kulski, W. W. (1968) *International Politics in a Revolutionary Age*. Philadelphia: Lippincott.

Kunz, Josef L. (1960) "Sanctions in International Law," *American Journal of International Law* 54 (April): 324–347.

———. (1945) "The Meaning and the Range of the Norm *Pacta Sunt Servanda*," *American Journal of International Law* 39 (April): 180–197.

Kupchan, Charles H., and Clifford A. Kupchan. (1992) "A New Concert for Europe," pp. 249–266 in Graham Allison and Gregory F. Treverton, eds., *Rethinking America's Security: Beyond Cold War to New World Order*. New York: W. W. Norton.

———. (1991) "Concerts, Collective Security, and the Future of Europe," *International Security* 16 (Summer): 114–161.

Lalman, David, and David Newman. (1991) "Alliance Formation and National Security," *International Interactions* 16 (No. 4): 239–253.

Landy, Joanne. (1992) "Peace from Below," *Boston Review* 17 (November/December): 8–9.

Langsam, Walter Cunsuello. (1954) *The World Since 1919*. New York: Macmillan.

Lasswell, Harold D. (1950) *World Politics and Personal Insecurity*. New York: Free Press.

Lauren, Paul Gordon. (1983) "Crisis Prevention in Nineteenth-Century Diplomacy," pp. 31–64 in Alexander L. George, ed., *Managing U.S.–Soviet Rivalry*. Boulder, Colo.: Westview.

Lauterpacht, Hersch. (1933) *The Function of Law in the International Community*. Oxford: Clarendon.

Lawrence, Thomas J. (1915) *The Principles of International Law*, 6th ed. Boston: D. C. Heath.

Layne, Christopher. (1993) "The Unipolar Illusion: Why New Great Powers Will Rise," *International Security* 17 (Spring): 5–51.

Leng, Russell J. (1983) "When Will They Ever Learn? Coercive Bargaining in Recurrent Crises," *Journal of Conflict Resolution* 27 (September): 379–419.

Leng, Russell, J., and Hugh B. Wheeler. (1979) "Influence Strategies, Success and War," *Journal of Conflict Resolution* 23 (December): 655–684.

Lepgold, Joseph. (1990) *The Declining Hegemon: The United States and European Defense, 1960–1990*. New York: Praeger.

Lerche, Charles O., and Abdul A. Said. (1963) *Concepts of International Politics*. Englewood Cliffs, N.J.: Prentice-Hall.

Leubsdorf, Carl P. (1991) "Gorbachev's Feats Go Beyond Most Optimistic Predictions," *The State* (Columbia, S.C.) (August 11): D3.

Levinson, Marc. (1992) "The Hand Wringers," *Newsweek* (October 26): 44–46.

Levy, Jack S. (1989a) "The Causes of War: A Review of Theories and Evidence," pp. 209–333 in Philip E. Tetlock, Jo L. Husbands, Robert Jervis, Paul S. Stern, and Charles Tilly, eds., *Behavior, Society and Nuclear War, Vol. 1*. New York: Oxford University Press.

———. (1989b) "The Diversionary Theory of War: A Critique," pp. 259–288 in Manus I. Midlarsky, ed., *Handbook of War Studies*. Boston: Unwin Hyman.

———. (1988) "Domestic Politics and War," pp. 79–99 in Robert I. Rotberg and Theodore K. Rabb, eds., *The Origin and Prevention of Major Wars*. Cambridge: Cambridge University Press.

———. (1985) "The Polarity of the System and International Stability: An Empirical Analysis," pp. 41–66 in Alan Ned Sabrosky, ed., *Polarity and War*. Boulder, Colo.: Westview.

———. (1983) *War in the Modern Great Power System, 1495–1975*. Lexington, Ken.: The University Press of Kentucky.

———. (1982) "Historical Trends in Great Power War," *International Studies Quarterly* 26 (March): 278–300.

_____. (1981) "Alliance Formation and War Behavior," *Journal of Conflict Resolution* 25 (December): 581–613.

Lewis, Flora. (1991–1992) "The 'G-7 1/2' Directorate," *Foreign Policy* 85 (Winter): 25–41.

Lewis, Paul. (1993) "U.S. Backs Council Seats for Bonn and Tokyo," *The New York Times* (January 29): 16.

Lieber, Robert J. (1991) *No Common Power: Understanding International Relations,* 2nd ed. New York: HarperCollins.

_____. (1989) "British Foreign Policy: The Limits of Maneuver," pp. 1–26 in Roy C. Macridis, ed., *Foreign Policy in World Politics: States and Regions.* Englewood Cliffs, N.J.: Prentice-Hall.

Lieberman, Bernhardt. (1968) "i-Trust: A Notion of Trust in Three-Person Games and International Affairs," pp. 359–371 in Louis Kriesberg, ed., *Social Processes in International Relations.* New York: John Wiley & Sons.

Link, Arthur S. (1965) *Wilson the Diplomatist.* Chicago: Quadrangle.

Lippmann, Walter. (1943) *U.S. Foreign Policy: Shield of the Republic.* Boston: Little, Brown.

Liska, George. (1967) *Imperial America.* Baltimore: Johns Hopkins University Press.

_____. (1962) *Nations in Alliance: The Limits of Interdependence.* Baltimore: Johns Hopkins University Press.

Lissitzyn, Oliver J. (1967) "Treaties and Changed Circumstances (Rebus Sic Stantibus)," *American Journal of International Law* 61 (October): 895–922.

Lockhart, Charles. (1978) "Flexibility and Commitment in International Conflicts," *International Studies Quarterly* 22 (December): 545–568.

Lorenz, Joseph P. (1992) "Collective Security After the Cold War," pp. 213–238 in Sheryl J. Brown and Kimber M. Schraub, eds., *Resolving Third World Conflict: Challenges for a New Era.* Washington, D.C.: United States Institute of Peace Press.

Luard, Evan, ed. (1992) *Basic Texts in International Relations.* New York: St. Martin's Press.

_____. (1987) *War in International Society: A Study in International Sociology.* New Haven, Conn.: Yale University Press.

_____. (1986) *War in International Society.* London: I. B. Taurus.

_____. (1976) *Types of International Society.* New York: The Free Press.

Luck, Edward C. (1992–1993) "Making Peace," *Foreign Policy* 89 (Winter): 137–155.

Lundestad, Geir. (1992) "The End of the Cold War, the New Role for Europe, and the Decline of the United States," pp. 195–206 in Michael J. Hogan, ed., *The End of the Cold War: Its Meanings and Implications.* Cambridge: Cambridge University Press.

Mahbubani, Kishore. (1992) "Japan Adrift," *Foreign Policy* 88 (Fall): 126–144.

Mandelbaum, Michael. (1988) *The Fate of Nations: The Search for National Security in the Nineteenth and Twentieth Centuries.* New York: Cambridge University Press.

Mansbach, Richard W., and John A. Vasquez. (1981) *In Search of Theory: A New Paradigm for Global Politics.* New York: Columbia University Press.

Mansfield, Edward D. (1993) "Concentration, Polarity, and the Distribution of Power," *International Studies Quarterly* 37 (March): 105–128.

_____. (1990) "The Concentration of Capabilities and the Onset of War." Paper presented at the Annual Meeting of the American Political Science Association, San Francisco, September 2.

Maoz, Zeev. (1990) *Paradoxes of War.* Boston: Unwin Hyman.

_____. (1982) *Paths to Conflict: International Dispute Initiation, 1816–1976.* Boulder, Colo.: Westview.

Maoz, Zeev, and Nasrin Abdolali. (1989) "Regime Types and International Conflict," *Journal of Conflict Resolution* 33 (March): 3–36.

Maoz, Zeev, and Bruce Russett. (1992) "Alliance, Contiguity, Wealth, and Political Stability: Is the Lack of Conflict Among Democracies a Statistical Artifact?" *International Interactions* 17 (No. 3): 245–267.

Masaki, Hisane. (1993) "Japan Adopts a New Asian Policy," *The Japan Times Weekly International Edition* (January 11–17): 1, 6.

Masters, Roger D. (1961) "A Multi-Bloc Model of the International System," *American Political Science Association* 55 (December): 780–798.

Mattingly, Garrett. (1971) *Renaissance Diplomacy*. Boston: Houghton Mifflin.

Maynes, Charles William. (1993) "The World in the Year 2000: Prospects for Order or Disorder." Address given at the Army War College Strategy Conference, February 24–25, 1993. Carlisle Barracks, Pa.: Strategic Studies Institute, U.S. Army War College.

McAllister, J. F. O. (1993) "Clinton's People," *Time* (January 11): 20.

McClelland, Charles A. (1966) *Theory and the International System*. London: Macmillan.

McDonald, H. Brooke, and Richard Rosecrance. (1985) "Alliance and Structural Balance in the International System," *Journal of Conflict Resolution* 29 (March): 57–82.

McGowan, Patrick J., and Robert M. Rood. (1975) "Alliance Behavior in Balance of Power Systems: Applying a Poisson Model to Nineteenth-Century Europe," *American Political Science Review* 69 (March): 859–870.

McNamara, Robert S. (1993) "Nobody Needs Nukes," *The New York Times* (February 23): A13.

———. (1991) "Alternative Visions of a Post–Cold War World," *Wingspread* 13 (Summer): 12.

Mead, Walter Russell. (1992) "On the Road to Ruin," pp. 332–339 in Charles W. Kegley, Jr., and Eugene R. Wittkopf, eds., *The Future of American Foreign Policy*. New York: St. Martin's Press.

———. (1987) *Mortal Spendor: The American Empire in Transition*. Boston: Houghton Mifflin.

Mearsheimer, John J. (1992a) "Disorder Restored," pp. 213–237 in Graham Allison and Gregory F. Treverton, eds., *Rethinking America's Security: Beyond Cold War to New World Order*. New York: W. W. Norton.

———. (1992b) "Why We Will Soon Miss the Cold War," pp. 48–62 in Charles W. Kegley, Jr., and Eugene R. Wittkopf, eds., *The Future of American Foreign Policy*. New York: St. Martin's Press.

———. (1990a) "Back to the Future: Instability in Europe After the Cold War," *International Security* 15 (Summer): 5–56.

———. (1990b) "Back to the Future, Part II," *International Security* 15 (Fall): 194–199.

Melko, Matthew. (1992) "Long-Term Factors Underlying Peace in Contemporary Western Civilization," *Journal of Peace Research* 29 (February): 99–113.

Melloan, George. (1993) "Military Cutbacks Will Crimp U.S. Foreign Policy," *The Wall Street Journal* (January 25): A17.

Michels, Roberto. (1949) [1911] *Political Parties: A Sociological Study of Oligarchical Tendencies of Modern Democracy*. New York: Free Press.

Midlarsky, Manus I. (1993) "Polarity and International Stability," *American Political Science Review* 87 (March): 173–177.

———. (1989) "Hierarchical Equilibria and the Long-Run Instability of Multipolar Systems," pp. 55–81 in Manus I. Midlarsky, ed., *Handbook of War Studies*. Boston: Unwin Hyman.

———. (1988) *The Onset of World War*. Boston: Allen and Unwin.

———. (1984) "Preventing Systemic War," *Journal of Conflict Resolution* 28 (December): 563–584.

Miller, Benjamin. (1994) *When Opponents Cooperate: Great Power Collaboration in World Politics*. Ann Arbor, Mich.: The University of Michigan Press, forthcoming.

———. (1992) "Explaining Great Power Cooperation in Conflict Management," *World Politics* 45 (October): 1–46.

Miller, Lynn H. (1985) *Global Order: Values and Power in International Politics*. Boulder, Colo.: Westview.

Modelski, George. (1987) *Long Cycles in World Politics.* London: Macmillan.

_____. (1978) "The Long Cycle of Global Politics and the Nation-State," *Comparative Studies in Society and History* 20 (April): 214–235.

_____. (1974) *World Power Concentrations: Typology, Data, Explanatory Framework.* Morristown, N.J.: General Learning Press.

_____. (1972) *Principles of World Politics.* New York: The Free Press.

Møller, Bjørn. (1992) *Common Security and Nonoffensive Defense: A Neorealist Perspective.* Boulder, Colo.: Lynne Rienner.

Moniac, Rüdiger. (1992) "NATO Revises Nuclear Strategy for the Post–Cold War Age," *The German Tribune* (October 30): 1–2.

Moran, Theodore H. (1992) "International Economics and U.S. Security," pp. 307–318 in Charles W. Kegley, Jr., and Eugene R. Wittkopf, eds., *The Future of American Foreign Policy.* New York: St. Martin's Press.

Moravcsik, Andrew. (1992) "Arms and Autarky in Modern European History," pp. 23–45 in Raymond Vernon and Ethan B. Kapstein, eds., *Defense and Dependence in a Global Economy.* Washington, D.C.: Congressional Quarterly Inc.

Morgan, T. Clifton, and Valerie L. Schwebach. (1992) "Take Two Democracies and Call Me in the Morning: A Prescription for Peace?" *International Interactions* 17 (No. 4): 305–320.

Morgenthau, Hans J. (1985) *Politics Among Nations: The Struggle for Power and Peace,* 6th ed. Rev. by Kenneth W. Thompson. New York: Alfred A. Knopf.

_____. (1970) "The Origins of the Cold War," pp. 79–102 in J. Joseph Huthmacher and Warren I. Susman, eds., *The Origins of the Cold War.* Waltham, Mass.: Ginn.

_____. (1959) "Alliances in Theory and Practice," pp. 184–212 in Arnold Wolfers, ed., *Alliance Policy in the Cold War.* Baltimore: Johns Hopkins University Press.

_____. (1958) *Dilemmas of Politics.* Chicago: University of Chicago Press.

Morita, Akio. (1993) "Toward a New World Economic Order," *The Atlantic Monthly* 271 (June): 88–98.

Moul, William Brian. (1988) "Balances of Power and the Escalation to War of Serious Disputes Among the European Great Powers, 1815–1939: Some Evidence," *American Journal of Political Science* 32 (May): 241–275.

Moynihan, Daniel P. (1990) *On the Law of Nations.* Cambridge, Mass.: Harvard University Press.

Mueller, John. (1992a) "Dueling, War and the Utility of Force," *Bulletin of Peace Proposals* 23 (March): 103–107.

_____. (1992b) "Quiet Cataclysm: Some Afterthoughts about World War III," *Diplomatic History* 16 (Winter): 66–75.

_____. (1990) "A New Concert of Europe," *Foreign Policy* 77 (Winter): 3–16.

_____. (1989) *Retreat from Doomsday.* New York: Basic Books.

Murphy, Cornelius J. (1982) "The Grotian Vision of World Order," *American Journal of International Law* 76 (July): 477–498.

Nathan, James A. (1993) "Can Japan's Commercial Dominance Continue?" *USA Today* 121 (January): 34–36.

Nau, Henry R. (1990) *The Myth of America's Decline: Leading the World Economy into the 1990s.* New York: Oxford University Press.

Neustadt, Richard A. (1970) *Alliance Politics.* New York: Columbia University Press.

Nicolson, Harold. (1946) *The Congress of Vienna.* New York: Viking.

Niebuhr, Reinhold. (1940) *Christianity and Power Politics.* New York: Scribner's.

Niou, Emerson M. S., and Peter C. Ordeshook. (1990) "Stability in Anarchic International Systems," *American Political Science Review* 84 (December): 1207–1234.

Niou, Emerson M. S., Peter C. Ordeshook and Gregory F. Rose. (1989) *The Balance of Power: Stability in International Systems.* Cambridge: Cambridge University Press.

Nish, Ian H. (1966) *The Anglo–Japanese Alliance: The Diplomacy of Two Island Empires, 1894–1907.* London: The Athlone Press.

Nitze, Paul H. (1992) "Visions of Leadership: The United States," pp. 27–47 in Steven Muller and Gebhard Schweigler, eds., *From Occupation to Cooperation: The United States and United Germany in a Changing World Order.* New York: W. W. Norton.

Nixon, Richard. (1993) "Clinton's Greatest Challenge," *The New York Times* (March 5): A17.

Nogee, Joseph. (1975) "Polarity: An Ambiguous Concept," *Orbis* 28: (Winter): 1193–1224.

North Atlantic Council. (1990) *London Declaration on a Transformed North Atlantic Alliance,* July 5–6.

Northedge, F. S. (1974) *Descent from Power: British Foreign Policy, 1945–1973.* London: Allen & Unwin.

Nye, Joseph S., Jr. (1992–1993) "Coping with Japan," *Foreign Policy* 89 (Winter): 96–115.

————. (1992a) "The Changing Nature of World Power," pp. 117–129 in Charles W. Kegley, Jr., and Eugene R. Wittkopf, eds., *The Global Agenda,* 3rd ed. New York: McGraw-Hill.

————. (1992b) "What New World Order?" *Foreign Affairs* 71 (Spring): 83–96.

————. (1990) *Bound to Lead: The Changing Nature of American Power.* New York: Basic Books.

————. (1989) "The Long-Term Future of Deterrence," pp. 81–89 in Charles W. Kegley, Jr., and Eugene R. Wittkopf, eds., *The Nuclear Reader.* New York: St. Martin's.

O'Brien, Conor Cruise. (1993) "Germany Resurgent," *Harper's* 286 (March): 15–17.

Odom, William E. (1993) "More Military Muscle, Not Less," *The New York Times* (February 17): A15.

————. (1992) "Who Really Won the Cold War?," *The Washington Post National Weekly Edition* 10 (August 24–30): 29.

Ohmae, Kenichi. (1990) *The Borderless World.* New York: Harper Business.

Olson, Mancur. (1982) *The Rise and Decline of Nations.* New Haven, Conn.: Yale University Press.

————. (1965) *The Logic of Collective Action: Public Goods and the Theory of Groups.* Cambridge, Mass.: Harvard University Press.

Oppenheim, Lassa F. L. (1928) *International Law: A Treatise,* 4th ed. London: Longmans.

Oren, Ido. (1990) "The War Proneness of Alliances," *Journal of Conflict Resolution* 34 (June): 208–233.

Organski, A. F. K. (1968) *World Politics,* 2nd ed. New York: Alfred A. Knopf.

Organski, A. F. K., and Jacek Kugler. (1980) *The War Ledger.* Chicago: University of Chicago Press.

Osgood, Robert. (1968) *Alliances and American Foreign Policy.* Baltimore: Johns Hopkins University Press.

Ostrom, Charles W., Jr., and John H. Aldrich. (1978) "The Relationship Between Size and Stability in the Major Power International System," *American Journal of Political Science* 22 (November): 743–771.

Oxnam, Robert B. (1992–1993) "Asia/Pacific Challenges," *Foreign Affairs* 72 (No. 1): 58–73.

Oye, Kenneth A. (1992) "Beyond Postwar Order and New World Order," pp. 3–33 in Kenneth A. Oye, Robert J. Lieber, and Donald Rothchild, eds., *Eagle in a New World.* New York: HarperCollins.

————. (1986) "Explaining Cooperation Under Anarchy: Hypotheses and Strategies," pp. 1–24 in Kenneth A. Oye, ed., *Cooperation Under Anarchy.* Princeton, N.J.: Princeton University Press.

Palmer, Norman D., and Howard C. Perkins. (1957) *International Relations: The World Community in Transition.* Boston: Houghton-Mifflin.

Parker, Geoffrey. (1987) *The Thirty Years' War.* London: Routledge.

Parry, Clive. (1968) "The Function of Law in the International Community," pp. 1–54 in Max Sørensen, ed., *Manual of Public International Law*. New York: St. Martin's Press.

Parsons, Talcott. (1961) "Order and Community in the International System," pp. 120–129 in James N. Rosenau, ed., *International Politics and Foreign Policy*. New York: Free Press.

Patchen, Martin. (1990) "Conflict and Cooperation in American–Soviet Relations: What Have We Learned from Quantitative Research?" Paper presented at the Annual Meeting of the International Studies Association, Washington, D.C., April 13.

Paterson, Thomas G. (1978) *On Every Front: The Making of the Cold War*. New York: Norton.

Pearson, Frederic S., Robert A. Baumann, and Jeffrey Pickering. (1991) "International Military Intervention: Global and Regional Redefinitions of Realpolitik." Paper presented at the Annual Meeting of the American Political Science Association, Washington, D.C., August 29–September 1.

Pelz, Stephen. (1991) "Changing International Systems, the World Balance of Power, and the United States, 1776–1976," *Diplomatic History* 15 (Winter): 47–81.

Perkins, John A. (1981) *The Prudent Peace: Law as Foreign Policy*. Chicago: University of Chicago Press.

Perle, Richard. (1992) *Hard Line*. New York: Random House.

———. (1991) "Military Power and the Passing Cold War," pp. 33–38 in Charles W. Kegley, Jr., and Kenneth L. Schwab, eds., *After the Cold War: Questioning the Morality of Nuclear Deterrence*. Boulder, Colo.: Westview.

Pinson, Koppel. (1966) *Modern Germany*. New York: Macmillan.

Porter, Michael E. (1990) *The Competitive Advantage of Nations*. New York: Free Press.

Possony, Stefan T. (1946) "Peace Enforcement," *The Yale Law Journal* 55 (No. 5): 910–949.

Powell, Colin L. (1992–1993) "U.S. Forces: Challenges Ahead," *Foreign Affairs* 71 (Winter): 32–45.

Preston, Richard. (1992) "Crisis in the Hot Zone," *The New Yorker* 68 (October 26): 58–81.

Prestowitz, Clyde, V., Jr. (1989) *Trading Places: How We Are Giving Our Future to Japan and How to Reclaim It*. New York: Basic Books.

Puchala, Donald J. (1992) "The History of the Future of International Relations." Paper presented at the Annual Meeting of the American Political Science Association, Chicago, September 3–6.

Puchala, Donald J., and Raymond F. Hopkins. (1983) "International Regimes: Lessons from Inductive Analysis," pp. 61–91 in Stephen D. Krasner, ed., *International Regimes*. Ithaca, N.Y.: Cornell University Press.

Ramphal, Sir Shridath. (1992) "Globalism and Meaningful Peace: A New World Order Rooted in International Community," *Security Dialogue* 23 (September): 81–87.

Ranke, Leopold von. (1973) [1833] *The Theory and Practice of History*. Edited by George G. Iggers and Konrad von Moltke. Indianapolis: Bobbs-Merrill.

Rapkin, David, and William Thompson with Jon A. Christopherson. (1979) "Bipolarity and Bipolarization in the Cold War Era," *Journal of Conflict Resolution* 23 (June): 261–295.

Rapoport, Anatol. (1992) *Peace: An Idea Whose Time Has Come*. Ann Arbor, Mich.: University of Michigan Press.

Rasler, Karen A., and William R. Thompson. (1992) "Concentration, Polarity and Transitional Warfare." Paper presented at the Annual Meeting of the International Studies Association, Atlanta, Georgia, March 29–April 2.

Ray, James Lee. (1995) "Promise or Peril? Neorealism, Neoliberalism and the Future of International Politics," forthcoming in Charles W. Kegley, Jr., ed., *Controversies in Inter-*

national Relations Theory: Realism and the Neoliberal Challenge. New York: St. Martin's Press.

———. (1994) Democracies and International Conflict. Columbia, S.C.: University of South Carolina Press, forthcoming.

———. (1992) Global Politics, 5th ed. Boston: Houghton Mifflin.

———. (1991) "Threats to Protracted Peace: World Politics According to Murphy," pp. 329–344 in Charles W. Kegley, Jr., ed., The Long Postwar Peace. New York: Harper-Collins.

———. (1990) "Friends as Foes: International Conflict and Wars Between Formal Allies," pp. 73–91 in Charles Gochman and Alan Ned Sabrosky, eds., Prisoners of War? Nation-States in the Modern Era. Lexington, Mass.: Lexington Books.

Raymond, Gregory A. (1980) Conflict Resolution and the Structure of the State System: An Analysis of Arbitrative Settlements. Montclair, N.J.: Allanheld Osmun.

Raymond, Gregory A., and Charles W. Kegley, Jr. (1987) "Long Cycles and Internationalized Civil War," Journal of Politics 49 (May): 481–499.

Remnick, David. (1993) "Dumb Luck: Bush's Cold War," The New Yorker 69 (January 25): 105–108.

Richardson, Neil R. (1995) "International Trade as a Force for Peace," forthcoming in Charles W. Kegley, Jr., ed., Controversies in International Relations Theory: Realism and the Neoliberal Challenge. New York: St. Martin's Press.

Risse-Kappen, Thomas. (1991) "Did 'Peace Through Strength' End the Cold War?" International Security 16 (Summer): 162–188.

Rochester, J. Martin. (1993) Waiting for the Millennium: The United Nations and the Future of World Order. Columbia, S.C.: University of South Carolina Press.

Rock, Stephen R. (1989) Why Peace Breaks Out: Great Power Rapprochment in Historical Perspective. Chapel Hill, N.C.: University of North Carolina Press.

Rosecrance, Richard. (1992) "A New Concert of Powers," Foreign Affairs 71 (Spring): 64–82.

———. (1990) America's Economic Resurgence: A Bold New Strategy. New York: HarperCollins.

———. (1986) The Rise of the Trading State: Commerce and Conquest in the Modern World. New York: Basic Books.

———. (1973) International Relations: Peace or War? New York: McGraw-Hill.

———. (1966) "Bipolarity, Multipolarity, and the Future," Journal of Conflict Resolution 10 (September): 314–327.

———. (1963) Action and Reaction in World Politics: International Systems in Perspective. Boston: Little, Brown.

Rosen, Steven. (1970) "A Model of Alliance and War," pp. 215–237 in Julian R. Friedman, Christopher Bladen, and Steven Rosen, eds., Alliance in World Politics. Boston: Allyn and Bacon.

Ross, Robert S. (1993) "U.S. Policy toward China," pp. 338–357 in Robert J. Art and Seyom Brown, eds., U.S. Foreign Policy: The Search for a New Role. New York: Macmillan.

Rothenberg, Gunther E. (1988) "The Origins, Causes, and Extension of the Wars of the French Revolution and Napoleon," pp. 199–221 in Robert I. Rotberg and Theodore K. Rabb, eds., The Origins and Prevention of Major Wars. Cambridge: Cambridge University Press.

Rothgeb, John M., Jr. (1992) Defining Power: Influence and Force in the Contemporary International System. New York: St. Martin's Press.

Rothstein, Robert L. (1968) Alliances and Small Powers. New York: Columbia University Press.

Ruggie, John Gerard. (1992) "Multilateralism: The Anatomy of an Institution," International Organization 46 (Summer): 561–597.

Rummel, Rudolph. (1983) "Libertarianism and International Violence," *Journal of Conflict Resolution* 27 (March): 27–71.

Rusi, Alpo M. (1993) "Military Threats to Regional Security—Back to the Future?" forthcoming in Regina Cowen-Karp and Adam Rotfeld, eds., *Stability and Instability in East Central Europe and in the New Independent States*. Oxford: Oxford University Press.

Russett, Bruce M. (1989) "The Real Decline in Nuclear Hegemony," pp. 177–193 in Ernst-Otto Czempiel and James N. Rosenau, eds., *Global Changes and Theoretical Challenges*. Lexington, Mass.: Lexington Books.

———. (1985) "The Mysterious Case of Vanishing Hegemony, or Is Mark Twain Really Dead?" *International Organization* 39 (Spring): 207–231.

———. (1974) *Power and Community in World Politics*. San Francisco: W. H. Freeman.

Russett, Bruce, and Harvey Starr. (1989) *World Politics: The Menu for Choice*, 3rd ed. New York: W. H. Freeman and Company.

Russett, Bruce, and James S. Sutterlin. (1991) "The U.N. in a New World Order," *Foreign Affairs* 70 (Spring): 69–83.

Ryan, Alan. (1993) "Twenty-first Century Blues," *The New York Review of Books* 40 (May 13): 20–23.

Sabrosky, Alan Ned. (1985a) "Alliance Aggregation, Capability Distribution, and the Expansion of Interstate War," pp. 145–189 in Alan Ned Sabrosky, ed., *Polarity and War*. Boulder, Colo.: Westview.

———, ed. (1985b) *Polarity and War*. Boulder, Colo.: Westview.

———. (1980a) "Allies, Clients, and Encumbrances," *International Security Review* 5 (Summer): 117–149.

———. (1980b) "Interstate Alliances: Their Reliability and the Expansion of War," pp. 161–198 in J. David Singer, ed., *The Correlates of War II: Testing Some Realpolitik Models*. New York: Free Press.

Safire, William. (1993a) "Bush's Summation of When to Use Force Instructive," *The State* (Columbia, S.C.) (January 4): A8.

———. (1993b) "NATO on the Brink," *The New York Times* (January 28): A21.

Sagan, Carl. (1992) "Between Enemies," *The Bulletin of the Atomic Scientists* 48 (May): 24–26.

Salmore, Steven A., and Charles F. Hermann. (1969) "The Effect of Size, Development and Accountability on Foreign Policy," *Peace Research Society Papers* 14: 15–30.

Sandholtz, Wayne, Michael Borrus, John Zysman, Jay Stowsky, Ken Conca, Steven Vogel, and Steve Weber. (1992) *The Highest Stakes: The Economic Foundations of the Next Security System*. New York: Oxford University Press.

Saperstein, Alvin M. (1991) "The 'Long Peace'—Result of a Bipolar Competitive World?" *The Journal of Conflict Resolution* 35 (March): 68–79.

Sayrs, Lois W. (1993) "The Long Cycle in International Relations: A Markov Specification," *International Studies Quarterly* 37 (June): 215–237.

Scalapino, Robert A. (1991–1992) "The United States and Asia: Future Prospects," *Foreign Affairs* 70 (Winter): 18–40.

Schelling, Thomas C. (1966) *Arms and Influence*. New Haven, Conn.: Yale University Press.

———. (1960) *The Strategy of Conflict*. New York: Oxford University Press.

Schlesinger, Arthur M., Jr. (1993) "The Radical," *The New York Review of Books* 40 (February 11): 3–8.

———. (1992a) "Some Lessons from the Cold War," *Diplomatic History* 16 (Winter): 47–53.

———. (1992b) "Who Really Won the Cold War," *The Wall Street Journal* (September 14): A10.

———. (1986) *The Cycles of American History*. Boston: Houghton Mifflin.

Schlesinger, Jacob M. (1992) "Japan's Military Stirs Just Enough to Worry Citizens and Neighbors," *The Wall Street Journal* (December 1): 1, 12.

Schlesinger, James. (1993) "Quest for a Post–Cold War Foreign Policy," *Foreign Affairs* 72 (No. 1): 17–28.

Schmemann, George. (1993) "Russia and Predicaments: Irritation on U.S. Policies," *The New York Times* (January 27): A4.

Schroeder, Paul W. (1989) "The Nineteenth Century System: Balance of Power or Political Equilibrium?" *Review of International Studies* 15 (April): 135–153.

———. (1986) "The 19th-Century International System: Changes in the Structure," *World Politics* 39 (October): 1–26.

Schuman, Frederick L. (1969) *International Politics*. New York: McGraw-Hill.

Schweller, Randall L. (1993) "Tripolarity and the Second World War," *International Studies Quarterly* 37 (March): 73–103.

———. (1992) "Domestic Structure and Preventive War: Are Democracies More Pacific?" *World Politics* 44 (January): 235–269.

Seaman, L. C. B. (1963) *From Vienna to Versailles*. New York: Harper & Row.

Serfaty, Simon. (1992) "Defining Moments," *SAIS Review* 12 (Summer–Fall): 51–64.

Shalom, Stephen Rosskamm. (1993) *Imperial Alibis: Rationalizing U.S. Intervention After the Cold War*. Boston: South End Press.

Sheehan, Michael. (1989) "The Place of the Balancer in Balance of Power Theory," *Review of International Studies* 15 (April): 123–134.

Shiina, Motoo. (1992) "American Foreign Policy: A Japanese View," *SAIS Review* 12 (Summer–Fall): 73–80.

Simmel, Georg. (1956) *Conflict*. Glencoe, Ill.: Free Press.

Singer, J. David. (1991) "Peace in the Global System: Displacement, Interregnum, or Transformation?" pp. 56–84 in Charles W. Kegley, Jr., ed., *The Long Postwar Peace*. New York: HarperCollins.

———. (1980) "Accounting for International War: The State of the Discipline," *Annual Review of Sociology* 6: 349–367.

Singer, J. David, Stuart Bremer, and John Stuckey. (1972) "Capability Distribution, Uncertainty, and Major Power War, 1820–1965," pp. 19–48 in Bruce M. Russett, ed., *Peace, War, and Numbers*. Beverly Hills: Sage.

Singer, J. David, and Melvin Small. (1968) "Alliance Aggregation and the Onset of War," pp. 247–268 in J. David Singer, ed., *Quantitative International Politics*. New York: Free Press.

———. (1966) "Formal Alliances, 1815–1939: A Quantitative Description," *Journal of Peace Research* 3 (January): 1–32.

Sivard, Ruth Leger. (1991) *World Military and Social Expenditures 1991*. Washington, D.C.: World Priorities.

———. (1989) *World Military and Social Expenditures 1989*. Washington, D.C.: World Priorities.

Siverson, Randolph M., and Joel King. (1980) "Attributes of National Alliance Membership and War Participation, 1815–1965," *American Journal of Political Science* 24 (February): 1–15.

———. (1979) "Alliances and the Expansion of War," pp. 37–49 in J. David Singer and Michael Wallace, eds., *To Augur Well*. Beverly Hills: Sage.

Siverson, Randolph M., and Michael P. Sullivan. (1983) "The Distribution of Power and the Onset of War," *Journal of Conflict Resolution* 27 (September): 473–494.

Siverson, Randolph M., and Michael R. Tennefoss. (1984) "Power, Alliance, and the Escalation of International Conflict, 1815–1965," *American Political Science Review* 78 (December): 1057–1069.

———. (1982) "Interstate Conflicts: 1815–1865," *International Interactions* 9 (July): 147–178.

Small, Melvin, and J. David Singer. (1982) *Resort to Arms: International and Civil Wars, 1816–1982*. Beverly Hills: Sage.

_____. (1976) "The War-Proneness of Democratic Regimes, 1816–1965," *Jerusalem Journal of International Relations* 1 (March): 50–69.

Smith, W. Y. (1992) "Principles of U.S. Grand Strategy: Past and Future," pp. 264–275 in Charles W. Kegley, Jr., and Eugene R. Wittkopf, eds., *The Future of American Foreign Policy*. New York: St. Martin's Press.

Smoke, Richard, and Andrei Kortunov, eds. (1990) *Mutual Security: A New Approach to Soviet–American Relations*. New York: St. Martin's Press.

Snyder, Glenn H. (1990) "Alliance Theory: A Neorealist First Cut," *Journal of International Affairs* 44 (Spring/Summer): 103–123.

_____. (1984) "The Security Dilemma in Alliance Politics," *World Politics* 36 (July): 461–495.

Snyder, Jack. (1992) "The Transformation of the Soviet Empire," pp. 259–280 in Kenneth A. Oye, Robert J. Lieber, and Donald Rothchild, eds., *Eagle in a New World*. New York: HarperCollins.

_____. (1991) *Myths of Empire: Domestic Politics and Strategic Ideology*. Ithaca, N.Y.: Cornell University Press.

Spiezio, K. Edward. (1990) "British Hegemony and Major Power War, 1815–1939: An Empirical Test of Gilpin's Model of Hegemonic Governance," *International Studies Quarterly* 34 (June): 165–181.

Spykman, Nicholas J. (1942) *American Strategy and World Politics*. New York: Harcourt Brace Jovanovich.

Stalin, Joseph V. (1946) *Speech Delivered at a Meeting of Voters, February 9, 1946*. Washington, D.C.: Embassy of the U.S.S.R.

Stares, Paul B., and John D. Steinbruner. (1992) "Cooperative Security in the New Europe," pp. 218–248 in Paul B. Stares, ed., *The New Germany and the New Europe*. Washington, D.C.: Brookings.

Starr, Harvey. (1972) *War Coalitions*. Lexington, Mass.: D. C. Heath.

Stedman, Stephen John. (1993) "The New Interventionists," *Foreign Affairs* 72 (No. 1): 1–16.

Steel, Ronald. (1993) "Mission Control: Beyond Interventionism," *The New Republic* 208 (January 25): 16–19.

_____. (1992) "Europe after the Superpowers," pp. 164–173 in Charles W. Kegley, Jr., and Eugene R. Wittkopf, eds., *The Future of American Foreign Policy*. New York: St. Martin's Press.

_____. (1967) *Pax Americana*. New York: The Viking Press.

Stein, Arthur A. (1991) *Why Nations Cooperate: Circumstance and Choice in International Relations*. Ithaca, N.Y.: Cornell University Press.

Stoessinger, John G. (1969) *The Might of Nations: World Politics in Our Time*, 3rd ed. New York: Random House.

Strange, Susan. (1987) "The Persistent Myth of Lost Hegemony," *International Organization* 41 (Autumn): 551–574.

Sullivan, Michael P. (1990) *Power in Contemporary International Politics*. Columbia, S.C.: University of South Carolina Press.

Sullivan, Michael P., and Randolph M. Siverson. (1981) "Theories of War," pp. 9–37 in P. Terrence Hopmann, Dina A. Zinnes, and J. David Singer, eds., *Cumulation in International Relations Research*. Denver: University of Denver Monograph Series in World Affairs, vol. 18.

Suryanarayana, P. S. (1992) "Time to Break the Yalta Order," *World Press Review* 39 (October): 13–14.

Talbott, Strobe. (1992) "Beware of the Three-Way Split," *Time* (June 15): 46.

_____. (1990) "Rethinking the Red Menace," *Time* (January 1): 66–72.

Taylor, A. J. P. (1954) *The Struggle for Mastery in Europe, 1848–1918*. Oxford: Oxford University Press.

Teune, Henry, and Sig Synnestvedt. (1965) "Measuring International Alignment," *Orbis* 9 (Spring): 171–189.

Thies, Wallace J. (1991) "Randomness, Contagion and Heterogeneity in the Formation of Interstate Alliances—A Reconsideration," *International Interactions* 16 (No. 4): 335–354.

Thompson, Kenneth W. (1953) "Collective Security Reexamined," *American Political Science Review* 47 (September): 753–772.

Thompson, William R. (1992) "Dehio, Long Cycles and the Geohistorical Context of Structural Transitions," *World Politics* 45 (October): 127–152.

———. (1988) *On Global War: Historical–Structural Approaches to World Politics.* Columbia, S.C.: University of South Carolina Press.

———. (1986) "Polarity, the Long Cycle and Global Power Warfare," *Journal of Conflict Resolution* 30 (December): 587–615.

———. (1983) "Cycles, Capabilities and War: An Ecumenical View," pp. 141–163 in William R. Thompson, ed., *Contending Approaches to World System Analysis.* Beverly Hills: Sage.

Thompson, William R., and Karen A. Rasler. (1988) "War and Systemic Capability Reconcentration," *Journal of Conflict Resolution* 32 (June): 61–86.

Thurow, Lester C. (1992a) *Head to Head: Coming Economic Battles Among Japan, Europe, and America.* New York: Morrow.

———. (1992b) "The 21st Century Belongs to Europe," *The Washington Post National Weekly Edition* 10 (April 27–May 3): 23–24.

Tillema, Herbert K. (1991) *International Armed Conflict Since 1945.* Boulder, Colo.: Westview.

Tillema, Herbert K., and John R. Van Wingen. (1982) "Law and Power in Military Intervention: Major States After World War II," *International Studies Quarterly* 26 (June): 220–250.

Tonelson, Alan. (1993a) "Clinton's World," *Atlantic Monthly* 271 (January): 71–74.

———. (1993b) "Superpower Without a Sword," *Foreign Affairs* 72 (Summer): 166–180.

Toynbee, Arnold J. (1967) "Anarchy in Treaties, 1648–1967," pp. xii–xxix in Fred L. Israel, ed., *Major Peace Treaties of Modern History, 1648–1967.* New York: Chelsea.

Treverton, Gregory F. (1992) "The New Europe," *Foreign Affairs* 71 (No. 1): 94–112.

Treverton, Gregory F., and Barbara A. Bicksler. (1992) "Conclusion: Getting from Here to Where?" pp. 407–433 in Graham Allison and Gregory F. Treverton, eds., *Rethinking America's Security: Beyond Cold War to New World Order.* New York: W. W. Norton.

Truman, Harry S. (1955) *Memoirs.* Vol. I. Garden City, N.Y.: Doubleday.

Tuchman, Barbara. (1962) *The Guns of August.* New York: Macmillan.

Tucker, Robert W., and David C. Hendrickson. (1992) *The Imperial Temptation: The New World Order and America's Purpose.* New York: Council on Foreign Relations Press.

Tyler, Patrick J. (1992) "Pentagon Drops Goal of Blocking New Superpowers," *The New York Times* (May 24): 1, 14.

Ullman, Richard H. (1991) *Securing Europe.* Princeton, N.J.: Princeton University Press.

Urquhart, Brian. (1993) "For a UN Volunteer Military Force," *The New York Review of Books* 40 (June 10): 3–4.

U.S. Arms Control and Disarmament Agency. (1992) *World Military Expenditures and Arms Transfers, 1990.* Washington, D.C.: U.S. Government Printing Office.

———. (1980) *World Military Expenditures and Arms Transfers, 1980.* Washington, D.C.: U.S. Government Printing Office.

———. (1973) *World Military Expenditures and Arms Transfers, 1973.* Washington, D.C.: U.S. Government Printing Office.

U.S. Army War College. (1960) *Power Analysis of the Nation-State.* Carlisle Barracks, Pa.: U.S. Army War College.

Van Alstyne, Richard W. (1974) *The Rising American Empire.* New York: Norton.

Van Dyke, Vernon. (1966) *International Politics,* 2nd ed. New York: Appleton-Century-Crofts.

Van Evera, Stephen. (1992a) "American Intervention in the Third World: Less Would Be Better," pp. 285–300 in Charles W. Kegley, Jr., and Eugene R. Wittkopf, eds., *The Future of American Foreign Policy.* New York: St. Martin's.

———. (1992b) "Preserving Peace in the New Era," *Boston Review* 17 (November/December): 4–5.

———. (1992c) "The United States and the Third World: When To Intervene?" pp. 105–150 in Kenneth A. Oye, Robert J. Lieber, and Donald Rothchild, eds., *Eagle in a New World.* New York: HarperCollins.

———. (1985) "Why Cooperation Failed in 1914," *World Politics* 38 (October): 80–117.

Vasquez, John A. (1993) *The War Puzzle.* Cambridge: Cambridge University Press.

———. (1992) "World Politics Theory," pp. 839–861 in Mary Hawkesworth and Maurice Kogan, eds., *Encyclopedia of Government and Politics,* Vol. 2. London: Routledge.

———. (1991) "The Deterrence Myth: Nuclear Weapons and the Prevention of Nuclear War," pp. 205–223 in Charles W. Kegley, Jr., ed., *The Long Postwar Peace.* New York: HarperCollins.

———. (1990) "The Role of Alliances in the Spread of War." Paper presented at the Peace Science Society (International) Meeting, New Brunswick, N.J., November 16.

———. (1987) "The Steps to War: Toward a Scientific Explanation of Correlates of War Findings," *World Politics* 40 (October): 108–145.

———. (1986) "Capability, Types of War, Peace," *Western Political Quarterly* 39 (June): 313–327.

Väyrynen, Raimo. (1983) "Economic Cycles, Power Transitions, Political Management and Wars Between Major Powers," *International Studies Quarterly* 27 (December): 389–418.

Vernon, Raymond, and Ethan B. Kapstein, eds. (1992) *Defense and Dependence in a Global Economy.* Washington, D.C.: Congressional Quarterly, Inc.

Vernon, Raymond, and Debra Spar. (1989) *Beyond Globalism: Remaking American Foreign Economic Policy.* New York: Free Press.

Wagner, R. Harrison. (1993) "What Was Bipolarity?" *International Organization* 47 (Winter): 77–106.

———. (1986) "The Theory of Games and the Balance of Power," *World Politics* 38 (July): 546–576.

Walker, Jenonne. (1991) "Keeping America in Europe," *Foreign Policy* 83 (Summer): 128–142.

Walker, Stephan F., ed. (1987) *Role Theory and Foreign Policy.* Durham, N.C.: Duke University Press.

Wallace, Michael D. (1985) "Polarization: Towards a Scientific Conception," pp. 95–113 in Alan Ned Sabrosky, ed., *Polarity and War.* Boulder, Colo.: Westview.

———. (1979) "Arms Races and Escalation: Some New Evidence," *Journal of Conflict Resolution* 23 (March): 3–16.

———. (1973) "Alliance Polarization, Cross-Cutting, and International War, 1815–1964: A Measurement Procedure and Some Preliminary Evidence," *Journal of Conflict Resolution* 17 (December): 575–604.

Wallensteen, Peter. (1984) "Universalism vs. Particularism: On the Limits of Major Power Order," *Journal of Peace Research* 21 (No. 3): 243–257.

Wallerstein, Immanuel. (1993a) "Foes as Friends?" *Foreign Policy* 90 (Spring): 145–157.

———. (1993b) "The World-System After the Cold War," *Journal of Peace Research* 30 (February): 1–6.

———. (1980) *The Modern World-System II.* New York: Academic Press.

———. (1979) *The Capitalist World-Economy.* Cambridge: Cambridge University Press.

———. (1974) "The Rise and Future Demise of the World Capitalist System: Concepts for

Comparative Analysis," *Comparative Studies in Society and History* 16 (September): 387–415.

Walsh, Kenneth T., with Louise Lief, and Bruce B. Auster. (1993) "The Clinton Doctrines," *U.S. News & World Report* (January 11): 16–18.

Walt, Stephen M. (1992a) "Alliances in Theory and Practice: What Lies Ahead?" pp. 187–195 in Charles W. Kegley, Jr., and Eugene R. Wittkopf, eds., *The Global Agenda*, 3rd ed. New York: McGraw-Hill.

――――. (1992b) "Revolution and War," *World Politics* 44 (April): 321–368.

――――. (1987) *The Origins of Alliances.* Ithaca, N.Y.: Cornell University Press.

Waltz, Kenneth N. (1992a) "Nuclear Myths and Political Realities," pp. 49–58 in Charles W. Kegley, Jr., and Eugene R. Wittkopf, eds., *The Global Agenda*, 3rd ed. New York: McGraw-Hill.

――――. (1992b) "The Origins of War in Neorealist Theory," pp. 39–52 in Robert I. Rotberg and Theodore K. Rabb, eds., *The Origin and Prevention of Major Wars.* New York: Cambridge University Press.

――――. (1991a) "America as a Model for the World? A Foreign Policy Perspective," *PS* 24 (December): 667–670.

――――. (1991b) "Realist Thought and Neorealist Theory," pp. 21–38 in Robert L. Rothstein, ed., *The Evolution of Theory in International Relations.* Columbia, S.C.: University of South Carolina Press.

――――. (1990) "The Emerging Structure of International Politics." Paper presented at the Annual Meeting of the American Political Science Association, San Francisco, August 28–31.

――――. (1979) *Theory of International Politics.* Reading, Mass.: Addison-Wesley.

――――. (1964) "The Stability of a Bipolar World," *Daedalus* 93 (Summer): 881–909.

Wang, Kevin, and James Lee Ray. (1991) "The Initiation and Outcome of International Wars Involving Great Powers, 1495–1985." Paper presented at the Annual Meeting of the International Studies Association, Washington, D.C., April 10–14.

Watson, Adam. (1992) *The Evolution of International Society.* London: Routledge.

――――. (1987) "Hedley Bull, State Systems and International Societies," *Review of International Studies* 13 (April): 147–153.

Wayman, Frank. (1985) "Bipolarity, Multipolarity, and the Threat of War," pp. 115–144 in Alan Ned Sabrosky, ed., *Polarity and War.* Boulder, Colo.: Westview.

Weede, Erich. (1984) "Democracy and War Involvement," *Journal of Conflict Resolution* 28 (September): 395–411.

――――. (1983) "Extended Deterrence by Superpower Alliance," *Journal of Conflict Resolution* 27 (June): 231–254.

――――. (1975) "World Order in the Fifties and Sixties: Dependence, Deterrence, and Limited Peace," *Papers of the Peace Science Society* (International) 24: 49–80.

Wegener, Henning. (1990) "The Transformed Alliance," *NATO Review* 38 (August): 1–8.

Wehberg, Hans. (1959) "Pacta Sunt Servanda," *American Journal of International Law* 53 (October): 775–786.

Weinberger, Caspar. (1990) *Fighting for Peace.* New York: Warner Books.

Weiner, Tim. (1993) "C.I.A. Says Chinese Economy Rivals Japan's," *The New York Times International* (August 1): 6.

Wildavsky, Aaron. (1989) "Serious Talk About the Nuclear Era," *The Wall Street Journal* (March 16): A16.

Williams, William Appleman. (1980) *Empire as a Way of Life.* New York: Oxford University Press.

Williamson, Samuel R., Jr. (1969) *The Politics of Grand Strategy: Britain and France Prepare for War, 1904–1914.* Cambridge, Mass.: Harvard University Press.

Wittkopf, Eugene R. (1990) *Faces of Internationalism.* Durham, N.C.: Duke University Press.

Wolf, John B. (1968) *Louis XIV*. New York: W. W. Norton.

Wolfe, Thomas W. (1970) *Soviet Power and Europe, 1945–1970*. Baltimore: Johns Hopkins University Press.

Wolfers, Arnold. (1968) "Alliances," in David L. Sills, ed., *International Encyclopedia of the Social Sciences*, pp. 268–271. New York: Macmillan.

––––––. (1962) *Discord and Collaboration: Essays on International Politics*. Baltimore: Johns Hopkins University Press.

Working Group on U.S.–Soviet Policy. (1987) *U.S. Policy Towards the Soviet Union: A Long-Term Western Perspective, 1987–2000*. Washington, D.C.: Atlantic Council of the United States.

World Bank. (1993) *World Development Report, 1993*. New York: Oxford University Press.

Wright, Quincy. (1965) *A Study of War*, 2nd ed. Chicago: University of Chicago Press.

––––––. (1955) *The Study of International Relations*. New York: Appleton-Century-Crofts.

Wriston, Walter B. (1992) *The Twilight of Sovereignty*. New York: Charles Scribner's Sons.

Yergin, Daniel. (1977) *Shattered Peace*. Boston: Houghton-Mifflin.

Zakaria, Fareed. (1992–1993) "Is Realism Finished?" *The National Interest* 30 (Winter): 21–32.

Zhdanov, Andrei. (1947) *The International Situation*. Moscow: Foreign Languages Publishing House.

Zuckerman, Lord. (1993) "The New Nuclear Menace," *The New York Review of Books* 40 (June 24): 14–19.

NAME INDEX

A

Aaron, Henry J., 173
Abdolali, Nasrin, 63, 228
Acheson, Dean, 35, 36
Acton, Lord, 187
Adams, John Quincy, 187
Aldrich, John H., 53
Alexander I, 135
Alexander VI, Pope, 108
Aliano, Richard A., 96, 109
Alperovitz, Gar, 169
Altfeld, Michael F., 91
Ambrose, Stephen E., 181
Andropov, Yuri, 29
Angell, Norman, 228
Arbatov, Georgi, 29, 40
Aron, Raymond, 38
Art, Robert J., 230, 231
Aspin, Les, 5, 157, 200
Attali, Jacques, 191, 205
Attlee, Clement, 124
Austin, Walter F., 208
Auton, Graeme P., 208

B

Babst, Dean V., 63
Baker, James A., 22, 201
Baldwin, David A., 13, 16
Baldwin, Lord, 164
Bandow, Doug, 182, 185
Barnathan, Joyce, 206
Barnet, Richard J., 36, 72
Baum, Richard, 206
Baumann, Robert A., 26

Beer, Francis A., 94
Bell, Coral, 196, 203, 227
Bell, David, 11
Benevolenski, Vladimir, 43
Bennett, A. LeRoy, 219
Bentham, Jeremy, 228
Berger, Sandy, 185
Bergesen, Albert, 79n, 81
Bergsten, C. Fred, 168
Bethmann-Hollweg, Theobald von, 128, 207, 208
Betts, Richard K., 214
Beveridge, William, 212
Bird, Kai, 169
Bismarck, Otto von, 208, 219
Black, Jeremy, 68n, 77
Blitzer, Charles, 129
Bolton, John, 214, 222n
Bonaparte, Napoleon, 20, 76, 85, 95, 111, 133, 142, 206, 210
Borrus, Michael, 11
Boswell, Terry, 85
Boutros-Ghali, Boutros, 223
Boylan, Delia M., 216
Bozeman, Adda B., 218
Brademas, John, 173
Branigin, William, 222, 223
Braudel, Fernand, 175
Brawley, Mark R., 95
Brecher, Michael, 25, 88, 130
Bremer, Stuart A., 86, 228
Brenner, Michael J., 197
Brewer, Anthony, 80n
Brezhnev, Leonid, 29, 31

265

Brierly, James Leslie, 90n
Brodie, Bernard, 39
Brooks, David, 183
Brougham, Lord Henry, 93
Brown, Seyom, 218, 219
Brueggemann, John, 85
Brzezinski, Zbigniew, 205, 212
Buchan, Alastair, 98
Bueno de Mesquita, Bruce, 53, 89, 100, 104, 119
Bull, Hedley, 122, 124
Bullock, Alan, 22
Burke, Edmund, 142
Burke, Kenneth, 235
Burman, Stephen, 171n, 172, 186, 187
Burns, Arthur Lee, 33, 68, 127
Bush, George, 9, 27, 37, 42, 183, 185, 186
Bynkershoek, Cornelius van, 127
Byrnes, James F., 22, 36, 162

C
Calleo, David P., 7
Canning, George, 137
Caporaso, James A., 215
Carlsson, Ingvar, 183
Carpenter, Ted Galen, 7, 43
Carr, Edward H., 19
Carter, Jimmy, 31, 36
Castlereagh, Viscount, 135, 136, 137, 219
Catherine II (Czarina), 110
Catherine the Great (Czarina), 70
Chace, James, 11, 199, 203, 206, 218
Chaliand, Gérard, 114
Chamberlain, Joseph, 192, 193
Chan, Steve, 228
Charles II (King of England), 77, 129
Charles V (Holy Roman Emperor), 61, 76, 79
Charles VIII (King of France), 108, 109
Charles X (King of France), 136
Charney, Jonathan I., 122
Cheney, Dick, 169, 182
Christensen, Thomas J., 49, 94, 111
Christopherson, Jon A., 55
Churchill, Winston, 38, 46, 90n, 93, 142, 194
Cicero, Marcus Tullius, 173n
Clark, G. N., 133
Claude, Inis L., Jr., 18, 94, 155, 158, 160, 162, 210, 214, 219
Clinton, William Jefferson, 5, 45, 46, 166, 172, 173, 180, 182, 183, 185, 188n, 198, 200, 214
Cobden, Richard, 228

Cohen, Benjamin J., 80, 81, 84
Cohen, Eliot A., 194, 230
Colbert, Jean-Baptiste, 173n
Conable, Barber B., Jr., 7, 206, 207
Connor, W. R., 58n
Cooper, Richard N., 228
Coplin, William D., 135
Courbet, Gustave, 138
Crabb, Cecil V., Jr., 14
Cresson, Edith, 204
Crocker, Chester A., 168, 172, 190
Crowe, Eyre, 165, 192
Cumings, Bruce, 183

D
Dahl, Robert A., 13
David, Arie E., 129
De Callières, François, 143
Dehio, Ludwig, 60, 77, 105
Deibel, Terry L., 31
Delcassé, Théophile, 127
De Michelis, Gianni, 220
DePorte, Anton W., 35
De Redcliffe, Stratford, 137
Destler, I. M., 205
Deudney, Daniel, 41
Deutsch, Karl W., 13, 51, 52, 64, 71
Dickens, Charles, 138
Diehl, Paul F., 69
Dimitrov, Philip, 43
Djilas, Milovan, 30
Dockrill, Michael, 83
Domke, William K., 228, 229
Doran, Charles F., 20, 69n, 72, 88n
Dougherty, James E., 144
Doyle, Michael W., 17, 63, 187, 196, 198, 228
DuBois, Pierre, 157
Dulles, John Foster, 30, 31
Dumas, Alexander, 158

E
Eagleburger, Lawrence S., 3, 9, 168
Eden, William, 149
Eisenhower, Dwight D., 84
Elizabeth (Czarina), 110
Elliott, J. H., 187, 194
Elrod, Richard, 219
Encarnation, Dennis J., 204
Erasmus, Desiderius, 92

F
Feinberg, Richard E., 11, 216
Fénelon, François, 92

Ferguson, Gordon, 227
Ferguson, Tim W., 172, 197
Finkelstein, Lawrence S., 158, 159
Finkelstein, Marina S., 158, 159
Finlay, David J., 104
Francis I (King of France), 61, 76
Frederick the Great (King of Prussia), 19, 110, 126, 142
Friedberg, Aaron L., 7
Friedheim, Robert L., 122
Friedman, George, 204
Friedrich, Carl J., 129
Fukuyama, Francis, 8, 25, 196, 228

G
Gaddis, John Lewis, 4, 202, 203
Galo, Daniel P., 198, 200
Galtung, Johan, 122
Garten, Jeffrey E., 199, 204
Gärtner, Heinz, 195
Gasiorowski, Mark J., 229
Geiger, Theodore, 168
Gelb, Leslie H., 44, 184, 188, 222
Geller, Daniel S., 18, 77, 79n, 85, 105
Gellner, Ernest, 44
George II (King of England), 110
George III (King of England), 110
George, Alexander L., 34
Gilpin, Robert, 21, 67, 85, 123, 156
Gladstone, William Ewart, 164
Gleditsch, Nils Petter, 63
Glynn, Patrick, 37, 43, 209
Gochman, Charles, 35, 69, 77, 139
Goertz, Gary, 69
Goldberg, Andrew C., 203, 211
Goldstein, Joshua S., 79n
Gondomar, Count, 92
Gorbachev, Mikhail, 29, 36, 38, 42, 44
Gould, Wesley L., 130
Gowa, Joanne, 174
Gregg, Robert W., 223
Grey, Edward, 37, 113, 209
Grieco, Joseph M., 75, 154
Gross, Leo, 133
Grotius, Hugo, 124
Gulick, Edward Vose, 51, 94, 97, 98, 161
Gurr, Ted Robert, 117
Gwin, Catherine, 11

H
Haas, Michael, 88, 104
Hanrieder, Wolfram F., 208

Harriman, Averell, 23
Hart, Jeffrey A., 102, 200
Hartmann, Frederick H., 14, 94, 98, 110, 117, 209
Haushofer, Karl, 22
Hendrickson, David C., 210
Henry VII (King of England), 58
Henry VIII (King of England), 109
Hermann, Charles F., 228
Hinsley, F. H., 60n, 138, 219
Hitler, Adolph, 22, 23, 63, 72, 76, 94, 134n, 185, 210
Hoagland, Jim, 180, 188
Hobbes, Thomas, 47, 96n
Hoffmann, Stanley, 41, 51, 122, 123, 135, 146, 181, 191n, 197
Holbraad, Carsten, 137, 191n
Holsti, Kalevi J., 150, 151
Hopf, Ted, 53, 109
Hopkins, Raymond F., 122
Hopkins, Terrence K., 62, 80
Horne, Charles F., 208
Horne, Thomas A., 80, 81
House, Karen Eliot, 48
Hovet, Thomas, Jr., 104
Howard, Michael, 97
Howell, Llewellyn D., 173
Hudson, G. F., 99
Hughes, Barry B., 11
Hull, Cordell, 143
Huntington, Samuel P., 8, 45, 171n
Hurd, Douglas, 212, 223
Hussein, Saddam, 230n
Huth, Paul, 33
Hyland, William G., 173, 175, 180, 199, 203n

I
Ibsen, Henrik Johan, 138
Ikenberry, G. John, 41
Iklé, Fred Charles, 41, 42, 157, 201n
Ismay, Lord, 35

J
Jagow, Gottlieb von, 127
James, Patrick, 88, 130
Jensen, Lloyd, 63
Jervis, Robert, 10, 196, 218
Joffe, Josef, 197
Johansen, Robert C., 38
Johnson, Lyndon, 31
Joll, James, 193, 209

Jönsson, Christer, 95
Jordan, Amos A., 90
Joyner, Christopher C., 122
Judis, John B., 214
Julius II, 108

K
Kahler, Miles, 208, 229
Kaplan, Morton A., 51, 154, 155
Kapstein, Ethan B., 228
Katzenstein, Peter J., 205
Kautilya, 46
Kegley, Charles W., Jr., 17, 41, 87, 119, 125n, 131, 150, 204
Kelleher, Catherine McArdle, 226
Kennan, George F., 8, 23, 29n, 97, 229n, 235
Kennedy, John F., 31
Kennedy, Paul M., 6n, 11, 19, 78, 84, 85, 111, 167, 171n, 172, 179, 181, 186, 188, 192
Keohane, Robert O., 18, 123, 169
Kester, W. Carl, 204
Keylor, William R., 115
Khrushchev, Nikita, 30, 39
Kielinger, Thomas, 166, 199, 200
Kilpatrick, James J., 187
Kim, Woosang, 86, 88, 119
Kindleberger, Charles P., 155
King, Joel, 100
Kinkel, Klaus, 224, 226
Kissinger, Henry A., 38, 136, 144, 169, 181, 183, 188, 190, 211, 214, 219
Klare, Michael T., 8
Knorr, Klaus, 13, 171
Kober, Stanley, 9
Kohl, Helmut, 199
Kokoshin, Andrei A., 200
Kondratieff, Nikolai, 79n
Kortunov, Andrei, 43, 200
Krauthammer, Charles, 10, 172, 173, 234
Kristol, Irving, 44
Krugman, Paul, 11
Kugler, Jacek, 33, 39, 85, 86, 119
Kulski, W. W., 14
Kunz, Josef L., 129
Kupchan, Charles A., 158, 216
Kupchan, Clifford A., 158, 216

L
Lalman, David, 91, 104
Lampton, David M., 206
Landy, Joanne, 216

Langsam, Walter Cunsuello, 114, 116
Lansdowme, Lord, 193
Lasswell, Harold D., 229
Lauren, Paul Gordon, 219, 220
Lauterpacht, Hersch, 123
Lawrence, Thomas J., 124
Layne, Christopher, 11
Le Bard, Meredith, 204
Leng, Russell J., 35
Lepgold, Joseph, 171n, 188
Lerche, Charles O., 14
Leubsdorf, Carl P., 44
Levinson, Marc, 172, 174
Levy, Jack S., 63, 68, 75, 108, 133
Lewis, Flora, 227
Lewis, Paul, 221
Lieber, Robert J., 49, 208
Lieberman, Bernhardt, 104
Lincoln, Abraham, 4
Link, Arthur S., 113
Lippmann, Walter, 119, 169
Liska, George, 95, 101, 157n
Lissitzyn, Oliver J., 96, 129
Lodge, Henry Cabot, 93
Lorenz, Joseph P., 223n
Louis XI (King of France), 58, 159
Louis XIV (King of France), 20, 76, 92, 95, 121, 126, 129, 173n, 210, 227
Luard, Evan, 39, 95, 104, 109, 122, 134n, 140, 219
Luck, Edward C., 184, 216
Lundestad, Geir, 11

M
Mahbubani, Kishore, 204
Machiavelli, Niccolò, 128, 142
Macintosh, James, 94
Mandelbaum, Michael, 219
Mansbach, Richard W., 35
Mansfield, Edward D., 55n
Maoz, Zeev, 63, 69, 77, 86, 139, 228
Marinus, Antonius, 159
Masaki, Hisane, 205
Masters, Roger D., 205n
Mattingly, Garrett, 60
Maynes, Charles William, 166, 172
Mazzini, Guiseppe, 5, 93, 142
McAllister, J. F. O., 185
McClelland, Charles A., 13
McDonald, H. Brooke, 112
McGowan, Patrick J., 112
McNamara, Robert S., 7, 8

Mead, Walter Russell, 172, 173
Mearsheimer, John J., 7, 37, 49, 50
Melloan, George, 42, 190
Metternich, Prince Klemens Wenzel Nepomuk
    Lothar von, 135, 137, 219
Michels, Roberto, 235
Midlarsky, Manus I., 35, 49, 75, 88, 100
Mill, John Stuart, 137
Miller, Benjamin, 11, 71, 219
Miller, Lynn H., 133
Milton, John, 149
Mitterand, François, 205
Modelski, George, 20, 85, 87, 132
Møller, Bjørn, 95, 211
Moniac, Rüdiger, 225
Montesquieu, Charles de, 228
Moravcsik, Andrew, 173n, 174
More, St. Thomas, 142
Morgan, T. Clifton, 63
Morgenthau, Hans J., 14, 25, 29, 47, 51, 52,
    91, 94, 98, 104, 110, 117, 122, 146,
    154
Morita, Akio, 11
Moul, William Brian, 90
Moynihan, Daniel P., 8
Mueller, John, 25, 39
Mun, Thomas, 81
Murphy, Cornelius J., 133
Mussolini, Benito, 94

N
Nacht, Michael, 205
Nathan, James A., 204
Nau, Henry R., 11, 171n, 172
Neustadt, Richard A., 208
Newman, David, 91
Nicolson, Harold, 135, 212
Niebuhr, Reinhold, 47
Niou, Emerson M.S., 53, 201
Nitze, Paul H., 9
Nixon, Richard M., 43, 168, 190, 202
Nogee, Joseph L., 60n
Northedge, Fred S., 208
Nye, Joseph S., Jr., 7, 11, 13, 18, 39, 168,
    175, 178, 196, 204, 205

O
O'Brien, Conor Cruise, 199
Odom, William E., 7, 9, 26
Okawara, Nobuo, 205
Olivares, Count-Duke (Don Gaspar de Guz-
    mán), 194

Olson, Mancur, 215
Oppenheim, Lassa Francis Lawrence, 123
Ordeshook, Peter C., 53, 201
Oren, Ido, 100
Organski, A.F.K., 15, 33, 78, 85, 86, 119,
    190
Orwell, George, 205n
Osgood, Robert, 94
Ostrom, Charles W., Jr., 53
Otte, Max, 199, 200
Oxnam, Robert B., 203, 205
Oye, Kenneth A., 49, 182

P
Palmer, Norman D., 15
Palmerston, Lord (British Foreign Secretary),
    137, 142, 154, 164
Perkins, Howard C., 15
Parker, Geoffrey, 97
Parsons, Talcott, 122
Paruta, Paolo, 92
Patchen, Martin, 42
Paterson, Thomas G., 36
Pearson, Frederic S., 26
Pelz, Stephen, 25, 150
Perkins, John A., 123
Perle, Richard, 37
Peter III (Czar of Russia), 110
Peter the Great (Czar of Russia), 70, 77
Pflatzgraff, Robert L., Jr., 144
Philip II (King of Spain), 126
Philippe, Louis, 136
Pickering, Jeffrey, 26
Pinson, Koppel, 137
Plato, 235
Podebrad, George, 159
Porter, Michael E., 19, 75
Possony, Stefan T., 157, 159
Powell, Colin L., 37, 195
Preston, Richard, 6n
Prestowitz, Clyde, V., Jr., 204
Puchala, Donald J., 81, 86, 122
Pufendorf, Samuel, 127

R
Rageau, Jean-Pierre, 114
Ramphal, Sir Shridath, 216
Rapkin, David, 55
Rasler, Karen A., 71, 72
Ray, James Lee, 17, 26, 63, 86, 97, 100, 113,
    228
Raymond, Gregory A., 87, 88, 119, 125n,
    131

Reagan, Ronald, 9, 29, 31, 36, 37, 38, 43, 44
Remnick, David, 42
Richardson, Neil R., 229
Richelieu, Cardinal (Armand-Jean du Plessis), 96n, 143
Risse-Kappen, Thomas, 38
Rochester, J. Martin, 8, 223
Rood, Robert M., 112
Roosevelt, Franklin D., 22, 99, 158n, 165
Rose, Gregory F., 201
Rosecrance, Richard, 12, 112, 135, 158, 171n, 172, 183, 234
Rosen, Steven, 72, 94
Ross, Robert S., 207
Rothenberg, Gunther E., 63
Rothgeb, John M., Jr., 16, 118
Rothstein, Robert L., 128
Rousseau, Jean-Jacques, 47
Ruggie, John Gerard, 215
Rummel, Rudolph, 228
Rusi, Alpo M., 200
Russett, Bruce M., 33, 40, 90, 101, 171n, 223, 228
Ryan, Alan, 6n

S
Sabrosky, Alan Ned, 131n
Safire, William, 185, 227
Sagan, Carl, 36
Said, Abdul A., 14
Saint-Pierre, Abbé de, 164
Salisbury, Lord, 129, 193
Salmore, Steven A., 228
Sandel, Michael, 8
Sanders, Liman von, 129
Sandholtz, Wayne, 11, 173
Santayana, George, 53
Saperstein, Alvin M., 50
Sargon I (of Agade), 57
Satakarni, Yajna, 57
Sayrs, Lois W., 78
Scalapino, Robert, 206
Schelling, Thomas C., 34
Schlesinger, Arthur M., Jr., 38, 44, 146
Schlesinger, Jacob M., 204
Schlesinger, James, 180, 186, 233
Schmemann, George, 5
Schoenberg, Ronald, 79n, 81
Schroeder, Paul W., 219
Schuman, Frederick L., 19, 70, 113, 127, 134
Schwebach, Valerie L., 63
Schweller, Randall L., 22

Seaman, L. C. B., 161
Shalom, Stephen Rosskamm, 187
Sheehan, Michael, 190
Shinna, Motoo, 212
Simmel, Georg, 63
Singer, J. David, 24, 51, 52, 63, 71, 77, 89, 90, 112, 117, 131n, 139, 228
Sivard, Ruth Leger, 24
Siverson, Randolph M., 100, 121, 139
Small, Melvin, 63, 77, 90, 112, 117, 131n, 139, 228
Smith, Adam, 81, 228
Smith, W. Y., 45
Smoke, Richard, 200
Snyder, Glenn H., 99, 104
Snyder, Jack, 49, 94, 111, 169, 213
Soboul, Albert, 63
Spar, Debra, 182
Spenser, Herbert, 228
Spiezio, K. Edward, 81, 84
Spinoza, Baruch, 47
Spykman, Nicholas J., 19, 123
Stalin, Joseph V., 22, 23, 30
Stares, Paul B., 217
Starr, Harvey, 101
Stedman, Stephen John, 8, 187, 222
Steel, Ronald, 7
Steinbruner, John D., 217
Stoessinger, John G., 15
Strange, Susan, 171n
Suarez, Francisco, 127
Sullivan, Michael P., 121
Suryanarayana, P. S., 221n
Sutterlin, James S., 223
Sweat, Mike, 85
Synnestvedt, Sig, 89

T
Talbott, Strobe, 8, 29, 205n
Tarnoff, Peter, 188n
Taylor, A. J. P., 67
Taylor, William J., Jr., 90
Tennefoss, Michael R., 139
Teune, Henry, 89
Thies, Wallace J., 91
Thompson, Kenneth W., 162
Thompson, William R., 20, 53, 55, 71, 72, 77, 87, 88
Thucydides, 46
Thurow, Lester C., 8, 174, 198
Tillema, Herbert K., 24
Tirpitz, Alfred von, 127

Tocqueville, Alexis de, 23
Tonelson, Alan, 11, 198
Toynbee, Arnold J., 124
Treverton, Gregory F., 227
Truman, Harry S, 23, 32, 36, 40, 84
Tyler, Patrick J., 189

U

Ullman, Richard H., 226
Urquhart, Brian, 223

V

Van Dyke, Vernon, 15
Van Evera, Stephen, 128, 174, 227
Vasquez, John A., 33n, 35, 39, 87, 91, 99,
    100, 101, 119
Vattel, Emerich de, 104, 143
Väyrynen, Raimo, 79n
Vernon, Raymond, 182, 228
Vitoria, Francisco de, 127

W

Wagner, R. Harrison, 28, 45, 68
Walker, Jenonne, 227
Walker, Stephan F., 151
Wallace, Michael D., 119, 139
Wallensteen, Peter, 201
Wallerstein, Immanuel, 9, 62, 78, 79, 80,
    232n
Walpole, Sir Robert, 93
Walt, Stephen M., 94

Waltz, Kenneth N., 16, 37, 48, 95, 182, 183
Wang, Kevin, 86
Washington, George, 93, 97, 100, 164
Watson, Adam, 59
Wayman, Frank, 88, 102, 119
Weede, Erich, 34, 228
Wegener, Henning, 200
Wehberg, Hans, 127
Weinberger, Caspar, 36
Wellington, Duke of (Arthur Wellesley), 89
Wheeler, Hugh B., 35
Whitehead, John C., 7, 207
Wildavsky, Aaron, 38
Wilkenfeld, Jonathan, 25, 88
William I (King of Holland), 137
Williamson, Samuel R., Jr., 129, 157
Wilson, Woodrow, 113, 134n, 164
Wittkopf, Eugene R., 150, 180, 204
Wolfe, Thomas W., 32
Wolfers, Arnold, 89, 97, 151
Wotton, Sir Henry, 92
Wright, Quincy, 104, 139, 161

Y

Yeltsin, Boris, 6, 201n
Yergin, Daniel, 22

Z

Zakaria, Fareed, 195, 234
Zhdanov, Andrei, 23
Zuckerman, Lord, 8
Zysman, John, 11

SUBJECT INDEX

A

Abkhazia, 225
Acid rain, 6
Afghanistan, 38, 107, 116, 171, 194
Age of reason, 143
AIDS, 6
Aix-la-Chapelle, Congress of, 135, 218
Albania, 101, 107, 116
Algeciras conference, 194
Alliances, military, *see also* Balance of power;
    Polarization
  defined, 89
  and deterrence, 32–33
  life cycle of, 98
  of movement versus position, 30–31
  and norm formation, 34–36
  types of, 90
Amphictyonic League, 159
Anarchy, 6, 17, 99, 127, 149, 186, 218
Anglo-Dutch Naval War, 73
Anglo-French Entente, 156–157, 201, 209
Angola, 31, 222
ANZUS, 30
Arms race, 38, 102, 155
Assyria, 218
Atlantic Charter, 30
Austria, 61, 68n, 69, 76, 94–95, 97, 106–
    107, 109–111, 113, 116, 128, 133,
    135–136, 138
Austria–Hungary, 61, 69–70, 76–77, 96,
    101, 112–113, 208
Austrian State Treaty, 35
Austrian Succession, War of the, 74

Austro-Turkish War, 73
Autarky, 213
Azerbaijan, 32

B

Babylonia, 218
Baghdad Pact, 160
Balance-of-bloc system, 205n
Balance of power, 17, 19, 34, 48, 78, 85, 87–
    88, 150, 180–181, 186, 209, 211, *see*
    also Realism
  and alliances, 99–116, *passim*, 190
  compared to collective security, 160–163
  within concerts, 158
  incentives for unilateralism, 154–155
  and norms, 122–123, 135, 219
  and special relationships, 192, 195, 210
  and system change, 167, 182
Balancer, 111, 129, 154, 181, 190
Bandwagoning, 31, 94–95, 127
Bavaria, 106–107
Bavarian Succession, War of the, 74
Belgium, 81, 107, 116, 137, 199, 207
Berlin blockade, 32
Billiard ball model, 68
Bipolarity, 3, 12, 28, 54, *see also* Cold War;
    Long peace
Blocs, *see* Alliances, military; Polarization
Boer War, 193
Brazil, 221
British–Spanish War, 74
Bruges, synod of, 159
Buck-passing, 49

C

Cambodia, 167, 222
Canada, 227
Capabilities, national, 13–15, 54, *see also* Power
Carlsbad Decrees, 135
Carthage, 53n
Central Treaty Organization (CENTO), 31, 34
Chaco, War, 213
Chain-ganging, 49
Chaumont, Treaty of, 61, 133
China, 81, 107–108. 158n, 193
  ancient, 57
  People's Republic of, 6, 10, 30, 168–169, 176–178, 190, 196–197, 203n, 205–206, 221, 225–227, 234
City–state systems
  ancient Greek, 57–58
  Maya, 57–58
  Renaissance Italian, 10, 57–58, 108–109
  Sumerian, 57–58
Civil War, 8, 77, 179
  internationalized, 87
Clayton–Bulwer Treaty, 193
Cold War, 4–5, 7, 22–45 *passim*
  and bipolarity, 56
Collective defense, 160
Collective security, 113–114, 151–153, 158–165, 210–211, *see also* League of Nations
Colonialism, 79n, 81–84
COMECON, 167
Concert, 151–152, 157–158, 163–164
Concert of Europe, 10, 111, 133–140, 153, 158, 203, 216, 218–219
Condominium, 132, 157, 201, 205
Conference on Security and Cooperation in Europe (CSCE), 220
Containment, 27–36 *passim*
Cooperative security, 217–218
Cordon sanitaire, 132
Cretan Federation, 218
Crimean War, 74, 111, 138
Croatia, 200
Cross-cutting loyalty, 51, 71
Cuba, 31, 35, 81
Cuban missile crisis, 40
Cultural divisions, 8
Cyprus, 226
Czechoslovakia, 32, 107–108, 116–117

D

Defensive restructuring, 217
Deforestation, 6
Democracy, 8
  and war, 17, 50, 60, 63, 228, *see also* Neo-liberalism
Denmark, 108, 197
Deterrence, 5, 94, 96, 99, 129, 202, 213
  by denial versus punishment, 32
  extended, 29, 198
  nuclear, 38–40, 231
Devolutionary War, 73
Diversionary theory of war, 63
Dual Alliance, 111
Dutch Wars of Louis XIV, 73

E

Egypt, 107–108, 157n, 194, 218
Elam, 218
El Salvador, 222
End of history thesis, 8, 25
England, *see* Great Britain
English–Spanish War, 73
Entente, 90, 156–157, 201
Estonia, 108, 116
Ethiopia, 213
Ethnonationalism, 185, 197, 212, 226, 231–232
  and irredentism, 230
European Community, 10, 166–167, 174, 176–178, 196–199, 204, 224
European Free Trade Association (EFTA), 224

F

Falkland Islands, 157
Finland, 30, 100, 108, 116
Formosa, *see* Taiwan
Four policemen plan, 158n
France, 61, 69, 76, 85, 101, 110–113, 126–129, 197, 199–200, 203, 221, 234
  alliances, 94–97, 106–108, 116
  and Concert of Europe, 133, 135–136, 218
  colonial expansion, 80–81
  entente, 157, 159, 194, 207, 209
  membership in international organizations, 224, 226–227
  "new" monarchy, 58
Franco-Prussian War, 26, 74, 96, 111
Franco-Spanish War, 73
Free-riding, 214
Free trade, 79n, 81, 84, 173–174, 181, 187, 232

Friendship and Peace, Treaty of, 90n
Functional integration, 218

G
Geopolitics, 6
Germany, 10, 35, 134n, 135, 138, 157, 166,
    183, 193–195, 202–203, 207, 213–
    214, 218, 226–227, 231
  alliances, 69–70, 76–77, 81, 107–108,
    111–113, 116–117, 127–129
  as ascending power, 6, 167, 169, 171, 174–
    178, 199–200, 221, 234
  reunification, 4
  and World War II, 22–23, 100, 210, see
    also Prussia
Global warming, 6
Great Britain, 61, 69–70, 76, 85, 110, 128–
    129, 158n, 188, 199–200, 234
  alliances, 95, 101, 106–108
  colonial expansion, 80–81
  Concert of Europe, 111–113, 133, 136–
    137
  membership in international organizations,
    221, 224, 226–227
  "new" monarchy, 58
  role of balancer, 154, 157, 192–194
  special relationships, 192–194, 207–209
Great Northern War, 73
Greece, 46, 116, 226, see also City–state sys-
    tems
Group of Seven (G-7), 220
  as basis of collective security, 227–229

H
Hawaii, 81
Hay–Pauncefote Treaty, 193
Hegemony, 69n, 232
  and stability, 85, 122–123, 155, see also
    Power; Unipolarity
Helsinki Accords, 35, 201–224
High politics, 8, 16, 20, 198
Holland, see Netherlands, the
Holy League, War of the, 73
Holy Roman Empire, 95, 105
Honduras, 31
Hubertusburg, Treaty of, 110
Hungary, 70, 107, 116, 200

I
Idealism, 181
Imperial overstretch, 84–85
Imperialism, 80–85

India, 46, 193, 196, 207
  ancient, 57
Indivisibility, 215
Indonesia, 221
INF Treaty, 8
Interaction opportunity, 51–70
Inter-American Treaty of Reciprocal Assis-
    tance, 30
Interdependence, economic, 50, 132, 198,
    227–229
Intervention, 25–26, 135, 187–188
Iran, 116, see also Persia
Iraq, 31, 108, 222, 230
Isolationism, 151, 226
  Splendid isolation, 157, 192
Italian Unification, War of, 74
Italy, 69–70, 76–77, 81, 107–108, 111, 117,
    226
  alliances, 96–98, 100–101, 116, 129, 208
  and Group of Seven, 227
  invasion of Ethiopia, 213

J
Japan, 7, 30, 32, 61, 76–77, 81, 100–101,
    193–197, 213–214, 225–226
  alliances, 107, 116–117
  as ascending power, 6, 10, 70, 167–169,
    171, 174–178, 183, 190, 203–207,
    221, 234
Just war, 124

K
Korea, 167, 222
  North and South, 31, 35
Korean War, 32
Kuwait, 222, 230, see also Persian Gulf War

L
Laibach, Congress of, 136
Latvia, 108, 116
Law, international, see Normative orders
League of Augsburg, War of, 73, 95
League of Cambrai, 108
League of Nations, 10, 113–114, 117, 125,
    158–159, 161, 215, 220, 230
League of Venice, War of the, 73
Lithuania, 107, 116
Little Entente, 89
London, Treaty of, 97
Long cycles
  economic, 78–84
  world leadership, 85, 87

Long peace, 4, 23–27, 32
Luxembourg, 199

M
Maastricht Accords, 8, 197
Marshall Plan, 33
Mercantilism, 80–81, 200
  neomercantilism, 6
Middle powers, 12, 191n
Mitanni, 218
Moldovia, 225
Mongolia, 30, 108
Monroe Doctrine, 180
Morocco, 31, 127, 194, 209
Most Holy League, 58
Mozambique, 31
Multipolarity, 3, 12, *see also* Balance of
    power; Balancer
  and alliances, 92–93, 102–117 *passim*
  criticisms of, 48–51
  and norms, 140–146
  range of policy choice in, 151–165 *passim*
  size, 68, 71–76
  stability of, 179, 196, 209
  support for, 51–53
  types of, 53–57, 67
Mutual transparency, 217–218

N
Nagorno-Karabakh, 225
Napoleonic Wars, 61, 87, 130, 203, *see also*
    Vienna, Congress of
Nationalism, 5, 63, 227, *see also* Ethnona-
    tionalism
National Security Council Memorandum, No.
    68, 33
Neapolitan War, 73
Neoliberalism, 17, *see also* Democracy
Neorealism, *see* Realism
Netherlands, the, 61, 69–70, 76–77, 80, 85,
    106, 129, 188, 199
Neutrality, 132, 154, 160, 185
Nigeria, 221
Nonintervention principle, 132
Normative orders, 119–120, 140, 209
  defined, 55
  permissive versus restrictive, 124, 127, 132,
    144
Norms, international, 34, 40, *see also* En-
    tente; Concert
  defined, 122
  source of, 122–124

and special relationships, 201, 209
and stability, 132–146 *passim*, 179, 233
types, 124–132
North American Free Trade Area (NAFTA),
    204
North Atlantic Cooperation Council (NACC),
    220–225
North Atlantic Treaty Organization (NATO),
    30, 33–34, 160, 167, 184, 199–200,
    220
  as basis for collective security, 225–227
Northern Ireland, 157

O
Oman, 31
OPEC, 16
Ottoman, Empire, 61, 68n, 69, 76–77, 97,
    159, 193
Ottoman War, 73
Ozone depletion, 6

P
Pact of Steel, 94
Pacta sunt servanda, 127–131
Pactomania, 30
Pakistan, 31
Peace through strength, 36–37
Peacekeeping, 222–223
Peace of Lodi, 58
Peloponnesian War, 87
Persia, 107, 193–194
Persian Gulf War, 221, 223n, 230, 232–233
Philippines, the 30, 81
Poland, 70, 95, 100–101, 106–108, 110,
    116, 137, 200
Polarity, defined, 12, 68, *see also* Unipolarity;
    Bipolarity; Multipolarity
Polarization, defined, 54–55, 102
  as mediating variable, 101
Polish Succession, War of, 74
Portugal, 34, 61, 69–70, 76, 80–81, 107,
    137, 188
Power, 3, 19, 179, 232, *see also* Balance of
    power; Capabilities, national; Polarity
  concept of great power, 68n
  dimensions of, 16
  economic, 11, 171, 173
  as performance trait, 13
  relational quality of, 12
Power transition, 72, 79n, 85–88
Preventive war, 86
Proliferation, weapons, 5, 8, 37, 179, 185,
    202, 212, 232

Protectionism, trade, 6, 8, 179, 226
Proto-alliance, 31–32
Proxy war, 25
Prussia, 61, 69–70, 76, 95–96, 106, 110–111, 133, 136–137
Public good, 95
Puerto Rico, 81
Punic Wars, 87

Q

Quadruple Alliance, 61, 133
Quadruple Alliance, War of the, 74

R

Rank instability, 72–88 *passim*, 123
Rapallo, Treaty of, 200
Rastadt, Treaty of, 61
Realism, 16, 19, 41, 72, 75, 154, 156, *see also* Anarchy; Balance of power
    assumptions of, 18
    classical, 46–47
    interpretation of alliances, 91–101
    neorealism, 47–51
Rebus sic stantibus, 128–131
Reciprocity, diffuse, 215
Relative advantage, 75
Roman Empire, 10, 53n, 157n
Romania, 107, 112, 116
Rules of the game, *see* Norms, international
Russia, 10, 61, 69, 76–77, 95, 101, 110–113, 128–129, 167, 169, 190, 193–197, 206–208, 221, 224, 231, 234
    alliances, 106–107
    in Concert of Europe, 133, 135–137
    prospects for entente with United States, 200–203
    relative strength, 175–179
Russo-Japanese War, 75

S

Saudi Arabia, 31
Second Milanese War, 73
Second Northern War, 73
Secret diplomacy, 113
Serbia, 107, 113, 128, 208, 226
Seven Weeks' War, 74, 208
Seven Years' War, 74, 110
Siam, *see* Thailand
Soft power, 13, *see also* Power
Somalia, 222, 232–233
Southeast Asian Treaty Organization (SEATO), 30, 35

Sovereignty, 53, 132, 154
Soviet Union, 4, 6–7, 20, 61, 69, 76, 100, 151, 167–168, 174–175, 185–186, 189, 198, 200, 212, 225, *see also* Russia
    alliances, 107–108, 116
    Cold War, 22, 27, 30, 46, 61
Spain, 20, 30, 34, 61, 68n, 69–70, 76, 95, 106–107, 109, 199
    imperialism, 80–81
    rebellion, 135–136
    relative decline, 187–188, 194
Spanish Succession, War of, 61, 95
Spanish–Turkish War, 73
Specialized relationship, 151–153, 156–157, 163–164, *see also* Entente
    between Great Britain and the United States, 152
Sphere of influence, 132
Stability, crisis versus general, 39n
Stag hunt, allegory of, 47
Strategic Defense Initiative (SDI), 43, 217
Sudan, 157
Sweden, 61, 69–70, 76–77, 94–95, 97, 106, 110
Swiss Confederation, 106

T

Taiwan, 81
Teheran conference, 22
Thailand, 31, 81
Thirty Years' War, 61, 94, 132, *see also* Westphalia, Treaty of
Threats, nonmilitary, 5–6
Three Emperors League, 90, 112
Tibet, 194
Tordesillas, Treaty of, 34, 61
Transnational Rules Indicators Project (TRIP), 125n, 130n
Trends, systemic, 5
Triple Alliance, 98, 111, 113, 129, 208
Triple Entente, 113
Troppau, Protocol of, 135
Truman Doctrine, 32
Turkey, 107–109, 111–112, 116, 129, 126, *see also* Ottoman Empire

U

Ukraine, 200
Uncertainty, 71–72, 127–129
    risk aversion, 52
Uneven growth, 78

Unilateralism, 151–156, 163–164
Unipolarity, 3, 10, 12, 54, 232
United Nations, 8, 10, 34, 159, 161, 183–
    184, 214, 230
  as basis for collective security, 215, 221–
    223
  Declaration of, 30
  Security Council, 126
  support for, 179
United States, 7, 10, 20, 22, 30, 46, 61, 69,
    76, 100, 126, 193, 200–203, 205,
    208–209, 212, 214
  debt, 38
  future policy choices, 166–190 *passim,*
    195–199
  hegemonic position of, 80–81, 85
  isolationism, 150
  relative decline, 9, 11, 192
  role in future security system, 221–234
    passim
Utrecht, Treaty of, 10, 61, 109–110

V
Venezuela, 192
Versailles, Treaty of, 61, 113, 116, 125, 218
Vervins, Peace of, 61

Vienna, Congress of, 63, 111, 133, 137–138,
    158
Vietnam, 31, 171, 207

W
War, 23–25, 27–45 *passim, see also* Balance
    of power; Collective security; Concert;
    Deterrence
  as a cause of resource redistribution, 77–78
  great-power, 73–75
  legal control of, 124–126, 141
  system-transforming, 18, 77, 87
Warsaw Treaty Organization, 30, 34, 151,
    160, 167, 220, 224–225, 231
Western European Union, 199, 226
Westphalia, Treaty of, 9, 61, 132–133, 168
Win–hold–win strategy, 188n
World War I, 61, 87, 112–113, 125, 194,
    207–208, *see also* Versailles, Treaty of
World War II, 22, 61, 87, 100, 117, 125, 204

Y
Yalta conference, 22
Yemen, 31
Yugoslavia, 107–108, 116, 225

ABOUT THE AUTHORS

Charles W. Kegley, Jr. (Ph.D., Syracuse University) is Pearce Professor of International Relations at the University of South Carolina. President of the International Studies Association (1993/1994), he has also taught at Georgetown University, the University of Texas, Rutgers University, and the People's University of China. With Eugene R. Wittkopf, his books include *World Politics: Trend and Transformation, 4/e* (St. Martin's Press, 1993); *The Global Agenda, 3/e* (1992); *American Foreign Policy: Pattern and Process, 4/e* (St. Martin's Press, 1991); and *The Nuclear Reader: Strategy, Weapons, War, 2/e* (St. Martin's Press, 1989). He was also the editor, with Wittkopf, of the first editions of *The Future of American Foreign Policy* (St. Martin's Press, 1992) and *The Domestic Sources of American Foreign Policy* (St. Martin's Press, 1988). He is editor of *The Long Postwar Peace: Contending Explanations and Projections* (1991) and *International Terrorism, Characteristics, Causes, Controls* (St. Martin's Press, 1990). He has also published many articles in a wide range of scholarly journals.

Gregory A. Raymond (Ph.D., University of South Carolina) is Chair of the Department of Political Science at Boise State University. His most recent books include *The Other Western Europe: A Comparative Analysis of the Smaller Democracies, 2/e* (1983) and *Third World Policies of Industrialized Nations* (1982). He has also published many articles on foreign policy and world politics in various scholarly journals. Raymond has spoken on international issues at numerous professional conferences throughout Europe, the United States, and Latin America.

Together Kegley and Raymond have previously published *When Trust Breaks Down: Alliance Norms and World Politics* (1990), and *International Events and the Comparative Analysis of Foreign Policy* (1975). They have also co-authored 15 articles in a diverse range of periodicals, including *International Studies Quarterly*, the *Journal of Conflict Resolution*, the *Harvard International Review*, and *USA Today*. Both Kegley and Raymond were Pew Faculty Fellows at the John F. Kennedy School of Government at Harvard University.